FISCAL POLICY AND BUSINESS CYCLES

FISCAL POLICY
and
BUSINESS CYCLES

By Alvin H. Hansen
HARVARD UNIVERSITY

Publishers
W · W · NORTON & COMPANY · INC ·
New York

PRINTED IN THE UNITED STATES OF AMERICA
FOR THE PUBLISHERS BY THE VAIL-BALLOU PRESS
3456789

CONTENTS

PART THREE. FISCAL POLICY AND FULL USE OF RESOURCES

PART FOUR. INVESTMENT INCENTIVES PAST AND PRESENT

PART FIVE. DEFENSE AND ITS AFTERMATH

INTRODUCTION

THE twin scourges that afflict the modern world—Depression and War—are not altogether unrelated. Bad as the Treaty of Versailles was, a steady improvement in international political relations could have been expected had we had the vision and courage to stop the Great Depression dead in its tracks and to move forward to higher levels of real income and employment.

The war now afflicting, directly and indirectly, the entire world cannot be explained by overly simplified dogmas running in terms of competitive capitalism and imperialistic rivalries. But it has, nonetheless, an economic basis—the inability of the great industrial nations to provide full employment at rising standards of real income. The disastrous economic breakdown of the thirties let loose forces which have set the world in flames. The ultimate causes of the failure to achieve a world order in the political sphere must be sought in the facts of economic frustration.

It is against the background of the past decade of economic and political futility that this book is written. It deals with the changing role of government, and particularly with fiscal policy as an instrument for regulating the national income and its distribution.

In June, 1939, it was my privilege to present a preliminary report on *Fiscal Policy and Business Cycles* to a conference of specialists in the fields indicated, called together under the auspices of the Social Science Research Council at Rye, New York. This conference proved to be extraordinarily stimulating and helpful, and I am deeply in debt to all those who participated. They included Roy Blough, J. M. Clark, Gerhard Colm, Lauchlin Currie, Gottfried Haberler, C. O. Hardy, Simeon E. Leland, Abba P. Lerner, Arthur W. Marget, Lawrence H. Seltzer, Carl Shoup, and John H. Williams.

Especially am I under obligation to Dean Williams and members of the Seminar on Fiscal Policy at the Graduate School of Public Administration, Harvard University, for a thoroughgoing, critical analysis of the report referred to above and of oral presentations of my views. These, together with the discussion at the conference referred to above, have frequently forced me to clarify my thinking and to alter or restate my position. I have, moreover, learned much from conversation with, and from the writings of, my colleagues—Professors Schumpeter, Haberler, and Harris—and from prolonged discussions on many points with graduate fellows and younger faculty members, especially J. Keith Butters, Emile Despres, John T. Dunlop, J. K. Galbraith, R. V. Gilbert, Benjamin H. Higgins, G. G. Johnson, Martin Krost, Richard A. Musgrave, Kenyon E. Poole, Walter Salant, Paul A. Samuelson and Paul M. Sweezy.

In view of the controversial character of many of the issues discussed, it is especially important to say that none of the persons named above are responsible for the arguments presented or the conclusions reached in this book. With respect to the basic underlying philosophy, some are, as I understand them, in substantial agreement, while others are highly skeptical though splendidly sympathetic and open minded to ideas differing from their own.

I wish also to express my deep obligation to the Graduate School of Public Administration, Harvard University, for the seminar and research facilities which it has provided. In the preparation of certain chapters I have had the assistance of Willard D. Arant, Virginia Coughlan, Benjamin H. Higgins, and Mortimer Kaplan. In addition, David W. Lusher and Saul

R. Srole aided in assembling basic data. In a part of Chapter V, I have relied heavily upon the work of George Jászi, published in *Public Policy,* 1940 yearbook of the Graduate School of Public Administration. I am particularly happy to include the Appendix to Chapter XI, on "A Statistical Analysis of the Consumption Function," written by Assistant Professor Paul A. Samuelson, Massachusetts Institute of Technology.

Permission has kindly been granted to use parts or all of articles or addresses published elsewhere. These include the following: "Economic Progress and Declining Population Growth," *American Economic Review,* Supplement, March, 1939; "Extensive Expansion and Population Growth," *Journal of Political Economy,* August, 1940; "The Dynamic versus the Circular Flow Economy," an address delivered September 17, 1940, at the Bicentennial Celebration of the Founding of the University of Pennsylvania; "Price Flexibility and the Full Employment of Resources," *The Structure of the American Economy,* Part II: Toward Full Use of Resources, National Resources Planning Board, 1940; "Monetary and Fiscal Controls in War Time," *Yale Review,* Winter, 1940; "Defense Financing and Inflation Potentialities," *The Review of Economic Statistics,* February, 1941; "Some Aspects, Near-term and Long-term of the International Position of the United States" (joint author with A. R. Upgren), *American Economic Review,* Papers and Proceedings, February, 1941.

Finally, my sincere thanks and appreciation are due Miss Virginia Coughlan for her highly efficient secretarial work in the preparation of the manuscript and in seeing it through the press.

Part One

TOWARD AN UNDERSTANDING OF THE THIRTIES

Chapter I

THE THIRTIES VIEWED AGAINST THE BACKGROUND OF EARLIER CYCLES

THE Great Depression, beginning in 1929, which had only partially been overcome, at any rate in the United States, by the end of the thirties, has been characterized as something quite unique in the long history of business cycles. To be sure, in a sense every cycle is unique and has special characteristics of its own. When, however, it is said that the Great Depression was a unique phenomenon, something else is meant than the ordinary degree of variation in duration and depth which we find from cycle to cycle.

There is not, however, unanimity of opinion among business cycle students with respect to the uniqueness of the Great Depression. There are those who hold that the severity of this depression and the difficulty of overcoming it fit quite well into the general scheme of cycle development over the last one hundred and fifty years.

Whether the Great Depression was indeed unique or not, it is at any rate true that it will be much better understood if it is set off against the background of the history of business cycle movements. To do so, it is necessary to differentiate various cycles or wavelike movements in the process of modern economic development.

Whether these movements may strictly be characterized as *cyclical* is at least debatable. Some would defend the use of the term "fluctuations" as more accurate, since the movements of output, employment, and prices vary so greatly from time to time and are highly irregular. On the other side, those who run to abstract theorizing, and desire as far as possible to fit concrete data into a mold or pattern, will be inclined to search for greater regularity in the movements than can properly be described under the term "fluctuations." And, indeed, the data lend a good deal of support to this point of view. It is, at any rate, a reasonably defensible proposition that the movements of industry and business run in cycles sufficiently regular so that, within limits, a period may be assigned to their duration. Moreover, the analysis of the cycle gives strong support to the view that a movement, once started in one direction, tends to cumulate and grow stronger and stronger up to a certain point beyond which the generating forces weaken until a reverse movement finally develops in the opposite direction. If this is true, the movement is wavelike in character, and not merely an erratic fluctuation.

Into this discussion—on which there is an extensive literature—we shall not enter. We shall follow the view that economic development does run in cycles. We believe that there is sufficient justification in the historical and statistical record, supported by the theoretical analysis of the cumulative process, to warrant this assumption.

The upward and downward movements, which together make business cycles, are now commonly believed to be mainly associated with fluctuations in the volume of real investment. We distinguish between real investment and financial investment. When one purchases a share in a corporate enterprise or a bond or a mortgage, one is making a financial investment. When one, however, builds a house or a factory or a machine, one is making a real investment. Real investment may, of course, be measured either in value terms or in quantitative terms.

The fluctuations of cyclical movements may be characterized in terms of either money income, real income (the output of material goods and services), or employment. These three categories, to be sure, are not identical. Money income is a function both of real income and of price movements, while real income or output differs from employment by reason of changes in productivity. Cyclically, however, the three move more or less in consonance, though the trend movement is likely to differ considerably under varying circumstances. For certain problems it is extremely important to differentiate sharply between them. But frequently in discussing economic fluctuations or cyclical movements all three may be regarded without serious error as moving together, whether in the upswing or in the downswing. This is particularly true for the short-run movements but less true for the longer-run developments.

We have noted that the upswing and downswing movements of income, output, and employment are mainly characterized by fluctuations in the rate of real investment. It is true, as we shall develop later, that the fluctuations in income, output, and employment involve more than fluctuations in real investment alone. Consumption also rises and falls with the cycle movement, but less violently proportionally than the rise and fall of real investment. Moreover, consumption rises or falls, in large part, in response to movements in real investment, though to some extent, as we shall see later, these movements are of an independent character unrelated to the movements of real investment.

We distinguish real investment from consumption in a more or less arbitrary manner, though following conventional terminology. By real investment we mean the purchase of capital goods, by which is usually meant: (1) producers' goods, including (a) industrial, public utility, commercial and financial plant and equipment and (b) inventories of stocks of goods in process or held for future sale; and (2) consumers' capital, including (a) residential building and (b) public works of all kinds, such as public buildings, roads, and the like.

In consumption we include purchases of: (a) personal services, (b) nondurable consumption goods, such as food and the like, (c) semidurable consumers' goods, such as clothing, and (d) durable consumers' goods, such as automobiles and household equipment.

The most general, all-inclusive statement of the essential character of cyclical movements is that they consist in an increase or decline, as the case may be, in the purchase of real investment goods and of durable consumers' goods as defined above. While the role of durable consumers' goods plays an increasingly important part, it is nevertheless still true, and formerly almost exclusively so, that the causes of business fluctuations are to be found mainly in the factors which bring about a rise and fall in the rate of real investment. This analysis will be developed with the necessary qualifications in subsequent chapters.

Major and Minor Cycles

Quite commonly, particularly in America, the term "business cycle" is applied with reference both to what is called the minor cycle and to the major cycle. And with respect to the term "depression," equally the term is applied both to minor recessions and to major depressions. In Europe, when the business or trade cycle is spoken of, reference is usually made to what we call the major cycle.

On the whole it is, we think, preferable to concentrate attention upon the major cycle in business cycle analysis. But it is not possible in doing so to overlook the fact that, particularly in the upswing phase of the major cycle, there regularly occurs, especially in American experience, one or sometimes two interruptions to the upswing movement. In seven of the fifteen major cycles in the period from 1807 to 1937 there were two minor recessions, and in eight of the major upswings there was one minor recession. Since 1883, out of six major cycles two were interrupted by two minor recessions and four by one minor recession.[1]

The major upswing, as we have already noted, can be char-

[1] The figures given in this chapter on the number of cycles, major and minor, are based on the data in W. C. Mitchell, *Business Cycles, the Problem and Its Setting,* National Bureau of Economic Research, 1927, Chapter IV; W. M. Persons, *Forecasting Business Cycles,* John Wiley and Sons, 1931; and the *Cleveland Trust Bulletin.*

acterized essentially as an expansion in the rate of real investment. For the purpose currently at hand, it is most useful to classify real investment into the two categories suggested above: (a) inventories of commodity stocks and (b) real investment in fixed capital, including plant and equipment, housing and public construction. When an upsurge in real investment occurs, it is not unusual for the spurt in inventory accumulation to run ahead of the normal requirements indicated by the rising trend. When this is the case, sooner or later a temporary saturation in inventory accumulation develops, leading to an inventory recession. Not infrequently the minor setbacks experienced in the major upswings may be characterized as inventory recessions. But sometimes other situations may initiate or aggravate these minor recessions. Thus, for example, in the beginning of the major upswing it may be that large investment in improved machinery occurs and that after a time a temporary saturation is reached in this type of investment leading to a recession. The general buoyancy of the upswing, however, soon starts the economy upward again with a further burst of real investment after the temporary setback thus sustained. Sometimes special situations are partly responsible for minor recessions, such as critical international developments, labor disturbances, or even special factors having to do with major industries, such as the Ford shutdown in 1927. Regularly, however, inventory movements play an important role.

It is to be noted that very rarely do minor upswings interrupt the downturn of the major cycle. One notable case, however, was the temporary recovery which occurred in 1895 in the major downswing from 1893 to 1897. Following this very brief recovery, the economy continued downward in a deep and prolonged depression. There are very few other clear cases in our history of a temporary upturn in the period of the major downswing of the business cycle. There are, however, the brief recoveries of 1818, 1828, and 1841, all of them coming in the period of the long, difficult readjustment after the Napoleonic Wars. About this period we shall have more to say later in connection with a discussion of the so-called "long waves." For the most part, the minor cycle in American experience has appeared in the form of a temporary recession in the general upswing of the major cycle.

It has been suggested (and to some extent this view is tenable) that both the Great Depression from 1929 to 1932 inclusive and the recovery from 1933 to 1939 follow a pattern which is fundamentally similar to other cycles. This is not to say, however, that those who advance this view would necessarily argue that there is implied in such correspondence anything in the nature of inevitableness about the course of the cycle development, whether in the downswing or in the upswing. Indeed, it is highly probable that wiser and sounder public policy could have modified very greatly the development both in the depression and in the recovery phases. What is true is that the experiences of this decade certainly become more understandable if we set them out against the background of the history of earlier American business cycles.

One generalization stands out very clearly from this record —one which apparently has been lost sight of in the current period, particularly with respect to the recovery movement from 1933 on. The generalization referred to is the highly important one that every prolonged upswing period has been interrupted by minor recessions. From the record of past American experience it is clear that a continuous upswing has rarely occurred extending without interruption beyond a period of about four years, and usually the period is somewhat shorter. From this we may deduce that the major upswing represents a discontinuous, jerky spurt in the rate of real investment; that the rapid expansion of real investment proceeds by fits and starts. Particularly, as we have noted, is it difficult in the upswing period, when demand and prices are rising, to hold to an appropriate pace the accumulation of inventories.

The American experience indicates that the major business cycle has had an average duration of a little over eight years. Thus, from 1795 to 1937 there were seventeen cycles of an average duration of 8.35 years. In the hundred-year period 1837 to 1937 there were twelve major cycles of an average duration of 8.33 years. In the eighty-year period from 1857 to 1937 there were ten major cycles of an average duration of 8.0 years. And in the period from 1873 to 1937 there were eight major cycles of an average duration of 8.0 years.

Since one to two minor peaks regularly occur between the major peaks, it is clear that the minor cycle is something less than half the duration of the major cycle. In the one hundred and thirty-year period 1807 to 1937 there were thirty-seven minor cycles with an average duration of 3.51 years. In the eighty-year period from 1857 to 1937 there were twenty-three minor cycles with an average duration of 3.48 years. And from 1890 to 1937 there were fourteen minor cycles with an average duration of 3.36 years.

The major cycles vary in length from a minimum of six years to a maximum of twelve years, though with rare exceptions they fall within the range of seven to ten years, the average being slightly over eight years. The minor cycles have a range of from a minimum of two years to a maximum of six years, though they usually fall within the range of three to four years, with the average slightly over three and one-third years.

Building Cycles

But there are other factors, altogether aside from those which bring about the temporary interruptions in the broad sweeps of the major cycle, which profoundly alter the course of its development and influence the intensity and violence both of the upswing and of the downswing. One of the most important is one that, strangely enough, has been greatly neglected in the analysis of business cycles. And this factor is of peculiar significance for us, for it has an important bearing upon an understanding of the Great Depression of the nineteen-thirties.

The factor to which we refer is the fluctuation in building construction. This follows, in large measure, a wavelike movement much longer than the major business cycle. Notable studies have been made by Riggleman, Newman, Long, and the Federal Reserve Bank of New York City of building construction, both residential and nonresidential.[2] Riggleman's study extends over a century from 1830 to 1935 and covers, in the earlier period, three cities and, in the later period, sixty-five cities. Long's study covers the period from 1864 to 1934 and includes twenty-nine cities. Newman's study is for seventeen cities and covers the period 1879 to 1934, while the study of the Federal Reserve Bank of New York City covers the years 1877 to 1934 and is for seven of the leading cities of the United States. All of these studies relate either directly to volume or to the value of building corrected for price changes.

From these studies it appears, according to the American experience, that building construction over the last hundred years has followed a fairly regular cyclical pattern. The Riggleman study reveals six building cycles from 1830 to 1934, with an average duration of 17.33 years. The studies of Long and Riggleman reveal four cycles from 1864 to 1934, with an average duration of 17.5 years. All four studies cover the period from 1878 to 1934 and reveal three cycles with an average duration of 18.7 years, while the period from 1900 to 1937 gives two cycles of an average duration of seventeen years. Thus, it appears that the building cycle averages somewhere between seventeen and eighteen years in length, or almost precisely twice the length of the major business cycle.

Question may be raised why building construction should have a cycle of its own different in length from that of the major business cycle. In this connection it is well to point out that building is not the only field of economic activity which reveals a periodicity varying from that of the major cycle. Thus, for example, we know that there is a cycle in textile

[2] See G. F. Warren and F. A. Pearson, *World Prices and the Building Industry*, John Wiley and Sons, 1937; W. H. Newman, *The Building Industry and Business Cycles*, University of Chicago Press, 1935; J. R. Riggleman, "Building Cycles in the United States, 1875–1932," *Journal of the American Statistical Association*, 1933; C. D. Long, Jr., *Building Cycles and the Theory of Investment*, Princeton University Press, 1940.

production, which fits neither the minor cycle nor the major business cycle, of about two years' duration; that there is a cycle of hog production of about three to five years; and, indeed, a cycle of greater or shorter duration in the production of several of the more important domestic animals.

The corn-hog cycle, for example, has been explained by the interrelation of the price of corn and the price of hogs. When there is a large production of corn, and feed prices are low, farmers find that it is desirable to produce more hogs, but it takes some time to make the decision and some time to raise the new hog crop. Thus, after an interval an excessively large supply of hogs appears on the market, causing a low price of hogs in relation to the price of corn. Thereupon, the farmers conclude that it is better to sell the corn in the market and raise fewer hogs. Again, it takes some time to make the decision and to adjust the hog crop to the new price situation, and after a lag a relative shortage appears in hog production, causing a high price of hogs in relation to the price of corn. Thus, in the lag of reaction of producers to the market situation one finds the explanation of the hog production cycle.

In somewhat similar fashion one may advance a tentative explanation of the seventeen-eighteen-year cycle of building construction. We shall apply the argument particularly with respect to residential building, though the same analysis holds in large part for other kinds of construction. Let us suppose that residential building has for a period been depressed and that increasingly rental space is becoming scarce. Rents thus rise. But it takes some time before the building industry is sufficiently convinced of the permanence of the higher rents to be stimulated into activity. Moreover, the building industry by its very nature cannot be set going on a large scale suddenly. In a period of building depression many contractors, particularly the smaller ones, have gone into other industrial activities, and the same is true of the skilled workmen. It follows that it takes considerable time to recruit a sufficient number of new entrepreneurs and skilled laborers to develop construction on a large scale. Once expansion is under way, the construction continues so long as the rents appear favorable. Structures and plans are in process which cannot be completed for many months, and sometimes even years, after it appears that the rent situation, owing to the increasing surplus of available houses, is becoming less favorable. Thus, the adjustment of the supply of houses to the demand for houses takes place with a very considerable lag, and this, it appears, accounts in part for the cyclical movement in residential building.

The fluctuation in rents resulting from the failure of quick adjustment of available housing space to the number of families seeking accommodations is the major cause of the fluctuation. There are, however, other factors which have a bearing on the building cycle, including fluctuations in the cost of building, availability of investment funds, changes in the national income, changes in the rate of urban population growth, and general pessimism or optimism with respect to the long-run future.[8]

Some of these factors are themselves affected by the building cycle itself and, therefore, are in part caused by, as well as causes of, the building cycle movement. Thus, as building construction increases, the cost of building is advanced by reason of activity in the industry. And the ever-mounting cost is itself a factor causing, in part, a cessation of building operations. Much the same may be said about the availability of real-estate investment funds. Moreover, changes in the national income are, in part, affected by the building cycle and often act in a manner to reinforce and accelerate the upswing or the downswing of constructional activity.

As we have already noted, the building cycle on the average is almost exactly twice as long as the major business cycle. It is therefore not true, as has sometimes been suggested, that the building cycle has no relation whatever to the major business

[8] Cf. J. Tinbergen, *Statistical Testing of Business Cycle Theories, A Method and Its Application to Investment Activity,* League of Nations, 1939; C. F. Roos, *Dynamic Economics,* The Principia Press, Inc., 1934; J. B. D. Derksen, "Long Cycles in Residential Building: An Explanation," *Econometrica,* April, 1940; see also extended bibliography cited in C. D. Long, Jr., *op. cit.,* pp. 9–10.

cycle. On the contrary, American experience indicates that with a high degree of regularity every other major business boom coincides roughly with a boom in building construction, while the succeeding major cycle recovery is forced to buck up against a building slump. In the former case the peak of the building boom usually antedates the peak of the major cycle.

The periods of the six building cycles of the last hundred years are as follows:

TABLE I

	Low	*High*	*Low*
Cycle 1	1830	1836	1843
Cycle 2	1843	1853	1864
Cycle 3	1864	1871	1878
Cycle 4	1878	1890	1900
Cycle 5	1900	1909	1918
Cycle 6	1918	1925	1934

The major depressions which coincide with a sharp curtailment in building construction following pronounced booms are as follows: 1837, 1857, 1873, 1893, and 1929. It will be noted that every one of these depressions was of unusual severity and duration. This is precisely what one would expect. If temporary saturation in other forms of real investment coincides with a temporary saturation in investment in building structures, it is reasonable to suppose that the total decline in real investment will be far greater than would otherwise be the case. Moreover, since it takes longer to overcome the temporary saturation in building construction—indicated by the average length of the downswing in the building cycle, eight to nine years—it is not difficult to see that recovery of general investment activity is made more difficult so long as building construction, which has always been such an enormously important industry in American life, is declining or running along on a very low level. Thus, the depressions which have fallen in the interval of the construction downswing are typically deep and long. And the succeeding recovery is held back and retarded by the unfavorable depressional influence from the slump in the building industry.

With respect to the Great Depression of the thirties, it is worthy of note that the constructional boom of the twenties was the greatest in our history and that the precipitate decline in building after 1928 exceeded that in any earlier period. The only earlier building construction boom which at all approaches that of the nineteen-twenties in magnitude, relative to the then prevailing size of the economy, was that from 1843 to 1853; the subsequent decline was, however, considerably less serious than that experienced in the thirties.

The major depressions which have fallen in the periods when building construction was on the upgrade, or about to revive, are as follows: 1847, 1864, 1883, 1900, and 1920. It is a notable fact that each of these depressions was relatively short in duration and did not fall to any extreme depth. This also conforms with what one would expect. If the depression of the major business cycle occurs at a time when building construction is reviving, it is reasonable to suppose that the decline in general business activity will be cushioned by this fact, and that the moment forces making for revival appear, such forces will be powerfully reinforced and strengthened by the upsurge of building activity. The succeeding business boom is powerfully reinforced by a strong building boom.

There remain two major business cycle depressions which have not been included in the above analysis—those of 1907 and 1913. The 1907 major depression coincides with a downturn in building activity, which, however, was quickly checked. The succeeding level of building activity reached an even higher point than that which had prevailed in 1906. The major depression beginning in 1913 also coincides with a very minor downturn of building construction. As would be expected from these facts, both of these major depressions, while fairly sharp, were relatively short in duration. The recovery after 1907 could not, to be sure, be characterized as a pronounced boom but only as a period of moderate business prosperity. The recovery after the 1913 depression was, of course, profoundly influenced by the impact of the first World War. The generally sustained high level of building activity during the interval of both these depression periods, however, doubtless helps to explain the fact that both depressions were relatively mild and short lived. It is, of course, true that after the war began building construction fell to a very low level, reaching bottom in 1918. But investment expansion in other directions, stimulated by the vast war exports, caused the pronounced war boom.

It is reasonable to suppose that the most important single explanation for the speed of the recovery from the 1921 depression was the phenomenal upturn in building construction which began in 1921 and which rose to an unprecedented crest in 1925 and remained at an extraordinarily high level until 1928, when a drastic curtailment of constructional activity set in. No explanation of the boom of the twenties or the severity and duration of the depression of the thirties is adequate which leaves out of account the quite extraordinary record in building activity. Probably at no time in our history had we reached as complete a temporary saturation in building construction, including apartment houses, residences, office buildings, and other commercial structures, as was the case in the late twenties. Under these circumstances it was to be expected that it would take a long time to work through this period of oversaturation.

It is thus apparent that it is not possible to give an adequate analysis of the major business cycle (of eight to nine years' duration) without taking account of the impact on that cycle of the longer cycle of building construction. This factor is one of the most profound of the various influences which cause one major business cycle to differ from another. And in this factor we are able to see against the background of earlier American experience a part of the explanation of the severity of the Great Depression starting in 1929.

The role of the construction cycle in the boom of the twenties and the depressed conditions of the thirties is strikingly revealed when one compares real investment in fixed capital in the high prosperity period 1923–29 with the partial recovery years 1936–39. We include in fixed capital: (1) producers' equipment, (2) plant, (3) housing (including private nonprofit construction), and (4) public construction. The record is as follows:

TABLE II

Average Annual Real Investment[4]

(in billions)

	1936–39	*1923–29*
Equipment	$4.3	$4.8
Plant	1.9	3.9
Housing (plus nonprofit)	1.9	5.1
Public Construction	3.3	2.1

Investment in producers' equipment was $4.3 billions annually in 1936–39, very nearly equal to the annual investment of $4.8 in 1923–29. Considering the lower price level of 1936–39, the real investment was at least equal to that of 1923–29. The failure to achieve full recovery was not due (at least not to any appreciable extent) to inadequate expenditures on new equipment.

The next two categories reveal clearly where the deficiency lay. Investment in producers' plant amounted to only $1.9 billions annually in 1936–39, compared with $3.9 billions in 1923–29. Plant investment was down $2.0 billions per year. Housing averaged $1.9 in 1936–39, compared with $5.1 in 1923–29. The shortage here amounts to the vast figure of $3.2 billions per annum. Together, private construction of plant and housing ran annually $5.2 below the 1923–29 level. It is in this area that one must find the explanation for the incomplete recovery of the thirties.

The building cycle which we have been considering is, of course, nothing more or less than just the cycle in the con-

[4] Data from George Terborgh, *Federal Reserve Bulletin*, September, 1939, and subsequent estimates.

struction of plant and housing. According to our century-old experience with the building cycle, we should expect a slump in housing and in plant construction in the first recovery period following the intense constructional boom of the twenties. From this standpoint we could have expected, quite apart from the war and the defense program, that the major recovery of the forties would have made a more favorable record than that made in the thirties.

The construction areas in which the highest saturation was reached in the twenties were also the areas most depressed in the thirties. Office buildings and housing are leading examples. With respect to railroad plant, it is to be noted that expenditures in this area rose progressively (with a very slight recession in 1925 and 1927–28) to the peak of the boom, and even continued (despite the growing encroachment of trucks) into the depression, reaching the highest point in 1930. Similarly, investment in electric power plant, after a moderate decline from the 1924 peak, rose again in 1929 and even in 1930. Despite a sharp decline in electric power output in 1930, plant capacity was greatly increased. Installed capacity of plant and equipment remained far in excess of current output requirements for several years. Not until the relatively high electric power production of 1936 and 1937 was capacity sufficiently utilized to justify further large capital outlays. Thus, the thirties offer a conspicuous illustration of the prolonged saturation following a high constructional boom—the basic factor in the long building cycle.

The So-called "Long Waves"

But there are still other factors of a long-run character which influence the major business cycle and which help to explain the depressed thirties. Many writers, including Kondratieff, Spiethoff, Mitchell, Thorp, Schumpeter, Woytinsky, Ciriacy Wantrup, and others, have noted the important fact that the past experience of the Western world indicates prolonged periods of relatively good times, extending far beyond the boundaries of the major business cycle and even of the building cycle; and similarly prolonged periods of more or less chronic depression, within which, however, the swings of the business cycle occur. In the long periods of good times it has been noted that the upswing of the business cycle is vigorous and reaches high levels of activity, while the downswing phase is of relatively brief duration and comparatively easily overcome. The long periods of good times are apparently periods in which there is present a strong undercurrent of buoyancy, a powerful upsurge in investment activity, interrupted, to be sure, at fairly regular intervals by more or less severe depressions. In the long periods of chronic hard times, on the contrary, it has been found that depressions are regularly deep and prolonged and that recoveries are weak and anemic and fail to reach a level of reasonably full activity.

Among the characteristics which, from the statistical standpoint, most clearly distinguish these prolonged periods of good times and bad times are (a) secular movements of prices and (b) secular movements of interest rates. Always in the long periods of good times the trends of prices and interest rates are upward, while in the long periods of hard times the secular movements of prices and interest rates are downward. Some writers have sought to find in these phenomena the causal explanation. It is, however, more probable that the movements of prices and interest rates are *indicators* registering the impact of the deeper factors which cause the periods of good times or bad times, as the case may be. They are statistical thermometers, so to speak, registering the fact of prolonged buoyancy or chronic depression.

Attention should be called to the fact that it is scarcely appropriate, as has frequently been done, to speak of these prolonged periods as "upswing" and "downswing" periods. The long periods of hard times, at any rate, do not reveal an absolute decline in production, though they do reveal falling prices and interest rates. The trend of per capita output and real income continues to rise, though probably at a somewhat retarded rate

The periods of prolonged hard times are regularly associated with an exceptionally large amount of unemployment. Indeed, much convincing data with respect to these periods are to be found in social and labor history.[5] The periods of hard times are regularly periods of profound social unrest, of revolutionary movements designed to cure by more or less drastic procedures the social structure which caused or permitted such vast unemployment. A part of the political turbulence of these periods is, to be sure, to be explained in terms of the increasing weight of debt in view of falling prices. To this extent, the movement of the price level must be regarded as, at any rate, an intermediate causal factor intensifying the social and political disturbances commonly encountered in these periods. It is, however, necessary to look deeper into the underlying factors and to ascertain the fundamental causes of the general price decline.

Within these long periods of good times, on the one side, and bad times, on the other, there occur, modified however as indicated above, the more or less regular swings of the major business cycle, the temporary recessions of the minor cycles, and also the more or less regular swings of the eighteen-year building cycle. But since the long periods of buoyant prosperity or chronic depression extend beyond any of these phenomena, there is reason to suppose that there are other factors which have not been fully taken account of in the discussion either of the major and minor business cycles or of the building cycles.

Some writers have referred to these prolonged periods of good and bad times as "long waves." Whether or not it is appropriate to do so cannot yet be established in view of the fact that the record reveals thus far only three such "waves," the last of which is yet incomplete and, indeed, in some respects somewhat obscure. It is a fact, however, that as high a degree of periodicity has prevailed for these three waves as any which we find for the major business cycle. Moreover, it

[5] See John R. Commons, *et al.*, *Documentary History of American Industrial Society*, A. H. Clark Co., 1910–11; and also John R. Commons, *History of Labor in the United States*, Macmillan, 1918.

is a tenable hypothesis that the process of economic development tends to run not only in terms of the regular business cycle movement, but also in terms of these long waves. Indeed, as also with the business cycle, each phase of these long waves tends, in some measure, though we think less clearly than with respect to the business cycle, automatically to develop into the next succeeding phase.

The dates usually assigned to these periods [6] of preponderantly good times and bad times—or "long waves," if this term is preferred—are approximately as follows:

Good Times	*Bad Times*
1787–1815	1815–1843
1843–1873	1873–1897
1897–1920	1920– ?

It is interesting to note that in each of the long periods of good times there developed four major recoveries and three major depressions, while in each downswing there occurred two major recoveries and three major depressions. The turning point both at the top and at the bottom of the "long waves" coincides with the turning point of a major business boom or depression. This may be represented schematically as follows: If one measures the average duration of the three complete business cycles which occurred in each of the long periods of good times, one gets the following results: 6.67 years for the major business cycle in the first long period of good times, 8.67 for the second period, and 6.67 for the third. On the other hand, if one measures the two complete major cycles in each of the periods of prolonged hard times, one gets the following

[6] See J. A. Schumpeter, *Business Cycles,* McGraw-Hill, 1939; A. Spiethoff, "Krisen," *Handwörterbuch der Staatswissenschaften,* 4th ed., 1923; N. D. Kondratieff, "Die Langen Wellen der Konjunktur," *Archiv für Sozialwissenschaft und Sozialpolitik,* December, 1926 (translated in abridged form in *Review of Economic Statistics,* November, 1935); W. C. Mitchell, *Business Cycles, The Problem and Its Setting,* National Bureau of Economic Research, 1927, pp. 441–42; S. von Ciriacy Wantrup, *Agrarkrisen und Stockungsspannen,* Paul Parey, 1936; and Alvin H. Hansen, *Economic Stabilization in an Unbalanced World,* Harcourt, Brace and Co., 1932, Chapter VI.

results: eleven years for the major business cycle in the first period, ten years for the second period, and 8.5 years for the third period. Thus, it is evident that on the average the major cycle in the long periods of good times had a duration of 7.3 years, while on the average the length of the major cycle in the long hard times was 9.8 years.

Just as the major business cycle has not always been completely synchronous in the various industrial countries, so also it is not always possible to fit all countries neatly into the intervals designated as long periods of buoyant expansion or prolonged bad times. For the most part, however, the experience of different countries conforms with the periods outlined above. With respect to the current phase, the thesis is perhaps defensible that for the western European countries the economic development from 1920 on justifies characterizing it as the beginning of a prolonged period of hard times. With respect to the United States, however, in view of the high prosperity of the twenties, it is difficult to justify placing the United States in such a category. There is, however, the undoubted fact, of which cognizance must be taken, that the decade of the twenties was preponderantly a period of hard times for agriculture. From the standpoint of employment in urban industry as a whole, the twenties must clearly be characterized as a decade of preponderantly buoyant prosperity. It is possible that the most reasonable classification is to make 1920 the turning point for the European countries and 1929 the turning point for the United States.

On balance, we believe it is a defensible thesis, though certainly not proven, that the basic underlying economic conditions from 1920 were relatively unfavorable, but that special factors growing out of the first World War, along with certain technological developments especially favorable to the United States, differentiate the experience of our country from that of western Europe. Moreover, with respect to certain European countries the underlying unfavorable economic factors were, even in the period of the twenties, in some measure offset by deliberate governmental intervention stimulating economic activity. Eventually, out of the depth of the Great Depression and the heightened international tension incident thereto, sprang the enormous military expenditures preparatory to the 1939 European War.

Whether or not the future economic development will justify any continuing classification of periods into eras of good times and bad times only the future can reveal. For one thing, the strong impact of governmental intervention in recent decades may vitiate any such classification. On the other hand, it is too early to say precisely what will be the impact of governmental intervention upon even such long-run tendencies as we are here discussing. After the first World War there were those who argued that the intervention of new central bank techniques and other governmental policies made it quite impossible to speak any longer of the movements of the business cycle. This contention, thus far at any rate, appears not well founded, and it may be that we need similarly to postpone any hasty decision with respect to the impact of governmental policy upon longer-run fundamental economic forces related to eras of buoyant prosperity and chronic depression which transcend the shorter movement of the business cycle.

Three major explanations have been offered for these long periods of good and bad times. One runs in terms of technological developments, innovations, exploitation of new resources, and the opening of new territory. This explanation has been advanced notably by Spiethoff, Wicksell, and Schumpeter. A second explanation runs in terms of war. This explanation has been advanced prominently by Ciriacy Wantrup and has also been noted by Kondratieff and Wicksell. A third, running in terms of gold and price movements, has been advanced by Cassel,[7] Warren and Pearson,[8] Woytinsky,[9] and others.

[7] *Report of the Gold Delegation of the Financial Committee,* Geneva, 1932; G. Cassel, *On Quantitative Thinking in Economics,* Oxford, 1935; Cassel, *The Theory of Social Economy,* Harcourt, Brace and Co., 1923.

[8] C. F. Warren and F. A. Pearson, *Gold and Prices,* John Wiley and Sons, 1935.

[9] W. Woytinsky, *Internationale Hebung der Preise als Ausweg aus der Krise,* 1931.

According to the first theory, the periods of prolonged good times are periods in which there is a favorable underlying basis for the growth of real investment in the development of technology, innovations, and the discovery of new resources. In such periods, it is said, the pace of technological progress is accelerated far beyond what may be expected from the usual run of multitudinous inventions, each of relatively small significance. In the long periods of good times quite revolutionary new techniques are introduced which profoundly change the character of the whole economy. In the periods of the prolonged hard times these exceptional technological developments are damped down or run out. The great investment opportunities exploited in the preceding period of good times are now largely exhausted. General technological improvements of a less profound character are, to be sure, going on, gradually raising the productivity of labor and increasing the real income. Indeed, the great technological advance and the vast real investments completed by the end of the long period of good times become the foundation upon which an advancing real income is projected into the succeeding period of preponderantly hard times. The rise in income experienced in this period is a function of the higher productivity of the factors of production achieved by the technical advance of the preceding period, but the preponderance of hard times reveals itself in a marked degree of unemployment and in the failure of the upswings of the major business cycles to reach a condition of full economic activity.

Professor Schumpeter, with his emphasis on the role of innovations, explains the prolonged good times of the first long wave by the emergence of the Industrial Revolution and the first long period of hard times by the readjustments and adaptations necessary once this new structure had become more or less firmly incorporated into the economic system. The second period of buoyant good times he explains by the admittedly new revolutionary technique which perhaps more than anything else has profoundly altered the character of modern industrial civilization, namely, the railroad. There can be no question that the development of the railroad opened up vast real investment outlets throughout the Western world, and that this gave a continuous upward push to the economy, making every burst of investment associated with the major business cycle a pronounced and strong one and tending to weaken the forces making for depression. In the last quarter of the nineteenth century, however, came a sharp decline in the rate of growth of the railroad industry. The third period of prolonged good times Professor Schumpeter explains by the emergence of the electrical, chemical, and automotive industries. Wicksell, in his famous Chapter XI in *Interest and Prices,* published in 1898, emphasized fundamentally the same technological factors which are heavily relied upon in Professor Schumpeter's explanation. Spiethoff similarly stresses technological developments in his analysis.

The view that these periods of prolonged good times ("Aufschwungsspanne") and bad times ("Stockungsspanne") have been caused by wars has been most effectively presented by Ciriacy Wantrup. According to this analysis, the long periods of good times are basically caused by the vast governmental expenditures relating to preparation for war and the war itself, while on the other side the periods of chronic hard times are caused by the difficult readjustments incident to the sharp curtailment of war expenditures. The best case for this thesis can probably be made out for the first so-called long wave. The long period of the Napoleonic Wars, the vast governmental expenditures which they entailed, and the stimulus which these expenditures gave to the changes in the economic system ushered in by the Industrial Revolution all indicate that the impact of these wars played a very considerable role. Similarly, the sharp curtailment of expenditures, together with the difficult readjustments to a peacetime basis after the whole of western Europe had for a quarter of a century adjusted itself to war conditions, goes far to explain the difficulties of the long period of chronic hard times from 1815 to the middle forties. A much poorer case can be made for this thesis with respect to the second so-called long wave. It is true that in the "Aufschwungsspanne" (1843–73) there occurred a number of important wars at various intervals, including the Crimean War, the American Civil War, the Danish-Prussian and the Austro-Prussian Wars of the sixties, and the Franco-Prussian War of 1871.

For the "Aufschwungsspanne" of the third cycle also the case for the war thesis seems relatively weak and would have to rely upon the expansion of armament expenditures, since the first World War did not come until the very end of the long period of good times. At all events, there is much force in the contention that the difficulties confronted by countries in western Europe since 1920 were in large measure related to the aftermath of the war.

On balance, it may perhaps be said that, in the "upswing" phase of the first so-called long wave, wars occupied a position of major importance, perhaps equal to that of the innovations introduced by the Industrial Revolution. Each reinforced the other, and it is difficult to disentangle the relative potency of each factor. For the second "Aufschwungsspanne" it appears reasonable to conclude that the major factor was the railroadization of the world and that wars played a relatively minor part, with respect to both the good times and the ensuing period of chronic hard times which followed. For the third period the most reasonable conclusion appears to be that the electrification and motorization of the Western world played by far the dominant role, reinforced toward the end of the period by the first World War, and that for the succeeding period of economic difficulties postwar readjustments played an important role, though it may well be that the adaptation of the economic structure to the innovational developments of the preceding period was of equal significance.

Those who have stressed price factors in the so-called long waves have tended to lay great emphasis upon the effective supply of monetary gold, a function, on the one side, of the annual net additions to the gold stock from gold production and, on the other side, of the increasing volume of trade. Those, like Cassel, who have stressed this analysis have usually limited their discussion to the period from 1850 to 1913. Cassel calculated the effective gold supply by correcting the monetary gold stock by an index of an estimated rising trend of the physical volume of trade assumed to increase at a compound rate of 3 per cent per annum. He found that the effective gold supply rose from 1850 to the early seventies, fell from the early seventies to the middle nineties, and rose again to 1913. This movement correlates closely with the general movement of commodity prices and also with the dates usually assigned for the second so-called long wave and the first half of the third. According to this type of analysis, the price movements are caused by the gold movements.

Gold production is clearly more or less a result of accidental discoveries and the development of new mining and refining techniques. While these may themselves, to a certain extent, be related to changes in the profitableness of producing gold, they are certainly, in large part, independent developments. In addition, it is quite clear that the fluctuation of gold production is, in part, related to the changes in the price level which alter the costs of gold production and, therefore, the profitableness of producing gold.[10] From this standpoint, gold production may be looked upon as a result of price movements, and not a cause. Thus, the farther prices fall the more profitable it becomes to produce gold, and a progressively increasing stimulus to output develops, so that after prices have fallen a certain distance gold production increases more and more. There is a lag in the cycle of gold production relative to the cycle of prices of about fifteen years. For example, in the period from 1873 to 1920—one complete long cycle of commodity prices from peak to peak—there is a corresponding cycle of gold production, lagged fifteen years, extending through the period from 1888 to 1935.[11] Thus, in the period of high prices gold production was discouraged, and this influence continued on for a considerable interval of time. As

[10] Similarly the increased market or legal price of gold in terms of most currencies in recent years has stimulated gold production.

[11] Warren and Pearson, *op. cit.*

prices, however, fell from 1873 on, the impact of this decline finally revealed itself in an upturn of gold production about fifteen years later. Similarly, as prices reached bottom in the nineties, the continued stimulus to gold production carried on over a considerable period after prices began to rise. Thus, with a lag of about fifteen years gold production followed the price movement and from this standpoint may be regarded as a result and not a cause of the price movement.

While it is not possible at this point to go into any extended discussion of the theory of money and prices, it may be said that the trend of monetary thinking is in the direction of laying less stress than formerly upon the purely monetary factors and still less stress upon gold. It is clear that the more credit instruments are developed the farther modern money is removed from gold. The development of deposit currency, and also the development of central banking, permits a high degree of variation between the volume of the means of payment and the gold supply. There is no longer any close connection between them. But more than that, the trend of modern monetary thinking runs in the direction of emphasizing the factors which influence fluctuations in total money income rather than factors influencing the constituent elements in the total volume of money payments, namely, the amount of money, including demand deposits (M), and the velocity of turnover (V). If forces are present tending to cause a rise in the money income, the possibilities under modern conditions of increasing the quantity of money regardless of the gold base, or of utilizing any given quantity of money more efficiently through changes in turnover or velocity, are so great that it may within broad limits safely be said that there are no serious limits, from the side of the money supply, to movements of money income. We must look for other factors, notably those affecting the prospective rate of profit, rather than limitation or superabundance of the money supply, to explain secular movements in income and prices.

Thus, if technological developments and innovations tend to favor a rapid expansion in real investment, money incomes may be expected to rise, and the money supply and its utilization (MV) may be expected to adjust itself to these conditions. If, on the other hand, the underlying technological developments are unfavorable to a rapid expansion of real investment, money income will fail to keep pace with output and the secular trend of prices will be downward. Here again the money supply (M) and its utilization (V) adjust themselves to the demands of the underlying real factors. Still more obvious is the fact that, in periods of vast war expenditures, governments, through radical readjustments in the monetary system, such as the abandonment of the gold standard, adapt the money situation to their own demands. Inflation in wartime has never encountered any limits in terms of the monetary situation. Such limits as have been imposed run mainly in terms of direct price controls and of governmental policies with respect to expenditures and the methods employed for obtaining revenues, whether by taxation or by borrowing. Thus, on balance, we conclude that gold and monetary factors play a subsidiary role and that the main causes of the long periods of good times and of chronic depression must be sought in technological and innovational factors, and at times in greater or less degree in the fiscal policies of governments hitherto related mainly to the conduct of war.

According to the technological and innovational thesis, the electrification and motorization of the American economy dominated the period from the late nineties to 1929. From this standpoint this epoch may be compared with the period of rapid expansion in railroadization from the middle forties to the decade of the seventies. Both of these innovations caused a profound structural change in economic life and institutions. Both relate mainly to speed of communication and transportation. Both opened up enormous opportunities for real investment, not only directly in the railroads, in automobile factories, and in roads, but also in a vast network of underlying and supplementary industries, including for the last period, glass, rubber, steel, cement, electrical appliances, petroleum, and the like. These epochs are clear illustrations of the profound impact of the rise of quite new techniques giving birth to a range of new industries and expanding and developing old ones into new lines. Both epochs represent a period of rapid growth and expansion. But all new developments finally reach the stage of maturity. Thus, new railroad mileage experienced a rapidly rising trend from the middle forties to the decade of the seventies, and thereafter flattened out with, however, a major spurt in the middle eighties, and eventually in the nineties sharply declined. Similarly, the production of automobiles and the construction of roads experienced a rapid growth into the decade of the twenties. But this rate of growth could obviously not be continued indefinitely. Automobile production gradually reached an asymptotic level after 1923, and the curve of the construction of roads similarly flattened out toward the end of the twenties and thereafter declined.

In the long sweep of technological and innovational developments the decade of the thirties is, therefore, in many respects not unlike the fourth quarter of the nineteenth century,[12] with its deep depressions of the seventies and the nine-

12 It was in this period, when the railroadization of the country was increasingly reaching a saturation point, that Colonel Carroll D. Wright, Commissioner of Labor, made his famous declaration with respect to the exhaustion of real investment opportunities. Up to that time the central barometer of prosperity and economic activity, of which everyone was more or less consciously aware, was activity in the railroad industry. The declining role of the railroad was, indeed, the most significant single fact for this period and offers the most convincing explanation for the chronic hard times, particularly of the decade of the nineties. Colonel Wright's analysis has attracted, particularly in recent years, widespread attention and received much comment. Some, in view of the tremendous expansion ushered in by the electrification and motorization innovation beginning at the end of the century, have been disposed to criticize his analysis as shortsighted. But others regard his observation as the most penetrating and valid analysis of the economic difficulties of his time which anyone of his generation made. The investment saturation to which he called attention is evidenced by the continued difficulties which confronted not only the United States, but also the countries of western Europe for more than a decade following his lucid exposition of the deep, underlying, real factors in the situation. While others were stressing superficial aspects, Colonel Wright placed his finger upon the really significant cause of the world-wide stagnation.

See U. S. Commissioner of Labor, First *Annual Report,* Government Printing Office, 1886, dealing with Industrial Depressions.

ties. Thus, against the background of earlier experience the decade of the thirties is more understandable.

The early expansion of the railroad served to promote vigorous booms and to cut short temporary lapses into depression. But progressively the railroad reached maturity and eventually ceased to grow. The mere slowing down in the *rate* of growth caused an absolute decline in the volume of new investment required in the plant and equipment of subsidiary industries, such as iron and steel, which manufactured the materials that went into railroad construction. Those who point to the high level of new railroad construction which continued on into the eighties miss the point. It is not enough that new railroad construction should continue at the high level reached. New construction must *continue to rise at a constant rate* if new investment in the underlying, subsidiary industries is to be maintained at the pace set. Thus, the mere slowing down in the *rate of increase* in new railroad construction was already beginning to have a damping effect on the economy long before there was an actual decline in the volume of new construction. This is the important lesson which we learn from the acceleration principle. The sharp decline in railroad construction in the decade of the nineties was a significant factor in that depressed decade.

But now a new era of buoyancy superseded the railroad era —the era of electricity and motorcars. The three decades 1900–29 witnessed the rise of four new giant industries.[13] Street cars led the way in the nineties and reached its investment peak ($2.5) in the decade 1900–09. Capital outlays on telephones increased rapidly after 1900 and doubled in each of the two succeeding decades, rising to $2.5 billions in the twenties. Electric power investment first assumed large proportions in the decade 1900–09 ($1.7 billions), increased 50 per cent in the following decade, and leaped forward with a capi-

[13] I am indebted to John Wilson, formerly instructor in economics at Harvard University and now economist in the Department of Commerce, for the use of data in his unpublished manuscript.

tal expenditure of $8.1 billions in the twenties. Automobile production, from only 4,000 units in 1900, rose to 187,000 units in 1910, 1,000,000 in 1915, 2,200,000 in 1920, 4,400,000 in 1925, and 5,600,000 in 1929. Garages, repair shops, and service stations multiplied throughout the country. Thus, the automobile industry not only fostered gigantic production plants, largely concentrated in a single industrial area, but also opened opportunities for thousands of small business units located in all sections of the country roughly in proportion to the consuming population. Major subsidiary industries were created or expanded on the tide of the vast purchasing power of the automobile industry, including such giants as Petroleum, Rubber, Glass Plate, and Steel. Finally, outlays on public roads, largely induced by the rise of the automobile, reached the figure of $9.9 billions in the decade 1920–29.[14]

Thus, an era of buoyant prosperity was generated by the growth of four great industries: street railways, telephone, electric power, and automobile industries (including Petroleum, Rubber, and Glass Plate, largely accessory to the Automobile). Also important, but nevertheless dwarfed by the four giants, were the movie, chemical, and electrical equipment industries.

Just as the railroad expansion came to an end, so also the buoyant era of 1900–29. Street railway development was largely completed in the first decade, telephone and automobile expansion in the third decade. Electric power alone remains with large prospects for further growth. The great era of expansion was over by 1930. Thus, the decade of the thirties resembles the conditions in the nineties. Technological developments making for expansion had temporarily spent their force. This does not mean, however, that eras of buoyant expansion are permanently a thing of the past. The progress of technology, we can be reasonably certain, will sooner or later open outlets for enlarged streams of investment in great new industries.

14 From Temporary National Economic Committee Hearings, Part 1, p. 232.

Structural Changes in American Economy

Thus far we have seen that the decade of the thirties is largely understandable in terms of past experience. But our analysis would remain incomplete if we neglected to consider one important structural change in our economy for which we have no precedent in the past. Always, in the past century, expansion has rested not merely on *intensive* investment arising from technological progress, but also on extensive growth—the occupation of new territory and the growth of population. The nineteenth century was a unique era of *extensive* growth.

Approximately in the period of 1915–30, the rate of extensive growth rapidly slowed down. The decennial increment of population growth in northern and western Europe, including the three great powers, the United Kingdom, Germany, France, and the smaller northern and western countries —Scandinavia, Finland, Belgium, Holland, Switzerland, and the Irish Free State—continued to rise, or at any rate did not decline materially until the first World War. The following table (calculated from Kuczynski's *The Balance of Births and Deaths,* p. 9) gives the approximate increases for the *eleven* countries of northern and western Europe referred to above. The period 1913 to 1926 is omitted, since the war abnormally reduced the rate of population growth. The decade 1926–36 may be regarded as representative of postwar normal rate of growth.

TABLE III

Decade	*Increase*
1883–93	10,290,000
1893–03	14,950,000
1903–13	14,510,000
1926–36	9,468,000

In the United States the decline came later, as shown in the table which follows:

TABLE IV

Decade	*Increase*
1900–10	16,138,000
1910–20	14,923,000
1920–30	15,901,000
1930–40	9,218,000

In northern and western Europe the turning point came with the first World War. In the United States it came in 1924.

The expansion of Europe into new territory (in terms of both migration and foreign investments) came to an abrupt halt in the first World War and, while resumed in the twenties, did not again attain its former level. In the United States the expansion into the great West was followed by several decades of urbanization; and then we turned (via capital export) on a large scale to less developed countries. This movement ended in the Great Depression. Doubtless, under more favorable political conditions, there is still room for considerable foreign investment in the less industrialized parts of the world, and it may be expected again sooner or later to be resumed on a fairly large scale. But no one is likely to challenge the statement that the era of development and settlement of new territory is largely over. The role of territorial expansion is likely to be much less in the next half century than was the case in the nineteenth century relative to national income.[15]

The rapid decline in population growth and the exhaustion of the world frontier may well have a causal interconnection. Certainly it is true that, so long as there were great new territories to be opened and developed, rapid population growth was a healthy economic development. With an increasing exhaustion of opportunities for settlement and exploitation of new territory, the continuation of the nineteenth-century rate

[15] See Isaiah Bowman, *Limits of Land Settlement,* Council on Foreign Relations, 1937.

of population growth would rapidly have given rise to insoluble economic problems.

It is true that the sudden and drastic decline in the rate of population growth so far has affected mainly western Europe, and highly developed industrial countries, such as the United States. It is also true that there are still areas which have a long way to go in the process of industrialization. But just as the rate of population growth in the highly industrialized countries has rapidly declined and in some is approaching zero, so also the possibilities of large outlets for foreign investment by these countries appear meager, in terms of national income and wealth, in comparison with those of the nineteenth century. While it is not possible statistically to measure the rate of decline in investment opportunities with the precision that is possible with respect to population growth, in general the two movements appear to exhibit a somewhat parallel development.

In this connection, it is well to emphasize that the economic frontier of any country must always be conceived of not in terms of its own boundaries, but in terms of the possibility of capital investment throughout the entire world. Thus, Great Britain, despite the fact that her own territory was, of course, from the beginning of the modern capitalist period fully occupied, enjoyed equally with the United States a great economic frontier throughout the nineteenth century. From this standpoint, it is clearly a mistake to speak of the passing of the American frontier as the end of extensive expansion, for after this phase was over, investment abroad played an important role in the general world expansion, and this in turn reacted upon the speed of our own internal development. Moreover, of course, as far as general economic expansion is concerned, it must always be remembered that throughout the era of modern industrialization there are three strands to the process—technological innovations, the development of new territory, and the growth of population. Each has reinforced the other, but at times, when one or the other has slackened, another factor has taken an exceptional spurt. This was notably true in the United States in the period of electrification and motorization of her economy.

Population growth [16] and territorial expansion opened vast outlets for *extensive* investment of capital. But, it is argued, may not equally favorable opportunities for *intensive* investment take their place? The answer appears to be that in the past we have enjoyed opportunities for *both* extensive and intensive investment. Now *extensive expansion* is largely over, and there remains only the possibility of intensive developments. But intensive investment is not something new. Intensive and extensive developments have proceeded together, each reinforcing the other. New technological developments underlie the nineteenth century of expansion. But population growth and the penetration into new territory, in turn, played an important role in the widening of the market and the development of mass production techniques. Extensive expansion minimized the risks of technological innovations and encouraged bold experimentation. Thus extensive expansion stimulated intensive expansion. On the other side, the pressure to find investment opportunities, in view of the slowing down of extensive growth, will be greater in the future. Industrial research is now far more systematic and more generously financed than ever before.

The era of buoyant prosperity (1844–73), based largely on the railroad, was intimately linked up with extensive growth and expansion. The next buoyant era (1900–29), based on electricity and the automobile, had less to do with mere extensive growth and expansion into new territory, and involved a much more radical transformation in consumption

[16] It has been argued that cessation of population growth should be favorable to employment, since the supply of new workers in the labor market would be reduced. But it is easy to show that population growth, if it occurs in a period of territorial expansion, raises the demand for labor more than it raises supply. Thus, the volume of extensive investment associated with the net addition of one worker involves capital outlays on a house, amounting to, say, $4,000, and outlays on plant and equipment amounting to an additional $4,000. Eight thousand dollars of investment represents a far greater effect on the demand for labor than the effect on supply of one additional man-year of labor.

habits and ways of living. This sort of transformation, involving vast investment of capital, can take place without extensive growth, and under the progress of technology we shall doubtless experience again far-reaching revolutionary innovations of this sort. There is, perhaps, inherent in the process of innovation a cumulative tendency which may be described in terms of a geometric progression. That this was true, even of the past century, is at least in part supported by the fact that the percentage rate of increase in per capita real income was approximately a constant. It is, of course, always possible that the rate of technological development may in the future exceed the geometric rate of the past, but here obviously one enters a field of speculation which can be settled only by the actual course of future historical events. It is, at any rate, a question whether intensive investment can attain the buoyancy and tempo of earlier periods when technological developments were stimulated by population growth and territorial expansion.

The decline in the rate of extensive expansion may partly account for the structural change which we are witnessing in economic institutions. The economic order is undergoing progressively changes in its internal organization which affect its functioning and operation—defense mechanisms, they may be, which seek more or less blindly and experimentally to adjust the economy to an era of less rapid extensive growth. These changes are commonly described in terms of a shift from a free market economy to a planned economy.

In the nineteenth century an automatic price mechanism functioned with relatively little intervention or control from organizational influences, whether governmental or private. Each individual unit in the process of production constituted, so to speak, only a small atom, unable to control but instead controlled by the general forces inherent in the price mechanism. And while, particularly from 1870 on, institutional interferences with the automatic functioning of the price system were gradually developing, it is, broadly speaking, true that these played a relatively minor role until the first World War.

Just as wars have frequently acted as a profound stimulus upon technological development, so also the first World War enormously accelerated the development of institutional interferences with the price mechanism. An increasing degree of regimentation by both public and private organization developed with startling rapidity. Instruments of control that had gradually been taking shape were perfected and utilized on a wide scale. This revealed itself in monetary and fiscal policy and also in corporate, labor, and other private control mechanisms.

In a free market economy no single unit was sufficiently powerful to exert any appreciable control over the price mechanism. In a controlled economy the government, the corporation, and organized groups all exercise a direct influence over the market mechanism. Many contend that it is just this imperfect functioning of the price system which explains the failure to achieve reasonably full employment in the decade of the thirties. Some place the blame on corporate price policies, some on trade-union practices, and some on the restrictions imposed by government.

There can be no doubt that these profound changes in institutional arrangements are significant. It is not possible to go back to the atomistic order. Corporations, trade-unions, and government intervention we shall continue to have. Modern democracy does not mean individualism. It means a system in which private, voluntary organization functions under general, and mostly indirect, governmental control. Dictatorship means direct and specific control. We do not have a choice between "plan and no plan." We have a choice only between democratic planning and totalitarian regimentation.

Chapter II

INVESTMENT AND CONSUMPTION, 1920–1939

IT may be well to remind the reader again that we have chosen to follow the common-sense classification adopted by Kuznets in his study of *National Income and Capital Formation, 1919–1935,* and have included in real consumption not only the flow of personal services, nondurable consumption goods (e. g., foodstuffs), and semidurable commodities (e. g., clothing) reaching consumers' markets, but also such durable consumers' goods as automobiles and household equipment. By real investment we mean the flow of production of (a) fixed capital goods, including plant and equipment, residential housing, public construction, and (b) net increases in inventories of commodity stocks held by business firms, whether finished, semifinished, or raw. Real consumption means the annual flow of consumers' goods and services; real net investment means the annual flow of additions to stocks of plant, equipment, and inventories. Together, the annual output of consumption and investment goods constitutes the real income.

The money expenditures made on consumption and investment goods in any given period are the source of the stream of money income received by the society as a whole for the stream of goods and services produced. The money income equals consumption plus investment expenditures. We shall designate the money income (or net income) by the letter Y, consumption expenditures by C, and investment expenditures by I. Thus $Y = C + I$. When the terms "income," "investment," and "consumption" are used alone, it is understood that they refer to money income and to the money expenditures on consumption and on investment.

For certain purposes it is convenient to use gross investment (I′) which includes expenditures on capital replacement (I_r) plus net additions to capital (I). When gross investment expenditures are added to consumption expenditures, we obtain gross income (Y′). Thus $Y' = I' + C$.

It is characteristic of the cyclical fluctuations in the money income that its two component parts—consumption and investment—tend to rise and fall together. But this is a very general statement. We shall want to know more specifically about the *timing* and *amplitude* of these movements.

With respect to timing, it appears that, while investment and consumption fluctuate together, the movements are not entirely synchronous. Kuznets' data show that investment tends to lead, with consumption following. Thus, the recovery of 1921 begins with an increase in investment expenditures. Gross investment rose by $1.8 billions from 1921 to 1922, while consumption continued to fall (though at a diminished rate) by $0.7 billions. In the following year both moved strongly upward together. Again, in the recovery of the thirties, investment started up first, rising by $0.7 billions from 1932 to 1933, while consumption was still falling by $1.8 billions. In the downturn of 1929 both investment and consumption declined simultaneously. It should be noted, however, that investment fell sharply from 1929 to 1930, while consumption receded by a relatively small amount. This would indicate that also in the downswing consumption tends to follow.

The lead of investment over consumption can be traced (though less clearly) not merely at the turning points of the major business cycle, but also in the minor fluctuations. Thus, there was a minor recession from 1923 to 1924, evidenced by a decline in investment; while consumption continued to rise, though at a reduced rate. In the following year investment leaped forward, with consumption rising but little, indicating a lag in consumption. In the next year (from 1925 to 1926) investment continued at the high level reached, while consumption (under the stimulus of the preceding year's upsurge of investment) moved strongly forward. Again, it appears that consumption followed investment. Thereafter, both remained high (with some decline of investment in 1928) through 1929.

Thus, the statistical data during the last two decades tend to support the thesis that the active dynamic factor in the cycle is investment, with consumption assuming a passive, lagging role.

The problem is further illuminated if investment and consumption are broken up into various constituent elements. With respect to investment, this involves a number of components, which we shall presently consider. We shall first consider the consumption components.

Consumption is divided by Kuznets into four parts as follows: (a) durable [1] consumers' commodities (automobiles, household equipment), (b) semidurable [2] consumers' commodities (shoes, clothing, etc.), (c) perishable [3] consumers' commodities (food, etc.), and (d) services. In general, it is possible to discern a sequence in the expenditures on these four categories in the order mentioned. But the most pronounced lead is that of durable consumers' commodities over the other three combined. Because of this definite lead it will be useful for our purposes to concentrate upon a twofold classification of consumption expenditures: (a) durable consumers' commodities, and (b) "all other" consumers' goods (commodities and services).

Expenditures on durable consumers' goods increased over $600 millions from 1921 to 1922, while the outlay on "all other" consumers' goods decreased nearly $1,400 millions. In

[1] "Durable commodities" include those whose use ordinarily extends over three years.

[2] "Semidurable commodities" include those ordinarily used less than three years, but more than six months.

[3] "Perishable commodities" include those whose use ordinarily extends over less than six months.

1923 expenditures for both rapidly increased. In 1924 expenditures for "durables" remained at the level of 1923, while "all other" moved strongly upward. In 1925 "durables" moved up, while "all other" remained about stationary. In 1926 "durables" held the new level, while "all other" again shot up. Thereafter, the fluctuations around the high level reached were relatively small through 1929. Thereafter "durables" began a sharp decline, with "all other" responding more sluggishly to the general downswing. In 1933 "durables" made a small step toward recovery, while "all other" continued to decline. Thereafter, both rose until 1937. The lead of "durables" over "all other" can be seen in Chart 1 (Kuznets' data).

In general (see Chart 2), the turning points in the fluctuations of durable consumers' goods expenditures synchronize fairly closely with outlays on producers' equipment. Durable consumers' commodities bear a resemblance to producers' equipment in several important respects. They require an investment of funds during the interval in which they are used. Moreover, since they have a durability which is not rigorously fixed, it is possible to postpone the purchase of a new unit, if necessary, beyond the normal period of use. On the other hand, the purchase of perishable commodities [4] cannot readily be postponed without great inconvenience and a serious decline in consumption standards. Further, durable consumers' goods, like producers' equipment, are subject to obsolescence in the event that new innovations are introduced. Finally, since they are durable, it is possible to buy them on credit by permitting the seller to retain title until the last installment is paid.

In all these respects, durable consumers' goods resemble producers' equipment, and, indeed, investment goods in general; and, from a strictly logical standpoint, they might well be included in the investment category.[5] This procedure,

[4] This, however, does not apply to luxuries, the purchase of which is also postponable.

[5] This Kuznets has, indeed, done in his Variant II classification. See pp. 34–39 in *National Income and Capital Formation, 1919–1935*, National Bureau of Economic Research, 1937.

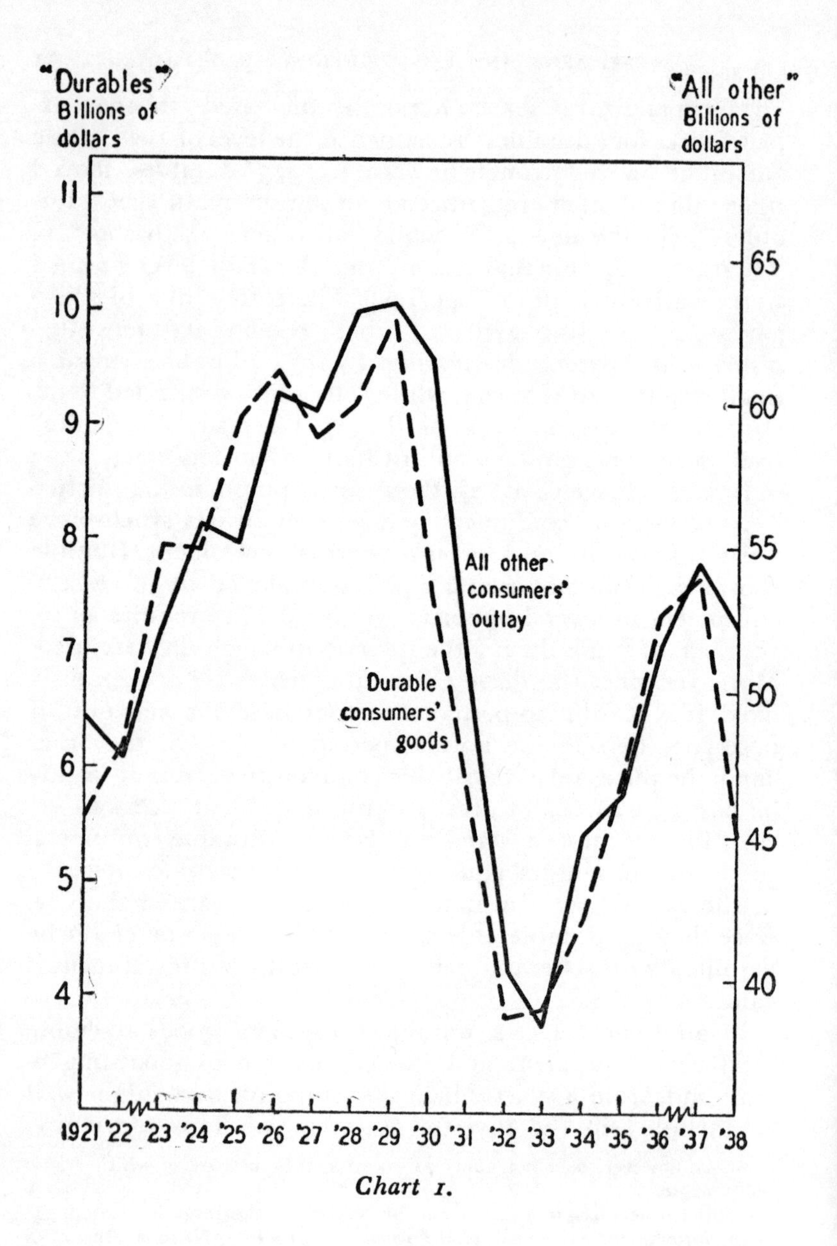
"Durables"
Billions of
dollars
"All other"
Billions of
dollars
11
10
9
8
7
6
5
4
65
60
55
50
45
40
All other
consumers'
outlay
Durable
consumers'
goods
1921
'22
'23
'24
'25
'26
'27
'28
'29
'30
'31
'32
'33
'34
'35
'36
'37
'38

Chart 1.

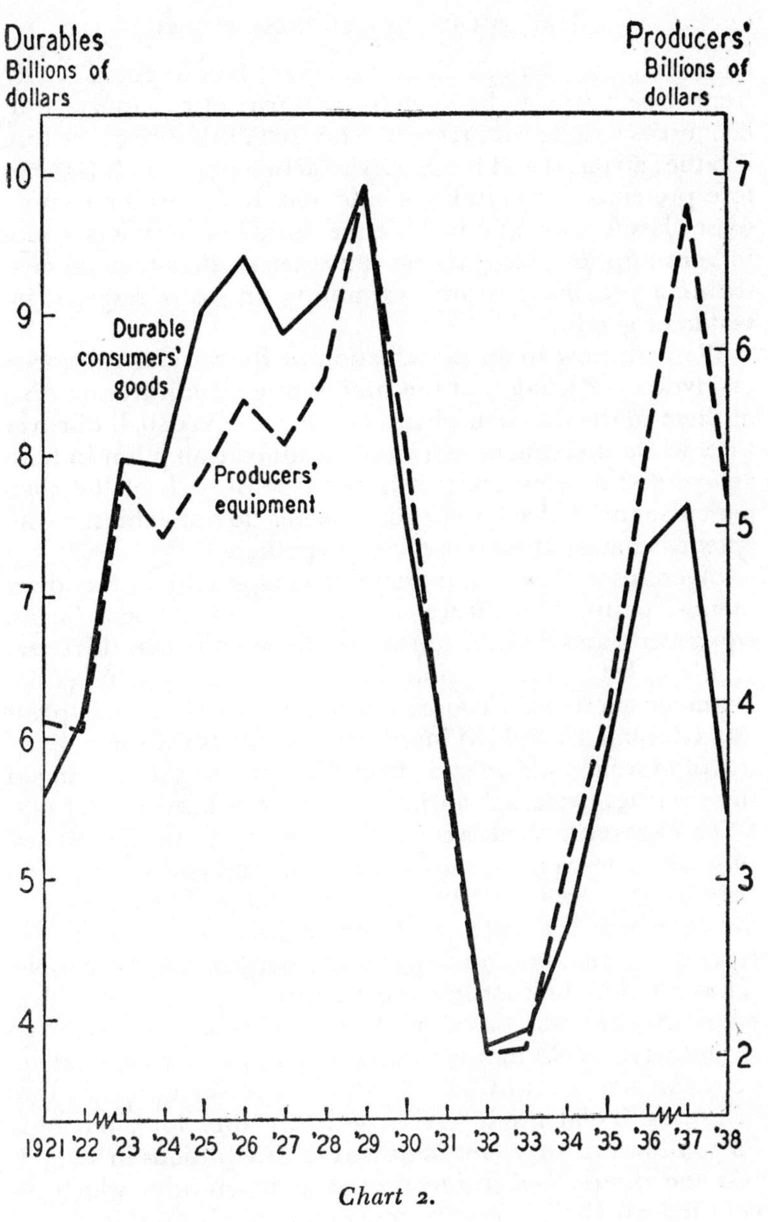
Durables
Billions of
dollars
Producers'
Billions of
dollars
10
9
8
7
6
5
4
7
6
5
4
3
2
Durable
consumers'
goods
Producers'
equipment
1921
'22
'23
'24
'25
'26
'27
'28
'29
'30
'31
'32
'33
'34
'35
'36
'37
'38

Chart 2.

however, would require the calculation of an imputed "rent" from these goods, to be included as a part of consumers' outlay, just as is done with respect to housing. But such procedure is rather artificial and is contrary to actual practice. It is therefore preferable, everything considered, to follow a common-sense classification and include the durable consumers' goods in consumption, recognizing, nonetheless, that they do constitute a peculiar category resembling, in many respects, investment goods.

We turn now to an examination of the various categories of investment goods and the timing of expenditures on each of these in the different phases of the cycle. We shall discover that, while investment as a whole leads consumption in both recovery and recession, this is not true of each of the components; and, indeed, some components do not exhibit a consistent behavior from one cycle to another.

Inventories play an important role, especially in the lower turning point. Thus, if we consider producers' goods (plant, equipment, and inventories) as a whole, we find that this series regularly leads consumption. But if we divide producers' investment goods into two categories: (a) fixed capital (plant and equipment) and (b) inventories, we discover some diversity of movement from cycle to cycle. Thus, in the upswing of the twenties there was an increase in both fixed capital outlays and inventory outlays from 1921 to 1922. In the thirties' upswing, however, the outlays on plant and equipment from 1932 to 1933 remained approximately stable. The large liquidation which had been going on in inventories since 1930 reached the maximum in 1932 and declined sharply in 1933. Thus, the $3.1 billions investment (gross) in plant and equipment in 1932 was offset by $2.4 billions *disinvestment* in inventories, while in 1933 the $3.0 billions fixed capital investment was offset by only $1.1 billions disinvestment in inventories. Total producers' investment, therefore, was only $0.7 billions in 1932, but increased to $1.9 billions in 1933. It was the *diminished disinvestment* in inventories which accounted for the increase in total producers' investment and which gave the upward stimulus, as far as business expansion was concerned, to the revival of 1933. Thus, the mere cessation of inventory liquidation (or indeed slowing down of the rate) may initiate the revival, provided other investment expenditures streams have reached substantial stability.

Inventories regularly play an important role in helping to initiate the upturn. But inventories, as we have already seen, do not continue to accumulate through the whole major cycle upswing. At intervals of from three to four years' disinvestment of inventories takes place, and the ensuing temporary damping of the upswing constitutes the so-called minor recession. During this interval investment in plant and equipment frequently holds approximately the level reached but fails to advance further. After this temporary "pause," inventory stocks again rise, and investment in plant and equipment moves on to still higher levels. These interrelations may be seen in detail in Chart 3.

We have already noted that investment in producers' fixed capital contributed to the upswing in the 1921–22 turning point, but scarcely maintained itself in 1932–33. We must now consider the constituent parts of producers' investment goods: (1) equipment and (2) plant.

From 1921 to 1922 outlays on equipment decreased from $3,926 millions to $3,848 millions. From 1932 to 1933, however, there was a slight increase from $2,019 millions to $2,051 millions. Thus, equipment expenditures contributed to the revival in the 1932–33 turning point, but not in 1921–22. The changes are small and Terborgh's data are somewhat at variance with those of Kuznets. On balance, investment in equipment appears to play no significant role in the turning points.

Outlays on producers' plant in all forms of enterprise as a whole contributed $597 millions to revival in the 1921–22 turning point, but declined $161 millions from 1932 to 1933. With respect to the various fields,[6] investment in manufacturing and mining plant moved sideways (declined very slightly) in both turning points. Railroad plant outlays declined in

[6] See Terborgh's data, *Federal Reserve Bulletin,* September, 1939.

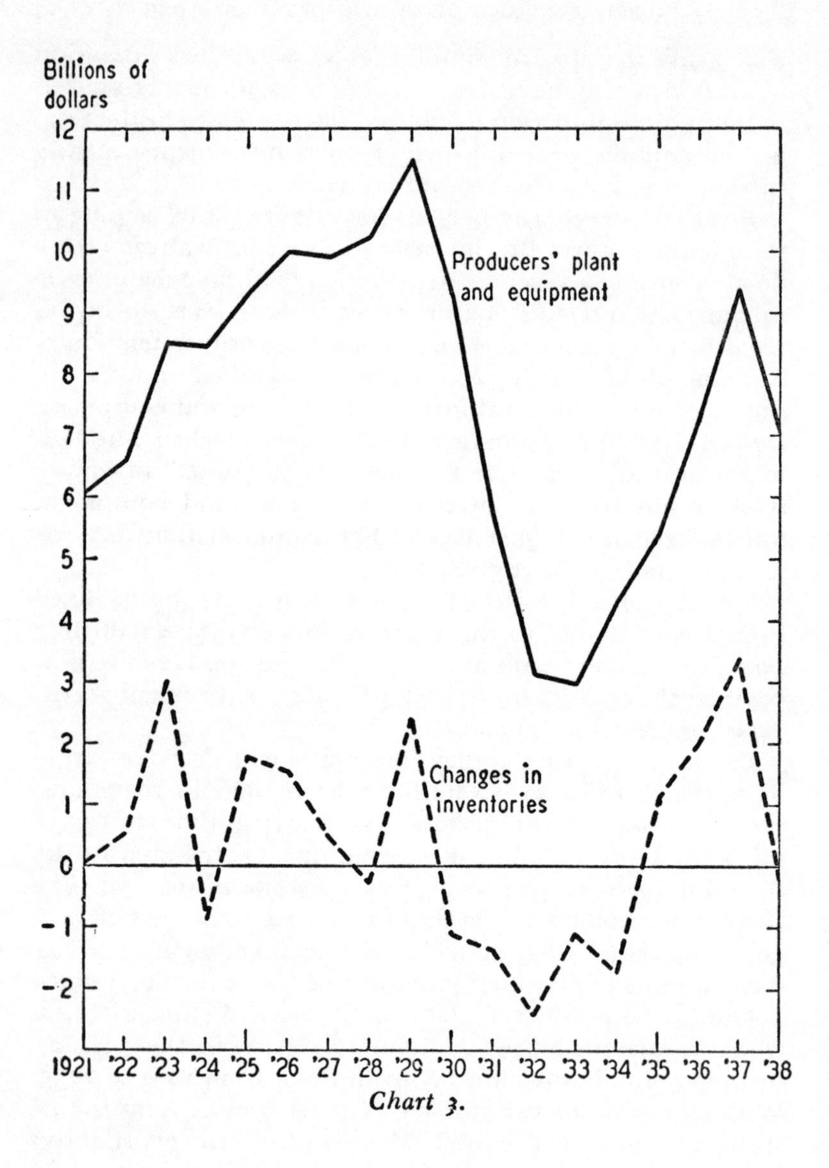
Billions of dollars
12
11
10
9
8
7
6
5
4
3
2
1
0
-1
-2
Producers' plant and equipment
Changes in inventories
1921
'22
'23
'24
'25
'26
'27
'28
'29
'30
'31
'32
'33
'34
'35
'36
'37
'38

Chart 3.

both, while for other public utilities combined investment in plant contributed $173 millions to revival in the 1921–22 turning point, but declined by $166 millions from 1932 to 1933. Commercial and miscellaneous plant outlays contributed $45 millions to revival in 1921–22, but declined by $133 millions from 1932 to 1933. Investment in agricultural plant aided revival (about $30 millions) in both turning points.

Investment in housing (Chart 4) played by far the most conspicuous role in the upturn from 1921 to 1922, the increase being $1.3 billions over the 1921 level. Outlays on housing rose year by year, until a peak was reached in 1925 at $5.2 billions. Receding slowly from this high point, the volume of capital expenditures on housing continued annually above the $4.0 billion level through 1928. The drastic decline from 1928 to 1929 of $1.2 billions undoubtedly exerted a heavy downward pressure upon the whole economy and contributed largely to the general collapse which started in 1929.

But, while investment in housing led the recovery in 1921–22, it lagged far behind in 1932–33. This behavior accords with a long experience already discussed with respect to the cyclical behavior of residential building. In view of the familiar eighteen-year construction cycle, every other major recovery is usually led and reinforced by housing construction, while the intervening major recovery is compelled to move forward under the handicap of a slump in residential building. A similar analysis applies to the construction of producers' plant, the second main constituent (the third being public construction) in the building cycle. As will be seen in Chart 5, outlays on producers' plant led (though far less vigorously than housing) in the 1921–22 turning point and strongly supported the recovery clear up through 1929. Plant investment, however, lagged behind and continued depressed throughout the recovery of the thirties in a manner closely corresponding to the behavior of housing.

Chart 6 discloses the role of construction as a whole (including producers' plant, residential construction, and public construction) in the two major cycles 1921 to 1938 relative to that

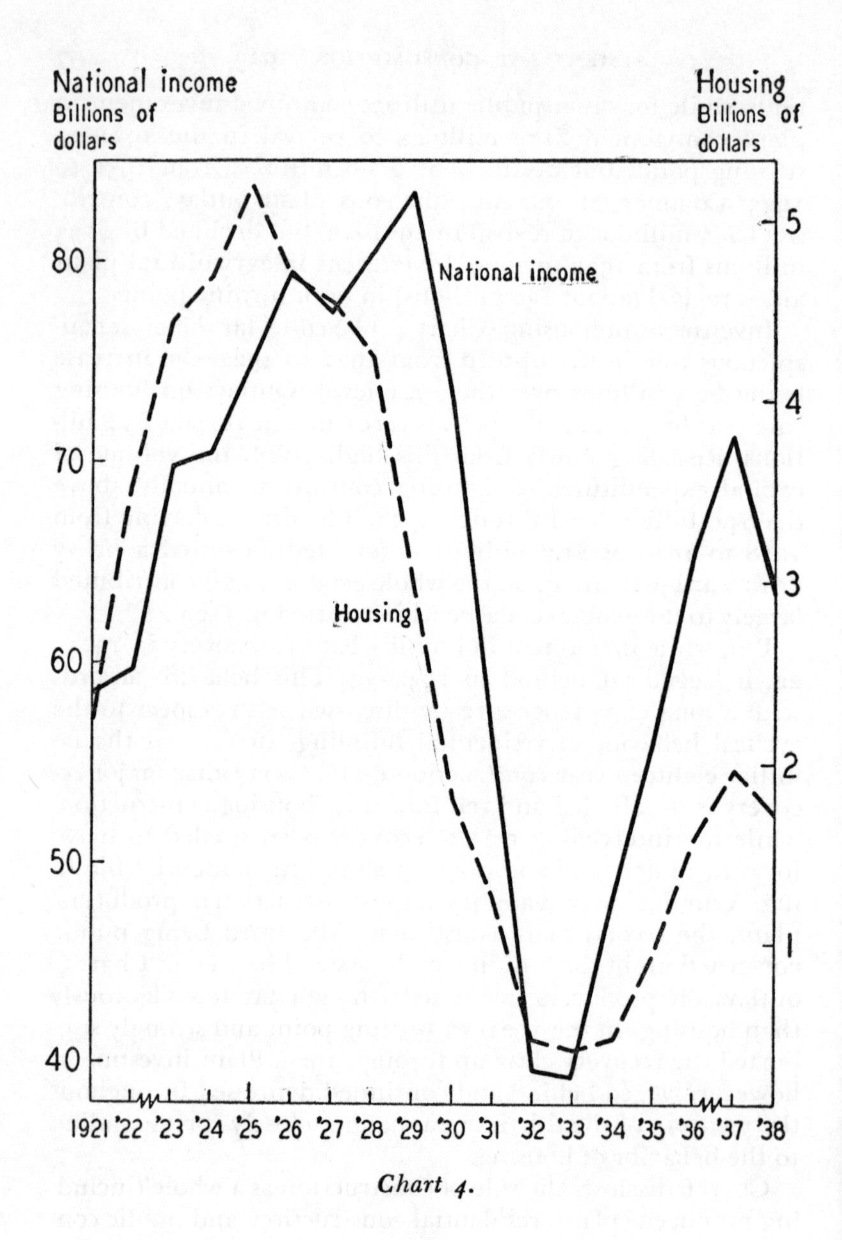
National income
Billions of
dollars
Housing
Billions of
dollars
National income
Housing
80
70
60
50
40
5
4
3
2
1
1921
'22
'23
'24
'25
'26
'27
'28
'29
'30
'31
'32
'33
'34
'35
'36
'37
'38

Chart 4.

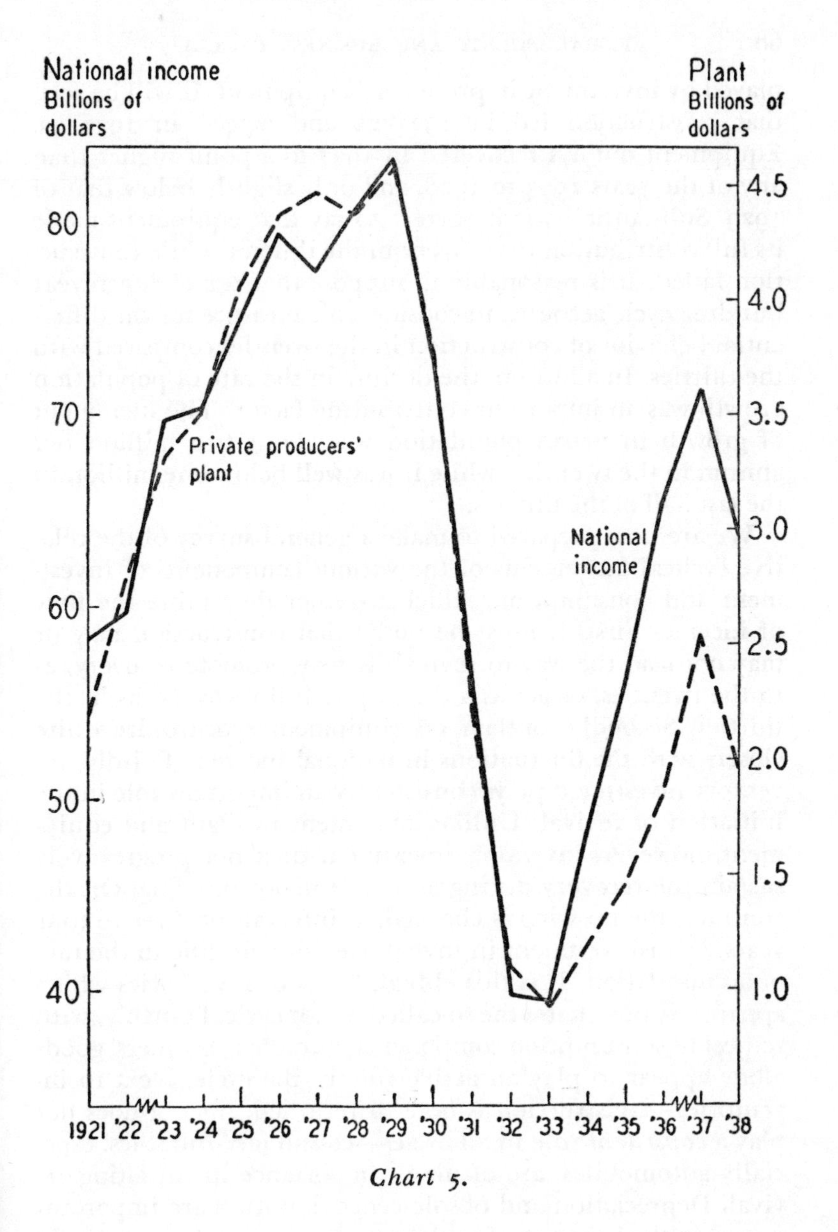
National income
Billions of dollars
Plant
Billions of dollars
80
70
60
50
40
4.5
4.0
3.5
3.0
2.5
2.0
1.5
1.0
Private producers' plant
National income
1921
'22
'23
'24
'25
'26
'27
'28
'29
'30
'31
'32
'33
'34
'35
'36
'37
'38

Chart 5.

played by investment in producers' equipment. It will be seen that construction led in 1921–22 and lagged in 1932–33. Equipment outlays recovered in 1937 to a point higher than any of the years 1923 to 1928, and only slightly below that of 1929. Substantially, it is correct to say that equipment made its full contribution to recovery in the thirties, while construction failed. It is reasonable to suppose that the eighteen-year building cycle accounts in considerable measure for the differential behavior of construction in the twenties compared with the thirties. In addition, the decline in the rate of population growth was an important contributing factor. The increment of growth in urban population was about two million per annum in the twenties, while it was well below one million in the last half of the thirties.

We are now prepared to make a general survey of the relative cyclical movements of the various components of investment and consumption, which together determine the flow of income. First, it must be noted that construction may or may not lead the way to revival. It may promote recovery, as in the twenties, or act as a drag upon full recovery, as in the thirties. Secondly, outlays on equipment synchronize quite closely with the fluctuations in national income. Thirdly, inventory investment plays consistently an important role in the initiation of revival. Unlike investment in plant and equipment, however, inventory investment does not progressively sustain the recovery during an entire major upswing. On the contrary, the upswing is checked, at intervals of three to four years, by disinvestment in inventories, or a decline in the rate of accumulation. It is this ebb and flow of inventories which apparently dominates the so-called minor cycle. Fourthly, with respect to consumption components, durable consumers' goods alone appear to play an active role in the cycle. Next to inventories—construction is here disregarded, since it does not play a *consistent* role in all cycles—consumers' durables, especially automobiles, are of major importance in initiating revival. Depreciation and obsolescence doubtless are important factors in the behavior of outlays on durable consumers' goods.

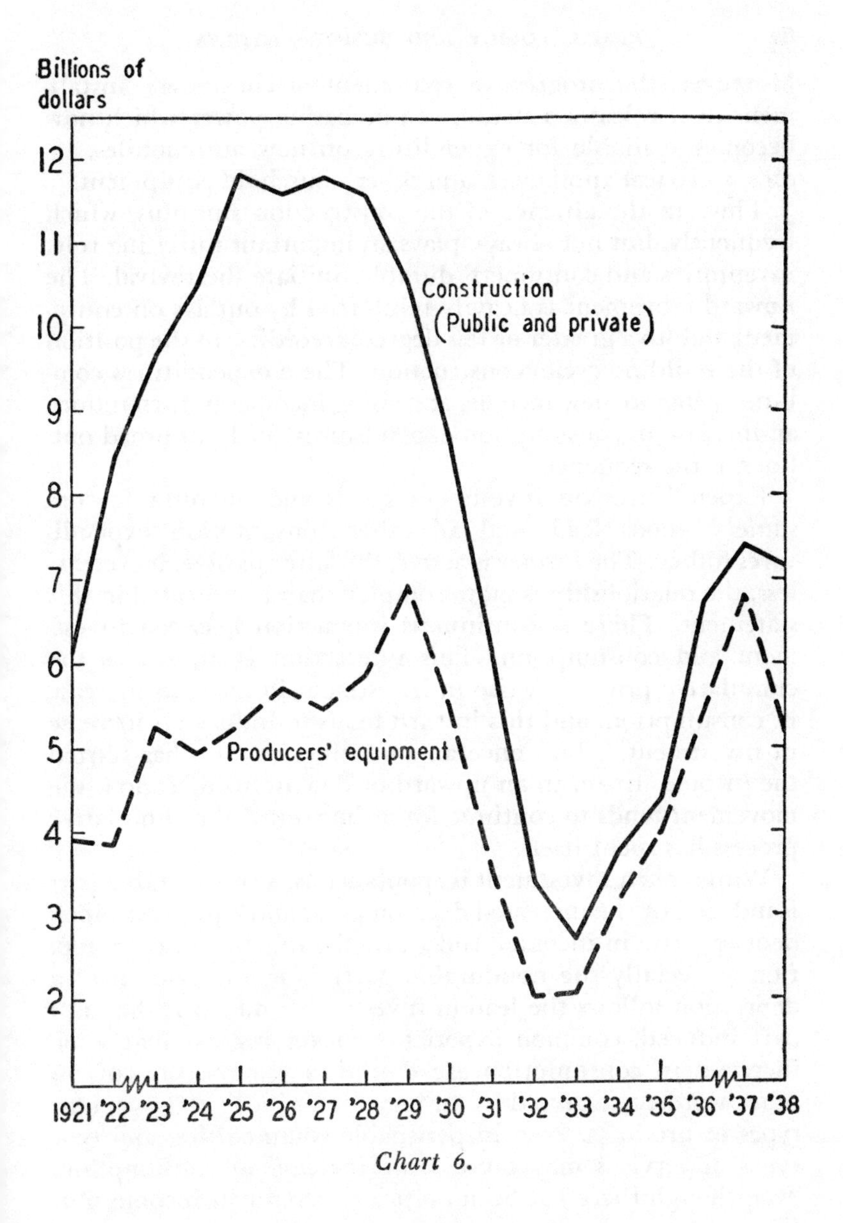
Billions of dollars
12
11
10
9
8
7
6
5
4
3
2
Construction (Public and private)
Producers' equipment
1921
'22
'23
'24
'25
'26
'27
'28
'29
'30
'31
'32
'33
'34
'35
'36
'37
'38

Chart 6.

Moreover, the progressive retirement of consumers' installment debt releases a stream of purchasing power which now becomes available for expenditure on new automobiles, radios, electrical appliances, and other household equipment.

Thus, in the absence of the construction stimulus, which frequently, but not always, plays an important initiating role, inventories and consumers' durables initiate the revival. The upward movement is heavily reinforced by outlays on equipment and (to a greater or less degree, according to the position of the building cycle) construction. These expenditures combined generate new income, and rising incomes in turn induce an increase in consumption expenditures. Such, in broad outlines, is the sequence.

Expenditures on investment goods and on durable consumers' goods lead, and all other consumption expenditures follow. The former is active, the latter passive. Nevertheless, the relationship is more complex than is indicated in this statement. There is continuous interaction between investment and consumption. This interaction is known as the cumulative process. A rise in investment induces an increase in consumption, and this in turn tends to induce an increase in investment. Thus, once an initiating impulse has started the income stream in an upward or downward direction, the movement tends to continue for a time, until the cumulative process has spent itself.

While much investment is spontaneous, a considerable part is induced by the increased draft on plant and equipment incident to a rise in income. And while the increase in consumption (especially the nondurable part) from the bottom of a depression follows the lead of investment and is for the most part induced, common experience makes it clear that some increases in consumption are doubtless spontaneous, or, in other words, not caused by an increase in income. Thus, new types of products, even in perishable commodities, and new types of services may cause some increase in consumption, even though there has been no prior increase in income. But this is relatively unimportant. For the most part, spontaneous expenditures—expenditures not caused by a prior rise in income—are likely to be made on investment goods or upon durable consumers' goods, but not upon other forms of consumption.

It does not follow, however, that all investment is spontaneous. Much of it is, in fact, induced. It is, however, quite

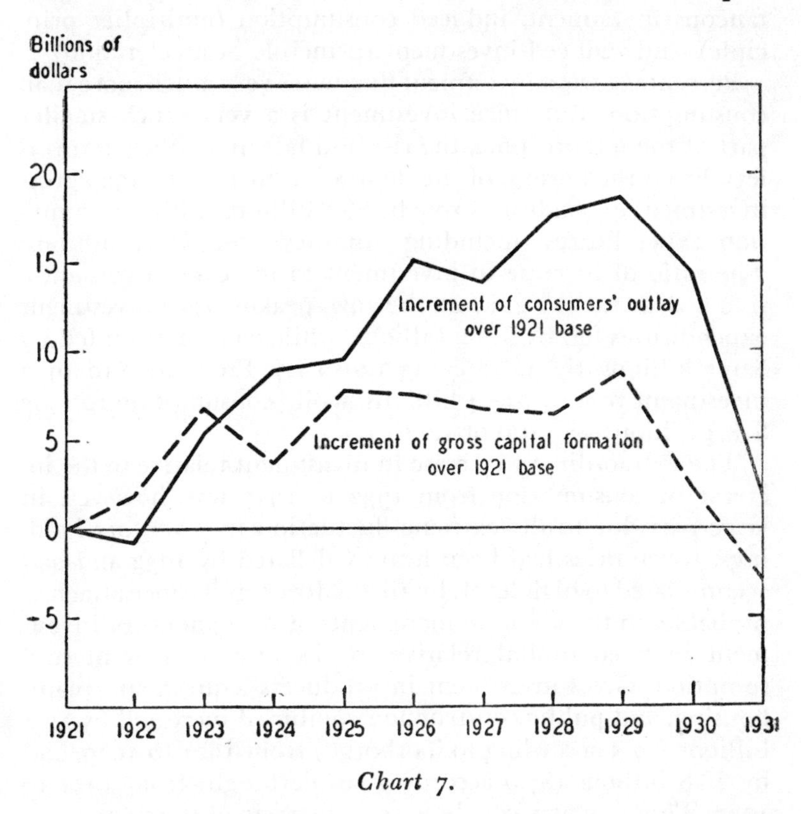

Chart 7.

impossible to determine statistically what part is spontaneous and what part is induced.

Chart 7 compares the absolute increments of fluctuations from the 1921 level of (1) investment and (2) consumption for the period 1921 to 1931. The lag of consumption behind investment we have already referred to above.[7] The chart indicates that a continuous flow of investment progressively induces an advancing volume of consumption, until the upper turning point is reached. The more technical aspects of the interconnection between investment and consumption are treated in Chapter XII, dealing with the "leverage" of spontaneous investment, induced consumption (multiplier principle), and induced investment (principle of acceleration).

Percentage-wise, investment fluctuates very much more than consumption. But since investment is a very much smaller part of the total income, the rise and fall in absolute terms is less. From the bottom of the depression in 1921 to 1929 gross investment expenditures rose by $8.8 billions, while consumption expenditures (including durables) rose $18.7 billions. The ratio of increase in investment to increase in consumption was as 1.0 to 2.2. From the 1929 peak to 1932 investment expenditures fell by $17.2 billions, while consumption fell by $29.3 billions, the ratio being 1.0 to 1.7. From 1932 to 1937 investment rose by $14.4 billions, while consumption rose by $18.4 billions—a ratio of 1.0 to 1.3.

The extraordinary increase in investment relative to the increase in consumption from 1932 to 1937 was, however, in large part due to the extreme fluctuation in inventory holdings. Inventories had been heavily deflated by 1932 and had accumulated to high levels by 1937. More significance attaches, probably, to the absolute increments or decrements of investment in fixed capital relative to absolute changes in consumption. Gross investment in producers' equipment, plant, housing, and public construction combined increased by $7.4 billions ($7.3 according to Terborgh) from 1921 to 1929, and by $8.8 billions ($7.0 according to Terborgh) from 1932 to 1937. Thus, we may conclude that the ratio of the increase in fixed investment to consumption was approximately the same in the two upswing periods. The increase in producers' plant and equipment from 1921 to 1929 was $5.4 billions according

[7] This lag would be all the more pronounced, as we have seen, if we had excluded "durables" from consumption and included them with investment.

to Kuznets, and $4.9 according to Terborgh. For 1932 to 1937 the figures are $6.3 billions (Kuznets) and $4.8 billions (Terborgh). Thus, again, the ratio of increase in producers' capital outlays to increases in consumption was approximately the same in the twenties and in the thirties. When all forms of investment are included, however, it is clear that the increase in consumption was relatively smaller in relation to increases in investment from 1932 to 1937 than had been the case from 1921 to 1929.[8]

[8] Throughout this chapter, including the charts, the data used are Kuznets', unless otherwise stated.

Chapter III

MONETARY POLICY IN THE DEPRESSION

INCREASING use of the term "Public Policy" indicates a change in the role of government in modern economic life. It is, of course, nothing new that a governmental policy is more and more coming to the fore. The tradition of *laissez faire*—never, in fact, fully applied—so dominant in the first half of the nineteenth century increasingly gave way to an ever-expanding measure of governmental control and intervention. But governmental control in the last half of the nineteenth century, and indeed up to the first World War, assumed almost exclusively the form of (a) regulation of the competitive process under which it was sought to check monopoly tendencies and to maintain, to the utmost possible degree, protection, on the one side, to consumers and, on the other side, to free and independent producers from organizational interferences with the functioning of the price system; (b) protection to labor in the form of minimum standards of work, including regulations with respect to hours, working conditions, and to a much lesser extent wages; (c) general efforts at social betterment, including protection to the public health, provision for recreation principally through parks and playgrounds, and a broad extension of public education; and (d) minimum provision for relief of poverty and old age. The latter, to be sure, just before the first World War was rapidly being extended in England through the development of old-age, unemployment, and health insurance, and it had for several decades past become an accepted part of social policy in various continental countries, notably Germany, Denmark, Belgium, and Holland. Only in the United States was this expansion of public welfare activities of the state postponed and delayed until the exigencies of the Great Depression forced upon a reluctant public the necessity of these measures.

With respect to the business cycle, not until the postwar period was there any serious thought of governmental intervention and control. Indeed, not until the publication of Wesley Mitchell's *Business Cycles* in 1913 was there any general awareness of the business cycle problem as such. Businessmen, of course, had experienced crises and depressions, some of them, as in the seventies and nineties, long and deep. But these were always regarded as disasters, something quite pathological—interruptions to a normal state of business prosperity. Some indeed, like Veblen, impressed by the chronic depressed conditions of the last quarter of the nineteenth century, had come to regard depressions as the normal condition of the modern economy. But this view was an exception to the rule. That the cycle of prosperity and depression was something which normally could be expected to recur with more or less regularity, each phase containing within itself the seeds of the succeeding phase of the cycle, was nowhere generally accepted by the public, nor even for the most part by economists, until the advent of Mitchell's great book. Rarely, indeed, has the central thesis of any book become so much an accepted part of the thinking of an entire society. Henceforth, neither prosperity nor depression was regarded as normal in the modern economy, but instead the cyclical progression from one phase to another was accepted in a quasi-fatalistic manner as a characteristic feature of the functioning of the modern economy.

Monetary Control Inadequate

Attention was at once centered, however, upon the possibility of minimizing the fluctuations of the cycle. A number of more or less accidental developments directed this type of thinking, notably in the United States, toward monetary control as the means to that end. In the first place, the United States had just before the war instituted for the first time in its history a centralized control over the money and credit supply through the establishment of the Federal Reserve System. In the second place, traditional economic thinking in the Anglo-Saxon world, both England and America, had laid large, though not exclusive, emphasis upon money and credit as a fundamental cause, or at least a controlling factor, in the business cycle. Already in England as far back as the eighteen-forties it had been thought that a reform in the Banking Act would eliminate the disrupting crises which periodically shook the financial and industrial structure. Disillusionment, to be sure, quickly followed this experiment and the problem was superseded by others which proved more pressing during the remainder of the century.

English economic literature, with notable exceptions, such as the writings of D. H. Robertson, had mainly stressed monetary aspects of the cycle. Not until the postwar period was the Anglo-Saxon world impressed with the penetrating analysis running in terms of investment and saving, which had long been current on the Continent, starting with the great work of Tougan-Baranousky and Spiethoff.

The Continental writers who had found the deeper causes of cyclical development in the factors underlying economic progress—technical innovations, the discovery of new resources, the opening up of new territory, and the growth of population—had tended to minimize the role of institutional factors, including money and credit. The investment theories of the cycle had an essential kinship with the doctrine of natural law in economic life and economic development. Institutions were regarded as results and not causes of the process of economic change, rooted essentially in the progress of technology. If the violence of the cycle were to be toned down, this it was thought would, if it ever came, be the result of a damping down of the extensive expansion of the economy in terms of growth of population and the occupation of new territory. Thus, Spiethoff believed that the violence of the cycle was a function of the highly dynamic nineteenth century, with its rapid rate of extensive expansion and of economic progress. The cycle was regarded as a manifestation of the extraordinarily rapid growth and transition from a rural economy to an urban, industrialized economy and of the expansion of modern industry into all parts of the globe. Once the process of industrialization and territorial expansion was completed, it was thought that the powerful ground swells throwing up the periodic tidal waves of economic activity would increasingly come to rest and the fluctuations of economic life would approach greater and greater stability.

Robertson's views especially bear, in many respects, a resemblance to those of Spiethoff. But, in general, considerations such as these were not incorporated in Anglo-Saxon thinking. In the English-speaking world the monetary and financial institutions were stressed, and from this point of view it was not unnatural that the fluctuations of the cycle should be regarded by many as easily amenable to control.

Preoccupation with fluctuations in prices and the monetary causes of these fluctuations contributed to this approach to the problem. The work of Irving Fisher and Kemmerer on the quantity theory of money and prices and the attempt at statistical verification of this theory had attracted widespread interest and attention. Moreover, the war upheaval and the price disturbances to which it gave rise concentrated attention upon the problem of price stabilization. The fluctuation of prices and the business cycle became almost synonymous. The establishment of the Federal Reserve System, the unique position occupied by the United States with respect to the world's gold supply, and the postwar uncertainties with respect to price movements inevitably pointed to monetary stability as the problem par excellence of the postwar period.

The relative success of price stabilization in the decade of the twenties, in view of the importance attached to this problem, diverted attention away from the more deeply significant developments of the decade—the developments in the field of real investment. Because of this diversion of interest and attention and the importance attached to monetary and price factors, the coming of the Great Depression was not only not anticipated but appeared to be quite inexplicable. Indeed, from the monetary and price standpoint, no satisfactory explanation of the depression was possible, and as the depression deepened the more ardent adherents of the monetary school persisted in the view that the mere multiplication of currency by the central banks would have prevented the depression, and that even then all that was required to restore full economic activity was vigorous monetary expansion and price reflation. That the prosperity of the twenties was, at bottom, an investment boom, and that the depression was inevitable once the investment outlets of the postwar period had temporarily become saturated, was in general not recognized by monetary theorists,[1] though many businessmen close to the facts saw quite clearly the real nature of both the boom and the depression.

The monetary theory of the cycle held that the road to stability lay mainly through price stabilization. If a price-inflated boom could be prevented, the succeeding depression, it was believed, could be averted. When the boom manifested no price inflation, as in the twenties, other monetary and financial factors, such as the rise of debt, were introduced to explain the initiation of the deflationary process which, it was believed, could alone be stopped by monetary measures. And when monetary action was at long last undertaken, it was always charged that either it had been undertaken too late or that it had not been pursued with sufficient vigor.

It is, moreover, of interest to note that the monetary approach, so popular in the twenties, invaded even the camp of the investment cycle theorists, or, at any rate, one section of this school—the Viennese group led by Mises and Hayek. Granted that the expansion of investment was the underlying

[1] My own book, *Business-Cycle Theory,* published in 1927, emphasized nonmonetary aspects of the cycle, and stressed the rate of investment, especially in Chapters IV and VIII.

basis of the prosperity phase, it was argued that if the investment boom were held in check by monetary methods and were restrained within the limits of such investment as could be financed from the flow of voluntary saving, the subsequent collapse could be averted. Others, agreeing that the important thing was to slow down the spurt of investment, argued that if you lop off the top of the investment bulge, the investment thus abstracted from the boom would subsequently fill up, in part, the succeeding depression gulch. Thus, stabilization meant a leveling out of investment activity. It was not expected that the high activity of a boom period could for long be maintained, but rather that stabilization would involve an averaging process, leaving the level of activity somewhere between the peak of the boom and the bottom of the depression. It was suggested that this leveling process could be accomplished by monetary action which would knock an excessive investment boom in the head. Thus, until the Great Depression, attention was peculiarly centered on the boom phase as the period which required restrictive action. The central basis of stabilization policy rested upon the firm belief that the boom was the progenitor of the depression and, if it could be controlled, stability would result. It would not do to wait until depression was already upon us to introduce control measures. The time for action was in the preceding phase of the cycle. Once the boom had been allowed to run its course, depression was regarded as inevitable and it, in turn, would perforce have to be permitted to run its course. Preventive, not remedial, measures were required.

The events of the Great Depression have profoundly shaken the foundations of this type of analysis. Question is raised whether the monetary weapons designed to check an excessive boom do not inevitably, once they are applied with sufficient vigor to become effective, start a cumulative downward spiral. Lopping off the boom will not automatically fill up the depression gulleys. The monetary weapons can, indeed, be applied effectively to check an expansion. But if the factors making for expansion of investment are vigorous, the monetary brakes have to be applied with great rigor in order to choke off the highly alluring speculative ventures which are driving the economy on toward the boom. If the discount rate is to be raised sufficiently high to choke off the new developments which are the driving force of the investment boom, the more stable segments of the economy will be choked off by a degree of contraction quite incompatible with the aim to level off and stabilize.

Elsewhere, the view gained ground that there was nothing inherently wrong about the boom itself; indeed, the boom was regarded as highly desirable per se, not only because it offered full employment and a high level of income but also because it equipped society with new productive forces. The aim of public policy should be, it was now argued, not to choke off the boom but to maintain it at its high level. Obviously, to do so would require, as the continued investment in more and more capital facilities progressively brought nearer the prospective fall in the marginal efficiency of capital, either a lifting of consumption expenditures to fill the gap of the receding investment expenditures or else the expansion of investment expenditures through governmental measures or by a public investment program.

The feasibility of such action would obviously depend, in large measure, upon the magnitude of the gap to be filled. If the propensity to consume is high, the gap to be filled by investment expenditures to secure full employment and to maintain activity at a full-income level would be relatively small. Attention was accordingly shifted away from leveling down the top to leveling up at the bottom of industrial fluctuations. The problem became essentially not one of cracking the boom but of fitting a fairly high bottom to the depression. What was to be feared was not the boom, but the terrific shock of a drastic fall in income and employment from which the economic organization could only with the greatest difficulty recover.

All through the decade of the twenties economic policy was directed at the dangers of an excessive boom characterized mainly in terms of price and credit inflation. Preventive measures of a monetary character were deemed adequate. Thus, countries all over the world were caught unprepared to deal with the problem of checking the cumulative fall of investment and income once the decline set in. Had great industrial nations in the twenties concerned themselves not so much with the alleged dangers of a boom, but rather with instruments of control designed to check the depression at a relatively high income and employment level, the history of the decade of the thirties in terms of both economics and world politics might have been very different. The decade of the thirties has taught us the lesson that we cannot afford at whatever cost to permit the national income and the volume of employment to fall below a tolerable level.

With respect to this central conclusion there can probably be little difference of opinion. Opinion will diverge as to what the tolerable level is, below which at all costs the economy must not be permitted to fall. Some will wish to set the goal high and will wish to achieve continuously an approach toward full employment. Others will wish to minimize the role of government policy to the more modest aim, not of achieving continuously full employment, but of preventing the economy from falling below the assigned level.

The less ambitious goal has much to recommend it. In the first place, it fixes a limit to the role of governmental policy. In view of the magnitude of the problem involved, it is clearly a more manageable and realizable goal. It interferes less with established institutional arrangements and leaves to the functioning of free enterprise itself the problem of fuller employment beyond the minimum level. In a manner, it thus divides the field between governmental activity and the activity of private enterprise. It becomes the function of government to establrsh a minimum below which the health, continuity, and workability of the economic system is endangered, and indeed the workability of government itself and particularly of international political relations. If a reasonable bottom had been put to the Great Depression throughout the world, either by the action of each of the more important industrial countries separately, or by international co-operation, there might very probably have developed no successful Hitler movement and no new outbreak of warfare.

We are familiar in the history of social reform with the concept of the minimum. Governmental policy has, in large part, in this area been directed not at regularizing the whole of economic life, but merely at establishing minimum standards below which the automatic functioning of the price system and the system of free enterprise is not permitted on grounds of social policy to fall. This is the theory of the minimum wage, of maximum hours, and of minimum requirements with respect to working standards. This is the theory back of the minimum standards set by government for education, health, and sanitation regulations.

It is at this point that depression policy emerges in a new role as an important element in a positive governmental program. But an economic minimum cannot be insured by reliance exclusively upon monetary policy.

Federal Reserve Policy

In the decade of the twenties the Federal Reserve System experimented with various tools of monetary control.[2] An unwarranted optimism prevailed with respect to the efficacy of monetary action to stabilize prosperity. Emphasis on the forty-month cycle had the unfortunate effect of slurring over the essential difference between inventory recessions and major depressions caused by the sharp curtailment of fixed capital investment. Thus, the mild depressions of 1924 and 1927 were not clearly recognized as minor ebbs in a great tidal wave of investment activity. Relatively minor open-market operations in both these periods were given more credit than was warranted for the resumption of recovery to still higher levels.

[2] See C. O. Hardy, *Credit Policies of the Federal Reserve System*, Brookings Institution, 1932; S. E. Harris, *Twenty Years of Federal Reserve Policy*, Harvard University Press, 1933; Arthur Hersey, "Historical Review of Objectives of Federal Reserve Policy," *Federal Reserve Bulletin*, April, 1940.

The apparent success of these measures distracted attention away from the deeper causes of the sustained prosperity of the twenties—the powerful upsurge of investment activity in building and in a half-dozen growing industries especially related to the automobile and electrical industries. Like Rostand's Chantecler (with his faith in the causal connection between his morning crowing and the rising sun), monetary enthusiasts watched with satisfaction the apparently favorable results of monetary policy. But most economists, while not overlooking the usefulness of open-market operations, remained skeptical of far-reaching business cycle consequences, and some stressed the deeper factors of technical progress and investment opportunities. Central bankers themselves, while studying the new monetary experiments, were not too sure what results might with confidence be expected. On the whole, however, hopes ran high that a large measure of stability could be achieved by purely monetary devices.

The Reserve System had been established on the commercial banking theory. The member banks ideally were to extend credit only on the basis of self-liquidating loans. They were to "monetize" the credit of producing and marketing units. Bank loans were to finance goods during the process of production or marketing. And when the process was completed, the sale of the goods would supply the funds to repay the loans. Thus, the process of production would be facilitated by bank credit accommodation. But investment in plant and equipment ought to be financed, it was believed, from savings and not by the banking system. Unlike the neutral money proposal of Hayek, the commercial credit theory held that bank credit might legitimately finance the current production and might expand as such production expanded. The "neutral money" theory, however, held that bank credit ought not to be permitted to finance inventories any more than fixed capital. Both theories, however, agreed that fixed capital investment should be financed from savings and not from bank credit.

In practice, however, the member banks were not able to

live up to the rigid standards imposed by the commercial banking theory. Commercial loans of the self-liquidating type were not available in sufficient quantity. Hence, banks turned increasingly to other assets. Thus, the investments of member banks increased from about six billions of dollars in 1920 to about ten billions in 1929. The exigencies of war finance more or less forced this development not long after the Reserve System was established. Loans on government securities and bank purchases of governments and industrials thus became established practices. After the war was over, the policy of the Board was at first directed toward achieving a return to purely commercial banking practice. But this policy failed, simply because it did not square with the facts. Business was increasingly so organized that bank loans were less necessary. Banks were forced to employ an increasing part of these funds in long-term investments or in loans based on securities. While the Federal Reserve Banks were forbidden by law to rediscount investment paper, the law did not prohibit member banks from acquiring security loans and investments. Thus, regardless of what might be regarded as desirable practice, the Board recognized that it had no power to hold the banks to self-liquidating loans.

In the famous 1923 Report of the Board, it was argued that open-market operations of the System should be managed with an eye to the general credit situation. Concern was felt not only for the quantity of credit, but also for the uses to which it was put. Especially, it was felt that "speculative" uses should not be encouraged. Speculative activities were broadly conceived to include not merely stock market operations, but also excessive accumulation of inventories and abnormal spurts in capital expenditures, foreign exports, and consumer installment credit. The wave of speculative activity in the stock market in the late twenties became the occasion of grave concern. Brokers' loans reached extravagant proportions. The Board wished to direct adequate funds toward production and to check speculation. But it had no effective power to deal with the situation. The ease of capital flotations undoubtedly carried the investment boom farther than was economically justified. Errors of optimism played a role in pushing investment to a higher degree of saturation than would otherwise have occurred. This much may be granted to those who stress the importance of monetary policy. But, on the other side, it should be underscored that had banking policy successfully stopped investment plans short of the errors engendered by the monetary situation, a true investment saturation would nevertheless have been reached, leading to a deep depression.

The failure to check the speculative movement revealed the essential weakness of monetary policy, even as a device to check the boom. It was not possible, by means of Central Bank control over credit, to ensure adequate funds for productive uses and to choke off funds for speculative uses. The generalized controls were not adequate. Tightening the money market only meant that the stable run of industries were checked, while the speculative parts of the economy forged ahead, lured by prospects of profits far in excess of the cost of money. Thus, the conviction grew that more direct methods—such as the control of margin requirements on collateral loans—were necessary if the speculative sector were to be brought under control.

With the coming of the Great Depression, attention was necessarily directed toward the problem of checking the deflation and promoting recovery. Toward this end, discount rates were reduced. But this availed but little, since, under the process of liquidation and debt cancellation, banks strove to reduce their borrowings at the Reserve Banks. Federal Reserve credit declined from around $1.5 billion in 1928–29 to around $1.0 billion in 1930–31. This contraction occurred despite the fact that the sharp reduction in rediscounted paper was in considerable measure offset by open-market operations in early 1930. This purchase of United States securities helped (a) to cushion the stock market crash, (b) to supply the increasing demand for currency and gold, and (c) to enable the banks to reduce their indebtedness to the Reserve Banks without effecting too drastic a decline in member bank reserves.

With the British abandonment of the gold standard in 1931, member bank borrowing at the Reserve Banks sharply increased. Moreover, after the Glass-Steagall Act of February, 1932 had freed the gold (in excess of the minimum 40 per cent requirement) formerly held to secure the Federal Reserve notes, the System was able to extend greatly its open-market operations. Over a billion dollars of government securities were purchased in 1932. Thus, the total Federal Reserve credit was increased from less than one billion dollars to about $2.2 billions, thereby creating for the first time a large volume of excess member bank reserves. This action helped the banks to weather for some time the successive liquidation crises. Eventually, however, the terrific decline in security and real-estate values, the increasing volume of frozen loans, together with the continued withdrawals of deposits, forced the temporary closing of all the banks and the liquidation or reorganization of the weaker members.

By the end of 1933 the banks had repaid most of their borrowings at the Reserve Banks. Federal Reserve holdings of government securities were now increased to nearly $2.5 billions and these constituted from now on almost the whole of the earning assets of the Reserve Banks. In consequence of these open-market purchases, member bank excess reserves increased to nearly one billion dollars. Beginning with 1934 the excess reserves were progressively augmented by gold imports, until at the beginning of 1936 they amounted to about three billion dollars. The combined program of gold sterilization and raising the reserve requirements cut the excess back to well under a billion in midyear 1937. The reversal of this program, in the form of approximately a one-eighth reduction in the reserve requirements, and especially in the release of the sterilized gold, together with additional gold imports, shot excess reserves back to three billions by the midyear 1938. The accelerated gold inflow after the Munich crisis raised excess reserves to six billions by the middle of 1940.

This unprecedented development was mainly the result of gold imports into the United States. While deliberate Central Bank action would doubtless never have pushed an easy money policy to such extremes as we have recently experienced, the outcome, more or less accidental, has given us a striking laboratory experiment. We have been privileged to observe what contribution can be made by the utmost limit of Central Bank action toward economic recovery.

Cheap Money

The result is very illuminating. The rate of interest on Treasury bills has fallen close to zero from the level of 4½ to 5 per cent in 1929. Short-term commercial paper and trade acceptance rates would have followed a similar course had not the banks, by collective agreement, fixed the rate at 1 per cent. The yield on Treasury notes fell from around 3 per cent in 1933 to one half of 1 per cent in 1939. Commercial loan rates of city banks fell from 4½ to 5 per cent in 1932 to 2½ per cent in 1938. United States Government long-term rates fell from 4 per cent in 1929 to 2½ per cent in 1939 and just over 2 per cent in 1940. High-grade corporate bond rates fell from 4¾ per cent in 1929 to 3 per cent in 1939.

A characteristic of what may be regarded as a normal, cyclical interest-rate pattern is the narrowing of the spread between short-term and long-term yields as recovery develops. In an intense boom the short-term rate may even rise above the long-term rate, while in deep depressions the short-term rate is normally far below the long-term rate, and, indeed, in extraordinary depressions approaches the zero limit. Thus, the intensity of a boom can be measured, in a degree, by the relation of the short-term rate to the long-term rate, and similarly the intensity of a depression.

But this pattern is by no means fixed, since numerous factors operate to modify and distort it. Under certain conditions it is not impossible that a fairly high level of prosperity may be reached with short-term rates rising scarcely at all. This, indeed, was the case in 1937 and again in 1939–40. There was no strong, surging investment boom adequate to absorb all of the funds available in the long-term capital market. Thus, borrowers were not compelled to go to the banks for funds on a scale adequate to mop up all, or even any appreciable fraction, of the surplus funds available in the banking system. This condition was caused: (1) partly by the meagerness of private investment outlets, particularly in residential housing and in public utility and manufacturing plants; and (2) partly by the abnormally large banking resources created: (a) by the vast inflow of gold, and (b) by the new money created by the issue of silver certificates.

The extraordinary willingness to hold cash in recent years —a function partly of the greatly increased supply of money, partly of increased risk and uncertainty throughout the world, and partly of inadequate investment outlets—has affected profoundly the short-term rate and the rate on gilt-edged securities.

The areas in the interest-rate structure that can be reached by Central Bank policy are the short-term rates and the gilt-edged, long-term rates. But they are not the only areas, very probably not even the most important ones. Low interest rates in these areas do indeed "spill over," in a measure, into other areas, but not very effectively. The interest-rate structure is not as fluid and flexible, nor are the various parts in as sensitive interconnection as has frequently been supposed, or as one might wish for. The flooding of the banking system with excess reserves can bring the rates down in the areas enumerated above, but it has little effect on real-estate mortgage rates, the more speculative securities, or on commercial or personal loans in the smaller cities and rural communities. Six and even 8 per cent remains the traditional rate for small borrowers outside of the larger cities. "In 1938 about one-fifth of all member banks received on the average more than 7 per cent on their loans, and the proportion must be larger for non-member banks." [8]

[8] Woodlief Thomas: "The Banks and Idle Money," *Federal Reserve Bulletin*, March, 1940, p. 197. See also E. A. Goldenweiser, "Cheap Money and the Federal Reserve System," *Federal Reserve Bulletin*, May, 1940.

Thus, for the extremely important area of residential building, for the general run of intermediate and small-scale enterprise, for the more risky ventures, and for small cities and communities, cheap money in the banking system offers no adequate remedy. For these areas fantastically high excess reserves and a high degree of bank liquidity are apparently of little avail.

The inadequacy of Central Bank action in these important areas forced the development of other types of institutions designed to cope directly with the problem. To this end, scores of governmental corporations have been organized. These include the various lending agencies now grouped under the Federal Loan Agency. The R.F.C., from February 2, 1932, to December 31, 1939, poured altogether $4,075,000,000 into the banking system, including loans to open and closed banks to meet depositors' claims and purchase of preferred stock to bolster up weakened bank capital structures. To railroads with weakened credit it has made loans aggregating $1,372,000,000. In addition, $2,443,000,000 was advanced for the benefit of agriculture, including loans on cotton, corn, tobacco, and other commodities, loans to agricultural and livestock credit corporations, and other aids to agriculture. Loans to business enterprises amounted to $519,000,000, and $1,032,000,000 was advanced to self-liquidating public projects.[4] Altogether, $10,627,000,000 has been loaned or invested by action of the Directors of the Corporation and, in addition, $2,921,000,000 by direction of Congress in allocations and loans to various governmental agencies and for relief. The Federal Farm Mortgage Corporation and the Federal Land Banks have refinanced about two billion dollars of farm mortgages. This action had the combined effect of lowering the debt charges to overburdened borrowers and of protecting the lenders—banks, insurance companies, and other investors—who were caught with sour mortgages on their hands. In a similar manner, the Home Owners' Loan Corpora-

[4] See article by Emil Schram, Chairman of the Board, Reconstruction Finance Corporation, in *Britannica*, 1940 Yearbook. p. 574.

tion refinanced about three billion dollars of frozen urban mortgages. All these salvaging operations were important in order to start again a flow of expenditures on current production, whether of consumption or investment goods.

In addition, certain lending agencies, such as the Rural Electrification Administration, made funds available directly for new investment. Further, the Federal Housing Administration, by guaranteeing loans on residential construction, encouraged banks, insurance and other financial companies to enter a field where, without a guarantee, they would not venture without demanding rates so high as to preclude willingness to borrow.

These lending agencies supplement in an important manner the Central Bank devices, effective only in restricted areas, to reduce the rate of interest. Both of these mechanisms—Central Banks and government lending agencies—aim to stimulate investment and consumption expenditures by making the terms of borrowing favorable. Some of the agencies offer government funds directly to the borrower. Others, like the F.H.A., tempt private funds into the field at rates that can be borne by the borrowers through guaranteed financing on the principle of insurance. Thus, we have witnessed in the thirties a very broad supplementation of Central Bank policy designed to supply funds at low cost to the borrower.

But the decade of the thirties offers abundant evidence that cheap money alone is not adequate. Cheap money will not tempt borrowers if there are not available reasonably satisfactory outlets for profitable investment. Cheap money can encourage investment if conditions are favorable. But it will not of itself produce an adequate volume of investment and consumption. This is the lesson which we have learned, or which has at least been heavily reinforced, from the experience of the thirties.

Chapter IV

FISCAL POLICY IN THE RECOVERY

RECOVERY from the deep depression of 1932–33 proceeded by fits and starts, but on the whole at a fairly satisfactory rate, until 1937. The speed of the recovery, up to this point, was clearly one of the most rapid in our history, and probably about as rapid as the economic organism could digest. The recovery was, moreover, one of the longest in American experience.

In 1937, however, the recovery was checked at a point barely exceeding the 1929 total output level, but about 7 per cent below 1929 in terms of per capita output, and far below 1929 in terms of the degree of full employment reached. Thus, before a full recovery was reached, a major depression was allowed to develop until well into 1938. In the second quarter of that year the tide was turned by a positive program of federal expenditures, and by late 1939, stimulated by the war, the 1937 level was recovered, but no new ground conquered. In broad outlines, the recovery made satisfactory progress until August, 1937, and since then has been operating at about 70 to 80 per cent of reasonably full employment.

A combination of circumstances produced the depression of 1937. A part of these could have been avoided, but in part it was a normal reaction from a prolonged upswing. With respect to the mistakes made, careful account should be taken of them for future guidance,[1] and every effort made to avoid them. Some (for example, the labor difficulties) were related

[1] See my discussion of the causes of the 1937 depression in *Full Recovery or Stagnation?*, W. W. Norton and Co., 1938, Part IV.

to fundamental changes which the American economy was undergoing. But whatever the causes, once the downturn was started, it was a mistake to permit an acceleration of the recession and to countenance contraction at just the point when vigorous expansion should have been undertaken. If a bold program of federal expenditures had been undertaken in September, 1937, when danger signals were sufficiently in evidence, the precipitous stock market crash of October could have been largely averted, and the recovery pushed forward after a moderate and wholesome (in terms of the cost-price situation) setback. Federal expenditures on useful public projects should have been shot up, in fiscal 1938, $2 to $3 billions in excess of the 1937 level—or, in other words, to $10 or $11 billions. We may remind ourselves that $13.5 billions is the figure contemplated for the fiscal year 1941. Had the defense program, or something equivalent, been started in the autumn of 1937, the national income could have been lifted to $85 or $90 billions by 1940.

Expansionist Program vs. Salvaging Operation

Despite the fairly good showing made in the recovery up to 1937, the fact is that neither before nor since has the administration pursued a really positive expansionist program. Until 1936, public works outlays [2] fell far short of the level of the twenties, and since then have only slightly exceeded that level. For the most part, the federal government engaged in a salvaging program and not in a program of positive expansion. The salvaging program took the form of refinancing urban and rural debt, rebuilding the weakened capital structure of the banks, and supporting railroads at or near bankruptcy. As we have seen, the Reconstruction Finance Corporation, the Home Owners' Loan Corporation, and the Farm Credit Administration poured $18 billions into these salvaging operations. The federal government stepped into the

[2] Account is here taken of all public works, federal, state, and local. Federal public works, of course, ran much higher than in the twenties.

breach and supported the hard-pressed state and local governments—again a salvaging operation. One has only to consider the items accounting for the increase in recent years in the federal budget to see how true this is. Unable to carry the relief burden and to continue a normal program of public works, the local units turned to the federal government. From 1934–39 inclusive, $13.8 billions of the federal deficit of $18.7 billions is accounted for by the single item of unemployment relief. Other items which greatly relieved the fiscal position of local governments were the Agricultural Adjustment program, involving expenditures of $3.2 billions, and public works (largely as grants-in-aid or as substitutes for diminishing local outlays), amounting to $5.4 billions in the same period.

That a salvaging program of this magnitude was necessary was, of course, due to the unprecedented depth of the depression reached by early 1933. An important lesson that we can learn from this experience is the waste of funds for salvaging purposes which must be incurred if a depression is allowed to cumulate until the national income is cut in two. Under such circumstances the economy dries up like a sponge. Vast governmental expenditures, designed to float the "sponge" to a high level of prosperity, are instead absorbed by the sponge itself. The expenditures seemingly run to waste. This is the salvaging process. Only when the economy has become thoroughly liquid can further funds float it to higher income levels. A deep depression requires vast salvaging expenditures before a vigorous expansionist process can develop.

It is evident that governmental expenditures during the thirties were not of a character well calculated to take the place of private investment as a means to stimulate employment expansion. The deficit was not the result of a long-range program to fill the gap left by the receding tide of private investment. The spending was rather of an emergency type forced upon the government by reason of (1) the distress of unemployed urban workers, (2) the distress of farmers with declining income and overburdened with debt, (3) the weakened capital position of banks, railroads, and other industries, and (4) the weakened fiscal position of state and local governments.

In the early stages of the depression the local governments were forced to bear the brunt of the onrushing deflationary movement. In 1930–31 they made considerable loan expenditures for relief and public works. State and local outlays for construction and maintenance of government plant averaged over $3 billions in 1930–31. By 1932, however, the resources of the local governments were largely exhausted, and a sharp curtailment set in. Federal expenditures on construction and maintenance did not, however, take up this slack until as late as 1936.

TABLE V

Outlays for Construction and Maintenance of Public Works[8]
(millions of dollars)

Year	*Total gov't public works*	*State and local funds expended on public works*	*Federal public works and federal aid to local units*
1929	3,309	2,952	357
1930	3,733	3,288	445
1931	3,424	2,884	540
1932	2,539	1,949	590
1933	1,918	1,133	785
1934	2,474	1,208	1,266
1935	2,548	1,125	1,433
1936	3,496	1,316	2,180
1937	3,329	1,391	1,938
1938	3,711	1,612	2,099

From the above table it is evident that the rising federal outlays were quite inadequate until 1936 to hold total government construction to the predepression level. Total outlays were $1.4 billions short of the 1929 level in 1933, and $800 millions in 1934 and 1935. Before one makes a judgment of the efficacy of the federal public works program in the

[8] T.N.E.C. Hearings, Part 9, *Savings and Investment*, p. 4064.

years 1933–35, one must take cognizance of what was happening to state and local outlays on construction. The federal government only helped to hold back the receding tide. Government as a whole made no positive contribution, through public works, toward recovery.

Had it been possible to maintain private fixed capital investment, including producers' plant and equipment, residential and private nonprofit construction, at the $14 billion level of the period 1925–29, it is reasonable to suppose that state and local construction would have remained high and that the total national income could have been sustained. The measure of the decline in private investment in the thirties indicates the magnitude of the task confronting the government.

The following table gives the deficiency of private investment expenditures below the $14 billion level, together with the induced deficiency of consumption, in each year of the decade in terms of current dollars.

TABLE VI

(Billions of dollars)

Year	*Private Investment Deficiency below the 1925–29 level of $14 billion*	*Consumption Deficiency below the 1925–29 level of $70 billion* [4]
1930	$3.4	$0.9
1931	7.1	13.7
1932	10.5	25.5
1933	11.1	27.7
1934	10.1	20.3
1935	8.7	17.8
1936	6.8	11.1
1937	4.5	7.9
1938	6.8	12.4
1939	5.6	8.6
Total	$74.6	$145.9

[4] It should be noted, of course, that in real terms the deficiency was much smaller than this—indeed, had been wiped out by 1937.

Over against this deficiency of private investment and consumption, let us consider the record of the federal budget during the decade. The following table gives the expenditures, tax receipts, and deficits in each fiscal year in the decade.

TABLE VII

Fiscal year ending June 30	*Federal Budget, 1931–40 (billions)* Expenditures	Tax Receipts	Deficit
1931	$3.7	$3.2	$0.5
1932	4.5	2.0	2.5
1933	3.9	2.1	1.8
1934	6.0	3.1	2.9
1935	7.0	3.8	3.2
1936	8.7	4.1	4.6
1937	8.2	5.0	3.2
1938	7.2	5.9	1.3
1939	8.7	5.2	3.5
1940	9.0	5.4	3.6
Total	$66.9	$39.8	$27.1
Annual average 1931–40 (10 fiscal years)	$ 6.7	$ 4.0	$ 2.7
Annual average 1926–30 (5 fiscal years)	$ 3.2	$ 4.1	$ 0.9 (surplus)

During the first three years of the depression, federal expenditures continued, for the most part, along traditional lines at approximately the usual rate to which they had settled down in the twenties. It is true that in the fiscal year 1931 public works had increased to $421 millions, and loans amounted to $263 millions. In the fiscal year 1932, owing especially to the financial difficulties encountered by the banks and the railroads, loans increased to nearly $873 millions. In addition, federal public works were expanded to half a billion dollars, about double the level of the late twenties. In the next fiscal year total expenditures were reduced by $700,000,000 and, except for public works amounting to $472,000,000 and loans of $181,000,000, were close to the predepression level.

Thus, during the first three years of the depression there occurred an average increase in public works and loans of nearly $700 millions per annum. These items account almost wholly for the increase in total expenditures to $4.0 billions, compared with $3.2 billions in 1926–30.

From 1933 on, the picture is changed, mainly by: (1) an increase in public works expenditures from an average of $464 millions in 1930–33 to $940 millions per annum in 1934–40; [5] (2) relief expenditures (including direct relief, work relief, W.P.A., C.C.C., etc.) which had grown from zero in 1930–32, and $360 millions in 1933, to $2,243 millions per annum in 1934–40; and (3) the Agricultural Adjustment program, averaging $592 millions per year. Together, these three items account for $3.8 billions, or a half of the $7.8 billions annual expenditures in the period 1934–40. They account for practically all of the excess expenditures of this period over the average of the period 1926–30.

It is evident that the major effort was directed toward salvaging human and capital resources. Altogether, for this purpose, direct federal expenditures amounted to $26 billions during 1934–40, while indirect expenditures through governmental agencies account for some $18 billions.

Tax receipts averaged in the thirties almost exactly the same as in the fiscal years 1926–30, while expenditures averaged $3.5 billions more per annum. Thus, the federal government poured $6.7 billions per year into the income stream and took back $4.0 in the form of taxes, the "net contribution" measured in this crude manner being $2.7 billions per annum. A somewhat more refined, but still not wholly satisfactory, method of measuring the net contribution of the federal government to the money flow has been attempted by Martin Krost. According to this calculation, the net annual contribution of the federal government in 1931–40 was $2.66 billions.[6]

[5] Loans declined from $439 millions per annum in 1930–33 to $304 millions in 1934–40.

[6] An effort was made to eliminate from expenditures items which did not enlarge the income stream, and from the tax receipts items which did not

While there are important differences from year to year, the average for the entire decade scarcely varies at all from the average excess of all expenditures over all tax receipts.

The so-called "net contribution" of the government may be regarded as similar to private investment expenditures in so far as both are offsets to saving. It is important, however, to take the "net" figure rather than total expenditures, for the reason that a part of government expenditures are financed from funds which are taken from the consumption and not from the savings stream. In contrast, private investment expenditures are in the usual case financed from the savings stream or from new bank funds. These funds ordinarily are not abstracted from consumption. But the statistical materials necessary to get the ideal "net contribution" of government are not available. The calculation as currently made is an understatement. It is, at any rate, clear that we have no right to take all of the governmental expenditures and regard them (along with private investment) as income-producing expenditures that offset saving. Nor can we take as a satisfactory measure the capital expenditures (public construction) of the government. This is true for the reason that such expenditures may be financed from consumption taxes and, therefore, may not form an outlet for saving as private construction does.[7]

There is, moreover, a very important difference between various kinds of governmental expenditures with respect to their potency in generating employment and income. As we have already indicated, the major new expenditure by the federal government was made in the form of relief. Such expenditures, especially in a period of general depression, are likely to be less effective in raising income and employment

---

abstract from the income stream. Thus, the "net income-creating expenditures," so called, are total expenditures that make a positive contribution to the income stream minus total taxes which abstract from the income stream.

[7] It is, of course, a coincidence that, when one takes all governmental bodies into consideration—federal, state, and local—the so-called "net contribution" ($20.5 billions per annum) was not very different in 1933–39 from the average annual volume of public construction of $18.5 billions.

than expenditures on public works. This thesis, to be sure, is often denied. It has been argued by some that relief expenditures are more potent because the funds are paid out to very needy individuals who will at once spend all, or nearly all, of it in the consumers' market and thereby at once, and to the fullest extent, stimulate employment and output. It is also said that, in the case of public works, the money is paid out to contractors who will use some considerable part of the money to pay off debts at the banks, or liquidate other indebtedness, and, in part, will simply hold the funds idle. Thus, it is said that the commodity market and employment are stimulated less in the case of public works.

Some comments with respect to this controversy are pertinent. In the first place, it should be noted that, while the utilization of the funds paid out in the commodity market is, in the first instance, quicker and more active in the case of relief payments than in the case of public works, this fact is true only for the first round of expenditures. Once the reliefers have bought goods at the stores, the storekeepers will use the money in the second round of expenditures, partly to liquidate debt and, in part, to hold funds idle. In the second and subsequent rounds of expenditures there is no clear presumption that one case is different from the other. Thus, this part of the argument, while valid up to a certain point, can easily be greatly exaggerated. On the other hand, more important, I think, is the difference in the induced consequences of the two kinds of expenditures upon investment and employment. In the case of relief expenditures, the additional purchases by reliefers is relatively small compared to the large volume of consumption expenditures made by the community as a whole, even in periods of deep depression. The additional purchases are spread very thinly over the vast consumption industries, thus giving very little stimulus to increased output, and are, therefore, likely to induce hardly any increase in employment. This is true because there is sufficient slack in the consumption industries to permit the additional output without taking on additional workers, and frequently even without increasing part-time employment. Thus, the induced employment from relief expenditures is likely to be very insignificant.

On the other hand, public works expenditures are likely to have a much greater induced effect on employment, for the following reasons. In a period of serious depression, it is the constructional and heavy industries—those relating to fixed capital production—which are seriously depressed. Employment has fallen to a mere fraction of the level reached in the boom, and construction and heavy industries output is at a low capacity level. Many constructional companies have gone into bankruptcy and passed out of the picture. Many heavy goods industries are largely shut down, and in these even replacement capital expenditures are likely to be running at a low level. But when orders come in for construction projects, workers are re-employed and the plant is reconditioned. Public works expenditures of $4 billions or $5 billions would have a tremendous effect upon re-employment and upon capital expenditures. It should be noted that an expenditure of the magnitude of $4 billions to $5 billions is fairly large, even in relation to total fixed capital construction in boom times. From 1925 to 1929, private fixed capital investment, including plant, equipment, housing, and nonprofit construction, amounted to $14 billions per annum. Thus, an injection of from $4 billions to $5 billions of public works would represent a really large figure in relation to even prosperity levels of activity in the capital goods industries. On the other hand, as noted above, a similar amount spent on relief is a very small proportion of the total consumption expenditures. A public works program of relatively moderate proportions will, therefore, induce a very large increase in employment in the construction and heavy goods industries. Thus, the leverage effect of a public works program on employment, taking account of both consumption and investment repercussions, is relatively large.

The magnitude of public expenditures, whether for governmental capital projects or for community consumption, required to counteract a depression as intense as that of the early thirties is enormous. If we underestimate the task to be performed, we are prone to disappointment over quite inadequate efforts from which too much was expected. The task confronting any government intent on a vigorous antidepression policy in 1930–35 can be gleaned from Table VI on page 87, giving the decline in private outlays on plant, equipment, and housing, including private, nonprofit construction.

It would not have been necessary for the government to fill the entire gap left by the receding tide of private investment. Yet in the earlier years—1930 and 1931—it is probable that, in order to have prevented any considerable decline, the outlays would have had to be approximately equal to the decline in private investment. It is a great mistake to assume, as some have, that a mere announcement by the government that it will fill the gap if private enterprise failed to do so would alone be sufficient, and that therefore very small expenditures would, in fact, be necessary. This overly optimistic view fails to take cognizance of the high degree of saturation reached by private investment at the end of a major boom. Private investment, on the scale of the late twenties, could not uninterruptedly have been maintained, even on the basis of favorable expectations with respect to vigorous government action and reasonably satisfactory maintenance of the national income. Not until depreciation, obsolescence, growth of population, and new technological developments had again enlarged the outlet for private investment could the government safely assume that private investment would again become reasonably adequate.

But one can also exaggerate the government's load. This is true for the reason that vigorous governmental action (for example, in 1930 and 1931) could have stopped the secondary cumulation of the deflation. While large private outlays on *new* investment could not have been expected in the early thirties, the disinvestment which occurred could have been largely prevented. Had the government stepped into the breach and maintained the national income on a moderately high scale, private capital expenditures would not have fallen anywhere near as low as they actually did. For these reasons, had the government decided to take vigorous action, the gap left by the declining private investment in 1930–35 would have had to be filled only in part by the governmental outlays.

It is in the first years of a depression that especially vigorous governmental policy is necessary.[8] Bold action at that stage can prevent the drastic disinvestment which the cumulative secondary deflation will surely bring if it is allowed to run its course. Moreover, if the secondary deflation can be prevented, it will not be necessary later to engage in large salvaging operations, which, valuable and necessary though they be, must nevertheless yield disappointing results from the standpoint of the goal of a positive recovery.

Not only are the timing, magnitude, and character of expenditures important; equally significant is the manner of financing. New and burdensome consumption taxes were imposed both by the federal government and by state and local units in the thirties. Federal consumption-tax receipts increased from $1.1 billions in 1933 to $2.2 billions in 1935. To this was subsequently added the social security payroll taxes. The local governmental units resorted more and more to consumption taxes, until by 1938 they were collecting $2.5 billions from these sources, not including the unemployment insurance payroll taxes. Consumption taxes are repressive in character and tend to place a drag on recovery.

Thus, to sum up, various factors tended to reduce the effectiveness of the fiscal recovery program as it actually developed. Large expenditures of a purely salvaging character

[8] There were, of course, peculiar difficulties in the early thirties. Tied, as the leading countries were, to the gold standard, expansionist policy would have had to have been engaged in simultaneously by many countries to be really effective. Separate action by one country alone on a large scale would have necessitated abandonment of the gold standard. In the state of public opinion in the early thirties, this was clearly impossible in the United States.

had to be made, especially in 1933–35. The gross inadequacy of public works expenditures forced undue reliance on the less stimulating relief expenditures. And, finally, a drag was placed upon recovery by reason of the increase in consumption taxes.

Chapter V
RECOVERY IN GREAT BRITAIN

IN a world in which international factors play so large a role it is somewhat astounding that two large trading countries could have had experiences so diverse as those of the United States and Great Britain in the two decades between the two World Wars. In the twenties Great Britain suffered from chronic unemployment and lagged behind the general world postwar recovery. The United States, on the other hand, enjoyed a prolonged boom. In the early thirties Britain escaped with only a moderate decline in income and employment, while the United States had her national income cut to one half its former level. In the middle and late thirties Britain made a very satisfactory recovery, reaching a level of employment and production considerably better than that of the late twenties. The United States made a more rapid recovery percentage-wise, but, having fallen to a much lower level in the depression, did not achieve, in the first recovery movement culminating in 1937, as high a per capita output as that of the late twenties and continued to face a vast unemployment problem.

And just as the unfolding of events was different, so also were the public policies pursued. Throughout the depression, with relatively unimportant exceptions, the British balanced their national budget, while the United States throughout the depression and the recovery ran a large deficit.

Depression in England Relatively Mild

In considering England's budgetary position [1] during the depression, it is especially important to remember that her national income fell by only 15 per cent.[2] Moreover, England's income and employment ceased to fall as early as 1931, remaining at substantially that level through the following two years. Owing to the comparative mildness of the depression, she was able to balance her budget without making any important changes in expenditures and tax receipts. It is true that in the financial year 1931–32 additional income taxes and unemployment insurance contributions [3] were imposed, netting nearly £70 millions, while economies of about £60 millions were achieved through reduction in unemployment benefits and other economies. These are, however, relatively small figures in a budget of £725 millions. Broadly speaking, the budget was balanced without making any substantial reductions in the regular services and functions of government and without raising the tax rates on ordinary sources of revenue.

Unique Measures and Circumstances

Without resorting to any drastic measures either of economy or of taxation, two measures, deliberately undertaken, helped to ease the budget problem. On the one side, the service on the public debt was greatly reduced owing to the conversion operations. A reduction in the rate of interest in a country having a large public debt can yield huge savings. The conversion operations contributed very greatly toward balancing

1 See George Jászi, "The Budgetary Experience of Great Britain in the Great Depression," pp. 176–211 in *Public Policy,* Harvard University Press, 1939, a model of careful analysis. I have drawn heavily upon Mr. Jászi's work, undertaken at my suggestion, for materials in this chapter. The reader is urged to turn to his illuminating statement.

2 See Colin Clark, "Determination of the Multiplier from National Income Statistics," *Economic Journal,* September, 1938.

3 The Unemployment Insurance Fund was incorporated into the Budget in order to save it from financial disaster.

the budget. But it is necessary to note that this sort of measure is, of necessity, nonrecurring in character, and that, moreover, it cannot be used effectively in a country unless its public debt is so large that the service on this debt constitutes an important fraction of the total budget.

On the other side, the imposition of high customs duties in 1932 brought in additional revenues and, at the same time, stimulated investment in the protected industries. This also is a measure, like the conversion, which can be applied only once, and was, moreover, not open to a country like the United States, which already had high tariff rates.

Yet despite the contribution made by the conversion operations and the new protective tariff, the budget could not have been balanced had England suffered a really serious depression. Had the national income declined heavily after 1931, there can be little question that the balanced budget program would have failed. And even had the national income continued for several years at the moderately low 1931–33 level, it is doubtful whether a rigorous balancing of the budget could have been achieved without growing public criticism. But by 1934 recovery was under way, larger governmental expenditures were thereby made possible, and so the strain was eased.

In April, 1933, the London *Economist*, commenting on the budget situation, remarked that the Chancellor had been compelled

> to abandon budgetary purism—only to be inhibited by innate conservative caution from the "expansionism" which is the only alternative to a ruthlessly logical, but politically impracticable deflation of expenditure. . . . To us the most disquieting aspect of Mr. Chamberlain's speech was the absence of any sign that the government even now appreciates that, unless the national income expands, a balanced budget on a £700 millions scale—and that too after realizing all the possible savings from conversions and low interest rates—becomes a patent impossibility. [The Chancellor] gave no indication that the Government are even thinking seriously of any bold scheme of housing or other productive "works." . . . A Government which lacks the will or the courage to stimu-

late economic activity by a bold loan policy outside the Budget gives the Budget-maker an impossible task.[4]

It is important to inquire into the circumstances that explain why the deflation stopped short at a decline of only 15 per cent in the national income and why subsequently a strong recovery developed. It is generally agreed by English economists that the depreciation of the foreign exchange value of the pound in 1931, vis-à-vis the United States and the gold countries in Europe,[5] was an important factor in stopping the further fall in prices and income. The firm adherence to the gold standard in these countries protected England from the danger of competitive currency depreciation. This enabled England to achieve an advantage in the world markets over her leading export competitors. On the other side, countries complementary to Britain—Canada, Australia, New Zealand, Argentina, and Scandinavia—depreciated their currencies and joined the so-called sterling bloc. This also was an advantage to England. Thus, England achieved the best of two worlds: (1) an export advantage over competitors, and (2) an improvement of trade through exchange stability with countries complementary to her economy. In this respect England occupied a quite unique position. No other country in the world was in so favorable a position to profit, on the one side, from the unfavorable trade position of the gold standard countries and, on the other side, from the improved trading position of the agricultural and primary producing countries which had depreciated their currencies.

An important result of the depreciation of sterling was the easing of the money rates. Cheap money undoubtedly contributed materially to the British recovery. Cheap money, as the American experience demonstrates, cannot of itself produce a strong revival. If a country has just experienced a vigorous investment boom and the depression largely reflects a temporary saturation in plant, equipment, and housing, low

[4] Quoted from Jászi *op. cit.*, pp. 180–81.
[5] Mainly France, Belgium, Holland, and Switzerland.

money rates will not avail. But England's situation was different. The prolonged chronic depression of the decade of the twenties left England, by 1931, with a large backlog of unsatisfied housing requirements. Moreover, for many reasons which we cannot here go into, British industry had not undergone any such extensive "rationalization" as that experienced by American and German industries. Thus, England was ripe, by 1932–33, for a considerable investment boom. In the twenties England had been starved, while the United States had been surfeited with capital or investment goods.

The United States had ridden to high prosperity in the twenties on the tidal wave of rising new industries centering in and around the automobile. In the twenties England could see no solution for her troubles except the recovery of her old position in the world market. She was looking to the revival of her old export industries. This proved a forlorn hope. In the thirties she turned to her home market. The Tariff Act of 1932 gave an impetus to important domestic industries. A free trade country like England was in a peculiarly favorable position to introduce a general protective tariff as a recovery measure. But, obviously, this remedy is of a nonrecurring character and could not be repeated as a regular recovery policy. Aided by a new protective tariff, England was able to build new industries—the automobile, electrical equipment, electric power, and the chemical industries. In view of the quite different investment possibilities, it is no mystery that cheap money worked in England but not in the United States.

When British total output is segregated into (a) output for the home market and (b) output for the foreign market, it will be seen that output for the home market was well sustained throughout the depression and increased by 50 per cent during the recovery. Output for the foreign market, however, declined heavily in the depression and never recovered the predepression level. Investment in industries catering to the home market and in residential structures constituted the core of British recovery. In this development the protective tariff, as we have just noted, played a role. But it was also greatly encouraged by the quite phenomenally favorable terms of trade which the depression brought to England's doorstep. England, as a great importer of foodstuffs and raw materials, profited from the drastic world-wide decline in the prices of these commodities in relation to the prices of industrial products. "The wage and salary earners of the nation, after buying their food, drink, tobacco, and clothes, had something like £250 millions a year *more* left over in 1932 than in 1924–27." [6] In other words, the depressional decline in total payrolls was far more than offset by the decline in cost of living. Thus, the wage and salaried classes actually enjoyed collectively a larger purchasing power at the bottom of the depression than they had had in the twenties, and this increased sum was available for the purchase of domestic products. No other fact is more basic to an understanding of the causes of the British boom in housing and the new domestic industries.

Thus, various favorable factors—some accidental, others of a character which in the usual case could not be implemented as recovery measures—combined to bring the balanced budget program through to a successful conclusion. The depreciation of the pound, the conversion operations, the cheap money rates, the protective tariff, the backlog of capital goods shortages inherited from the depressed twenties, the favorable terms of trade must all be chalked down more or less to good fortune. In other circumstances the results might have been very different.

British Budget Large

Finally, and of special significance for fiscal policy, is the role of the British budget in the maintenance of purchasing power during the depression and in the recovery which followed. The important fact about the British budget is not that it was balanced, but rather that it is a *large* budget—the fact that a

[6] The *Economist* (London), October 26, 1935.

very large percentage of national income is taxed away and spent by the government. . . . It is clear that the taxing away of such a large part of national income will have profound effects on the economic system—effects which will depend on the manner of taxation and on the way in which these funds are spent. . . . We are broadly aware of the fact that the system of British public finance is characterized by heavy progressive taxation and large expenditures on social services. The tendency of such a system would be to increase the share of consumption in national income and to decrease the share of investment, thus adding to the stability of the economic system.[7]

A profound shift has occurred, compared with the prewar period, in the ratio of consumption to income, at corresponding levels of employment. The Colwyn Committee found that prewar savings amounted to £350 to £400 millions. Taking account of the rise in prices and the increased population, an equivalent volume in the middle twenties would have amounted to £650 millions. Yet the estimates of savings for the middle twenties suggested a figure of only £450 millions, or at most £500 millions. Thus, at the prevailing value of money, savings had declined by some £150 millions to £200 millions.[8] Professor Pigou,[9] summarizing the data available in 1927, found that "as against 1911, total savings fell from about sixteen per cent to twelve or thirteen per cent of the total social income. . . ." Colin Clark's study of net investment, based on more adequate data, arrives at broadly similar results. In 1907 net investment was 12.2 per cent of national income, 8.1 per cent in 1924, and 7.3 per cent in 1937.[10] According to the Report on Economic Conditions, issued by the Royal Economic Society, new capital issues declined from £308 millions in 1928–29 to £194 millions in 1936–37.

These figures disclose a remarkable shift in the ratio of sav-

[7] Jászi, *op. cit.*, pp. 185–87.

[8] Report of the Committee on National Debt and Taxation (Colwyn Committee), Cmd. 2800, 1927, p. 17.

[9] A. C. Pigou, *The Economic Position of Great Britain*, Royal Economic Society, 1927, p. 22.

[10] Colin Clark, *National Income and Outlay*, Macmillan, 1938, p. 185; and *Economic Journal*, September, 1938.

ings to income, or, otherwise stated, in the ratio of consumption to income. It is striking how the mere manner of stating this shift—as a consumption-income ratio or as a savings-income ratio—affects one's judgment about whether the shift can be regarded as a favorable or an unfavorable one. When stated as an increase in the consumption-income ratio, an optimistic note is struck; when stated as a savings-income ratio, traditional instinctive reaction suggests a pessimistic conclusion. So long as one could feel assured that savings would always find an embodiment in real investment, a high ratio of savings to income indicated a high rate of economic progress, but also at the same time, because of the cyclical variability in investment expenditures, a condition of instability. A high ratio of consumption to income indicates a probable gain in stability and a possibility also of fuller employment at the peak of the cycle movements. At any rate, such a ratio makes possible full employment at a relatively low level of new investment. Thus, if investment outlets are relatively meager, a high consumption-income ratio makes it easier to achieve full employment. Obviously, one encounters here a matter of great significance, of which due account must be taken if one wishes to compare the recovery of the thirties in England and in the United States.

The increased consumption-income ratio can apparently be accounted for mainly by reference to the changed tax structure and the growth of social service expenditures. In 1913–14, of incomes wholly earned, only 6.7 per cent of incomes of £5,000 were taken in taxes, only 8.4 per cent of incomes of £50,000, while for incomes half earned and half derived from investment the respective figures were 9.6 and 13.6 per cent. By 1925–26 taxes took from the £5,000 income class 23.2 per cent (when earned) and 29.5 per cent (when half earned), while for the £50,000 class the figures are 44.4 and 57.7. On the other hand, the percentage taken in taxes from the lower income classes had increased little, if at all. The relevant data are given below. Both direct and indirect taxes are included.

TABLE VIII

Total Taxation: Percentage of Income [11]

Income	*Income Wholly Earned*	*Income Half Earned, Half Investment*
1913–14	*Per Cent*	*Per Cent*
£ 50	8.0	8.8
100	5.4	6.6
150	4.4	5.6
200	4.0	5.3
500	4.4	7.1
1,000	5.2	8.3
2,000	4.9	8.4
5,000	6.7	9.6
10,000	8.0	11.8
20,000	8.4	13.6
1925–26		
£ 100	11.9	13.0
150	11.6	12.7
200	10.2	11.3
500	6.2	8.4
1,000	11.0	14.4
2,000	15.2	19.3
5,000	23.2	29.5
10,000	31.2	40.1
20,000	37.5	48.7
50,000	44.4	57.7

Pigou noted that the drop in savings was very nearly equal to the excess of social service expenditures in 1924 over 1911.[12] In 1911–12 only 3.1 per cent of the national income was spent on social services, while 12.0 per cent was so expended in 1934–35.[13] In 1913–14, according to Colin Clark,[14] expendi-

[11] Report of the Committee on National Debt and Taxation, p. 95.

[12] A. C. Pigou, *The Economic Position of Great Britain* (1927), p. 22.

[13] A. L. Bowley, *Wages and Income in the United Kingdom Since 1860* (1937); Annual Return of Social Services.

[14] Colin Clark, *National Income and Outlay*, Macmillan, 1938.

tures benefiting the working classes amounted to £76 millions, and in 1935–36 to £429 millions. On the other hand, the total taxes borne by the well to do in 1913–14 amounted to £172 millions, and in 1935–36 to £685 millions. Clark estimates that before the war the taxation of the lower classes actually exceeded the social benefits derived from governmental expenditures. By 1929, however, they were taxed for only 85 per cent of the social benefits received, and by 1935 for only 79 per cent. According to his calculations the sum redistributed from the well to do to the lower income groups amounted to £91 millions in 1935–36, while Ursula Hicks,[15] on the basis of later data, puts the figure at £110 to £115 millions.

In addition to the high level of consumption, including community consumption expenditures, social services, and the like, local governmental units in England have made important capital outlays on public projects and low-cost housing, financed in large part by borrowing. The gross debt of the local authorities in England and Wales increased from £800 millions in 1923 to £1,400 millions in 1934.[16] Taking account of our greater population, this rise in local debt is very comparable with the annual rise in state and local debt in the United States in the decade of the twenties. In the thirties, however, state and local bodies in the United States, supported by federal aid, were able to reduce their net debt obligations.[17]

[15] U. K. Hicks, *The Finance of British Government, 1920–1936,* Oxford University Press, 1938, p. 59.

[16] Hicks, *op. cit.,* p. 130.

[17] According to a computation (derived from the *Statistical Abstract for the United Kingdom*) made by the National Industrial Conference Board, *Studies in Enterprise and Social Progress,* p. 282, the total debt, national and local, increased from £8,965 billions in 1930 to £9,972 billions in 1938. At the normal rate of exchange, the increase in debt in eight years thus amounted to over $4 billions. Translated into American magnitudes, our population being three times larger, this would be an increase in debt of $12 billions. The low *percentage* increase in total public debt in Great Britain is often referred to, but the percent is low only because the total debt upon which the increase is calculated is very large.

Part Two

THE CHANGING ROLE OF FISCAL POLICY

Chapter VI

FISCAL POLICY, NEW AND OLD

THE changing ideas about the nature and use of public credit, from ancient times through the early modern period, constitute a fascinating chapter in the history of thought. Scholastic theologians, like Thomas Aquinas, were bitterly opposed to loans.[1] This attitude was due not merely to the official church opposition to the payment of interest, but to a belief that public debt was itself immoral. Political philosophers of the early modern period continued to regard the prior accumulation of treasures as superior to borrowing. Jean Bodin, for example, approved only six sources of state revenue: the public domain, conquest, gifts (which are "rare"), annual contributions of allies, customs, and taxes. Traffic in rights and titles he considered pernicious, and borrowing at high interest rates "the ruin of princes." Emergencies should be met by accumulated hoards, and only war provided justification for extraordinary levies or loans.[2]

Thomas Hobbes was more realistic in his approach. He recognized the limitations of revenue from the public domain alone. In view of the widening scope of governmental expenditures, the monarch must resort to taxation, and occasionally even to public credit.[3] Adam Smith reverted to the

1 Cf. E. R. A. Seligman, article on "Public Finance," in the *Encyclopedia of the Social Sciences,* Vol. 12, p. 641.

2 *Six livres de la Republique,* Book VI. Chapter 2, especially pp. 655–56, 661, 671, 680–83, 690–92.

3 *English Works of Thomas Hobbes,* ed. Molesworth; Volume VI, Chapter 1. A Dialogue Between a Philosopher and a Student of the Common Laws of England, pp. 10–22.

older tradition, parting company on this point with Hobbes. He maintained that only "the want of parsimony in time of peace imposes the necessity of contracting debt in time of war." He observed that with the growth of commerce and manufactures European monarchs have unfortunately lost their "disposition to save," while the upkeep of standing armies and needless luxuries absorb ordinary revenue. Individuals follow the example of the state by running into debt, and "the enormous debts . . . will in the long-run probably ruin all the great nations of Europe." [4]

Hume likewise compared contemporary financing with the ancient practice of accumulating hoards, much to the disadvantage of contemporary methods. "Our modern expedient," he wrote, "is to mortgage the public revenues . . . a practice which appears ruinous." In former times the "opening of the public treasure" in wartime at least "served as a temporary encouragement to industry, and atoned, in some degree, for the inevitable calamities of war." Loan-financed wars are doubly calamitous, for the similarity between the "circulation" of "stocks" and the "circulation" of goods and money is illusory. The taxes raised to pay interest on the loans are a check on industry. Government securities have all the disadvantages of paper credit, give rise to speculation, confer advantages on the city at the expense of the nation, make the country dependent upon foreign financiers, and encourage "a useless and inactive life." [5]

Wars and the Rise of Credit Institutions

Whatever the ideas of the political philosophers, the expansion of commerce and the undertaking of wars were from the very beginning of the Middle Ages closely associated with loan financing, both public and private. Through several centuries credit institutions were slowly developing to meet

[4] *The Wealth of Nations,* Book V, Chapter 3, Stuart Edition, pp. 724–27.

[5] *Essays and Treatises on Several Subjects,* Volume II, London, 1760. Essay "Of Public Credit," especially pp. 134–42.

growing needs, leading ultimately to an organized capital market dominated by the stock exchanges and by large banks, operating on a fractional reserve basis. Through the development of these institutions it became possible to engage in extraordinary expenditures, such as those incurred in war, without imposing confiscatory taxes. The development of credit institutions made possible the financing of wars in a manner which added stimulus to the economy through the net additions of purchasing power injected into the community through the use of credit. To be sure, the dose of credit was frequently excessive, leading to price inflation. At any rate, public borrowing for war purposes removed the necessity for unduly severe and quasi-confiscatory exactions upon private wealth and income, and instead furnished a powerful stimulant to trade and enterprise. In so far as they were fought on foreign soil and with hired mercenaries, wars came to be regarded as by no means an unmixed evil. Indeed, the whole history from the late seventeenth century to the end of the Napoleonic Wars indicates a high correlation between: (a) the expenditures and use of public credit to which war gave rise, and (b) brisk trade, rising economic activity, and business prosperity. From the standpoint of the sovereign, wars were usually fought for dynastic reasons, for glory of empire, and frequently for acquisition of territory. The secondary consequences of wars during this earlier period in the history of capitalism are such as to give much support to the thesis that in this period in history wars stimulated the development of industrialism. This relatively complacent view of war was, however, shattered by the terrible experience of the first World War. Only in consequence of the disastrous effect on the economic system as a whole, and the revolutionary changes which emerged from the first World War, did there at last arise a conviction, in at least a large part of the Western world, that under modern conditions wars must be regarded as an economic, no less than a moral and social, disaster.

Thus, the emergence of private and especially public credit institutions aided the waging of expensive wars, and these, in turn, powerfully reinforced the development of the modern credit economy.

In 1691 the entire national debt in England was only £3 millions. By 1815 it amounted to over £800 millions. This enormous increase in the public debt created a haven of refuge —for capitalists both in England and abroad—for the investment of funds in a period of risk and uncertainty created by the international upheaval. The buying and selling of government obligations led to the development of the stock exchange, and throughout the eighteenth century dealings on the exchange were confined almost entirely to government securities. As late as 1843, 70 per cent of the securities listed on the London Stock Exchange consisted of securities of the English government, while an additional 10 per cent was composed of the debt obligations of foreign governments. Even as late as 1875 slightly over two thirds of the securities listed on the London Stock Exchange consisted of governmental securities.[6]

Moreover, in the very early stages of the development of modern industrialism public investments financed by public borrowing played a quite extraordinary role. In the case of the United States, internal improvements, such as turnpikes, canals, and, at the very beginning, railroads, were financed by lavish state expenditures. These wildly speculative promotional activities based on excessive optimism brought financial ruin, as is well known, to many American states and other local governmental units, leading to widespread defaults. But it must not be forgotten that, while individual investors—in very large part foreigners—lost their savings in these defaults, from a social standpoint these promotional developments played an important role in the emergence of the rapidly expanding industrialism. On the Continent of Europe the enormous financial needs incident to the development of modern systems of transportation, in particular the railroad, could not be financed from private sources under the prevailing state of financial institutional develop-

[6] G. W. Edwards, *The Evolution of Finance Capitalism*, Longmans, 1938.

ment. The great transportation undertakings, therefore, in contrast with the smaller requirements of manufacturing, were almost everywhere on the Continent financed by public borrowing and became established state enterprises. The tradition of an efficient bureaucratic civil service doubtless played an important role in the success of these ventures in contrast with the financially disastrous public ventures undertaken in America.

In England and the United States, however, and in the subsequent emergence of the manufacturing phases of modern industrialism on the Continent, governmental securities were increasingly supplanted, relatively speaking, by the emergence of the corporation and the issuance of private securities. Thus, the nineteenth century, particularly the last half, witnessed a prodigious growth of private corporate securities and the development (almost to the point of the exclusion of governmental credit as a factor in economic life) of private capitalism. In consequence of the first World War and its aftermath, and particularly as a result of the unprecedented unemployment incident to the Great Depression, public credit as an instrument of economic policy has again come powerfully to the fore. Thus, we witness a cycle in the role of public credit in the history of modern industrialism. Starting with public credit playing a major role in the period of the early rise of private capitalism, we now again see a re-emergence of the role of public credit in economic life.

We have noted how the emergence of public credit was related to the rise of war expenditures. Historically, this has been, and still remains, by far the major cause of the rise of public debt. The enormous increase in public revenues derived from taxes is, however, mainly a function of the widening scope of governmental activities, though in part it is a result of the growing necessity of financing from taxes the necessary interest payments on the public debt created mainly by war. Government services, starting from the limited function of giving protection to life and property, expanded under the requirements of a growing industrial system, the rapid agglomeration of population in huge cities, and the increasing problems of organization incident to these developments. Collective action had to be taken to protect against disaster from fire and flood; to provide for sanitation and hospitalization; to protect the public health and prevent the spread of contagious diseases; to provide methods of communication in the development of roads, postal services, and, in many countries, telegraph and telephone; to provide for protection against crime; and, increasingly with the rise of democracy, to provide on an ever more lavish scale for the education of the entire population. Services which, in large part, had formerly been provided by private agencies eventually had to be taken over by the government. Thus, provision for self-protection was transformed into a public police force. Settlement of private disputes through mutual arbitration or dueling was transferred to public courts, private education was transferred to public schools, private hospitals to public hospitals, and increasingly, particularly since the Great Depression, private charity has given way to enormous expenditures on public relief and social insurance. Moreover, the development of modern standards of living and a huge urban population have made necessary large expenditures on community consumers' capital in the form of playgrounds, recreational facilities, public schools, and public buildings of various types. Public activities have, therefore, spread from current services to the development of large expensive capital projects devoted to community consumption.

Public Finance Under Early Capitalism

The nineteenth century was preoccupied with the problem of attaining a volume of savings adequate for the requirements of a rapidly expanding economy. The dynamics of population growth and technological progress placed a premium upon freedom of enterprise and private initiative. Fiscal policy aimed at the least possible interference with the functioning of the private, capitalistic economy. The Jeffersonian ideal in America and the Gladstonian in England alike sought to minimize to the utmost the functions of governments so that, as far as possible, the entire disposable income might be expended by the individual citizen, whether for consumption or investment, for such ends as he might deem advisable. The productive resources of the community, it was believed, would be utilized most effectively if guided by a market responsive to the choices of individuals free to use as they wished their personal incomes. Public functions per se were regarded as a necessary evil. Taxes were "unproductive" expenditures, representing an unfortunate waste in the process of production. The flow of goods and services which the citizenry might enjoy could always be increased by tax reduction. Sound fiscal policy called for two things: (1) the reduction of public expenditures to the utmost possible limit, and (2) a tax structure which disturbed the pricing system as little as possible, including the pricing of the factors of production, thereby leaving intact the relative distribution of income as it would be in a tax-free society.

Such was the ideal of public finance in the heyday of private capitalism. The ideal was, of course, never fully realized. As the "high" capitalistic period receded before the advance of state interventionism, taxation was seized upon as a convenient and highly effective instrument for the regulation and control of economic life. Already in the mercantilist period taxation had been used as a police measure designed to prohibit certain activities regarded as undesirable, whether in the field of consumption or production.

Changing Role of Fiscal Policy

A far more revolutionary aim of social policy now appeared above the horizon, the full implications of which were at first not wholly visible. Indeed, it was introduced at first largely as a by-product of the imperious necessity of financing great wars and not in response to a well-thought-out social philosophy. While avowed socialists had their eyes fixed on the goal of social ownership of the means of production, the course of events had unexpectedly forged a powerful instrument for the socialization of income. The severe requirements of national defense had demonstrated the extraordinary possibilities of progressive income and inheritance taxation and had thus prepared the ground for the utilization of tax measures to accomplish far-reaching social ends, such as the more equal distribution of income and the expansion of collective consumption by the community as a whole.

In the meantime, devastating depressions brought to the foreground as never before the problem of business instability. Whereas it had been the concern of economic policy to raise the standard of living, now attention was centered on the promotion of security and stability. At first, main reliance was placed upon monetary policy, but the exigencies of the Great Depression compelled (or, at any rate, led to) enormous expenditures for the relief of the unemployed. These were made more willingly in the belief that they served the double purpose of giving relief and also of "curing" the depression. Thus, fiscal policy was forced into service as a compensatory device more by accident than by design. It was, therefore, not surprising that experience in the implementation of this policy turned up some rather surprising results. Part of the consequences, it appears, were due to the applications of orthodox canons of fiscal policy to a situation for which they were totally unsuited. It was the old story of putting new wine into old bottles.

Back of the menacing unfolding of violent industrial fluctuations there now appeared the specter of chronic unemployment. Many, perhaps most, competent observers professed to doubt its reality and conceived it to be an illusion springing from the distracted psychological atmosphere created by the Great Depression. Discussions with respect to the phenomena of "long waves" and of structural changes in the economy, together with the increasing development of the theoretical tools of dynamic analysis, produced challenging hypotheses in explanation of chronic or secular underemployment. And while the debate progressed, all the leading governments of the world were continuing to pour out vast funds for armaments or for the relief of depression—whatever its character, whether temporary or secular. Government debt was everywhere mounting and fiscal policy was being drafted willy-nilly to serve as an instrument to increase the volume of employment.

There is thus emerging a new aim of fiscal policy, vigorously assailed by some and staunchly defended by others—the aim of ensuring the full employment of the factors of production. This policy involves greatly enlarged governmental expenditures. Some would finance these wholly from progressive taxation, once a full-income level had been achieved, and thus "balance the budget." Others would finance them partly from a progressive rise in the public debt. The possible limits of this development are certainly far wider than is usually supposed, owing partly to the low rates of interest which, under an appropriate Central Bank policy, are adequate to tempt idle funds into short-term government obligations, and partly to the fact that taxes raised to pay interest on a public debt domestically held flow back again to the community as a part of the income receipts of individuals. The larger aspects of this problem and its implications in terms of the distribution of income and the price structure will be discussed subsequently in this volume.

Chapter VII

THE CHANGING CHARACTER OF GOVERNMENTAL EXPENDITURES

THE major developments which peculiarly characterize the economic life of the twentieth century, particularly after 1914, are to a large extent merely continuations of trends which were already present in the nineteenth century and which differentiate the industrial-capitalist era from the old regime. But the differential rate of change in the various areas of economic life is itself sufficient to yield us a new kind of world qualitatively different from that of the last century. And, in this respect, the rapidly growing role of government throughout the Western world above all challenges attention.

The growing activities of government could not fail to result in a great increase in governmental expenditures. And the changing character of expenditures is equally significant. In this connection some illuminating contrasts are evident between the prewar decade, the decade of the twenties, and the decade of the thirties.

In the United States there are three levels of government: federal, state, and local. The changing fiscal importance of each of these levels of government, as indicated in the size of expenditures, is stated in the table on page 119.

From this table it is evident that some significant changes have occurred. In 1929 state expenditures had increased relatively more than federal or local, compared with 1913. In 1937 increases of federal and state expenditures over 1913 were not significantly different, but both had far outstripped

TABLE IX

Governmental Expenditures in the United States [1]

	millions of dollars			*1929 as multiple of 1913*	*1937 as multiple of 1913*
	1913	*1929*	*1937*		
Federal [2]	964	3,735	9,080	4.0	9.3
Federal (Post-office expenditures, except postal deficit, omitted)	703	3,047	8,349	4.3	11.9
State [3]	379	1,955	3,068	5.2	8.1
Local [4]	1,846	6,719	6,340	3.6	3.4

the increase in local expenditures. In absolute figures, local expenditures in 1913 were twice as large as federal, while the federal outlays, in turn, were more than twice as large as the state expenditures. But, by 1937, the ratio ran approximately 3 for the federal, 2 for the local units, and 1 for the states.

Highways and Education

The large relative growth of state expenditures from 1913 to 1929 is the result mainly of increased outlays on highways and on education. The development of highways and of education had a unique history in the three decades ending in 1930. As late as 1913, state governments were spending only $28 millions on highways, while, in 1929, $669 millions were

[1] Sources: *Annual Report of the Secretary of the Treasury;* U.S. Bureau of the Census, *Wealth, Public Debt, and Taxation, 1913; Financial Statistics of States,* 1915; U.S. Bureau of the Census, Press Releases, *Summary of Finances of State Governments, 1937,* Nos. 1 and 17; *Report of the Commissioner of Education,* 1914; National Industrial Conference Board, *Cost of Government in the United States; Statistical Abstract of the United States.*

[2] Federal expenditures include all post-office expenditures, but exclude debt retirement, refunds of receipts, and District of Columbia expenditures.

[3] State expenditures exclude federal grants received, but include state grants to local governments.

[4] Local government expenditures exclude subsidies and grants received.

expended. State expenditures for education were only $61 millions in 1902, $129 millions in 1913, and had risen to $549 millions in 1929. In this thirty-year span a revolution had occurred in methods of transportation and also in education.

The coming of the automobile compelled the construction of an entirely new and extremely expensive system of highways, the building of which is comparable in magnitude with the gigantic task in an earlier period of covering the entire country with a network of railroads. In a like manner, these three decades witnessed a profound revolution in the system of secondary education. In 1900 the total attendance in secondary schools in America was only 696,000 boys and girls; by 1930 it was 4,800,000, and, by 1934, 6,088,000. Whereas in 1900 only 10.2 per cent of the boys and girls from fourteen to seventeen years of age inclusive were in high school, by 1930, 47.7 per cent, and by 1934, 56.2 per cent, attended.[5] This remarkable development bears testimony, perhaps more than any other single fact, to the prodigious rise in the American standard of living from 1900 to 1930.

Whereas formerly the local governments provided almost exclusively for highways and education, the tasks imposed by the development of these decades made the burden too heavy. Property taxes, the main source of local revenue, were not adequate. Hence the increasing sharing of the burden by the states, and also, especially with respect to highways, by the federal government. Altogether, expenditures on highways by all governments increased from $182 millions in 1902 to $1,936 millions in 1929, more than a tenfold increase. Meanwhile, expenditures on education increased from $281 millions to $2,490 millions, approximately a ninefold increase.

Social Welfare and Unemployment Relief

A third category of growing importance is that of social welfare, including relief for the poor, aged, blind, and sick; mothers' and widows' pensions; care of children; public

[5] ***Statistical Abstract of the United States,*** **1936, p. 108.**

health; hospitals; sanitation (including sewerage disposal, refuse collection and disposal); institutions for the care of the handicapped; recreation (including parks and playgrounds); pensions to civil employees; and workmen's compensation. Expenditures on these items amounted to only $170 millions in 1902, but had risen to $1,360 millions by 1929. But as late as 1929 most of these outlays were by local governments.

A fourth category disclosing an enormous expansion of governmental expenditures is that of public service enterprises. These include water, electricity, gas, rapid transit and other transportation, and all other enterprises operated on a commercial basis. Expenditures by all governments for these purposes increased from $199 millions in 1902 to $1,461 millions in 1929.

A summary view of the four categories discussed above—categories which peculiarly reveal the shift in government functions during the current century—is given for four intervals, covering nearly four decades, in Table X.

TABLE X

Governmental Expenditures [6] *(Federal, State, and Local)*

(millions of dollars)

Expenditure category	*1902*	*1913*	*1929*	*1937*
Highways	182	426	1,936	1,818
Education	282	565	2,490	2,372
Social Welfare	170	342	1,360	5,098
Public Service Enterprises	199	489	1,461	1,778

One, and only one, of these categories leaped to a sharply higher level during the last decade—social welfare. And this illustrates the characteristic shift in the decade of the thirties.

[6] Sources: U.S. Bureau of the Census, *Wealth, Public Debt and Taxation,* 1902; Report of the U.S. Commissioner of Education, 1903; M. O. Eldridge, *Public Roads Mileage, Revenues and Expenditures in the U.S. in 1904* (U.S. Office of Public Roads Bulletin no. 32, 1907); *Financial Statistics of Cities,* 1905; and references cited on p. 119.

While highways, education, social welfare, and public service enterprises represent the great fields of growth up to the end of the twenties, the extraordinary relief load—both urban and rural—growing out of the Great Depression offers the main explanation for the great rise of governmental expenditures during the thirties.

But the new burden had to be carried almost exclusively by the federal government. The financial incapacity of the state and local governments, resulting from the fall of the national income in the early thirties to half its former level, compelled retrenchment. Local governments can carry on their fiscal obligations quite well when the national income is high and rising. But only the federal government—and, to a lesser degree, state governments—with its vastly greater taxing powers (especially with respect to income taxation) and its capacity for borrowing, can carry on and even expand its expenditures in the face of a low and falling national income.

State and local expenditures for education declined from $2.5 billions in 1929 to $2.3 in 1937, while expenditures on highways declined from $1.8 billions in 1929 to $1.4 billions in 1937. State and local capital outlays of all sorts (including those on education and highways) declined from $3.0 billions to $1.4 billions.[7]

Total governmental expenditures increased from $12.4 billions in 1929 to $18.5 billions in 1937. But the expenditures of local governments fell from $6.7 billions in 1929 to $6.3 billions in 1937. Federal expenditures, however, increased from $3.7 billions to $9.1 billions in 1937, while those of state governments increased from $2.0 in 1929 to $3.1 billions in 1937.

From January, 1933, to July, 1938, total federal contributions to various relief and assistance measures amounted to $11,120,000,000, while state and local contributions amounted

[7] Hearings before the Temporary National Economic Committee, Part 9, p. 4064.

to $4,195,000,000. The data for each year are as follows, in millions of dollars: [8]

TABLE XI

(in millions of dollars)

Year	*Federal*	*State and Local*
1933	907	401
1934	2,087	577
1935	2,108	627
1936	2,664	895
1937	2,170	1,048
1938 (six months)	1,184	646

An analysis of the growth of expenditures since 1930 relates, therefore, almost exclusively to federal expenditures springing from the necessity of coping with the problems arising from unemployment and related recovery measures. The emergency made it necessary for the federal government to come to the aid of state and local governments to provide for relief for the unemployed; and the unprecedented economic difficulties confronting industry and agriculture alike led the government into a vast range of experiments intended to restore the national income. Unemployment relief expenditures of the federal government leaped to $1.8 billions in 1934, averaged $2.4 billions in the years 1935–37, and amounted to $2.0 billions in 1938, $2.7 in 1939, and $2.0 billions in 1940. The Agricultural Adjustment program rose from $289 millions in 1934 to $712 millions in 1935, $782 millions in 1939, and $1,017 millions in 1940. These are the major developments in federal expenditures growing out of the depression emergency. Public works expenditures, including grants to state and local bodies, rose from $388 millions in 1931 to $719 millions in 1935 and $1,062 millions in 1937. Loans and subscriptions to the capital stock of governmental agencies (made

[8] Works Progress Administration, *Report on Progress of the W.P.A. Program,* June 30, 1938, p. 113.

directly from the federal budget) amounted to $885 millions in 1932 and $882 millions in 1934. These lending agencies, largely from their own funds obtained by issuing their own obligations (guaranteed by the federal government), in turn poured billions of dollars into the work of rehabilitation.

Two major shifts in expenditures may thus be noted from the decade of the twenties to that of the thirties. The first has to do with a large relative increase in federal expenditures in relation to state and local expenditures. The second has to do with a change in the underlying reasons for increased expenditures. In the twenties the rise in expenditures was due largely to certain demands incident to a changing or rising standard of living, notably expenditures for roads and education. In the thirties the increased expenditures grew out of an effort to overcome the Great Depression or to mitigate its ravaging effects on the standard of living, especially of the unemployed.

Unemployment relief constitutes the biggest single item of expenditure under the New Deal, with a total for the seven years 1934–40 of $15.8 billions. Public works of all sorts absorbed $6.0 billions, the Agricultural Adjustment program $4.2 billions. Unemployment relief, aid to agriculture, and public works designed to promote employment together account for $26.0 billions, or nearly 50 per cent of the total federal expenditures in 1934–40.

Chapter VIII

THE TAX STRUCTURE

THE tax structure in the United States has undergone quite revolutionary changes during the last quarter of a century. Until 1914 tax revenue was derived almost wholly from property taxes and from customs duties and excises.

The burden of taxes was, accordingly, distributed with little relation to ability to pay. Customs and excises constituted in 1902 nearly one half of total tax receipts of all governments in the United States, and nearly 40 per cent in 1913. In so far as such taxes affect the prices of commodities of general consumption, the tax burden represents a diminishing percentage of income the farther one moves into the upper-income ranges. And even property taxes—and this applies particularly to rented residences—are, in large part, shifted by property owners to the general public. Thus, a tax structure based upon property and consumption taxes is likely to be heavily regressive and burdensome upon the low-income groups of the community.

Progressive vs. Regressive Taxation

The federal income tax was introduced in 1914. During the war surtax rates on upper-bracket incomes were sharply raised, and this helped to diminish the regressive character of the general tax structure. But indirect taxes weighing largely on consumption continued to be levied, and, moreover, the rates on the moderately well-to-do and lower rich class were comparatively low. Accordingly, the tax structure as a whole did not reveal any great progressivity over the entire income range, even though high surtax rates were imposed on the highest brackets. The introduction of the federal income tax—a reform which came astoundingly late in American history—did, nevertheless, shift the burden of taxation much more largely upon those most able to bear it.

In the postwar decade the high surtax rates were drastically reduced. The rates were again raised in 1932, and in 1935 the high surtax rates of the war period were restored and even exceeded. In Table XII the effective rates applicable to each income level in the three years 1918, 1929, and 1937 are given. This table reveals the extremely low rates which prevailed in 1929 in contrast to those of 1918 and 1937. The 1937 rates were relatively lighter on all incomes below $25,000 than those of 1918, but slightly higher for incomes above this level.

TABLE XII

Effective Tax Rate on Individual Net Incomes[1]

Net Income Classes (Thousands of dollars)	*1918*	*(Per cent) 1929*	*1937*
Under 1	....	0.02	0.23
1 under 2	1.19	.04	.48
2 under 3	.98	.07	.39
3 under 5	2.35	.05	.84
5 under 10	4.34	.21	2.63
10 under 25	8.20	1.49	6.66
25 under 50	13.32	5.24	13.60
50 under 100	21.69	9.77	23.60
100 under 150	33.68	12.92	37.49
150 under 300	44.64	14.64	48.06
300 under 500	54.77	15.49	57.45
500 under 1,000	58.65	15.86	64.82
1,000 and over	64.65	15.76	71.95

Even the 1935 rates were relatively low on the so-called middle brackets, from $5,000 to $100,000. In view of the

[1] U.S. Treasury Department, *Statistics of Income for 1937*, Part 1, pp. 40–41.

greatly increased need for revenue resulting from the growth of governmental expenditures, and in view of the Social Security program, higher rates in this income range might have been expected. Increases were made, but in large part resort was had to consumption and payroll taxes. On balance, this tended to make the tax structure, as a whole, weigh more heavily on consumption than had been the case even in the twenties.

This fact can be strikingly shown from a table published in the *Annual Report of the Secretary of the Treasury* for the fiscal year 1940. An estimate is made of the federal tax liabilities for the calendar year 1941 based on the tax structures prevailing: (a) under the laws of May, 1932, and (b) under the laws of December, 1940. On the basis of the revenue acts in force in early 1932, it is estimated that $1,871 millions might be collected in taxes on individual incomes, estates, and gifts, and on corporate incomes and profits, assuming a national income equal to that expected in calendar 1941. On the same basis, $991 millions might be expected from consumption taxes, including liquor, tobacco, miscellaneous internal revenue, and customs duties. Thus, the tax structure as of 1932 would yield a revenue (based on the expected 1941 income) of which 35 per cent was consumption taxes. Considering the sharp increase in the rates on individual incomes, estates, and gifts, and on corporate incomes and excess profits, notably in the Revenue Acts of 1935 and of 1940, one might have expected a drastic reduction in the ratio of consumption to total taxes. This, however, is not the case. Based on the tax law in effect on December 31, 1940, it is estimated that $5,953 millions could be collected in corporate income and profits taxes and in individual income, estate, and gift taxes, while $3,660 millions might be collected in consumption taxes (including those listed above) and taxes on payrolls. Thus, on the basis of the revenue laws in force at the end of 1940, 38 per cent of total federal taxes could be regarded as mainly consumption taxes. This fact is all the more striking in view of the relatively high income—the anticipated income of 1941—

on which the estimates are based. The higher the income, the greater the potency of a progressive income tax structure.

To offset so effectively the greater progressivity of the income tax in 1940 compared with 1932 it is evident that the taxes burdening consumption must have been very sharply increased. The repeal of the Eighteenth Amendment, together with increases in liquor tax rates, accounts for about $800 millions of the increase in the consumption taxes estimated in the hypothetical case referred to above. Miscellaneous internal revenue items, including gasoline taxes and manufacturers' excises, account for another $800 millions, while payroll taxes, including old age and railroad unemployment insurance, account for $950 millions.[2]

Turning from the comparison of the tax structure of early 1932 with that of late 1940, as revealed in the estimated tax liabilities of these two structures applied to a high national income, such as that expected in calendar 1941, it is of interest to consider the *actual* tax collections in the fiscal years 1933–40. The following table shows the relation, year by year, of consumption taxes (as defined above, including pay-

TABLE XIII

(in millions)

Fiscal Year	*Consumption and Payroll Taxes*	*Total Tax Revenues*
1933	$1,075	$2,080
1934	1,889	3,116
1935	2,211	3,800
1936	2,000	4,116
1937	2,478	5,294
1938	2,837	6,242
1939	2,804	5,668
1940	3,039	5,925

[2] Equally striking is the great strength of the tax structure in 1940 compared with that of 1932. On the basis of the anticipated national income of 1941, the tax strucure of 1932 would yield only $2,862 millions, while the tax structure of 1940 would yield $9,613 millions.

roll taxes) to total tax revenues for this eight-year period.

The broad sweep of changes in the tax structure during the last four decades can be seen from a few summary tables disclosing the main tendencies at work. First, let us consider the tax structure, federal, state, and local, at four intervals: at the turn of the century, pre-World War I, at the end of the twenties, and pre-World War II. All taxes are grouped into four categories: (1) property taxes, (2) income, corporation, inheritance and gift taxes, (3) consumption taxes, and (4) payroll taxes.[3]

TABLE XIV

Federal, State and Local Tax Revenues[4]

(in millions)

	1902	*1913*	*1930*	*1938*
Property	$ 707	$1,440	$4,959	$4,745
Income,[5] Inheritance, Gift, and Corporation Taxes	29	77	2,866	4,107
Consumption Taxes: Motor Fuel and Vehicles, Liquor and Tobacco, Sales and other excises, Customs	651	859	2,600	4,478
Payroll Taxes				1,502
Total Taxes	$1,387	$2,376	$10,425	$14,832

[3] Some difficulties are necessarily encountered in fitting all taxes into these four categories, and some arbitrary classification becomes necessary. Nevertheless, the broad conclusions stand out clearly and are but little modified by these somewhat arbitrary decisions.

[4] Sources: *Annual Reports of the Secretary of the Treasury;* U.S. Bureau of the Census, *Wealth, Public Debt and Taxation,* and *Financial Statistics of States; Tax Policy* Magazine, December, 1938–January, 1939; National Industrial Conference Board, *Cost of Government in the United States, 1929–30;* U.S. Bureau of the Census; *Financial Statistics of Cities; Dun's Review,* July, 1939.

[5] Poll and occupation taxes, inconsequential in amounts, ranging from $7 millions in 1938 to $26 millions in 1930, are included here.

Relative to 1902, property taxes and consumption taxes had increased in 1938 by precisely the same multiple, 6.7. Relative to 1913, however, the multiple for property taxes was 3.3, while that for consumption taxes was 5.1. Income, inheritance, gift, and corporation taxes had risen by 1938 from insignificant amounts in 1902 and 1913 to a figure comparable with property and consumption taxes.

Relative to 1930, property taxes were slightly lower in 1938. Consumption taxes had, however, increased by a multiple of 1.67, and income, inheritance and gift, and corporation taxes by a multiple of 1.43.

Consumption taxes constituted 36 per cent of total taxes in 1913, and 33 per cent in 1938, social security taxes excluded. Consumption and social security taxes together amounted to 40 per cent of the total in 1938.

Such, in broad outlines, are the major shifts in the tax structure as a whole, including all governments. But it will be useful also to consider the main tendencies at each level—federal, state, and local. With respect to local governments, there are no significant changes to report. The property tax remains, as before, the almost exclusive source of tax revenue. Sales taxes and other excises have been added in recent years, but the receipts from these sources in 1938 were less than one twelfth of the sum received from property taxes. Local property taxes declined slightly during the thirties, but were, nevertheless, more than sevenfold the amount collected in 1902 and 3½ times that of 1913. Service receipts increased greatly during the twenties, reaching a level more than ten times that of 1902 and nearly five times that of 1913. This latter increase represents the growth of public service enterprises, water, electricity, gas, rapid transit, and other enterprises operated on a commercial basis. The data relative to tax revenues are presented in Table XV on page 131.

In contrast to the situation with respect to local revenues, very striking changes have occurred over the last three decades in state taxation. In the first place, state tax receipts have in-

TABLE XV

Local Tax Revenues

(in millions)

	1902	*1913*	*1930*	*1938*
Property	$625	$1,300	$4,614	$4,531
Corporation, Inheritance, Poll, and Occupational Taxes	25	31	171	
Consumption Taxes: Motor Fuel and Vehicles, Liquor and Tobacco, Sales and other excises	58	82	232	359
Total Taxes	$708	$1,413	$5,017	$4,890

creased enormously, being twenty-five times larger in 1938 than in 1902. With respect to sources, until the first World War, property taxes represented about half the total. By 1930, income, inheritance, and corporation tax receipts combined were more than twice as large as those derived from property.

TABLE XVI

State Tax Revenues

(in millions)

	1902	*1913*	*1930*	*1938*
Property	$ 82	$ 140	$ 345	$ 214
Income, Inheritance, and Corporation Taxes	54	124	725	928
Consumption Taxes: Motor Fuel and Vehicles, Liquor and Tobacco, Sales and other excises	19	36	711	2,023
Payroll Taxes				748
Total Taxes	$155	$300	$1,781	$3,913

The same holds for gasoline and sales taxes and other excises. And, by 1938, these consumption taxes had again tripled, as disclosed in Table XVI.

Equally significant are the changes in federal taxation. Prior to the first World War almost the exclusive sources of revenue were customs duties and excises—about equally divided. By 1930, however, individual and corporate income taxes were far and away more important sources of revenue. But, between 1930 and 1938, federal consumption taxes (heavily, liquor and tobacco) doubled, and were two thirds of the income, estate, and corporation taxes combined. And there were added, moreover, the social security taxes. Table XVII on federal revenues follows:

TABLE XVII

Federal Tax Revenues

(in millions)

	1902	*1913*	*1930*	*1938*
Income, Estate (and Gift), and Corporation Taxes	$ 5	$ 35	$2,475	$3,179
Consumption Taxes: Motor Fuel and Vehicles, Liquor and Tobacco, Excises and Customs	254	628	1,152	2,096
Payroll Taxes				754
Total Taxes	$259	$663	$3,627	$6,029

It is of interest to note that in 1938 the federal consumption taxes were almost precisely equal to state consumption taxes, each being around $2 billions. Moreover, in each case payroll taxes of about $750 millions were collected. With respect to income, inheritance, and corporation taxes, the states collected relatively little compared with the federal government. The main sources of tax revenue are the same with respect to the state governments and the federal government. Both rely heavily on consumption taxes, but the federal government places a much larger reliance on corporate and individual income taxes.

Federal and state tax revenues have shown greater capacity for expansion than local tax revenues. Confronted with a difficult fiscal situation, local units have received increasing grants from the state and federal governments. Thus, in 1938, states made grants to local bodies amounting to $1,250 millions, while the federal government made regular grants to states of nearly $600 millions, and to local governments of $125 millions. In addition, federal emergency expenditures, amounting to nearly $4 billions annually for W.P.A., C.C.C., N.Y.A., P.W.A. grants, and agriculture, greatly relieved the fiscal position of both state and local governments.

Federal-state-local fiscal relations present a major problem currently and in the immediate future. Growing social responsibilities have been forced upon the state and local governments by the unprecedented volume of unemployment and by the progress of social reform. These responsibilities the local governments cannot carry without resort to heavy consumption taxes. Thus, for example, many states have been compelled to levy or to increase sales taxes in order to finance the Old Age Assistance program. If we are to cure this malady, either the federal government will have to take over more functions, or it will have to assume a larger responsibility with respect to the financing of social welfare projects.

Federal, state, and local consumption taxes (see table on page 129) amounted to the sum of $4.3 billions. These include sales taxes and other excises, taxes on motor fuel and motor vehicles, liquor, and tobacco. In addition, $1.5 billions of payroll taxes were collected, also largely abstracted from consumption. If we include these, we reach the vast total of $5.8 billions withdrawn through taxation from the stream of consumption expenditures. Such taxes are definitely deflationary, impose a heavy drag on the economy, and tend to prevent full employment.

The growing importance of consumption taxes has reversed the trend toward a more progressive tax structure which began with the federal income tax of 1914. Taking all taxes into account—federal, state, and local—the structure does not begin to be progressive until an income of $10,000 is reached. As far as state and local taxes, considered as a unit, are concerned, the tax rate structure remains apparently strictly proportional to income throughout the whole range from the $500 income to incomes of over $20,000. The federal tax structure begins to be fairly progressive at the $10,000 income level. The relevant data are disclosed in Table XVIII below.

TABLE XVIII

The American Tax Structure [6]

Income	*Taxes as Percent of Income*		
Class	*Federal*	*State and Local*	*Total*
$500 to $1,000	6.6	11.4	18.0
1,000 to 1,500	6.4	10.9	17.3
1,500 to 2,000	6.6	11.2	17.8
2,000 to 3,000	6.4	11.1	17.5
3,000 to 5,000	7.0	10.6	17.6
5,000 to 10,000	8.4	9.5	17.9
10,000 to 15,000	14.9	10.6	25.5
15,000 to 20,000	19.8	11.9	31.7
20,000 and over	27.2	10.6	37.8

Apparently the American tax structure, taken as a whole and including both direct and indirect taxes, is far less progressive than is commonly supposed.

[6] See Colm and Tarasov, *Who Pays the Taxes?*, Temporary National Economic Committee, Monograph No. 3, 1940.

Chapter IX

THE GROWTH AND ROLE OF PUBLIC DEBT

I. The Rise of Public Debt

HISTORICALLY, it is clear that opposition to public debt, like the medieval opposition to interest, gradually broke down by reason of exigencies which appeared more or less uncontrollable. Thus, state borrowing entered as a by-product mainly of the increasingly costly outlays incident to modern warfare. It was not a question of theoretical principles but of practical, hard necessities. The tradition against borrowing was set aside when grave emergencies, such as wars, forced the issue.[1]

It was, however, held that the government ought to establish sinking funds and reduce governmental debt incident to war as much as feasible. While the United States, owing to its rapid expansion, found it possible to approximate this maxim following the War of 1812, the Civil War, and again the first World War, older countries with larger debts and with smaller possibilities of extensive expansion found it much more difficult, and indeed on the whole impossible, to retire debt in any important degree. With respect to England, while there was little actual retirement of debt in the hundred years between the Napoleonic Wars and the first World War,

1 Even taxes in early modern English history were tolerated only as extraordinary levies to meet necessary emergency situations, notably war. Emergence from the feudal period into the modern period gradually brought a shift from feudal dues, and income from the king's private domain, to regularly assessed taxes on property, transactions, and income.

the debt at any rate did not rise. France, on the other hand, experienced a continually rising *trend* in her public debt throughout the nineteenth century.

Charts 8 and 9 show the historical trends in the public debt in England from 1690 to 1938 and in France from 1815 to 1938. Some interesting facts emerge from these charts. The period from 1690 to 1815 in England is divided almost equally into years of war and years of peace. Regularly in the war years the public debt rose, while in years of peace the budget was more or less balanced, and at times some reduction in the debt occurred. It is evident, however, that there is a marked upward trend throughout the entire period which assumes almost a straight line on a logarithmic scale. Thus, overlooking the relatively short-run fluctuations about the trend, it may be said that the British public debt for this period of one hundred and twenty-five years was rising at approximately a constant percentage rate of increase. Between 1815 and 1914 the public debt ceased to rise and, considering the whole period, declined by a very moderate amount, so that by 1914 it stood 21.8 per cent under the 1815 level. There were some fluctuations up and down, notably the temporary rise in the debt during the Boer War, followed by a subsequent fairly rapid retirement. Then came the prodigious rise in the public debt incident to the first World War, so that the postwar debt stood in relation to the total national income at about the same level as in 1815. In both 1818 and 1923 the debt was twice the national income.[2]

At the close of the Napoleonic Wars the French public debt, in contrast with the situation in England, was small.[3] Her experience from 1815 to 1914 was quite divergent from that of England. Whereas the English debt became stabilized and indeed gradually declined, the French debt rose with temporary interruptions through the nineteenth century up to

[2] See Report of the Committee on National Debt and Taxation, *Cmd. 2800*, 1927, p. 235.

[3] Napoleon, while confronted with grave financial difficulties, nevertheless resolutely opposed loan financing.

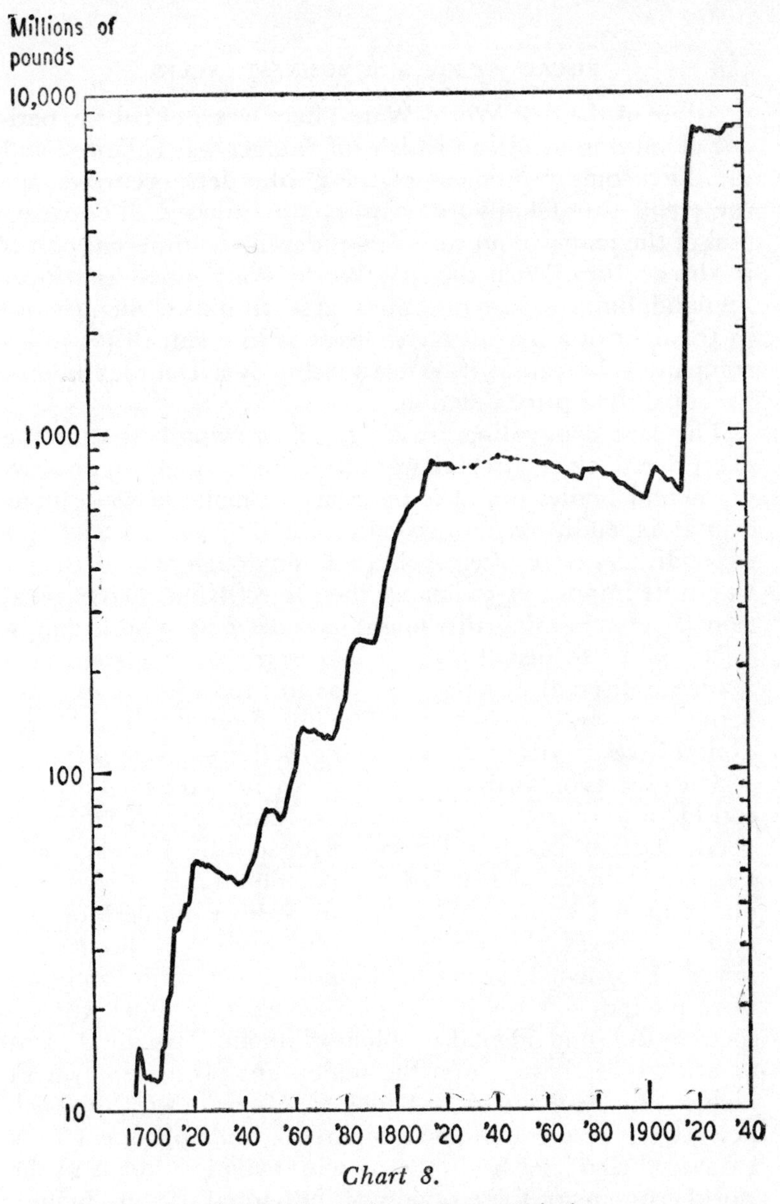

Chart 8.

The Public Debt of Great Britain

Sources: Figures for the years 1696–1825 from Elizabeth B. Schumpeter, "English Prices and Public Finance, 1660–1822," Review of Economic Statistics, *February, 1938. Figures for the years 1833, 1842, 1847, and 1854 from H. E. Fisk,* English Public Finance from the Revolution of 1688, *Bankers' Trust, New York, 1920. Figures for the years 1856–1937 from* The Statesman's Yearbook, *Macmillan, annually.*

the time of the first World War. There were, of course, periods of varying length in which the budget was balanced and in which some retirement of the public debt occurred, but the trend throughout the century was upward. The steepness of the rising trend varied considerably at different points in the century. With the first World War came—as also in England, but at a far more rapid rate—an unprecedented rise in the debt of a magnitude so great as to result in (or to accompany—the causal interrelationship is a complex one) a five- or sixfold price inflation.

The first compelling reason for borrowing was thus the exceptional emergency of war. But, increasingly, local governmental bodies found it necessary to make discontinuous capital expenditures on needed public improvements. These expenditures were often so large in any current year that it was quite impossible to finance the project from current taxation. Thus, a municipality might have decided to build a public school or to install a municipal water works system or a sewerage disposal plant so costly as to preclude the expense being borne by current taxes. The lumpiness of certain large capital investments made borrowing well-nigh imperative.

The objects of borrowing to which we have referred involve considerations with respect to apparently unavoidable expenditures, such as those for war or for socially necessary public improvements demanded by the community in order to maintain and improve modern standards of living. More recently, however, the sphere of public finance has been enormously broadened, owing to the political necessity imposed upon modern communities to pursue an active policy with respect to the fundamental problem of unemployment. This is true whether viewed from the standpoint of unemployment incident to the fluctuations which we associate with the business cycle, or from the standpoint of unemployment of a structural character having to do with maladjustments in the world economy or the economy of individual nations, including the problem of chronic unemployment.

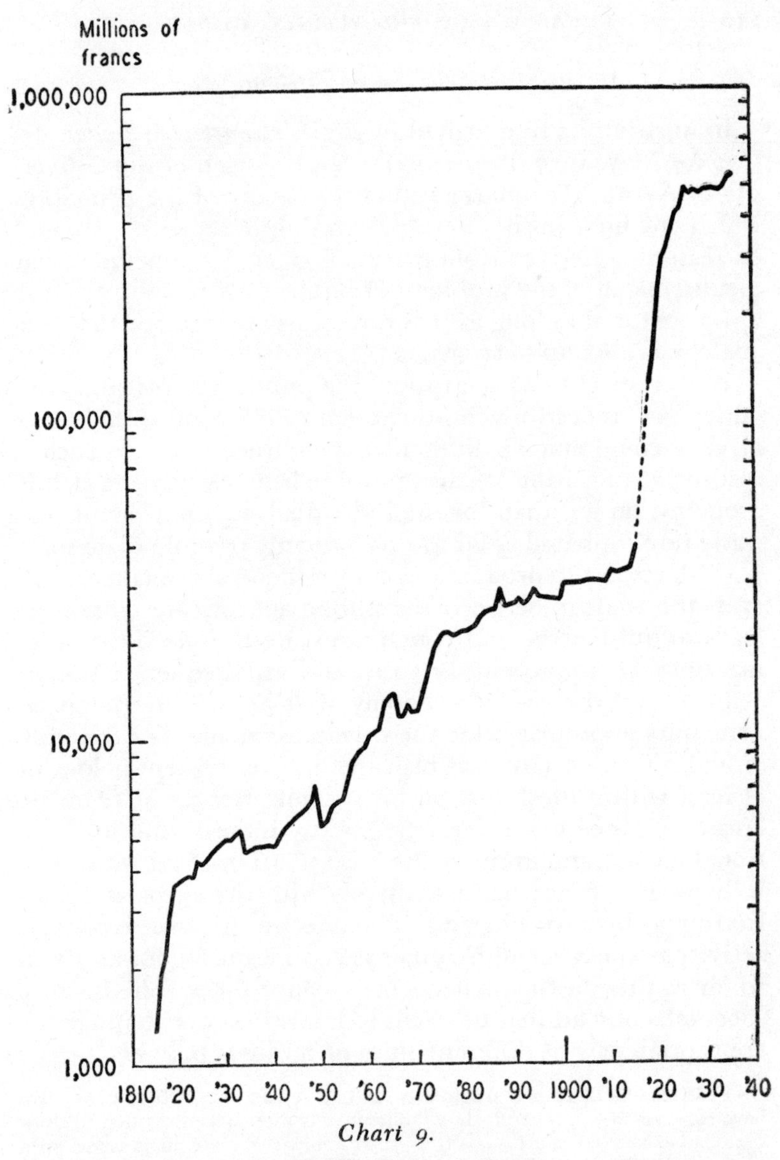

Chart 9.

The Public Debt of France

***Sources:** Figures for the years 1815–1932 computed from those given in* Statistique générale de la France—Annuaire statistique, *1933, pp. 204–06. Figures for the years 1932–36 from* The Statesman's Yearbook, *Macmillan, annually.*

II. Public Debt versus Private Debt

In an illuminating article in the *Weltwirtschaftliches Archiv* for May, 1937, Professor Jørgen Pedersen of the University of Aarhus, Denmark, argues that many of the principles which one finds in the literature on Public Finance are based on reasoning derived from private finance. He concludes that the discussion of the problems of public finance will continue to be confused as long as it is not clearly recognized that this analogy is false and erroneous.[4]

With respect to consumption, the public and private economies have indeed much in common. Both must distribute a given income among different expenditure items in such a manner as to get the greatest possible benefits. For the public economy, no less than for the individual, it is important that waste be eliminated as far as it is humanly possible to do so.

With respect to production, employment, and income, however, the analogy between the public and private economies leads to quite erroneous conclusions. Both, indeed, strive to maximize their income. But this end can frequently not be achieved by the public economy if it applies the financial principles appropriate for the private economy. For the individual it is important that his expenditures be kept below, or at least within the limits of, his income. For the state an increase of expenditures may frequently increase the total national income and improve the fiscal position of the state. The individual is concerned exclusively with the effect of his action upon his own business. The effect of his own economic activity upon other individuals is significant for him only in so far as this, in turn, affects his balance sheet. The balance sheet tells him all that he needs to know in order to judge the appropriateness of different lines of business policy.

[4] Pedersen disclaims any originality in this conclusion. "Other economists have come to the same result, but unfortunately most have forgotten to draw the relative concrete conclusions from their analysis. We are all so accustomed to the view of private business that it is difficult for us to liberate ourselves therefrom, even when we realize full well that in the case in hand another viewpoint is required." *Weltwirtschaftliches Archiv*, May, 1937, p. 469.

In the case of public finance, however, it is quite otherwise. The success or failure of public policy cannot be read from the balance sheet of the public household. It cannot be determined by whether or not debt is being retired or assets accumulated. The success or failure of public policy can be determined only by noting the effect of expenditures, taxes, and loans on the total national income and on how that national income is distributed.

The fiscal policies of the state cannot be conceived in terms of the calculations of private enterprise but in terms of regulation and control, in terms of the impact of public policies upon the functioning of the economy as a whole.

> We may therefore conclude [says Pedersen] that the financial transactions of the state, that is, the spending of money for certain purposes, the collection of taxes, the issuance of loans, and the creation of means of payment, the fixing of rates and prices for state-controlled goods and services, are not economic decisions arrived at with a view to the balance sheet of the business of the state as such. We conclude that such a balance sheet tells us nothing about the appropriateness or economic soundness of the measures taken. Such measures must rather be undertaken with a view to achieving an economic balance for the economy as a whole. Their appropriateness or soundness can be determined only in terms of their effect upon the welfare of the community as a whole. Politicians and statesmen are obsessed by the ideology of private business, and their good conscience therefore requires that their financial transactions correspond as far as possible to the requirements and practices of private business management. Through the force of circumstances they are often compelled to deviate seriously from this ideal, but such deviations are glossed over as much as possible. This ideological prejudice causes great damage, because it prevents statesmen from acting with conscious knowledge of the real aims of public policy and on the basis of the requirements of the relevant economic considerations.[5]

The familiar popular analogy between private debt and public debt internally held is especially misleading.

[5] *Ibid.*, p. 472.

Borrowing, as the term is commonly used, has two characteristics without which one could not speak of a loan: (1) there must be a transfer of the disposal over funds from one economic unit to another; (2) the burden of the borrower is distributed over a period of time during which repayment of the loan takes place. . . . When, however, the state borrows from its subjects, neither of the two characteristics is present. The state does not obtain the power of disposal over additional funds, for these funds were already within the realm of its power, and might, in fact, have been obtained through taxation.[6]

Thus an internal loan raised by the state is not really a loan in the ordinary sense, since it possesses none of the essential characteristics of such a transaction. There is no transfer of funds from one economic unit to another, and no burden is shifted to future generations. An internal loan resembles ordinary borrowing only in a purely formal way, and it is obvious that every analogy to private borrowing must be completely false. Yet the raising of a loan by the state is not a mere accounting phenomenon, such as would be the transfer of sums of money from one account to another within a given enterprise; on the contrary the process has far-reaching consequences upon production and distribution. Its actual significance arises from the fact that, like all other financial transactions of the state, it is a means of influencing production and the distribution of income, and it should be considered only as such.[7]

The statements just made on the nature of public debts are no new discoveries. It has been recognized by most economists that internal debts must not be considered as debts in the ordinary meaning of the term, and that they do not represent the shifting of the burden to future generations. In view of this fact it is surprising that economists, who after all may be considered experts in economic matters, regularly seem to fall back into popular views whenever they are called upon to advise their governments. Perhaps the most striking example is the Report of the British Committee on National Expenditure, the May Committee.[8] The majority of that Committee established the general principle that "existing financial difficulties make it necessary for the nation like

[6] *Ibid.*, pp. 472–73.

[7] *Ibid.*, pp. 473–74.

[8] Report of Committee on National Expenditure (May Committee), *Cmd. 3920*. London, 1931.

the private individual to consider seriously what it can afford and not merely what is desirable. Viewed from this standpoint much expenditure is unwarrantable at the present time, which, under more favorable circumstances, we should deem justifiable and even a wise investment of the national resources." This was written at the lowest point of the last depression when unemployment was the only alternative to additional governmental expenditures. The implied analogy with a private individual, who has to take account of income and outgo if he is not to go bankrupt and whose financial status can be read from his balance sheet, and at the same time the falsity of this analogy are so clear that no further comment is required.[9]

Another recent work which may be quoted in this connection is a book edited by Hugh Dalton entitled *Unbalanced Budgets*,[10] which offers a review of the financial problems in a number of countries. In almost all the contributions the idea prevails that the incapacity of most states to balance their budgets is a deplorable disadvantage, that the repayment of public debts as such is a virtue. Even in Myrdal's Report of 1934[11] there are traces of this layman's opinion. No author has more strongly insisted upon the untenability of the current analogy between public and private financial transactions than Myrdal himself. Nevertheless, he seems in his book to attach some importance to the nature of the state's capital and develops the idea that it is actually important, even apart from psychological effects, that the state's capital must be kept constant, or must even be increased in the long run. His arguments seem to imply that an increase in internal debt must burden the future budgets so much that no money would be available in the future for the normal and even probably increased social requirements; this is a view which cannot be maintained on the basis either of his own theoretical considerations or of experience. (Consider, for example, the enormous increase of internal debt in Britain during the war and the share of her social expenditures in comparison with those of Sweden which has not increased her debt in the same proportion.) This argument was at the basis of Dalton's proposal for a capital levy designed to extinguish a large part of the public debt; this proposal was prompted by the fear

9 *Weltwirtschaftliches Archiv,* May, 1937, p. 474.
10 Published by George Routledge and Sons, London, 1934.
11 G. Myrdal, *Finanzpolitikens ekonomiska verkningar*, Stockholm, 1934.

that the sums necessary for the service of the debt would burden the budget so much that the natural increase of other expenditures would have to be curtailed. This argument overlooks the fact that the sums spent for interest or repayment become income for the creditors, so that total income remains unaffected.[12]

While the above statement places the emphasis in the right place, it is nevertheless, unless properly qualified, an oversimplification. The tax structure, through which the transfer of interest payments to bondholders is implemented, may unfavorably affect the flow of consumption and investment. This fact is, however, implicitly recognized by Pedersen, for he keeps in mind the effect of fiscal policy as a whole—expenditures, loans, and taxes—upon the formation of income and upon the distribution of income.

Whether a public debt should be reduced or not depends exclusively upon the general economic situation and not upon judgments derived from private accounting considerations.

Whereas a single individual always improves his position by increasing his assets, the situation of a state does not necessarily improve by a corresponding procedure. It is quite conceivable that the reduction of public debt not only reduces the national income, but also that the fiscal position of the state may be deteriorated more by the repayment of debt than by the incurrence of further debt. . . . Whether retirement of debt should take place or not depends exclusively upon the expected effect upon production and income distribution and upon political circumstances which are connected with the political ends at the moment, and these will naturally vary from case to case.[13]

III. Public Expenditures and Productivity

Ursula Hicks[14] distinguishes three types of public debt: (a) dead-weight debt, (b) passive debt, and (c) active debt. Dead-weight debt is one which is incurred in consequence of

[12] *Ibid.*, pp. 475–76.

[13] *Ibid.*, p. 478.

[14] U. K. Hicks, *The Finance of British Government, 1920–1936,* Oxford University Press, 1938.

expenditures which in no way increase the productive power of the community, yielding neither a money revenue nor a future flow of utilities. The most conspicuous type of public debt thus incurred is, of course, that arising from war expenditures. Passive public debt is one incurred from expenditures which, while yielding utilities and enjoyments to the community, such as public buildings, public parks, and the like, neither return a money income themselves nor increase the efficiency and productivity of labor and capital. An active public debt is one incurred in consequence of (a) capital expenditures on projects which are self-liquidating, and (b) expenditures of a character which, directly or indirectly, increase the productive power of the community, such as expenditures on public health or education designed to raise the efficiency of the people, or expenditures on the conservation and improvement of the natural resources designed to increase the productivity of the nation as a whole.

The public debt in England is the leading example of the first category—the dead-weight debt. The same is, in large measure, also true of the French public debt and of the federal debt in the United States. Since 1930, the United States notably has incurred a large public debt, a considerable part of which must be placed in the dead-weight category, springing not from war expenditures but from the necessity of offering relief to the unemployed. In Germany the rise in the public debt since 1933 had indeed the effect, as in the United States, of relieving unemployment, but it was made incidental to a huge military program. Thus, the United States is the only great country which clearly shows a large addition to the dead-weight debt growing out of relief expenditures.

Historically, public debts in most countries have been mainly of the dead-weight type. Sweden is a notable exception to this rule. Her public debt is today far more than covered by productive assets. Indeed, in Sweden in recent years the net income from state enterprises was approximately twice as large as the interest on the public debt. The public debt of state and local bodies in the United States falls, in the main, in the passive public debt category. According to Edna Trull,[15] approximately 15 per cent of the total state debt in this country is of the self-liquidating, active type, while the remaining amount represents a passive type of public debt. It is always difficult to distinguish, however, between expenditures which merely yield consumption utilities and expenditures which indirectly increase the productive power of the community. Public playgrounds and recreational facilities give pleasure and enjoyment, but may also raise the morale of a people and make the nation vigorous and efficient. The distinction between active and passive debt has value for certain purposes, but it can also lead to the same confusion which is so often encountered in the history of economic thought with respect to so-called productive and unproductive labor.

Frequently one hears the comment that the payrolls of private industry are the source of the whole national income, that government is supported by business, that private enterprise alone is productive.

The early classical economists, led by Adam Smith, introduced a novel idea into economics—a new concept of productivity. The Physiocrats had held the view that agriculture alone was productive. Agriculture supplied the necessities of life for the agricultural population, and if there was a surplus left over, it was possible out of this "produit net" to support the "unproductive" town population.

It is not difficult to see how the Physiocratic concept of productivity was born out of the conditions emerging from the Middle Ages. Towns originally were simply the winter residences of great feudal lords. The town population grew up around the court. It performed personal services, prepared food, made rich clothing and ornaments, jewels, laces, velvets, tapestries, clocks, and furniture. All this activity was supported and sustained from the surplus which the lord was

[15] Edna Trull, *Resources and Debts of the Forty-eight States,* Dun and Bradstreet, 1937, p. 47.

able to draw from his domain. Without this surplus, life in the town would quickly ebb away. The town had no independent source of subsistence. It drew its sustenance from the country.

Town life was a luxury which could only be supported out of a richly productive countryside. Town life could develop only so far as an agricultural surplus could be produced and, through feudal rights and privileges, drawn off from the land to enrich the town life of the landed aristocracy. If king and country were to become rich and powerful, it was necessary to encourage agriculture. Agriculture alone was really productive. All other pursuits were sterile and unproductive.

As an explanation of the emergence of town life and the diversity of occupations, this line of reasoning was not without merit. But as an analysis of the functioning of a society advanced beyond the primitive stage of an exclusively rural community, it was hopelessly deficient. And as a basis for public policy, it led to ridiculous absurdities.

The thesis that agriculture was the fountainhead of all wealth, that agricultural pursuits alone were "productive," was once and for all disposed of in Adam Smith's great book *The Wealth of Nations.* The view he challenged had seemed so self-evident and plausible that none had seriously questioned it. Yet increasingly as manufacture and trade developed, it was inevitable that sooner or later it would become apparent to an original mind that this thesis simply did not fit the facts of a more highly developed society. Yet it held sway not only in the popular mind, but was rationalized into a complicated method of thinking by the Physiocrats.

The opening paragraph in *The Wealth of Nations* strikes directly at the foundations of the "produit net" philosophy. Smith regarded labor as the basic source of wealth. Through division of labor and exchange, productivity is increased. If one *exchanges* one's agricultural surplus against the products of specialized and efficient town craftsmen, one increases his own product. The surplus sent to the town is sold *in exchange for* products made more efficiently in the towns. The country does not *support* the town. Exchange with the town enriches the country.

Now, in point of fact, this analysis did not represent *merely* a new interpretation of the *same* facts. To some extent, the *facts* had changed. At the earliest emergence of town life the town, as we have noted, was simply a collection of families catering to the wants of the lord and his court. It had no independent existence. The activities of the town represented the lord's method of consuming his agricultural surplus.

But, gradually, some of the mechanics of the town acquired an independent status of their own. They offered their own wares in exchange. Country barons and squires *exchanged* their agricultural surpluses for the products of the towns' craftsmen. Thus, a real exchange developed between country and town. Both produced goods that satisfied wants, and both parties enhanced their productivity through the process of exchange.

The breakdown of feudal privileges in the French Revolution developed and expanded this exchange process. The peasant, having acquired a new status in relation to the land, was in a stronger position to retain control over his surplus product—the product in excess of his own consumption needs. This surplus he could exchange for manufactures made in the towns. By the time the development of social institutions had reached this point, it was possible to recognize that the country no longer supported the town any more than the town supported the country. Each enhanced the productivity of the other through the division of labor and the exchange of products. It no longer had any meaning to say that agriculture was productive while manufacture was not, or even that agriculture was more productive than manufacture. Both activities satisfied human wants. If all of the nation's productive effort had gone into agriculture, the real income would have been very much lower.

But while Adam Smith freed the thinking of his time from the Physiocrats' narrow concept of productivity, he failed to liberate himself and his generation wholly from the basic Physiocratic error. While urging that manufacturing was equally as productive as agriculture, he nevertheless held that only those workers engaged in making material goods were really productive. Thus, he argued that not only menial servants, but also "churchmen, lawyers, physicians, men of letters of all kinds, players, buffoons, musicians, opera singers, opera dancers, etc." were unproductive laborers. It is remarkable that, once he had taken the first step in the right direction, he should have made this error. If manufacture is productive, since it no less than agriculture satisfies human wants, surely the opera singer, the servant, the teacher are equally productive. Producers of personal services also play a role in the system of division of labor and in the exchange economy. At a later stage in economic thinking the logic of Adam Smith's own position, which he imperfectly applied, was pointed out and universally accepted by all economists.

But the logic of this thesis is frequently challenged with respect to governmental expenditures. Public investment (parks, roads, playgrounds, hospitals), it is asserted, is in some sense unproductive, while private capital expenditures are productive in character. Governmental payroll expenditures in order to carry out the activities of government are regarded as less productive, or even as nonproductive, compared with private payroll expenditures.

In discussing the productiveness of private business expenditures, it is important to make a sharp distinction between (a) the creation of a flow of real income of goods or services, and (b) the creation of new instruments of production which increases the efficiency of labor and results in a larger flow of real income than would otherwise be possible. The former is a utility-creating expenditure; the latter is an efficiency-creating expenditure. Investment which duplicates existing plants in accordance with the requirements of growth (as, for example, the erection of another radio factory) is of the former type. Investment in improved machinery is of the latter type.

The view that public investment is "unproductive," while private investment is productive, will not withstand careful analysis. Public investment, just as with private investment, may be merely utility-creating or it may also be efficiency-creating. The development of a public park, swimming pool, playground, or concert hall makes possible a flow of real income no less than the erection of a radio factory. Public investment in the national forest, by preventing soil erosion and floods, or the construction of school buildings, may contribute to raise the efficiency of labor no less than private investment in improved machinery. Public investment, like private investment, if wisely made will be utility-creating or both utility-creating and efficiency-creating.

In addition to being (a) utility-creating and (b) efficiency-creating, public expenditures may also be (c) income-creating in the sense that they tend currently to expand income and employment. Indeed, from this latter standpoint, expenditures which are not efficiency- or utility-creating (such as war expenditures) may be quite effective. Thus, wars not only promote employment during the emergency, but may stimulate postwar private investment by creating accumulated shortages in housing and in other investment areas.

It is sometimes said that there is an important difference between business expenditures and governmental expenditures, in that the former are self-sustaining while the latter are not. But this is not true. No private business can sustain its sales volume, unless the outlays of other businesses and the government continue to feed the income stream. Nor is private business as a whole self-sustaining. It was not self-sustaining when the national income fell from $80 billions to $40 billions in the early thirties, nor indeed in any other period of depression. The sales receipts of private business, no less than the tax receipts of government, depend upon the maintenance of a high national income. And the outlays of government can and do contribute to a sustained national income, no less than the outlays of private business. Indeed, when private business outlays decline, the government alone is in a position to go forward and sustain the income through increased expenditures.

When it is said that public expenditures are "sustained out of" private income, it will be disclosed, on careful analysis, that the reasoning is precisely similar to that of the Physiocrats. Manufactures were sustained, it was said, out of the surplus product of agriculture. The real fact, however, was that, instead of applying *all* the productive resources of society to agricultural production, the real income of the community was raised enormously by diverting [16] a part of the productive resources to manufactures. In like manner, under modern conditions, many wants can be satisfied at all only by governmental action, and in other cases more effectively by governmental action. Roads, streets, sewerage disposal, reforestation, flood control, parks, schools, public health, hospitals, low-cost housing, social insurance, public playgrounds, and other recreational facilities—all these represent ways of enlarging our real income far beyond what it could be if these things were not undertaken by government. These activities are utility-creating, and in part efficiency-creating, no less than the activities of private enterprise. The governmental expenditures are not "supported out of" private enterprise any more than manufacture is supported out of the agricultural surplus. Just as the manufacturing population buys the surplus of agriculture in exchange for its products, so also the services of government enter into the exchange process and enrich the income stream. It is true that part of the exchange payment is in the form of taxes, but this fact in no way alters the fundamental fact of exchange. The income of the population attached to any private enterprise is derived not merely from the sale of its product to other private industries, but also from the sale of its product to the population attached to governmental projects, including the construction of public works. In this process of exchange it is not true that any one segment of the exchange economy supports out of its surplus

[16] This is all the more true when it is a question not of *diversion* but of *employment* of idle labor and unused productive resources, as is the case in periods of depression or of chronic unemployment.

any other segment. Manufacturing is not maintained out of the surplus of agriculture, and government is not maintained out of the surplus of private enterprise. Each segment contributes to the total flow of real income, and each takes its share out of the income stream.

In the sense that the most essential necessity of life—food—is produced by agriculture, it may be said that agriculture is basic to all other economic activity. This seems to give it a sort of priority. But this priority has a meaning only in primitive societies where it is necessary to devote all, or nearly all, of productive resources to the procurement of food. As a society becomes more productive, agriculture loses its right of priority. The very superabundance of agricultural products implies that more emphasis must be placed upon other economic pursuits. Manufacture, indeed, may now become the really important branch in that its products are relatively scarce in relation to the products of agriculture. In an agricultural surplus society, manufactures may assert a claim to priority.

With increasing productivity, material wants are becoming more and more abundantly satisfied. It now becomes possible to satisfy more fully artistic and intellectual wants. Leisure itself becomes an economic good, more important than any further addition to food or clothing. And with leisure comes demand for recreational, artistic, and intellectual activities. And it is in this area that community and governmental activities play an increasingly important role.

IV. Economic Effects of Public Debt

The character of the expenditure for which debt is incurred will determine whether the effect is (a) employment-creating, (b) utility-creating, or (c) efficiency-creating, or some combination of these. The character of the expenditure will affect the standard of living. But once the debt has been incurred, its subsequent impact upon employment and the distribution of income will be the same regardless of the purpose for which the debt was incurred. The magnitude of subsequent real income will, indeed, vary according to the character of the expenditures made, but the functioning of the economy after the event will depend exclusively upon the magnitude of the debt and upon the type of tax structure designed to finance the interest payments.

It is of interest to inquire whether or not the enormous dead-weight debt in England, following the Napoleonic Wars, on balance impaired the great expansion of British industry in the nineteenth century. It must be remembered that this dead-weight debt was internally held and that, therefore, the high taxes required to service the interest on the debt flowed back directly again into the community. An examination of the tax structure prevailing in the early half of the nineteenth century would indicate that, in all probability, the huge dead-weight debt served to add to the flow of individual savings. This is true for the reason that the taxes were heavily of the indirect type, which did not weigh severely on the incomes of the rich, while on the other hand the rich, for the most part, held the government bonds. Thus, funds were taken through taxes from the community as a whole and paid in the form of interest to the wealthy holders of bonds, whose incomes flowed largely into the stream of savings. According to the Colwyn Committee, "taxation in 1818 hardly touched the saving power of the wealthy. . . ." The Committee reports that, of a total tax revenue of £56 millions, £40 millions was raised by customs and excise duties, levied largely on necessaries, the income tax having been repealed as from April, 1815.[17]

In a century which witnessed a rapid extensive expansion, revolutionary changes in technology, the emergence of new industries, the rapid development of new territory, and an unprecedented growth in population, an important limiting factor to expansion was the flow of savings. The dead-weight debt probably served to siphon a part of the stream of income

[17] Committee on National Debt and Taxation, *op. cit.*, p. 236.

from consumption into savings, and in this respect facilitated and encouraged the rapid expansionist development of the nineteenth century.

There were, indeed, periods of greater or less duration in which this compulsory saving process clearly tended to create depressed conditions. Chapter 7 of Malthus' *Principles of Political Economy* is a classic example of an illuminating analysis which interprets the post-Napoleonic War depression in these terms. But, viewing the period from a long-run standpoint, the investment outlets were over the century ample, and the scarcity of investment funds was, on the whole, a limiting factor.

> In the Victorian era it is generally true that saving was left as a monopoly in the hands of the wealthier classes, who were allowed to remain in almost complete control of their riches. In our view it is impossible to justify the old distribution of taxation, even though it reduced interference with saving to a minimum. It is true that under it industry advanced enormously, and the standard of living improved for the whole community more than in any comparable period. Nevertheless, a tax system falling less on the purchasing power of the poorer classes and more on the savings of the richer might have been beneficial to production, as it certainly would have been to immediate consumption.[18]

There are other directions in which the dead-weight public debt in the early nineteenth century acted as a stabilizing force. The fact that rapidly growing financial institutions—the stock market, commercial banks, savings banks, and finally life insurance companies—had available an asset which was virtually riskless could scarcely fail to have had great significance for the secure development of these institutions. Moreover, in the early period of capitalism, when enormous risks necessarily had to be taken in industrial ventures as yet untried and of a highly experimental nature, government bonds constituted a safety reserve which made it possible for capitalists to achieve a reasonable balance between investment

[18] Committee on National Debt and Taxation, *op. cit.*, p. 241.

assets and speculative assets. The "fact that a man holds a good block of War Loan and can rely on a nucleus of safe income may sometimes induce him to seek higher but less safe return on his other savings." [19] Had it not been possible to hold a large part of the assets in safe and secure government bonds, and to use these assets as a vantage point from which to make expeditionary excursions, so to speak, into untried and speculative investment territory, it can scarcely be doubted that the rate of bankruptcy in a highly dynamic and rapidly changing industrial system would have been greater than was the case. This holds true for the individual investing capitalist and for the rising industrial and trading firms and corporations. Indeed, it is difficult to see that the financial and industrial development of England in the nineteenth century could have proceeded with the degree of steadiness and security actually achieved had there been no large public debt available for secure investment.

The main disadvantage of the public debt in England in the nineteenth century was the weight which the taxation incident thereto imposed upon the wage-earning classes. From the short-run standpoint it depressed real wages. But in a highly dynamic society the curtailment of consumption rapidly brought about an expansion in the capitalistic process of production and thereby facilitated the progressive rise throughout the nineteenth century of the standard of living. It may be that the sacrifice of the present was too severe to be justified even by the rate of growth which it encouraged. It may well be that England in the nineteenth century, no less than Russia in the twentieth, but by different institutional processes, sacrificed present consumption too much in the interest of capital accumulation and a future rise in the standard of living.

Question may now be raised whether, in the altered conditions that currently confront Britain, an internal public debt today has any of the advantages or the degree of advantage which has been suggested above. In the England of the nine-

[19] Committee on National Debt and Taxation, *op. cit.*, p. 100.

teenth century a case can, we think, be made out for the thesis that a large public debt, substantially maintained but not allowed to rise, was, on balance, an advantage for expanding industrialism. It is probably true that, because of the economy imposed by a century of balanced budgets and even some retirement of debt, utility-creating public improvements, education and public health, were unduly neglected. Whether larger expenditures on such projects could have been financed adequately out of taxation without weighing unduly either upon the current necessities of life of the masses or upon the desirable volume of capital formation may be debatable. From the Napoleonic Wars to 1845, and again from the early seventies to 1895, a considerable portion of the country's productive resources was not fully employed. In the periods of prolonged depressions public expenditures of the character indicated could have been financed by borrowing (with some attendant monetary expansion) without, on the one side, encroaching upon capital formation or, on the other side, resulting in undue price inflation.

The assumption that a large public debt is inherently and necessarily under all circumstances an evil is not warranted. There are good grounds for believing that the post-Napoleonic debt exercised no depressing effect on the British economy and may, indeed, have played an important role in the economic progress of that country in the nineteenth century. Equally, we should not be justified if we concluded, without examination into the special circumstances of present-day economic tendencies, that the high public debt in England in the post-World War I period either depressed the standard of living, or prevented an otherwise attainable increase in productivity, or intensified the volume of unemployment. Indeed, it is not impossible that it may have acted in quite the opposite direction. While the post-Napoleonic era called for a large flow of savings, there are grounds for believing that the decade of the twenties called for a larger volume of consumption expenditures relative to income. And while the public debt, considering the manner in which it was held in conjunction with the then prevailing tax structure, encouraged saving in the post-Napoleonic era, in postwar England it may have acted to stimulate consumption, owing to the differences in the manner in which the debt was held and in the tax structure. Whereas the debt was formerly an instrument through which funds were siphoned from consumption into savings, so recently it has become, in part at least, an instrument to siphon funds from savings into consumption. This follows from the fact that the government debt has recently been held partly by savings and financial institutions, the beneficiaries of which constitute a large part of the British public, while on the other side the tax structure is sufficiently progressive as to weigh relatively heavily on savings and relatively lightly on consumption.[20] We suggest that quite possibly the public debt for different reasons and under different economic circumstances, then and now, has served a useful purpose.

There is no reason to suppose that it is not important now, as in the nineteenth century, for financial and business institutions to have available secure and safe investments, such as those offered by government bonds. Currently, the supply of government bonds relative to other securities is certainly very much higher than was true in the *latter* part of the nineteenth century, though clearly it is not as high as in the *early* part of the nineteenth century. From the standpoint of the quantity available, no case can be made for the thesis that the quantity is inadequate for the needs of a well-balanced investment portfolio of financial institutions and of business corporations. It is clear that gilt-edged private securities are now available in much larger quantity than formerly and that, correspondingly, there is less need for government obligations. Indeed, it may be argued that the current large volume of governmental securities is tending to displace and crowd out gilt-edged private securities which might otherwise have come into existence.

[20] "In regard to the *standard of saving,* we conclude that the increased direct taxes have contributed appreciably to a *pro rata* decline in saving—not startling, but very substantial—below the pre-war amount," Committee on National Debt and Taxation, *op. cit.,* p. 241.

Here we encounter the difficult question with respect to the advantages and disadvantages of a large volume of private, fixed-debt obligations. Private debt obligations may, indeed, be desirable enough from the standpoint of the investing institution, but from the standpoint of the issuing institution a large volume of such obligations, creating as it does a high burden of fixed charges, imposes a dangerous rigidity in an unstable economic world. Such rigidity is likely, in turn, to reinforce and augment the tendency toward economic instability, and has in certain instances, notably in the case of the American railroads, resulted in a serious impasse which almost precludes the possibility of making necessary new investments.

It is evident that we are developing more and more institutionalized sources of savings. These naturally seek fixed debt obligations, whether gilt-edged private securities or government bonds. Thus, from the standpoint of those who offer funds in the financial and investment market, there is clearly an incentive on the part of industrial enterprise to issue debt obligations which are preferred to equities by the investor. As the recent Twentieth Century Fund studies [21] have pointed out, however, this is a dangerous development, and legal regulations controlling financial investment institutions, notably savings banks and life insurance companies, ought probably to be liberalized so as to permit them to hold a certain proportion of their assets in the form of equities. Any considerable development in this direction, however, presupposes the combination of such equity holdings with an adequate volume of highly riskless assets, either in gilt-edged private securities or in government bonds. From the standpoint of the flexibility of the economy as a whole, it is desirable that the industrial borrower should issue stocks rather than bonds. If, however, the financial investing institutions are to be encouraged to hold equities so as to diminish the current ratio of private debt to private wealth, it is necessary that there shall be available an adequate volume of government secur-

[21] *Debts and Recovery, 1929–1937,* The Twentieth Century Fund, 1938.

ities in order to provide the appropriate balance for the portfolios of financial investing institutions.

We now encounter the question whether a public debt imposes any such serious rigidity upon the economy as is the case with private debt. We believe that it does not. The interest on the public debt is serviced by taxation, the successful collection of which depends upon the maintenance or increase from the long-run standpoint of the national income as a whole. The solvency of the government is not subject to the risk of structural changes which may cause the decline, or even death, of certain industries and thus profoundly affect the income of private corporations. Moreover, the cyclical fluctuations of income are less serious for the government than for the private sector of the economy. In the first place, the incomes of many private corporations fluctuate far more violently than the income of the economy as a whole. Much more important, however, is the fact that the individual corporation with a low income in the depression phase of the cycle is placed in a dangerous financial situation. Corporations with a heavy load of debt may, in seriously depressed conditions, be forced into bankruptcy and may be unable to carry the interest burden, or at any rate unable to raise necessary new funds for expansion in the subsequent revival period. The government is placed in no such dangerous situation by reason of cyclical fluctuations of income. Indeed, the government is not only able to, but may, to the advantage of the economy as a whole, engage in borrowing when the national income is temporarily low.[22] As long as the interest on the public debt is well within the practical taxable capacity of the government, taking the entire business cycle into consideration—and taxable capacity has very flexible limits, varying, however, with the financial integrity of the country—no question can arise with respect to the solvency of the government. And in advanced countries, in which

[22] The power of the government, through the open-market operations of the Central Bank, to increase the funds available for the purchase of government bonds is an important consideration.

there is a widespread interest on the part of the general public in the security of financial investments, such as savings and life insurance policies, the willingness to undertake taxation as an alternative to inflation is very strong. Such a community, on the one side, has an enormous capacity to submit to taxation and, on the other side, can be expected to resist the road of inflation so luring to more primitive economies in which the mass of the people had no stake whatever in the stability of the value of money.

Thus, a dual financial system, which on the one side affords a large supply of governmental debt obligations for secure financial investment, and on the other side encourages the issue of equity securities by private companies, may well be the desirable goal. Financial institutions with a large supply of government obligations may safely invest a very considerable portion of their assets in common stocks. A rise in the public debt is thus not necessarily inconsistent with the requirement that private industry should more and more turn to equity financing and eschew the tendency so prominent in the decade of the twenties toward mortgage and bond financing. As far as the late twenties are concerned, it is, of course, true that the extremely inflated stock market encouraged many large corporations to retire their bonds by the issue of common stocks.

In this connection it will be of interest to compare (a) the total amount of government debt obligations, federal, state, and local, (b) the total estimated volume of private debt [23] in the form of bonds and mortgages, and (c) the value of

[23] It is particularly noteworthy that, disregarding short-run fluctuations, private debt has remained substantially equal to the national income during the last 40 years, as shown in the following table. (See National Industrial Conference Board, *Economic Almanac,* and *Private Long-term Debt and Interest in the United States.)*

Year	*Nat'l Income* *	*Private Debt* *
1902	$18.4	$17.0
1913	31.5	32.2
1929	82.9	84.2
1937	71.2	70.3

* In billions.

common stock measured by the current market prices listed on the New York Stock Exchange. These data are given in the following table:

TABLE XIX

Gross Government Debt,[24] *Total Private Debt in Bonds and Mortgages,*[25] *Value of Common Stock*[26]

(in millions of dollars)

Gross Government Debt, 1937		
Federal	$36,715	
State and Local	19,152	
Total		$55,867
Private Debt, 1937		
Railway	13,109	
Industrial	7,762	
Public Utility	13,874	
Farm Mortgage	7,082	
Urban Mortgage	25,508	
Total		$70,335
Value of Common Stocks, 1935–37		$42,131

V. Public Debt Controversy in the United States

With respect to the role of public debt in the American economy, it is evident that a major revolution is already upon us. In three decades we have shifted from our nineteenth-century traditional position of virtually no public debt to a relatively high and rising public debt. For this there are three reasons: (1) the great increase in capital expenditures of local governments on capital projects, including roads, schools, sewerage disposal, etc.; [27] (2) the World War of 1914; and (3) the Great Depression. To these must now be added a fourth—defense expenditures incident to the second World

[24] and [25] *Survey of Current Business,* January, 1939, p. 11.

[26] *New York Stock Exchange Yearbook,* 1937, p. 105. Average of first-of-the-month figures for 1935–37 inclusive.

[27] See Temporary National Economic Committee Hearings, Part 9, *Savings and Investment.*

War. War, depression, and the growing need of large-scale consumers' capital, which can be supplied only by the collective action of the country as a whole—these are the developments which in the last quarter of a century have led, and are leading, the way to a large and increasing American public debt.

The history of the federal public debt over a span of one hundred and fifty years clusters around five major episodes: (1) the early period of federal expansion, (2) the War of 1812, (3) the Civil War, (4) the first World War, and (5) the Great Depression.

The increase in federal debt which occurred in each of the three middle periods has to do with war. Any controversy with respect to public debt in such periods is not likely to run in terms of fundamental considerations. Debate is likely to be limited largely to the practical problems of financing—the extent to which it is feasible or appropriate to finance the war from taxation.

In the first and last periods, however, discussion with respect to the role of public credit ran in more general terms and disclosed deeper issues. The problem was not so much, or at least not so exclusively: How can expenditures inevitably imposed upon the country by imperious necessity best be met? The problem was in part: Shall the public credit be used as a positive instrument of government in order to reach certain desired ends?

The first period was under the spell of the great leadership of Alexander Hamilton. Hamilton fought for a vigorous use of the public credit in order to strengthen the position and the power of the new federal government. He did not fear the growth of what, for his day, was a huge public debt. Having regard for the relative fiscal capacity of the federal government then and now, one may confidently assert that the federal debt was larger at the end of Washington's administration than it is at the present moment.

Hamilton wanted to achieve certain goals for the new government. He could not achieve the ends he sought without the federal government's incurring a large public debt. From this he did not shrink. Indeed, he argued that a considerable public debt, under certain circumstances, had definite advantages for the economy. He urged a fearless use of the public credit within appropriate limits, not merely for governmental ends, but also to achieve certain economic objectives.

To the horror of his opponents, who were eager to hold the public debt of the new federal government down to the lowest possible minimum, and whose aim it was to reduce it as soon as possible to zero, Hamilton proposed not only the assumption of the foreign-held debt (which was generally agreed to as necessary in order to preserve the nation's credit abroad), but also the assumption and funding of the Continental and Confederation domestic debt and even of the Revolutionary debts of the states. Together, these totaled $79,125,000. For a struggling young government to assume a debt of over $79 millions was regarded by his opponents as a highly dangerous proposal. Hamilton defended it, however, as the surest way of firmly establishing the new federal government.

He went farther than this. In his First Report on the Public Credit, issued January 9, 1790, he listed three benefits which he believed the economy would derive from the debt. He argued that merchants would, by reason of the public debt, be enabled to invest their unemployed capital in government bonds. This would yield an added source of revenue, and so enable them to trade for smaller profits. Moreover, the bonds would provide a ready source of credit when the merchant needed it for commercial operations. Similarly, agriculture and manufactures, he argued, would be promoted by the existence of public debt, not merely on their own account, but also because "the merchant whose enterprise in foreign trade gives them activity and extension" is benefited in the manner indicated above. Finally, he maintained that the rate of interest would be lowered by reason of the increased supply of liquid assets. Hamilton suggested that bonds were, for certain purposes, virtually the equivalent of money. Accordingly, a large public debt would lower the rate of interest, "for this is always in a ratio to the quantity of money and to the quickness of circulation." Hamilton's analysis is restated by Dunbar as follows:

Hamilton saw that the revival of industry could only be accomplished by the aid of a sound mercantile credit, and that for the growth of this the establishment and regular operation of public credit were necessary. He saw the advantage which must accrue to the community when the resources of individuals locked up in claims against the government should become mobile by being converted into negotiable securities having a recognized standing in the market.[28]

Such were the purely economic benefits which Hamilton saw in a public debt. From the standpoint of the new government, he saw in the assumption of state and Confederation debt a means of strengthening the central government.

Through the continual amortization of the funded debt he maintained that funds would be "liberated, and will be ready for any future use, either to defray current expenditures or be the basis of new loans, as circumstances may dictate." Thus managed the public debt was conceived of as a sort of revolving fund. The principle of debt amortization he regarded "as the true secret for rendering public credit immortal. . . . The successive liberation of the revenues, successively pledged, will afford resources that may almost be said to be inexhaustible." Public credit he regarded as "a means of accelerating the prompt employment of all the abilities of a nation." It is "not only one of the main pillars of public safety, it is among the principal engines of useful enterprise and internal improvement." [29]

Hamilton's opponents charged him with being merely a

[28] C. F. Dunbar, "Some Precedents Followed by Alexander Hamilton," *Quarterly Journal of Economics,* 1888, pp. 32–59.

[29] Hamilton, *First Report on the Public Credit; Second Report on the Public Credit.* (See pages 46, 156–7, 170–2 in McKee's edition *Papers on Public Credit, Commerce and Finance,* by Alexander Hamilton.)

slavish follower of Pitt and English financial theories. Jefferson wrote to Washington in 1792: "This exactly marks the difference between Colonel Hamilton's views and mine, that I would wish the debt paid tomorrow; he wishes it never to be paid, but always to be a thing wherewith to corrupt and manage the legislature." [80] Hamilton, however, denied the thesis imputed to him by his opponents that "public debts are public benefits" under all conditions. He was realistic and specific. He argued that with the problems then confronting the new government, both from the political and from the economic standpoint, the "proper funding of the present debt will render it a national blessing. . . ."

The Congressional debates disclose opposition to this view. A member from Georgia argued that England was a melancholy instance of the ruin attending funding systems.

> To such a pitch has the spread of funding and borrowing been carried in that country that in 1786 their national debt had increased to £230,000,000 sterling, a burthen which the most sanguine mind can never contemplate they will ever be relieved from. If future difficulties should involve that nation still further, what must be the consequence? The same effect must be produced that has taken place in other nations; it must either bring on a national bankruptcy, or annihilate her existence as an independent empire. Hence, I contend that a funding system in this country will be highly dangerous to the welfare of the Republic; it may for the moment raise our credit and increase our circulation by multiplying a new species of currency, but it must hereafter saddle upon our posterity a burthen which they can neither bear nor relieve themselves from.[81]

Hamilton was too keen to be befuddled over the "posterity burden" argument. He saw quite clearly what economists have always pointed out, that it is not a question of posterity versus the present generation, but rather a question of transfer from one group (the taxpayers) to another group (the bond-

[80] Jefferson, *Works,* Volume III, p. 464.

[81] Thomas Benton, *Abridgement of the Debates of Congress,* February 9, 1790.

holders)—both groups being members of the same generation. Hamilton argued that there was merely a transfer of capital to the amount of the annuity from those who pay to the creditor who restores it to circulation.[32]

Hamilton, arguing that certain positive economic benefits would accrue to the nation from a public debt, was confronted with the familiar *reductio ad absurdum* argument: If this is so, does it not follow that the more debt the better? Hamilton's answer was precisely the correct one to all such arguments, namely, that we must never lose sight of balance in economic life. It may be a good thing under certain circumstances to lower the price of steel by 10 per cent, but it does not follow that it must be good economic policy to force a reduction by, say, 90 per cent. It may be desirable to realign the foreign exchange value of a currency by 20 per cent, but it does not follow that an 80 per cent depreciation is desirable. And so for all economic policies. Hamilton put it as follows:

There are respectable individuals who, from a just aversion to an accumulation of public debt, are unwilling to concede to it any kind of utility; who can discern no good to alleviate the evil with which they suppose it pregnant; who cannot be persuaded that it ought, in any sense, to be viewed as an increase of capital, lest it should be inferred that, the more debt, the more capital, the greater the burthens the greater the blessings of the community.

But it interests the public councils to estimate every object as it truly is; to appreciate how far the good in any measure is compensated by the ill, or the ill by the good: either of them is seldom unmixed.

Neither will it follow that an accumulation of debt is desirable because a certain degree of it operates as capital. There may be a plethora in the political as in the natural body; there may be a state of things in which any such artificial capital is unnecessary.[33]

[32] Papers on Public Credit, Commerce and Finance by Alexander Hamilton (McKee edition, pp. 216–17).

[33] See Report on Manufactures, December 5, 1791 (McKee edition, *op. cit.*). Hamilton also notes the effect of an excessively large public debt on wealth concentration, the debt "serving only to pamper the dissipation of idle and dis-

Defending his own position, he admitted that he had

> explicitly maintained that the *funding* of the existing debt of the United States would render it a national blessing; and a man has only to travel through the United States with his eyes open, and to observe the invigoration of industry in every branch, to be convinced that the position is well founded.
>
> But whether right or wrong, it is quite a different thing from maintaining as a general proposition that a public debt is a public blessing; particular and temporary circumstances might render that advantageous at one time which at another might be hurtful.[34]

Hamilton's position was vigorously opposed by Gallatin, who consistently resisted any increase in debt and continually sought to reduce any existing debt. This was true long before he became Secretary of the Treasury. As Senator from Pennsylvania from 1795 to 1800, he fought the financial measures of the Administration. War was by many thought imminent, and this presented squarely the problem: Should the government increase its debt or neglect its defenses? The Federalists did not hesitate to choose an increase in the debt in order to achieve a substantial army and navy. Gallatin, holding a large public debt to be a menace, believed the national safety and security could best be promoted by spending less on defense and more on debt reduction. For him, the discharge of the public debt became an uncompromising dogma. Jefferson and Madison supported his principle, but were sufficiently realistic to modify the policy when circumstances justified large governmental expenditures necessitating an increase in the national debt. Thus, Jefferson's ideas with respect to the public debt did not prevent him from embarking upon large expenditures springing from the war with Tripoli and the purchase of the Louisiana Territory. Gallatin, however, with singleness of purpose and rigorously adhering to his dogma, opposed both. In 1807 the threat of war brought further

solute individuals," and making the sums required to pay interest oppressive. The latter would be particularly true in a society such as Hamilton's which relied mainly on consumption taxes.

[34] Letter to Philadelphia *Gazette*, September 11, 1792.

sharp increases in expenditures, followed by reductions in the next two years. But the War of 1812 blasted Gallatin's hopes of paying off the debt, and he resigned as Secretary of the Treasury. The debt had risen from $45 millions in 1811 to $100 millions in 1814.

The particular economic arguments advanced by Hamilton in support of the use of public credit have, of course, little relevance to the controversies of today. What is of interest for us is not the particular form of his argument (except for his recognition that an internally-held debt represents a transfer and not a burden), but rather the fact that he resisted the general dogma that public debts are inherently bad. He was realistic in his approach. His opponents were dogmatists who insisted that a public debt is, at all hazards, to be avoided except under the painful necessity of war; that no benefits may be derived from the use of the public credit from the standpoint of the economy; that its consequences are all harmful; and that, if unavoidably incurred, it should be reduced to a minimum at the earliest possible moment. Hamilton recognized public credit as a useful instrument of governmental policy. The economic ends he sought were, for the most part, not the ends we seek today, but the principle is still valid. It is necessary to look behind the instrument to the economic realities and to the results which can be expected to flow from the use of the public credit.

VI. Limits to the Public Debt [35]

Considerations with respect to the magnitude of the public debt involve an analysis of the very difficult concepts of taxable capacity and taxable income. Taxable income may be defined narrowly as that portion of the national income which passes through the commercial market and which is

[35] Compare David M. Wright, "The Economic Limit and Economic Burden of an Internally Held National Debt," *Quarterly Journal of Economics,* November, 1940; also chapter by R. A. Musgrave and B. H. Higgins in *Public Policy,* Vol. II, Annual Yearbook of the Graduate School of Public Administration, Harvard University, 1941.

received in the form of money. Obviously, however, a very considerable part of the national income is received in the form of services without passing through the money price mechanism. In the broader sense, therefore, taxable income may be said to include not only the monetary income upon which the tax collector can lay hands, but also that portion of the income received directly in the form of services, whether rendered by the government or by individuals (housewives, for example) without monetary recompense.

The term "taxable capacity" may thus be defined in various ways. Taxable capacity may be conceived of in terms of (a) the money income, (b) the money income plus the income derived from free governmental services to which, however, a fee might have been attached, and (c) the entire income of the community, whether derived within the price mechanism in the form of money receipts or outside of the price mechanism in the form of directly consumed utilities and services.

The question now arises what types of governmental expenditures may increase the taxable capacity or the taxable income. Clearly, governmental capital expenditures which are remunerative in character and produce a money income are precisely similar to private capital expenditures. Moreover, expenditures which increase the flow of utilities and services (such as parks and playgrounds), but for which no commercial price or fee is charged, may, nevertheless, furnish quite legitimate ground for permitting an increase in the national money income sufficient to permit the *transfer payments* without encroaching upon the monetary income remaining in the hands of the public, and which would be available for private investment and consumption expenditures. An increase in real income justifies a corresponding monetary expansion, whether springing from an increased output of goods and services placed on the market by private entrepreneurs, or from goods offered freely by the government without price or charge. Monetary expansion equal to the rise of real income does not mean price inflation. Indeed, without an increase in the money supply (assuming velocity constant) the *transfer* of funds through the public fisc would tend to cause deflation.

Thus, public investments, the services of which are offered without charge to the community, may through appropriate monetary expansion increase the taxable capacity in the sense of increasing the taxable money income. That they increase the taxable capacity is perfectly clear if the benefits from such investments are placed within the framework of the price mechanism by charging a fee for the services rendered, and if the monetary authority permits a sufficient monetary expansion to allow the collection of such fees without encroaching upon the monetary transactions of the private sector of the economy. All this will be equally true if we substitute a general tax levy in lieu of the special fee attached to each service rendered.

The monetary taxable capacity and monetary taxable income can, of course, quite easily be increased (once full employment by the loan expenditure method is reached) sufficiently to match the increased taxes, so that no encroachment upon the monetary funds available for the purchase of goods privately produced need occur. Thus, the receipt of a certain quantity of free goods would justify a monetary expansion. When private capital expenditures result in additional output of commodities or services, a monetary expansion adequate to circulate these goods at a profitable price is justified. Equally, when the government provides free services, some appropriate monetary expansion is justified. This would permit the collection of taxes sufficient to cover the expenses of operation, together with amortization and interest charges, without any reduction in the media available for monetary transactions. In so far as the governmental expenditures call forth the utilization of unemployed resources which otherwise would not be used, not only is the taxable income increased, but the increase is dependent upon such outlays. In the event that full employment has already been reached, any further expansion of governmental services would encroach upon, and become a substitute for, real income privately produced. But there is no a priori reason to suppose that the magnitude of the real income will be any smaller in the one case than in the other.

A second consideration with respect to the size of public debt has to do with the relation of debt to prices. The fear is frequently expressed that an increasing public debt must eventually produce a price inflation. This conclusion is not justified. No general statement can be made without an examination of the special circumstances in each case. The deficit may be financed by: (a) borrowing from the banks, (b) borrowing from accumulated idle balances held by corporations and individuals, and (c) borrowing from the current income of the individuals and corporations. The first method of financing results in an expansion of the money supply (demand deposits); the second results in an increase in the velocity of circulation. Whether new money is created or idle money is put to active use, in either case the income stream (MV) is increased. But this process will not cause a price inflation as long as it is possible to match the increasing stream of money income with a corresponding increase in flow of real income. In short, as long as there are unemployed resources neither of these methods of financing a deficit constitutes a dangerous threat to price stability.

Once full employment is reached, it is no longer possible to increase appreciably the flow of real income. At this point it becomes necessary, if price inflation is to be avoided, to stop any further increase in the money income stream. But it does not follow that even in this situation a continuing deficit must necessarily produce price inflation. What is true is that the deficit must no longer be financed by monetary expansion. If, however, the deficit is financed by diverting a part of the current income stream to the government through borrowing from the public, there is no ground for fearing inflation. A continuing deficit, even at full employment, need not result in price inflation.

Continued governmental expenditures would be necessary

to maintain full employment if, in the absence of such a program, a part of the income stream would otherwise be diverted into idle balances. Income, output, and employment would, accordingly, decline. By diverting these otherwise idle funds into spending channels, the money income stream can be kept flowing and the real income maintained. But this process would not result in price inflation. As long as the deficit is financed by borrowing from the current stream of savings, a continued increase in the public debt will not of itself produce inflation.

It is sometimes argued that the mere size of the public debt may cause inflation. This argument rests on the supposition that a huge debt represents a heavy burden upon the community and strains the taxable capacity of the government. It is said that the government may find it impossible to carry on its normal operations and, in addition, to meet the interest obligations on the debt. Accordingly, so it is argued, the government may be compelled to resort to the printing press, and thus an inflation will be produced.[36]

This reasoning is essentially erroneous. An internally-held debt represents a transfer of funds *within* the community. It is true that attention must be paid to the character of the tax structure through which the transfer payments are effected. Finally, in appraising taxable capacity it is necessary to keep in mind both aspects of fiscal policy—expenditures no less than taxation.[37]

[36] The inflation experience of Germany in the postwar period is sometimes cited. It is not possible at this point to consider the maze of special circumstances, including quite unsound public policies, on the part of both Germany and the Allies, which produced this inflation. For the purpose in hand, it is sufficient to point out that Germany's internal debt in relation to income was not as large as England's. The inflation can adequately be explained on other grounds.

[37] Confronted with a national debt equal to twice the British national income, the Colwyn Committee was nevertheless able to conclude as follows: "In our opinion the present taxation—even in conjunction with the loss of material wealth due to war expenditure, which lies behind the National Debt —is not one of the main causes of industrial difficulty. . . . So far as taxation is concerned, we think that, if general conditions improve and times become

Too frequently discussion with respect to the problems of a rising public debt and ability to service the interest charges, proceeds on the assumption of a static national income. This assumption is highly unrealistic. To make the system of free enterprise workable, it is absolutely necessary to ensure a rising national income. Should the income remain stationary, rising per worker productivity would imply an ever-growing volume of unemployment. A static national income, with or without a rising public debt, would wreck the economic order. During the nineteenth century, and up to the first World War, the real national income in the United States increased by around 4 per cent per annum. We cannot expect this rate of increase in the future, owing to a much slower rate of population growth. But we have a right to expect in the next half century a rate of increase in real and money income of 2 or 2½ per cent per annum. In fifty years this would give us a national income of around $250 to $300 billions of dollars at 1940 prices.

The popular belief that a large public debt tends to produce inflation has, no doubt, arisen in part from the fact that price inflation in wartime has usually been associated with a large increase in the public debt. It is, of course, true that vast war expenditures piled on top of private expenditures (inadequately curtailed by taxes or by borrowing from current income) will produce an inflation. But this is quite another matter. The question here has to do partly with the magnitude of the expenditures and partly with the manner in which they were financed. A too rapid *increase* in debt, particularly when it is accompanied by a rapid increase in bank credit, will produce an inflation. But it does not follow from this that a large debt *once reached* will result in inflation. Once the expenditures are over, the magnitude of the debt per se will not produce inflation.

It is true that a country with an enormous debt will have

---

more prosperous, the burden will be carried with comparative ease." Cmd. 2800, p. 245.

a larger budget owing to the interest charges. Accordingly, if the national income is allowed to fall drastically, tax receipts will fall sharply and a large deficit will be incurred—larger by reason of the debt. But under these circumstances the government will be compelled to cope with a deflationary situation, not an inflationary one.

The argument may, however, shift from inflation to deflation, and the question is raised: Is it not likely that a huge debt will cause deflation? This view appears superficially to draw support from the observed events following a great war. It is noted that, in these circumstances, countries saddled with a great debt frequently experience a serious postwar deflation. The difficulty, however, does not arise from the magnitude of the debt, but from the strenuous effort made to repay a large part of the debt. In the absence of a vigorous private investment boom, the retirement of any considerable part of the debt will produce deflationary consequences.[38]

What has been said with respect to inflation and distribution of wealth and income implies that there are limits to the public debt which, if exceeded, will tend to affect the workability of the economy. But these limits must be conceived of, not in terms of a fixed amount or a static situation, but in terms of a dynamic process. Account must be taken of rates of change and the magnitude of the public debt in relation to other magnitudes, especially the ratio of debt to national income. With respect to rates of change, a too rapid increase in loan expenditures at full employment will produce inflation. With respect to proportionality, a large debt in relation to national income may imply a disproportionate amount of wealth invested in government bonds and held by the wealthy classes.

[38] The case of the United States in the decade of the twenties is often cited as an example of the wholesome economic effects of a program of debt retirement. It should be noted, however, that public debt as a whole, including federal, state, and local, did not decline in this decade. Moreover, the accumulated shortages (housing, for example) caused by the war, together with other factors, produced a vigorous investment boom. Under these circumstances, some net retirement of total public debt (federal, state, and local) might have been desirable. The retirement of federal debt in fact, however, merely offset the rise in state and local debt.

The rentier class might accordingly become too large at the expense of the active elements in the country. Even an ideal tax structure will restrain more or less the inducement to invest, and a regressive tax structure will unduly restrict consumption. Diversion of a large part of the income stream into interest payments on government bonds would tend to raise the propensity to save, thus intensifying the savings-investment problem.

Much of the discussion about the limits of the public debt is wholly unrealistic. There are no rigid and fixed limits. The problem is a manageable one, and can best be taken care of by ensuring that taxation is adequate: (1) to prevent inflation and (2) to provide a reasonably equitable and workable distribution of wealth and income. Within the limits set by these criteria, it is possible to determine, according to varying circumstances, what proportion of public expenditures may advantageously be loan-financed and what proportion should be tax-financed.

VII. Controlled Borrowing

There are three ways in which governmental expenditures designed to secure full employment may be financed: (1) by the creation of interest-free, or virtually interest-free, money, (2) by borrowing at the market rate, and (3) by taxes.

There are many who favor a strong expansionist fiscal policy, but who wish nevertheless to avoid an increase in the public debt. Some wish by highly progressive taxes to balance the budget [39] at an expenditure level sufficiently high to produce full employment. Others would regard such a tax structure as altogether too repressive, and favor financing the expenditures from interest-free money.

Crude greenbackism, that is, the printing of paper money, is no longer seriously proposed. Even during the financial stress of the first World War no government resorted to this

[39] The phrase is here used in the sense commonly employed, namely, tax receipts adequate to cover all expenditures, including both operating and capital expenditures.

practice. The essential reason, of course, is that under modern conditions notes or currency are relatively little used as means of payment. Modern money consists of demand deposits, and so "modern greenbackism" seeks to devise schemes by which deposits can be created without the incurrence of interest-bearing debt.

Various methods to implement the latter proposal have been suggested. The Federal Reserve Banks might be required by law, at the request of the Secretary of the Treasury, to make interest-free loans to the government. Treasury deposits thus created at the Federal Reserve Banks would be spent in the usual manner by the government on public works and even on regular expenditures. Objection to this proposal could be raised on the ground that the spending of such deposits would create excess reserves, precisely as in the case of the spending of deposits created by the issue of gold certificates to the Federal Reserve Banks. To this some have replied that excess reserves are not important (and perhaps even to be welcomed), and others have suggested that this problem could quite well be taken care of by adopting the "hundred per cent reserve" plan, or else by giving the monetary authority unlimited powers over the reserve requirements. Another proposal which avoids the excess reserve problem is to compel the commercial banks to make interest-free, or virtually interest-free, loans to the government. Thus, the London *Economist*[40] suggested that in the case of war loans the banks should be compelled to take government bonds at one half of 1 per cent interest. In view of the extraordinarily low rate on short-term Treasury bills, and in view of the large amount of these purchased by the banks, it could be argued that this proposal was, in effect, substantially carried out in the United States in the period 1933–36.

The paper money issued by the American colonies, while

[40] See "The Technique of Inflation," London *Economist*, January 27, 1940. See also A. A. Berle's proposal in Hearings Before the Temporary National Economic Committee, Part 9, *Savings and Investment*.

at times used to help finance wars, was typically issued as loans to finance private business. The rate of interest was commonly 5 or 6 per cent. The loans were secured by mortgages on land and houses and were to be paid back in annual installments. Yet, in part, the issues were used to finance the government on an interest-free basis. These paper money issues were successfully made in the Middle Colonies, especially Pennsylvania, New York, New Jersey, and Delaware,[41] but with rather unfortunate consequences in some colonies. Benjamin Franklin relates in his *Autobiography* his part in the paper money movement in Pennsylvania. Besides publishing the first book supporting the issue of paper money, he himself wrote, in 1729, "A Modest Enquiry into the Nature and Necessity of a Paper Currency."

Pennsylvania made new issues periodically for about half a century, beginning with 1723. During the first half of this interval the price level remained substantially stable, but rose about 30 per cent during the second half under the impact of larger issues used to help defray the expenses of the French and Indian Wars. This successful paper money experiment is summarized by a contemporary as follows:

"The singular prosperity of the province may be attributed chiefly to the economical habits of the people and the genius of their jurisprudence, partly to the prudent policy of promoting enterprise by feeding circulation with loans of paper money, gradual yet moderate." [42]

The modern banking system, with its freedom to create demand deposits on a fractional reserve basis, essentially issues "paper money" through the loan-deposit operations. And this "multiplication of currency" has given us an ever-expanding money supply corresponding more or less to the increasing volume of trade. If, however, the banking system is called upon to finance the government deficit, there might

41 See Richard A. Lester, *Monetary Experiments,* Princeton University Press, 1939. This book, carefully documented, gives a wealth of information on paper money experiments in the American colonies.

42 George Chalmers, *Introduction to the History of the Revolt of the American Colonies,* quoted in Lester, *op. cit.*, p. 111.

be no relation between the requirements of trade and the money supply thus created. If the deficit is large—$3 or $4 billions per annum—the continued growth in demand deposits would quickly outrun the secular rise in output. Contrary to the crude monetary theory, we know, however, that this situation does not necessarily produce a price inflation, but may only result in a decline in the velocity of circulation. In the absence of private investment outlets adequate to produce full employment, the governmental expenditures could be controlled so as to prevent a price inflation. But if large governmental expenditures are required to promote full employment, and if the deficit is financed heavily by bank credit and not out of savings, the money supply will continue to rise, and may rise far more rapidly than the upward trend in the physical volume of trade.

The multiplication of the money supply at the beginning of a recovery from any considerable depression is desirable. The means of payment are inadequate at this point to circulate a full-employment output of goods and services. At this point it is, therefore, permissible to finance a part of a governmental recovery program through the sale to banks of low-interest-bearing, short-term bills. But a progressive multiplication of money beyond the requirement of market transactions drives interest rates on government and gilt-edged securities to an artificially low level. Not only are the banks deprived of reasonable earning assets adequate to support the expenses necessary to furnish the public banking services, but, in addition, social security trust funds, savings banks, life insurance companies, and educational and other nonprofit institutions are deprived of a reasonable return. These services must, therefore, be financed in some other way.

Thus, the apparent escape from the payment of interest charges, it turns out, entails expenditures by the community elsewhere. Moreover, there is something wholly artificial in the continued multiplication of money far beyond the requirements of trade. Pushed to its logical conclusion it means, in fact, the gradual "euthanasia of the rentier."

It is just here that a strong case can be made for a continuing deficit corresponding to the requirements of thrift savings streams. Life insurance, savings banks and other thrift institutions, baby bonds, and social security trust funds[43] have taken in recent years annually about $3 billions of government issues. Institutional thrift streams rightly seek, wholly or in large measure, the safest type of security: namely, government bonds. A wide diffusion of property ownership is thereby encouraged. There is thus a solid basis in these thrift streams for controlled borrowing. Here one finds a reconciliation between the principle of thrift and governmental loan expenditures.[44]

In so far as the government can borrow from small savers, an increase in the public debt will not prove unfavorable to an equitable distribution of wealth. But if the growth in the public debt is very rapid, it will not be possible for relatively small savers to take any large proportion of the new securities issued. They will be absorbed by the rich and the well to do, and by large corporations. A rapid growth in the public debt is, therefore, likely to intensify the inequality in wealth distribution. This is the most fundamental objection that can be raised against financing mainly by borrowing.

To mitigate this inequality in wealth and income it is necessary to finance the large proportion of government expenditures from taxation. Indeed, this is the primary function of a steeply progressive tax structure. Were it not for the fact that a rapidly mounting public debt tends toward wealth concentration, borrowing is always to be preferred to taxation, since borrowing is always a more expansionist method of financing expenditures. Expansion should, of

[43] As I have often stated, I do not favor large accumulations of social security reserves. Except for contingency reserves, this part of the current thrift stream should be eliminated.

[44] It is true that baby bonds have been taken largely by wealthy individuals. But it is believed that the "baby bond plan" could be implemented so as to reach a large number of small savers.

course, always be restricted to the point of reasonably full employment in order to prevent price inflation. In the event, however, that huge governmental expenditures *must* be made (as in wartime), taxation serves a further purpose. Diversion of resources from private consumption to war outlays becomes absolutely necessary, at least when the economy approaches full employment. If this diversion is not achieved, if the war expenditures are piled on top of private expenditures, inflation of commodity prices will inevitably follow. Taxation is a powerful device to achieve this diversion of resources. And this is especially true of taxes which weigh heavily on private consumption.

With respect to income distribution, it may be noted that historical studies, fragmentary as they are, point to the remarkable conclusion, suggested by Pareto, that the slope of income distribution has remained relatively constant in widely diverse periods in modern history and in different countries, despite the varying institutional arrangements which have emerged in consequence of modern social and political movements. It is a remarkable thing that the slope of income distribution in England, according to the studies of Sir Josiah Stamp and others, was apparently substantially the same in 1920 as in 1800, despite the fact that there had intervened between these periods the prodigious rise of modern machine industrialism, the emergence of trade-unions, the development of labor legislation, the rise of the modern corporation, the expansion of world trade, the revolution in the character of taxes weighing on production costs, and the upheaval of the first World War itself. Similarly, in the United States, the researches of Willford I. King and the National Bureau of Economic Research point to the conclusion that the slope of the income distribution was not greatly altered in this country over the period of the last century.

This remarkable apparent fact has led certain writers to the conclusion that some imperious necessity fixes the income distribution so that it may be regarded as more or less of a natural phenomenon. One basic ground for such an assumption is, of course, the distribution of native capacity in any population, which distribution has probably not changed materially over many centuries. Given this distribution of native capacity, there is at least some warrant for the belief that institutional arrangements are less powerful than is sometimes supposed in altering the manner in which the income is distributed. As long as we stick rigorously, as income statistics usually attempt to do, to the primary distribution of income—that is to say, the distribution of income to the factors of production prior to taxes on income—a sufficiently adequate reason for this historical development may, perhaps, be found in the pricing process. More and more, however, this primary distribution of income is likely to be modified by reason of the more equalitarian distribution resulting from a highly progressive tax structure. This, at any rate, would be true in so far as the secondary distribution—the distribution of income after taxes—affects property ownership and through this, in turn, the primary distribution of income. Thus far, apparently, the tax structure in the United States has not been sufficiently progressive to have had this effect.

The attack on chronic unemployment by means of public expenditures financed by a continually rising public debt is essentially a conservative proposal. This is true in the respect that it does not necessarily involve a redistribution of income unfavorable to property owners. Indeed, as we have noted, too great a reliance on borrowing could easily lead to an undue concentration of wealth. This would especially be the case if the interest (and amortization charges in the case of capital projects) were covered in large part by regressive taxation.

Yet, even though this undesirable method of taxation were applied, the effect on the lower income groups would not be nearly as serious as a condition of chronic unemployment. Moreover, the taxes collected would presumably represent payments for worth-while utilities flowing from public expenditures. These might quite conceivably be of such a character that they would raise the standard of living even higher than could be reached by the consumption of an equivalent amount of commercially-produced commodities. The payment, by means of regressive taxation, for public benefits flowing, for example, from capital projects over a long period of time would be no more burdensome upon the masses than the purchase of commercial products at a uniform price, the same alike for rich and poor.

No clear insight into the problem of borrowing and the interest charges incident to a rising public debt is possible without making a thoroughgoing integration of taxes with the general price structure. Taxes are compulsory prices, so to speak, charged for government services. Commercial prices are charges collected under voluntary choice (though affected by modern high-pressure salesmanship and advertising techniques) for utilities flowing from the stream of goods offered to the community by private business enterprise.

Nor can it be argued that loan-financed expenditures on capital projects, for which the annual charges are subsequently financed out of regressive taxation, have no stimulating effect on the economy. For the full effect of the loan expenditures on employment is felt when the project is constructed, and the subsequent taxation cumulates in small increments over the whole lifetime of the durable capital good. In contrast, if current expenditures were wholly financed by means of regressive taxes, they would have no expansionist effect, since they would merely divert a part of the income stream from private consumption to community expenditures.

Governmental expenditures may, however, be income-stimulating without being loan-financed. It is true, as just noted, that if the expenditures are financed from consumption taxes, the effect is obviously merely to divert resources without increasing the total income flow. But if financed from progressive taxation, thereby tapping a stream of savings which might not have found outlet in productive activity, adequate expenditures may be expected to drive the national income by a cumulative process up to the full income and full-employment level. At first, while the national income was still rising, the expenditures might be largely loan-financed. But after the national income had approached full employment levels, a sharply progressive tax structure would then draw in an amount of taxes sufficiently large to balance the budget, including both operating and capital expenditures.

There can, of course, be no assurance that this, in fact, would occur without further increases in expenditures or tax rates, or both. The closer one approaches full employment, the less effective expenditures become in raising the national income without causing a concomitant rise in prices. The higher the level reached, the smaller the effect on employment, and the greater the effect on prices. To check inflation, tax rates might have to be raised very high. A more stable equilibrium could be reached at a lower employment level. But even at a moderate approach to full employment, expenditures and tax rates would both have to be pushed to levels higher than necessary if some reliance were placed on loan expenditures. That this must be true of tax rates is, of course, obvious. That it is true also of expenditures follows from the fact that loan expenditures have a higher potency in income stimulation than tax-financed expenditures, even though the taxes are progressive. For even the funds raised from progressive taxation would, in part, have been expended for consumption or investment, had they not been taken in taxes. Taxation, though progressive, always involves some curtailment of consumption and, therefore, a mere *diversion* of the income stream. To the extent that tax-financed expenditures merely serve to *divert* income, they can obviously not be income-generating expenditures.

Governmental expenditures may thus appropriately be financed under certain conditions and within proper limits (a) by an increase in demand deposits through borrowing from the banks, (b) by borrowing from the public, and (c) by taxation. Main reliance must, on balance, be placed upon taxation in order to prevent too great concentration of wealth. But there is a legitimate place for loan financing within appropriate limits on a continuing basis. At times, the requirements of trade call for an increase in the money supply (demand deposits mainly), and this may properly be accomplished by borrowing from the banks at low, short-term rates of interest. But after the requirements of trade and the desire for liquidity have been reasonably satisfied, no useful purpose is served by a continued multiplication of the money supply such as would inevitably follow from a program to finance expenditures wholly through interest-free issues, or even from continued borrowing at the banks at market rates. The ensuing redundancy of money would drive the interest rate to a level which would strike at the position of thrift institutions and, in general, the creditor class. It would create an artificial degree of liquidity. It would result in the accumulation of vast unused cash resources which, in a world of changing and volatile expectations, might magnify the instability in the price structure.

If this analysis is sound, it points to the conclusion that the public debt, taxes, and changes in the money supply are all part of a balancing mechanism. How much reliance should be placed on each as a means of financing government expenditures depends upon a variety of considerations. It involves judgments with respect to the adequacy of the means of payment, adequate liquidity, the importance under certain conditions of using relatively expansionist and less restrictive methods of financing, the appropriate (socially desirable) degree of inequality of wealth and income, the relative desirability of tapping savings streams through borrowing (increasing the public debt) or through taxation. A limited increase in the public debt tends to promote a wide distribution of property in so far as the new issues are purchased by thrift institutions. On the other hand, a very rapid increase in the public debt necessarily implies a relatively light tax burden on upper-income groups and on corporations, tending to promote concentration of wealth and income. It is considerations such as these that one must bear in mind when one seeks to appraise the role of public debt and to determine how rapidly it may be permitted to rise.

A public debt, internally held, is not like a private debt. It has none of the essential earmarks of a private debt. The public debt is an instrument of public policy. It is a means to control the national income and, in conjunction with the tax structure, to regulate the distribution of income.

Chapter X

BUDGETARY THEORY AND PRACTICE

I. *Private versus Public Budgets*[1]

THE essential purpose of budgeting expenditures and receipts is to obtain a clear conception of the financial operations of an economic unit. This is true for the public economy no less than for private individuals or corporations. The significance of the accounts and the uses which one wants to make of them may, however, be very different in the public and in the private sphere.

It is customary for the layman, and also for many writers on public finance, to apply the same tenets of financial theory and practice to governmental bodies that are applied to private business. But even those who do so are far from consistent. Especially is this true in regard to budgetary theory and practice. Adapting the rules of private finance to the state, they nevertheless fail to carry this point of view over into public accounting procedure, particularly with respect to the budgeting of capital expenditures.

Expenditures on capital goods are given a special treatment in private accounting. Capital outlays are not lumped in with operating expenditures. Producers' capital is expected to yield a monetary return over its economic lifetime, and consumers' capital is expected to yield a flow of

[1] See the illuminating chapters on public budgets in *Public Policy*, Yearbook of the Graduate School of Public Administration, Harvard University, 1941, by Harvey S. Perloff, Spencer Thompson, Robert H. Rawson, and Charles Stauffacher.

utilities. It is accordingly recognized that expenditures in the operating budget ought to be treated by accounting theory and practice in such a manner that they will run parallel to the flow of money returns or utilities over time. A complete accounting of annual costs should include not merely the ordinary operating expenses, but also the capital charges of interest and depreciation. These latter must be charged against income in order to determine whether a year's operations have been profitable or not. And in the case of consumers' capital they must be charged against the value of the flow of utilities in order to measure accurately the economic validity of such projects. But the capital outlays initially made are not included in the current operating budget. Only by differentiating the capital expenditures from the current capital charges can we get a clear notion of whether or not the budget is balanced.

For the public economy, expenditures ought to be weighed not in terms of the profit and loss of the state itself, but rather in terms of the effect of such expenditures on the full and efficient functioning of the economy as a whole. Fiscal policy is an important instrument for maximizing the real income of the community and for regulating the distribution of income and wealth. At times it will be sound policy to balance the budget and at times it would be disastrous to do so. Only in the event that one applies the maxims of private finance to the public economy will one be concerned per se with the problem of balancing the budget.

All modern governments own and operate some state enterprises which yield a money return more or less covering all operating costs, including the capital charges of interest and depreciation. The United States Post Office is a gigantic business enterprise. Many European governments, and some American cities, own and operate public utilities. The federal government owns many so-called self-liquidating projects. Yet, as far as the federal government is concerned, private accounting practice is not applied to these projects. Capital expenditures are lumped in with ordinary operating expenditures and a quite distorted view is arrived at with respect to whether or not the budget is balanced.

Precisely the same applies to governmentally-owned consumers' capital, such as roads, parks, and public buildings. In private accounting no individual confuses capital outlays on a home with his ordinary living expenditures. No individual believes that his budget has become unbalanced merely because in building a home his expenditures exceed his income. Moreover, in budgeting his annual living expenditures he includes, or should include, not merely the cost of operating the home (fuel, light, etc.), but also annual capital charges—interest and depreciation. Governments, however, typically lump all expenditures, whether capital or operating, into a single budget. Thus, private accounting theory and practice is violated, and it becomes quite impossible to know whether or not the budget is really in balance.

The use of the capital budget in governmental accounting cannot, however, be justified by reference to private financial practice. If one adopts wholeheartedly the principle that governmental financial operations should be regarded exclusively as instruments of economic and public policy, the concept of a balanced budget, however defined, can play no role in the determination of that policy. One cannot examine with an unprejudiced mind the economic validity of a program of expenditures, loans, and taxes if one is hampered by the dogma that the budget must be balanced. From this point of view, if there is any value in incorporating into governmental accounting practice the technique of the capital budget, that judgment must rest on other grounds than that such a technique aids in determining whether or not the budget is really in balance.

There are, however, valid grounds for favoring the capital budget device. The essential purpose of accounting is to maximize efficiency in the use of productive resources and to eliminate waste. Waste in the use of public funds is no less reprehensible than the waste of private funds. The notion, so frequently expressed, that those who favor large governmental expenditures are unmindful of waste is, of course, quite mistaken. First and foremost, it is important to eliminate the waste of unemployment. It is true that full employment might be secured by wasteful expenditures. But such action has, of course, no economic justification. Once full employment is reached, it will be discovered that the real income falls far short of what is desired, and every effort should be made to employ the productive resources to the best possible advantage. Public accounting is a necessary instrument to secure efficiency in the government's financial operations. And it is essentially as a tool to further this end that the capital budget device deserves careful consideration. As an accounting tool, it may help to determine the appropriate *direction* of public expenditures and the degree of efficiency achieved. But it can tell us nothing about whether or not public expenditures ought to be increased or decreased or how they ought to be financed, whether by borrowing or by taxes. The capital budget is a valid tool of analysis, though for different reasons, whether one applies to governmental financial operations the principles of private finance or the criteria appropriate for public policy.

II. The Capital Budget

Whether a unitary budget or a multiple budget form is used by a government, it is, at all events, important that the principle of budgetary comprehensiveness shall not be lost sight of. The unitary budget, of course, fulfills automatically this requirement. There is, however, nothing incompatible between the principle of budgetary comprehensiveness and a multiple budget system. If a multiple budget system is used, involving a general budget and special budgets, it is nevertheless wholly feasible, and indeed urgently necessary, that a general over-all picture shall be presented.

It is particularly important that an over-all "liability balance sheet" of the government shall be clearly set forth. Such a balance sheet should include not only the direct liabilities of the government, but also the contingent liabilities incident to the issue of government-guaranteed bonds by more or less self-sustaining governmental corporations.

It is, moreover, desirable to give an over-all view of the cash-income, cash-outgo budget position of the government from year to year and from month to month. Such an accounting will indicate something more than the mere rise or fall in the government deficit. It will show the cash income and cash outgo, taking account not only of all governmental receipts (other than from the sale of obligations) and expenditures of whatever nature, but also of the receipts and expenditures of trust funds which come within the scope of Treasury management and control. A striking example of the divergence between the fiscal budget and the cash budget is found in the case of the Social Security trust funds. Beginning with January, 1937, with respect to the Old Age Reserve Account, sums were withdrawn through payroll taxes greatly in excess of the benefits which were paid out. For this and other reasons the cash budget deficit was only $198,000,000 in 1937, while the fiscal deficit was $1,450,000,000.

An over-all view of governmental fiscal operations may also make it desirable to present a monetary budget revealing the effect of the fiscal operations of the government upon the income stream. The cash budget differs from the monetary budget in that the net cash outlays differ from the net income-generating expenditures. The former takes account of cash receipts (except those from borrowing) and total cash outlays of all governmental agencies, including trust funds. The latter excludes those tax revenues which are not abstracted from the flow of private expenditures and which are drawn from idle balances.[2] On the other side, it excludes those outlays which do not add to the spending power of the

[2] The figures "net income-creating expenditures" as calculated by the Research Division of the Federal Reserve Board do not wholly conform to the definition given above, since they do not exclude all nonconsumption taxes. The following is an example illustrating my definition of net income-generating

community, such as those for debt retirement. Obviously, the monetary budget presents serious statistical difficulties and, at best, can be only an estimate in the determination of which judgment and hypothetical speculation play a large role.

It may, moreover, be desirable to present an over-all comprehensive picture of (a) the original cost and (b) the cost of replacement, less depreciation, of the stock of durable goods held by the government. Such an inventory kept up to date currently would certainly be of great significance for accurate accounting purposes, and particularly with reference to the planning of revenues and expenditures for amortization and replacement. The experience with respect to the valuation of the American railroads under the LaFollette Act indicates, however, that to attempt now a valuation of all of the properties of the government would be an extremely difficult and expensive undertaking, and serious question may be raised whether it is worth while. It is a different matter to apply such accounting procedure, however, to expenditures made in the future and thereby gradually develop over many decades a fairly complete inventory of public wealth.

A multiple budget can satisfy the requirements of comprehensiveness equally as well as a unitary budget. Moreover, it permits both greater flexibility of management and a clearer perception of the financial operations of the government. The following elements may be included in a comprehensive multiple budget setup.

I. Operating Budget
II. Capital Budget
  A. Public Works: Nonremunerative
  B. Self-liquidating Projects

---

expenditures. Assume government expenditures of $10 billions. Assume consumption taxes of $3 billions and nonconsumption taxes of $4 billions. The net income-generating expenditures will then be $7 billions. Net income-generating expenditures so defined can be added to private investment expenditures to get the total outlays offsetting saving.

C. Investment in Government Corporations and Independent Authorities

III. Annexed Budgets

A. District of Columbia
B. Post Office Department
C. Government Corporations
D. Self-liquidating Governmental Credit Agencies, Loans, and Revolving Funds
E. Trust Funds

The question of the appropriate classification of public expenditures is an important one. Expenditures have, in some countries, been divided into "ordinary" and "extraordinary"; and again into "operating expenditures" and "capital expenditures." Most commonly, all expenditures of whatever kind have been included within a single or unitary budget. Some countries have, however, used a double budget system. Under a true double budget, current and operating expenditures are accounted for in an operating budget and capital outlays in a capital or investment budget.

Professor Erik Lindahl, Swedish economist, has stated the problem of current and capital budgetary accounting and its significance for the concept of budget balancing as follows:

> Every budget is of course formally balanced, since the sum of the items on the expenditure side must always be covered exactly by revenue. A demand for a balanced budget must therefore mean that the sum of *certain* kinds of revenue must be equal to the sum of *certain* kinds of expenditures. The most natural procedure is to start either from total *current revenue,* i. e., revenue other than that arising from the sale of capital assets or from borrowing; or from total *current expenditures,* i. e., expenditure that does not lead to an increase in the aggregate net assets of the community. If these two are exactly equal, the budget is obviously balanced in the sense that the net value of total public assets remains unchanged. . . . If current revenue exceeds current expenditure, a corresponding rise in the net value of public assets occurs.

Thus the "problem of balancing the budget is concerned primarily with whether, and to what degree, the State (and local authorities) should increase or reduce their total net assets." [8]

Let us consider first the operating budget in a double budget setup. It is necessary to note at once that under conditions of fairly wide fluctuations in income and employment, such as modern countries undergo, it is virtually impossible to cover even the regular, operating expenditures of the government with adequate tax receipts in the depression years of the cycle. This fact is due to two causes. On the one side, the modern tax system is heavily composed of taxes which are highly sensitive to the cycle. This is especially true of the individual income tax, the corporate income tax, and customs duties. The receipts from these taxes fluctuate widely with the cycle, rising to high levels in boom years and falling to low levels in depression years. On the other side, under modern conditions certain expenditures of government, notably relief of unemployment, unavoidably increase in depression years. Thus, we experience not merely highly fluctuating revenues, correlated directly with the cycle, but also fluctuating expenditures correlated inversely with the cycle. The combined effect of these two diverse movements is to magnify the divergent movement of expenditures and tax receipts. If the tax structure is set sufficiently high so that tax receipts cover the total expenditures over an entire cycle, these diverse movements will produce a surplus of tax receipts over expenditures in the boom years, and a deficiency of tax receipts in relation to expenditures in the depression years.

[8] Erik Lindahl, *Studies in the Theory of Money and Capital,* London, 1939, pp. 352–53. Professor Lindahl calls attention (p. 354) to the fact that a program of public investment, or a program of debt retirement, financed by a system of stiff progressive taxation would increase the net assets of the state and would imply "some mitigation of the inequality of the present distribution of wealth. This is indeed the crux of the matter. The long-term solution of the problem of public investment is of primary importance for the distribution of wealth."

On the expenditure side many of the regular expenditures will go on from year to year, disturbed but little, if at all, by prosperity or depression. These are the regular expenditures growing out of the ordinary functions of government. But relief expenditures, if not otherwise provided for outside of the budget, must also be regarded in modern times as a normal function of government and one which it must face in every period when unemployment on a large scale prevails. It is an item of expenditure which it is difficult to regularize. But, even here, it is possible to go a considerable distance toward regularization through the development of unemployment insurance and other social security measures. By means of these special measures, the load of outright relief can, in large measure, be provided for outside of the government budget, thereby reducing the magnitude of the fluctuation of expenditures. Thus England, because of a well-developed system of unemployment and old-age insurance, was able to meet the relief needs of the depression with relatively small governmental support. Comparison with our own situation in the Great Depression must, of course, take cognizance of the greater depth of our depression and the correspondingly greater need.

Obviously, the failure to bring about a balance of receipts and expenditures in every single year, yet achieving a cyclical balance, involves deficits in the operating budget in some years and surpluses in others. Thus, temporary loan financing is necessary even in the case of the operating budget. If it is desired to ensure a balanced operating budget over the entire cycle, it is necessary to amortize such loans very rapidly. In order to facilitate this, Sweden has devised a system of amortization within five years of debt incurred to cover temporary deficits in the operating budget. It is possible that a better plan might be to use a varying amortization rate—each successive year carrying a higher and higher rate. Thus, the period of amortization would be longer with respect to deficits incurred in the earlier phase of depression and shorter for later deficits. At all events, in order to insure a cyclical balance of the operating budget, rapid amortization of such loans would be required.[4]

Some adjustment of tax rates to the cycle movement may be desirable as a compensatory measure. On balance, it may be suggested that taxes which bear heavily on the savings stream may, without damage to the economy, be raised in the boom phase of the cycle. This is true because high rates on incomes flowing largely into savings will simply take funds from the savings stream and, through the debt redemption process, place these same funds back again in the savings stream. This assumes that people owning the retired bonds will wish to reinvest the sums received. Taxes bearing mainly on savings rather than on consumption, and used for debt retirement, would, therefore, have neither an inflationary nor a deflationary effect. Such a procedure would leave the savings stream intact and would be neutral in its effects on the cycle movement.[5]

On the other hand, it might also prove desirable under certain conditions to fluctuate the rates on consumption taxes, raising them in the boom and lowering them in depression. The increase of consumption taxes in the boom will, however, tend to be deflationary in its effect, and should, therefore, be resorted to only in the event that the boom is proceeding at a pace which makes it desirable to hold it in check. In the event that the recovery lacks vigor, an increase in consumption taxes would be unfortunate, since this procedure would tend to dampen the recovery.

[4] Professor Erik Lindahl, in discussing the new Swedish budget plan, says. "The essential point is that the ordinary or current budget should include only such expenditures as should normally be covered by current revenue (and not by loan or capital assets). A positive or negative difference between current revenue and the corresponding expenditure should be expressly recorded as a surplus or deficit (as suggested above). But these surpluses or deficits are in this plan kept apart from the capital budget and transferred to a special fund, the so-called Budget Equalization Fund." See Lindahl's *Studies in the Theory of Money and Capital,* London, 1939, p. 379.

[5] The qualification must, of course, be made that diversion of funds through taxation, while it appears to leave aggregates unaffected, may nevertheless affect individual decisions to invest and to save in such a manner as to change the aggregates.

So much for the operating budget, which involves the regular, current expenses. We turn now to the nonrecurring expenditures on major capital projects, whether self-liquidating or not.

Under a fully developed double budget system, the operating budget must include as a part of its regular expenditures the depreciation, amortization, write-offs, and interest charges incidental to the capital outlays accounted for in the capital or investment budget. The interrelation between the operating budget, in a double budget system, and the capital or investment budget can perhaps best be illustrated by reference to the Danish budgetary system.[6]

Denmark's new budgetary system, inaugurated in 1927, offers the most logically consistent example of governmental accounting in the form of two separate but interrelated statements: (a) the Operating Budget, and (b) the Capital or Investment Budget. Every outlay on a capital good is entered in the capital or investment budget. No distinction is made between self-liquidating and non-income-yielding capital outlays. Durability, not profitability, is the criterion applied. Capital outlays on durable or capital goods are financed by (a) inheritance taxes, (b) borrowing, and (c) amortization or depreciation allowances transferred to the capital budget from the operating budget.

Self-liquidating capital projects are, of course, expected to earn an income adequate to cover the operating expenses of

[6] For an account of the Danish and Swedish budget systems see Brinley Thomas, *Monetary Policy and Crises,* London, 1936; *Fortune* magazine, September, 1938; *Swedish Yearbook;* K. Müller, "Die Neugestaltung des staatlichen Richnungs und Revisionswesens in Dänemak," *Finanz-Archiv,* 1928, pp. 131–39; G. Myrdal, *Finanspolitikens ekonomiska verkningar,* Stockholm, 1934; P. S. Runemark, "Den Föreslagna Omläggningen av Riksstatens Uppställning," *Föredrag Hállna Inför Svenska Ekonomföreningen,* Nummer 2, 1937; "Kungl. maj:ts proposition Nr 225," *Bihang till riksdagens protokoll,* 1937; Nr 199, protokoll, 1938; Erik Lindahl, *Studies in the Theory of Money and Capital,* appendix on "The Problem of Balancing the Budget," London, 1939; "The Financial Policy During Depressions and Booms," *Annals* of the American Academy of Political and Social Science, May, 1938.

the project and interest and depreciation charges. In the event that losses are sustained, these are carried by the operating budget. Non-income-yielding assets, on the other hand, since they earn no income directly, must look to the government's operating budget for income to cover not only expenses of operating, but also interest and depreciation charges. Thus, each branch of the government—for example, a state hospital or a state university—must include in its expenditure estimates not merely the usual operating expenses, but also an amount sufficient to cover interest and depreciation. These expense items entered in the government's operating budget are, of course, defrayed from general tax revenues. Thus, the operating budget carries the interest and depreciation charges originating in the capital or investment budget.

The Danish public accounting procedure is fully developed to include all state properties, and it is, therefore, possible to present annually a statement of the national debt and of the net cost minus depreciation of the national properties. And since a part of the capital outlays are, in fact, financed from inheritance taxes, the net cost minus depreciation of the national properties should exceed the debt obligations. If the ordinary budget shows a balance in any one year, such a balance would show up as a net addition to the assets in the state aggregate asset account; a deficit in the ordinary budget would reduce the net assets. The Danish budget thus illustrates a fully developed capital accounting procedure applied not only to the state's income-yielding assets, but also to public investments which do not yield a monetary income.

Too great significance should, however, not be attached to such an inventory. Indeed, it may well be argued that, at any rate with respect to non-self-liquidating projects, there is no legitimate warrant for setting up a balance sheet of assets against liabilities, since these so-called assets yield no income. The analogy to private business is a false one. The really important matter, however, with respect to the Danish procedure, is that for every capital outlay financed by borrowing, depreciation or amortization charges are assessed against the operating budget. The operating budget is in balance if its tax receipts are adequate to cover, in addition to expenses of operation, depreciation, amortization, and interest charges. But the initial capital outlay is thrown into a capital or investment budget and is not loaded onto the operating budget.

In the case of Sweden, the capital budget system grew naturally out of the fact that the Swedish state had for many decades past owned important state enterprises, including the railroads, bus lines, telegraph and telephone systems, large electric power plants, and forests, together with such factories and shops as are closely related to the operation of these projects. Thus, the state derived revenue not only from taxes, customs, and excises, but also from the net income from the State Productive Funds, including the Tobacco Monopoly, Iron Ore Company, the Post Office, Telegraphs, Railways, Waterworks, and Public Domains. Capital budgetary accounting also applies to income-yielding projects which are only partially self-sustaining, as, for example, low-cost housing projects. And the new Swedish budget plan proposes to extend the principle, following the Danish example, to nonremunerative public works, such as public buildings. It is proposed to do this piecemeal, if and when separate government agencies or authorities can effectively be set up to manage certain capital projects. As an example, the public roads might be placed under a government authority for the purpose of more efficient management and operating under its own budget. A public roads authority might, of course, have assigned to it a part or all of the gasoline taxes, which would make it in a sense more or less self-sustaining.

The capital or investment budget in Sweden applies, as yet, mainly to remunerative state enterprises. This is the simplest and clearest illustration of the capital budget principle. In Denmark, the principle has a more general application.[7]

With respect to our own country, the Swedish principle is particularly applicable to the various governmental corporations and credit agencies and to self-liquidating capital projects. How far, if at all, the capital budget principle could

[7] In Canada, although not always realized even by Canadians, a budgetary distinction between ordinary and capital expenditures has been made ever since confederation in 1867. The official reports show surpluses in fifty of the sixty-six years following 1867; but if the accounting were made on the United States basis, surpluses would appear in only fifteen of the sixty-six years. Receipts from the federal domain were credited to the "ordinary" budget, and capital expenditures in that field were charged to the "extraordinary" budget. From 1883 to 1914 railway subsidies, which, of course, yielded no return, were charged to the capital account. From 1896 to 1910 military equipment was so charged, and from 1897 to 1911 bounties to iron and steel producers. Thus, developmental expenditures, which however were not self-liquidating such as subsidies to railroads and private industry, and even military expenditures, were charged to the capital account. The financial position of the country, as revealed in the ordinary budget, was often made to appear better than it was. Since 1920, however, although the distinction between ordinary and capital expenditures has been retained, the Finance Ministers have balanced total expenditures against total revenue in their reports. (Cf. J. A. Maxwell, "The Distinction Between Ordinary and Capital Expenditure in Canada," *Bulletin of the National Tax Association,* Volume XIX, no. 5, February, 1934.)

In the case of France, the extraordinary budget was proverbially the dumping place for all expenditures which could not be balanced by tax receipts. France had, moreover, numerous autonomous budgets, but no logical consistency in the budget setup. The match and powder monopolies were handled through the regular budget; but the post office, telegraph, and telephone monopolies, as well as several minor state monopolies, had their own budgets. The tobacco monopoly, which was originally autonomous, since 1927 was managed by the Caisse d'Amortissement, established in 1926 as an autonomous fund with its own bonds, and paying the interest of the Bons de la Défense Nationale. The annexed budgets always appeared balanced, deficits being covered by a sum coming from the general budget, and surpluses being credited to the general budget. Capital expenditures since 1927 were financed in part by Treasury loans and in part from profits on state monopolies. In addition, there were "hidden budgets," such as that for gambling tax receipts. As in the case of Canada, the system seems to have led to underestimation of the true size of deficits. Haig reports that, whereas the official figures show an accumulated deficit of 54 billion francs for the period 1930–37, when extraordinary items are taken into account the figure should be around 70 billions. (R. M. Haig, "The National Budgets of France, 1928–1937," *Proceedings* of the Academy of Political Science, January, 1938, p. 27. See also Professor Haig's *The Public Finances of Post-War France,* pp. 356–64 and 413–14.)

be usefully extended to nonremunerative public works is a matter requiring further study. Before we embark upon any general program of capital budgeting, an exhaustive study should be made of the subject, including time for public education, so that the country would understand and accept as valid the principles involved in the new procedure.

The time is ripe for such an inquiry. We have already been stumbling piecemeal in the direction of a double budget system. Thus, for example, with respect to the Commodity Credit Corporation, its capital stock of $100 millions is held by the United States. It is authorized to issue its own obligations guaranteed by the United States in an aggregate amount of $500 millions. Under an Act of Congress, March 8, 1938, the Secretary of the Treasury is required to make an appraisal of all assets and liabilities of the Corporation as of the thirty-first of March in each year for the purpose of determining its net worth. If the net worth is below $100 millions, the Secretary is required, subject to appropriation of funds therefor, to restore such capital impairment. In the event that the net worth exceeds $100 millions, the excess must be deposited by the Corporation in the United States Treasury. Thus, the budget of the government is not affected by any debt which the Corporation incurs in pursuit of its loaning operations, but only in the event that a loss or surplus occurs in any given fiscal year.

Other governmental corporations and credit agencies are outside of the government budget in the sense that they are empowered to obtain funds by the sale of their own securities. Such securities are usually fully guaranteed as to principal and interest by the United States. Most of these corporations are making loans or engaging in activities which are expected to be wholly or mainly self-liquidating. In one important case—that of the United States Housing Authority —the loans made to local agencies for low-cost housing are only to a limited extent self-liquidating, since the rents received will not be sufficient to cover interest and amortization charges. The difference is covered by annual federal subsidies extending over a period of about sixty years, and these subsidies must be carried by the regular government budget.

These developments indicate that we are already moving, but without any systematic program, in some measure in the direction of the capital or investment budget. Yet the capital budget principle finds no recognition in the government's own budget, since we count our investments in the governmental corporations and credit agencies as operating expense, instead of charging them to an investment budget, as would be done in a true double budget system. In view of the tendencies indicated, it would appear that the time has come when a thoroughgoing re-examination of our budgetary procedure is called for.

Double budget accounting requires that the operating budget must carry year-to-year losses or write-offs sustained by governmental corporations or subsidiaries, together with depreciation and interest charges for nonremunerative capital projects accounted for in the capital or investment budget. This procedure has the merit that it helps to ensure a more adequate cost accounting than is likely to be the case when operating and capital expenditures are all lumped indiscriminately into a unitary general budget. Yet it is necessary to point out that there is not *necessarily* any advantage in this respect in the capital budget procedure. Under the unitary budget, accurate accounting for depreciation could equally be provided if one set about doing it. Similarly, a unitary budget could also provide for amortization charges. But, as a matter of fact, amortization of debt incurred from capital outlays has not been made a systematic part of current budget practice.

The double budget method, if it means anything at all, specifically makes provision in the operating budget for depreciation or amortization charges springing from capital outlays accounted for in the capital or investment budget. This has the merit of setting forth clearly what is the true cost of the annual services derived from the capital outlays.

If tax revenues adequate to cover depreciation and interest charges are provided in the operating budget, a true balancing of the budget over the life span of the capital project is achieved. Yet it must certainly be admitted that there is no magic about the double budget. It is all a question as to which mechanism—the unitary budget system or the double budget system—is likely to induce the most effective accounting control.

There is nothing about the capital budget device as such which helps us to determine whether or not a capital project should be financed from current taxes or from borrowing. Whether a country has a unitary budget or a double budget, it will have to decide on grounds of general economic policy which method of financing is, under any given situation, to be preferred. The double budget procedure, by stressing appropriate accounting of capital charges, serves as a helpful guide to policy. The capital project is worth what it costs if the annual benefits derived are at least equal to the depreciation and interest charges in addition to expenses of operation. The double budget procedure stresses the fact that a capital project is not consumed in the year in which it is constructed. It provides a more rational basis upon which the responsible authorities may decide the question whether to finance the construction of a capital project from taxes or from borrowing on the real merits of the case—that is to say, on grounds of appropriate economic policy, taking into account the effect of taxes versus borrowing on the prevailing economic situation. The question will then be decided, among other matters, on the basis of appropriate policy with respect to the prevailing state of employment.

III. Conflicting Views on the Capital Budget

It will be of interest to examine briefly the expressed opinion of American writers on the advisability of setting up "special" budgets. American economists, as Sundelson has pointed out,[8] have been less interested in "principles" of budgetary organization than have European students of public finance; but the subject has not been entirely neglected in the American literature. Discussion of federal budgetary principles antedates the introduction of our federal budget by at least a decade. H. C. Adams has a section on "What should be the form of the Budget Statement?" in his *Science of Finance* of 1909. True, the earlier discussion did not deal explicitly with the problem of "special" budgets, and even Professor Willoughby, in his article on Budgets for the *Encyclopedia of Social Sciences,* contents himself with the observation that extraordinary budgets have been passed "to finance war or war preparations or for such elaborate expenditures as were necessitated by the railroad building of European governments." [9]

Since the trend toward reformulation of the budget began in 1932, the problem of "special" budgets has received more attention in American economic literature. If we take three representative texts on public finance—Lutz, Buehler, and Jensen—we find that all three have lengthy sections on the budget, and devote some space to principles of formulation. All three are agreed that a budget should be "comprehensive." Buehler does not state whether this criterion excludes the possibility of "special" budgets. Jensen believes that "eliminating, from the ordinary budget, items of extraordinary character" is a "way of rendering the budget incomplete." [10] There is danger, he argues, that segregation will be regarded as a final solution, or that things will be put into the extraordinary budget that do not belong there. Lutz, on the other hand, suggests a "practical working classification" of expenditures in which the main headings are: Ordinary Government Activities, subdivided into "current" and "cap-

[8] "Budgetary Principles" in the *Political Science Quarterly* for June, 1935, p. 236.

[9] *Op. cit.,* Volume 3, p. 39.

[10] Jens P. Jensen, *Government Finance,* Crowell, 1937, p. 514.

ital" outlays; Commercial Enterprises, also divided into "current" and "capital"; Interest; Trust and Other Special Funds; Bookkeeping transactions.[11]

Sundelson includes in his own list of budgetary "principles" the principle of "unity," which he interprets to exclude "extraordinary, capital, annexed, emergency, special and industrial budgets." It also "requires that no part of the material in the budget system shall be considered as separate or apart from the ordinary finances and accorded a personality of its own." While one can find support for extraordinary budgets in the literature, "nevertheless, merely carrying to their logical conclusion the arguments for disunity will soon bring realization that independent budgets are, at best, dangerous." Disregard of the principle of unity is associated with "shady and doubtful practices, especially regarding the problem of balancing budgets." [12]

This vigorous polemic against extraordinary budgets is somewhat different from that of a paper published by the same author a year earlier, in which, on the whole, he approved of the introduction of an "Emergency Budget" by the federal government.[13] In its defense, Sundelson had argued that the huge New Deal expenditures were themselves "sufficient justification for their segregation"; other reasons given were that the recovery outlay was not a true government expenditure, since much of it was for self-liquidating construction work; that the emergency items were of a contingent nature and would not be disbursed entirely in one fiscal year; that they required a different sort of control and regulation than the expenditures of the regular departments; that a definite economic philosophy lay behind the expenditures—spending for recovery; that, after all, it is better for the federal government not to show a deficit, since it sets a bad example for the state and local governments. He pointed

[11] H. L. Lutz, *Public Finance*, Appleton-Century, 1936, p. 35.

[12] *Op. cit.*, pp. 247–48.

[13] "The Emergency Budget of the Federal Government," *American Economic Review*, March, 1934.

out, however, some "vices" of extraordinary budgets, but seemed to feel that these vices were not imminent in the American case. Perhaps the lesson is that one may adhere to the principles of "comprehensiveness" even though one abandon the principle of "unity," and that one may be fully aware of the possible "vices" of extraordinary and "special" budgets and still hold that such budgets can be made to serve the cause of clarity and accuracy.

F. R. Fairchild has emphasized the necessity for a clear distinction between revenue receipts and nonrevenue receipts (borrowing), and between governmental cost payments and nongovernmental cost payments (such as repayment of debt and capital expenditures on self-liquidating projects).[14] Equally important, in his view, is the distinction between gross and net debt, the latter being "simply the former reduced by the amount of cash and equivalent assets belonging to the government." He praises the Census Bureau for adopting these accounting concepts as early as 1907, and upbraids the Treasury Department for its failure to recognize the superiority of the Census classifications. The Annual Report of the Secretary for 1934, Fairchild says, fails to show the true revenue receipts, cost payments, and deficit, because it includes trust funds in its account and deals inadequately with the profits of devaluation of the dollar. Moreover, as far as principle is concerned, the deficit is undoubtedly exaggerated by the inclusion of expenditures on investments, such as the loans of the Reconstruction Finance Corporation, which "should be treated as a capital (nongovernmental cost) expenditure after the manner of private business accounting." However, one must be careful to avoid mistakes, such as that made by Willoughby in including among "assets" twelve billions of allied loans that clearly were not going to be repaid; and if expenditures of the R.F.C. or public works expenditures were going to be treated as capital items, reserves for loss and depreciation should be set up.

[14] "An Analysis of the Government's Financial Reports, with Special Reference to the Deficit," *American Economic Review,* March, 1935.

Thus, in 1935, Professor Fairchild seemed favorable toward the concept of a "capital" budget. Three years later, he vigorously attacked the "double" budget system as used by the government; yet this position could, perhaps, be reconciled with his former position, since no consistently logical capital budgeting procedure had, in fact, been set up.[15] "Without any intent to deceive, it can readily be shown that the use of the double budget has tended to obscure the true picture of the national finances." An erroneous impression has been given, he said, that the enormous deficits have been the result entirely of extraordinary expenditures. Moreover, whereas the official figure shows a substantial decline in emergency and relief expenditures since 1934, this result was obtained by a transfer (regarded by Fairchild as unjustified) of half the T.V.A. expenditures to the "general" account in 1936, and all of them in 1937 and 1938, together with the transfer of Emergency Conservation Work to the "general" budget in 1936. A "further distortion" resulted, he believed, from the inclusion of the net receipts of certain recovery loan agencies as a part of current revenues and the use of these funds to defray the expenditures of other agencies. When the proper adjustments were made, it was seen, he held, that the recovery and relief expenditures for 1937 amount to $3,827 millions instead of the reported $2,846 millions. Thus, Professor Fairchild accuses the "double" budget system of having underestimated the extraordinary expenditures.

Professor Gerhard Colm [16] points out that budgetary principles are a set of norms for the limitation and supervision of the budget administration. He justifies President Roosevelt's "double" budget on two grounds: (a) estimates concerning emergency expenditures are more uncertain, more subject to revision; and (b) separation promotes administrative thrift and maintains fiscal morale. Contrary to Fairchild, he defends the shift of the Emergency Conservation Work

[15] "The United States Budget in the Past Decade," *Proceedings* of the Academy of Political Science, January, 1938.

[16] "Comment on Extraordinary Budgets," *Social Research,* May, 1938.

(C.C.C.) from recovery and relief to the ordinary budget as "an example of accurate budgeting." Similarly, although the practice of including in the budget only the surplus and deficit of government corporations is a violation of the principle of "completeness," it must be regarded as an important improvement in budgetary procedure. Against the double budget, Colm argues that the line of demarcation is necessarily arbitrary, that it may violate the principle of "publicity," and may lead to a preference for self-liquidating projects which need not be shown in the ordinary budget, even though self-liquidating projects may be less desirable from the welfare point of view. He distinguishes between a "loan" budget, for which the criterion is that the items are financed by borrowing, and a "capital" budget, which involves expenditures on capital projects. The latter can be justified on grounds of administrative requirements. He argues that, whereas current expenditure estimates should be made by the spending department, such procedure for capital outlays leads to "dividing the kitty," each department securing its most pressing needs, even though all the needs of one department may be more important than the most urgent need of another. Colm believes that durability should not be the criterion for capital items. Expenditures on battleships, he thinks, ought not to be entered in the capital budget.

A more exhaustive treatment of special budgets is to be found in A. E. Buck's *The Budget in Governments of Today*. He believes that the experience of American municipalities and the Soviet government with the capital budget prove it to be an effective aid to long-term financial planning, provided the two parts of the budget are presented together. He mentions the unhappy experience of European countries with extraordinary budgets, but is of the opinion that the danger lies in making two distinct and unrelated budgets, and not in the division of a comprehensive budget into two parts. Annexed budgets are most appropriately applied to cases of self-supporting government undertakings or services.

IV. Federal Fiscal Documents

Four major documents, published by the federal government, give information on revenues, expenditures, and debt, actual or prospective: The *Daily Statement* of the United States Treasury, which is the primary source of information on actual receipts and expenditures; *The Budget of the United States,* which contains the President's annual budget message, together with summary and detailed tables; *The Annual Report of the Secretary of the Treasury,* which contains summary tables, charts, and written reports; *The Combined Statement of the Receipts and Expenditures, Balances, etc., of the United States,* which contains highly detailed tables.

Taken together, these documents provide as complete information on government finances as is necessary for most purposes. On the other hand, they are extremely difficult to use for anyone not familiar with their organization. There are discrepancies between the reports, and even within the same report when similar material is covered by different departments. The items one seeks are sometimes found under the most unpromising headings. Some items, like the Shipping Board, have the habit of popping in and out of particular tables from year to year without accompanying explanation. The form of classification is often different in each report for the same year. In short, it takes far more time and patience to discover what really is going on than the general public can be expected to devote to the matter. Standardization, systematization, and simplification are necessary to make these documents useful to the layman.

Let us suppose that a conscientious voter wants to see what expenditures were made on P.W.A. in 1937 and to compare the figure with the projected expenditures for 1938. He goes first to the *Annual Report,* since it is the least terrifying in aspect of the four documents. He turns to the table of "Expenditures" under "Budget Results" but finds no figure on P.W.A. On a wild guess he turns to "Estimates of Expenditures"; he finds here a much longer list of actual expenditures for 1937 than in the "Budget Results" table, including an item for "Administrative Expenses, P.W.A."—but no figure for actual P.W.A. expenditures. Under "Construction Activities" he finds a subhead, "Program under the P.W.A.," but the *Report* gives only a total figure for public buildings under P.W.A., and our conscientious citizen has an idea that there may have been other P.W.A. activities. He resigns himself to tackling the *Combined Statement* and consults the long table of contents. Finding no separate heading for P.W.A., he undertakes the wearisome task of going through the subheads for each department, item by item. As the best bet, he looks up "Procurement Division (including public buildings, Public Works Branch)" under "Treasury Department." In the sixteen pages of entries he finds only one item of less than a half a million dollars that is specifically labeled P.W.A. and—if he is diligent enough to consult all footnotes—two others that are "transferred from P.W.A." If he is not now utterly discouraged, he will find P.W.A. items under "Indian Affairs" of the Department of the Interior, Federal Emergency Administration of Public Works, "Nonmilitary activities" of the War Department, etc., which he is not certain how to classify. After these experiences, it is highly unlikely that our citizen is still conscientious enough to look at *The Budget* to see what appropriations have been made for P.W.A. for 1938. Under "General Public Works Program" he will find items of $2.00 for communications expenses, but he is not told whether or not all the twenty-one pages of items represent P.W.A. expenditures. From this single example, it should be clear that these documents in their present form cannot be regarded as a medium for informing the electorate of the government's finances.

After these disconcerting experiences, the inquiring citizen would be forced to recognize that his apparently simple query was in reality a research problem, and, if he had the time and the patience, he would tackle it as such. The research would begin with the various pieces of legislation creating the P.W.A. and providing the different appropriations which have financed its operations; it would lead through the statements made by that agency's officials in the course of hearings before the Congressional appropriation committees; and in all probability it would not end before the inquiring citizen had had some direct correspondence with the agency itself.

In the course of the search, it would be discovered that P.W.A. had originally been created with some very broad powers, including powers to make grants to other federal agencies, to make loans to railroads, and to make loans and grants to states, cities, and other units of government, and that by fiscal 1938 these powers had become restricted to the making of loans and grants to nonfederal units of government. It would be discovered that P.W.A., except for its own administration, spent no money itself, that it merely made loans and grants to be spent, under general P.W.A. supervision, by others. It would be discovered that, with respect to loans, the P.W.A. had functioned as a kind of quasi-investment banker for railroad and municipal issues, intermediate between the borrower and the capital market, and that this relationship had been complicated by the interposition of the R.F.C. between the P.W.A. and private purchasers of securities. Armed with this information, it would be possible to go to the appropriate items in the *Daily Statement,* and ascertain the volume of P.W.A.'s financial operations.

Despite the lack of standardization of expenditure classification in the government reports, one can discern a tendency toward the development of "special" budgets of the "extraordinary" type. The first step was taken in the Hoover Administration in the establishment of the Reconstruction Finance Corporation. Here was a government agency organized to meet an emergency, financed by a subscription to its capital stock of half a billion dollars out of the "General Fund." [17] In that year no special budget was set up for the R.F.C.; there is no report of its expenditures until 1933. But the very formation of a government-financed emergency corporation, authorized to make loans and undertake expenditures, was

[17] Cf. *Combined Statement.*

the first of several emergency measures which led directly to the President's recent demand for a separate budget classification. Clearly, the subscription to the capital stock of the R.F.C. represented an expenditure of an entirely different sort from administrative expenses, relief payments, or even public works. For presumably the capital subscriptions would provide the basis for investment in assets with a marketable value, and was, therefore, in some sense "balanced" by an acquisition of assets. The same is true of the subscription of $125 millions to the stock of the Federal Land Banks in the same year.[18]

The *Combined Statement* shows no changes in 1932 other than the addition of the subscriptions to the stock of the R.F.C. and the Federal Land Banks to the list of "other" (as opposed to "general") expenditures. The *Budget,* which previously had divided expenditures into "Ordinary" and "Reduction in Principal of the Public Debt Required to be Paid from Ordinary Receipts," divided them for the fiscal year 1932 into "General," "Special," and "Trust Funds." This division was not made according to departments; nearly every department had some items in all three categories. "Special" items consisted of such expenditures as the "Memorial to Women of the World War" under the heading "Legislative Establishment," and "Federal Reserve Board" under "Independent Establishments." Trust funds, which are funds held for particular groups or individuals, included items such as "Proceeds from Sale of Indian Lands."

In 1933 the form of the "budget results" table in the *Annual Report* was significantly changed. Whereas in previous years expenditures had been divided into two broad classes, "general" and "other," in 1933 there was an additional classification: "Major expenditures due to or particularly affected by the depression." Under this heading appeared the

[18] In the written report of the *Annual Report of the Secretary of the Treasury* for 1932 (p. 17), these two subscriptions to capital stock are described as "emergency" expenditures; but this term does not appear in the formal tabular statement of expenditures.

following items: Reconstruction Finance Corporation, Public Works, Special Aids to Agriculture, Distribution of Wheat and Cotton for Relief, Emergency Conservation Work (which latter became the C.C.C.), and Postal Deficiency. This classification is significant because it indicates a recognition by federal finance authorities that there are some sorts of expenditure that cannot properly be described as "ordinary," and which need some special kind of treatment.

In the text of the *Report,*[19] the new method of classification is explained in the following manner: "Expenditures for 1933 and prior fiscal years cannot be completely classified as between general and emergency outlays—a classification which was introduced into the Daily Treasury Statement on July 1, 1933. There is presented on page 7, however, a comparison of expenditures of the fiscal years 1932 and 1933, classified by major functional groups. In this table major items due to or particularly affected by the depression are shown separately."

The form of the *Budget* for the fiscal year 1933 (presented January 3, 1932) was the same as for the previous year. The *Combined Statement* showed no change except that four new "Independent Offices" were added and accounted for, namely, National Industrial Recovery, Emergency Conservation Work, National Banking Emergency Act, and Federal Home Loan Bank Board.

The "Federal Home Loan Bank Board" makes its first appearance in the *Budget* in 1934 (presented January, 1933), appearing under "Independent Establishments, Group I." The Reconstruction Finance Corporation also makes its first appearance under "Independent Establishments, Group II." The difference between these two groups is not explained. Most independent establishments are in Group I. One cannot conclude that Group II is regarded as the "emergency" group, since it includes the Shipping Board, Veterans' Administration, and the Federal Farm Board. Subscriptions to stock of Federal Land Banks are not shown under the same head-

[19] *Annual Report of the Secretary of the Treasury,* 1933, p. 5.

ing as subscriptions to stock of R.F.C., but under "Treasury Department, General Fund." About all that can be concluded from these revisions is that the Budget division at the beginning of 1933 was already feeling some need for reclassification of expenditures.

In the *Combined Statement* the only changes introduced in 1934 were the addition of a large number of new Independent Offices [20] and renaming the "Office of the Supervising Architect," which appeared under the Treasury Department, "Procurement Division, including public works, Public Works Branch."

A more important change was made in the *Annual Report*. The heading "Expenditures Due to or Particularly Affected by the Depression" gave way to the heading "Emergency and Other Expenditures."

Under the Roosevelt regime the trend toward setting up special budgets was considerably accelerated. In his first Budget Message—that for 1935, presented January 3, 1934—he tacitly accepted the principle of a balanced "regular" budget, which is made to balance by setting up an "extraordinary" budget for emergency expenditures. He emphasized the fact that, with the exception of debt retirement, the budget estimates for the fiscal year 1935 show a small surplus, but that this budget "does not include any additional expenditure for extraordinary purposes." [21] By making this distinction between the regular and the extraordinary budget, he sought to reconcile his election promise of balanced budgets with the expansion of those expenditures which, it was deemed, relief or recovery made necessary.

Roosevelt's distinction between "General" and "Emer-

[20] Viz.: Commodity Credit Corp., Electric Home and Farm Authority, Executive Council, Export-Import Banks, Fed. Alcohol Control Board, Fed. Board of Vocational Education, Fed. Civil Works Administration, Fed. Co-ordinator of Transportation, Fed. Deposit Insurance Corp., Fed. Emergency Housing Corp., Fed. Emergency Relief Admin., National Emergency Council, Fed. Savings and Loan Ass'n., Federal Surplus Relief Corp., National Industrial Recovery Admin., National Planning Board.

[21] *Budget,* 1935, pp. vi–viii.

gency" expenditures was carried into the *Budget* statement for 1935, in much the same manner as in the *Annual Report* for 1934. Under the heading "General," many items, not previously classified in that manner in the Budget statements, appear: Public Building Construction and Sites, River and Harbor Work, Agricultural Adjustment Administration, Farm Credit Administration, Agricultural Marketing Fund, Distribution of Wheat and Cotton for Relief, Subscription to the Stock of the Federal Land Banks, Interest on the Public Debt, Public Debt Retirements. From this list it is clear that the double budget was still a long way from being a "current" and "capital" budget, or even an ordinary and a "loan" budget.

In 1935 the *Combined Statement* adopted the classification introduced into the *Annual Report* of the previous year; expenditures are divided into "General" and "Emergency." The list of "emergency" expenditures is the same as in the 1934 *Annual Report,* except for the following additions: "Resettlement Administration" and "Chargeable against increment on gold: Melting losses, Payment to Federal Reserve Banks for retirement of national bank notes." Several new Independent Offices were added to the contents.[22]

By 1935, however, the form of the "budget results" table in the *Annual Report* had changed again. The main divisions were "General" and "Recovery and Relief" expenditures. Under the latter head is one main subhead: Federal Public Works Projects. The public works are redivided into two parts: nonrepayable and repayable. This distinction is still another step toward the accurate budgetary procedure. The "repayable" items include the Boulder Dam and other Reclamation Projects; Loans to the Commodity Credit Corporation, to the Joint Stock Land Banks, and Crop and Feed Loans; Public Works Administration; and Subscriptions to

[22] Viz.: Emergency Relief Appropriation Act, Railroad Retirement Board, Resettlement Administration, Rural Electrification Administration, Securities and Exchange Commission, Tennessee Valley Authority, Works Progress Administration. P.W.A. is not listed as a separate category, but appears under "Procurement Division" of the Treasury Department and other headings.

Capital Stock.[23] There is implied in the form of this table an argument that expenditures on income-yielding assets and on recoverable loans ought to be regarded differently from expenditures of other sorts.

This form of presentation of expenditures was adopted by President Roosevelt in his 1936 Budget Message (January 3, 1935). Still clinging to the principle of a balanced ordinary budget, the President pointed out that for the fiscal year 1934 "general receipts . . . approximately equalled the regular expenditures for the year, a fact which should be duly recognized," and noted that the 1936 estimates balanced "except for expenditure to give work to the unemployed." In this same Message attention is drawn to an important budget "reform." Henceforth, self-supporting or self-contained government units were to have their own separate and annexed budgets. There would also be a General Budget Summary, which would show surpluses or deficits from the annexed budgets in addition to the other items. Here we have the adoption of what is essentially the French system of annexed budgets for government corporations. In 1936 the departments so distinguished were the Post Office Department, the Reconstruction Finance Corporation,[24] the Tennessee Valley Authority, and the District of Columbia.

The *Budget* for 1936 divided expenditures into eight main divisions: I. Legislative, Judicial, and Executive; II. Civil Departments and Agencies; III. National Defense; IV. Veterans' Administration; V. Debt Charges; VI. Refunds; VII.

[23] These subscriptions included: Regional Agricultural Credit Corporations (1934), Federal Farm Mortgage Corporations (1934), Federal Intermediate Credit Banks (1935), Federal Land Banks, Home Loan Banks, Home Owners' Loan Corporation, Federal Savings and Loan Associations, Federal Deposit Insurance Corporation.

[24] The R.F.C. budget is subdivided in turn into a Summary Statement and "supporting statements" of the subsidiary organizations through which the R.F.C. operates. These included, in 1936, the Commodity Credit Corporation, the Export-Import Banks of Washington, the Federal Farm Mortgage Corporation, the Federal Home Loan Banks, Federal Housing Administration, Home Owners' Loan Corporation, and the Regional Agricultural Credit Corporation.

Recovery and Relief; VIII. Supplemental Items. Under Recovery and Relief the divisions were: (1) Agricultural Aid; (2) Relief; (3) Public Works; (4) Aid to Home Owners; (5) Miscellaneous; (6) Reconstruction Finance Corporation (from annexed budget); (7) Tennessee Valley Authority (from annexed budget).[25]

The reports of actual expenditures (*Annual Report* and *Combined Statement*) show little change in 1936. The items "Railroad Retirement Act," "Soil Conservation and Domestic Allotment Act," and "Social Security Act" were added to the list of "General" expenditures, and the debated transfer of Emergency Conservation Work to the "General" category from "Recovery and Relief" was made.

In his Budget Message for 1937 (January 3, 1936) Roosevelt reiterated his distinction between a balanced regular budget and an emergency budget. "In looking at the revised estimates for the fiscal year 1936 I am more than pleased to find that we have not only accomplished what I said we would in my Budget Message a year ago but that the results with respect to both expenditures and receipts have surpassed expectations." He included in the category of "regular activities," as opposed to "recovery and relief," "major public works, operations of the C.C.C., and agricultural benefit payments." He also announced that twenty emergency agencies had been brought under the administration of the Director of the Budget. In the *Budget* itself no significant

[25] The *Budget* for 1936 carries with it a "Supporting Schedule No. 3, Part III," in which is presented "Moneys for Recovery and Relief Classified as to Provisions for Repayment." Its outline is as follows: I. Nonrepayable, 1. Grants, aids and expenses: F.E.R.A.; C.W.A.; Emergency Conservation Work; Dept. of Agric. drought relief; P.W.A.; Surplus Relief Corp.; A.A.A.; Land Banks; R.F.C.; Regional Agric. Credit Corps.; Adm. for Industrial Recovery, 2. Federal public works projects; T.V.A.; Public highways; Boulder Canyon; Rivers and Harbors; Other; (Departmental). II. *Loans:* Comm. Credit Corp.; Joint Stock Land Banks; Crop and feed loans; P.W.A.; Emerg. housing; F.H.A.; Subs. homesteads; R.F.C.; Export-Import Banks. III. *Subscriptions to capital stock, etc.:* Production Credit Corps.; Banks for co-ops.; Regional agric. credit corps.; Fed. Farm Mtge Corp.; Fed. Interm. Credit Banks; Fed. Land Banks; Home Loan Banks; Home Owners' Loan Corp.; Fed. Savings and Loan Assns.; F.D.I.C. IV. Unallotted funds (by P.W.A.).

changes were made in 1937. In accordance with the reports of actual expenditure for 1936, the *Budget* for 1937 shifted the Emergency Conservation Work, under the heading Civilian Conservation Corps, from Recovery and Relief to the "General" category. The Boulder Canyon Project was taken out of the "Federal Public Works" division of the nonrepayable recovery and relief expenditures and entered under "Civil Departments and Agencies."

The "budget results" table in the *Annual Report* for 1937 divides expenditures into "Regular operating expenditures," "Public Works," and "Relief"—each with subdivisions; Loans, Subscriptions to Stock and Surplus, Agricultural Adjustment program, Social Security, Railroad Retirement, and Debt Retirement. A more significant classification makes its appearance in the "Estimates of Expenditures" table, which includes a report of actual expenditures for 1937. Under "General and Special Accounts" appear: I. General, II. Recovery and Relief, III. Revolving Funds, IV. Transfers to Trust Accounts (including for the first time the Old Age Reserve Account), V. Debt Retirements. "Trust Accounts, Increment on Gold, etc." are listed under that heading. As will be seen below, the 1939 budget organization is really an elaboration of this kind of formulation.

In the 1938 *Budget,* the "General Public Works Program" is eliminated from the "Civil Departments and Agencies" category and made a main division of its own, along with "Legislative," "Recovery and Relief," etc. "Social Security" is added as a main subdivision. The Federal Deposit Insurance Corporation follows the C.C.C. and Boulder Dam from "Recovery and Relief" to the regular division, under "Legislative and Executive." The Federal Surplus Commodities Corporation was added to the list of nonrepayable recovery and relief expenditures, while the Surplus Relief Corporation, Emergency Conservation Work, and Agricultural Adjustment program no longer appear there.

In his Budget Message for 1939, the President came out more definitely for a reclassification of expenditures. He divided expenditures into four major types: (1) Fixed charges that cannot be reduced by Executive action, e. g., interest on public debt, pensions, contributions to Old Age reserves, etc.; (2) Everyday operations of government that do not afford opportunity for large reductions, e. g., State Department salaries of diplomats, consuls, etc.; (3) "The major effort of the Government to help the economic security of large groups of citizens. . . ." Aids to save farms and homes from foreclosure, relief for unemployed, old-age pensions, etc.; (4) "The final category includes items of public expenditure for capital improvements—such as new highways, new river and harbor projects . . . ," etc.[26]

In his Budget Message for 1940, issued on January 3, 1939, President Roosevelt brought the issue of the capital budget specifically to the fore. He divided federal expenditures into "ordinary" and "extraordinary." The former relate to the "operating expenditures for the normal and continuing functions of government." "The ordinary expenses," said the President, "should be met out of current revenues." And he expressed the hope that in times of prosperity current revenues would so far exceed ordinary expenditures as to produce a "surplus that can be applied against the public debt that the Government must incur in lean years because of extraordinary demands upon it."

The extraordinary expenditures, which are concerned with loans, capital outlays, and relief of need, he deemed to be sufficiently flexible in character as to permit their contraction and expansion as a "partial offset for the rise and fall

[26] The general form of the 1939 *Budget* is unchanged. Among changes in the details, however, were the following: The Commodity Credit Corporation and the Farm Credit Assn. were eliminated from Recovery and Relief, and the Federal Farm Mortgage Corp., the Farm Security Corp., Administrative Expense, Boulder Canyon, Grants to States, Loans to Railroads, and the Resettlement Administration were added. The Commodity Credit Corp., Farm Credit Administration, Loans and Grants to States, Loans to Railroads, Export-Import Banks, and the R.F.C. were added to the Revolving Funds Account. The Old Age Reserve Account, Railroad Retirement Account, Adjusted Service Certificate Fund, Government Employees' Retirement Funds were placed in a new section called "Transfers to Trust Accounts."

in the national income." In this manner they "deal more particularly with the relationship between fiscal policy and the economic welfare of the country." Presumably, in periods of prosperity, these extraordinary expenditures could be greatly reduced. The current revenues, augmented by a rising taxable income, could be expected to yield a surplus which would be applied to debt retirement. The President's Message presupposed not merely highly fluctuating current revenues correlated directly with the business cycle, but also a highly fluctuating volume of extraordinary expenditures correlated inversely with the cycle.

This portion of the Message did not make it definitely clear whether it was expected that the surplus of current revenues during prosperous years shall be adequate to retire all the debt incurred by reason of the extraordinary expenditures made in depression years, or only a part of the debt so incurred. But other portions of the Message would indicate that the latter was intended. Reference was made to "criticism of the Government's practice of including in its budgetary expenditures amounts disbursed for loans or for self-liquidating projects or for other extraordinary capital outlays which increase the wealth of the nation." A change in the method of financing self-sustaining governmental corporations and credit agencies was recommended. An annual appraisal of the assets and liabilities of these corporations or agencies should be made and "any surplus from operations or impairment of capital resulting from losses" should be reflected as receipts or expenditures in the annual Government *Budget*. Thus "the *Budget* would be affected, not when the investment or loan is made, but in the fiscal year when the surplus or loss occurs." Capital expenditures made by these agencies would not result in an increase in the direct government debt. Moreover, it was recommended that the capital outlays incurred on self-liquidating public projects, like Boulder Dam, should likewise not be included in the annual budgetary expenditures. Such expenditures should be capitalized and should occupy a separate category in budgetary reporting. The implication clearly was that for self-liquidating capital outlays of this character a capital budget should be set up, separate and distinct from the extraordinary budget. Thus, in effect, it was suggested that four types of budget be created as follows:

I. Ordinary Budget
II. Extraordinary Budget
III. Capital Budget (including self-liquidating Public Projects and investment in government corporations and agencies)
IV. Annexed Budgets (for government corporations and agencies)

The implication was that both the ordinary and the extraordinary budgets should be financed over an entire cycle from current revenues, though not necessarily in each year in the cycle; and that the capital budget was to be financed by borrowing. According to this theory, the public debt might be permitted to rise *pari passu* with a rise in income-earning assets. Such increase in debt could be expected to liquidate itself over time and would represent no draft on the taxable wealth or income of the community.

The President's Message, however, went a bit farther, but how far is not definitely clear. He did say that our financial statements "should clearly reflect, in appropriate classifications, the amount of government outlays for physical improvements that are not self-liquidating in character." There followed a table which set over against the rise in the public debt during the decade 1931–40 the federal outlays for durable improvements and recoverable loans and investments. Recoverable loans and investments constituted, however, only 3.3 billions of dollars out of the total so expended. It is clear, therefore, that, in so far as the public debt had risen by reason of capital outlays, 80 per cent was due to expenditures on non-self-liquidating projects.

It is with respect to the rise in the public debt incident to these outlays that intelligent debate begins. The President did not commit himself. He suggested that a catalogue of such outlays at least helps to appraise the economic significance of our rising public debt. With respect to these outlays, at any rate, the money had not been thrown "out of the window or into the sea." The President insisted that we have been "buying real values with it." But he did not commit himself to the thesis that the public debt may properly rise commensurate with the growth of this type of public wealth. Indeed, he emphatically asserted that he was not suggesting "an ordinary budget which is always balanced and an extraordinary budget which is always unbalanced." Not only should the ordinary budget at all times be met from current revenues, but in good times any extraordinary expenditures which it was deemed necessary to make should, according to the Message, be met from taxes, and, in addition, a surplus should be produced in order to retire some of the debt incurred during depression. It is not clear, however, that the President advocated a complete balancing of ordinary and extraordinary expenditures over the cycle period, even after self-liquidating capital expenditures and governmental corporation outlays had been deducted from the "extraordinary" expenditure category. What can definitely be said is that he envisaged that extraordinary expenditures on non-self-liquidating public works and on unemployment relief shall, over the cycle, be met *in part* from current revenues.

Over the entire decade 1931–40, according to the President's table, total ordinary expenditures amounted to $40,515 millions and total current revenues to $41,033 millions. Except for the fiscal years 1932, 1933, and 1936, current revenues exceeded ordinary expenditures. But, for the entire decade, current revenues contributed only half a billion dollars to the total extraordinary expenditures of $27,797 millions. Of this total, $16,231 millions was for unemployment relief, $7,952 millions for public works, and $3,339 millions for loans and subscriptions to stock, etc. The unemployment relief total, however, included an estimated $2,687 millions of durable improvements constructed by the W.P.A. If this be added to the public works, loans, and stock subscription items, we get a total of $13,978 millions for public works and investments. There remains the almost exactly equal figure of $13,544 millions for unemployment relief expenditures of a sort which have left no material assets behind. According to these estimates, we have "something to show" for one half of the extraordinary expenditures; the rest went to relieve distress but added nothing to the public wealth.

In view of the stress laid on durable assets, it is important to note that the mere accumulation of tangible wealth is not an adequate criterion of the economic justification of public expenditures. Expenditures on public health and education may be more valuable than the construction of durable projects.

The trend toward reorganization of the federal budget to take account more adequately of the distinction between general expenditures and "special" expenditures of one sort or another has existed throughout most of the depression period, and the President's 1940 Budget Message represented a culmination of this trend. The time has now been reached when there should be undertaken a systematic budget reform.

Part Three

FISCAL POLICY AND FULL USE OF RESOURCES

Chapter XI

THE CYCLICAL CONSUMPTION-INCOME PATTERN

ONCE a revival is started, a cumulative process begins in which investment and consumption interact upon and stimulate one another—the first increment of investment induces an increase in consumption and this, in turn, induces further investment. This cumulative process, however, unless continually reinforced by spontaneous or independent investment, is likely to peter out rather quickly. This follows from the fact that a considerable part of the new income generated by investment is not used for consumption. Thus, the induced consumption expenditures tend continually to run down, and so, in turn, the induced investment slows up until the whole process comes to a standstill and thereafter rapidly develops into a cumulative downturn. The cumulative downward process similarly comes to a halt because, with lower incomes, consumption falls less rapidly than income and so offers an increasing resistance to a further decline.

The cumulative process, therefore, does not offer a valid theoretical basis upon which to predicate either a continued upward movement or a continued downward spiral. And it is equally precarious to pin one's faith upon the cumulative process to produce a sustained recovery. The recovery is not likely to reach any very high level, nor to be maintained for any considerable period of time, without the injection of a continuous flow of spontaneous or independent investment.

It is true that expenditures on durable consumers' goods

(especially automobiles) not only help to initiate an upturn, but also help to sustain the recovery as long as investment outlays are sufficiently large to maintain income at a high level. But there is not likely to be any important decline in the consumption of durables or of consumption in general until a decline in income has already set in. Whenever investment falls off, however, employment and income decline, and the decline in income is likely to bring about quickly a sharp reduction in the purchase of durable consumers' goods and more gradually a decline in consumption in general.

Thus, we must look to the continued flow of investment expenditures to sustain prosperity. Whenever this stops, income falls off, not only by the amount of the decline in investment expenditures, but also by reason of the induced decline in consumption. While consumption and investment both play a role in initiating recovery and in the cumulative process, it is peculiarly spontaneous or anticipatory investment which must carry on if a high level of income and employment is to be maintained. In the absence of governmental support, on a scale hitherto not realized, booms inevitably die sooner or later a natural death, because the investment flow dries up. It dries up because, after some years of large capital outlays, investment opportunities become temporarily exhausted.

A society so constituted that its consumption habitually falls, by a considerable percentage, below its income at reasonably full employment levels requires a large continued flow of new investment to keep it going at full activity. Thus, it is important not merely to inquire into a country's investment opportunities, and how fully these have already been satisfied, but also what proportion of its income is customarily consumed. The relation of consumption to income is apparently a highly stable function and certainly one of the most important in the whole field of economics.

The Consumption Function

A schedule giving the amount of consumption at various income levels is precisely analagous to the ordinary demand schedules for commodities. The consumption-income schedule and the ordinary demand schedule both show the functional relation between two variables, the former the relation of consumption to income, and the latter the relation of the amount demanded to price. The functional relation of consumption to income may be designated briefly by the phrase "the consumption function."

The relationship of percentage changes in demand to percentage changes in price may be described by the phrase "price elasticity of demand," while the relationship of consumption to income may be described by the phrase "income elasticity of consumption." A commodity demand schedule may, of course, also be set up in terms of the relation of quantity taken to income. The shape of such a derived curve may be described as the "income elasticity of demand" for a particular commodity. A summation or aggregate of all such individual commodity demand schedules for consumption goods of all sorts would, of course, give us the aggregate income-consumption schedule, which we are here discussing.

The income elasticity of consumption is a property or characteristic of the consumption function. Other properties of the consumption function are as follows: (1) the marginal propensity to consume and (2) the average propensity to consume.

The marginal propensity to consume may be defined as the percentage of an additional increment of income which the public wishes to consume; it may be designated as follows: $\frac{\Delta C}{\Delta Y}$, in which C is consumption and Y is income. The average propensity to consume may be defined as the proportion of any given aggregate income which the public wishes to consume; it is the ratio of consumption to income at any given income level and may be designated as follows: $\frac{C}{Y}$.

Both the marginal propensity to consume and the average propensity to consume may, of course, vary (as is also true of elasticity) at different income levels. But they need not both change in the same direction. Indeed, the average propensity to consume may, for example, increase steadily as income falls, while the marginal propensity to consume might remain constant at all income levels. This is illustrated in the table and chart on page 229.

Keynes' "propensity to consume" is merely another term for the consumption-income schedule or the consumption function. Keynes' terminology is perhaps more likely to be misunderstood, especially by the nontechnical reader, who is likely to conclude that "propensity to consume" means merely a *desire* to consume. On the contrary, it represents something quite specific with respect to *action*. The "propensity-to-consume" schedule indicates precisely the action which the public is prepared to take with respect to consumption purchases at various income levels, just as the demand schedule for individual commodities indicates the amount of the commodity which the public is prepared to buy at various prices. At times, the phrase "propensity to consume" is a peculiarly convenient expression to use, but more often the phrases "consumption-income schedule," or, more briefly, "consumption function," will be used in this book.

With respect to both the demand function and the consumption function, it is, of course, true that they are hypothetical in the respect that the amount which will be demanded in the former case, or the amount which will be expended on consumption in the latter case, is dependent upon a single variable—price in the former instance and income in the latter. It is assumed that everything else, not inherently connected with the change in price in the one case or the change in income in the other, remains constant. Thus, with respect to the demand curve, it is assumed that the tastes and relative preferences of consumers for different commodities remain unaltered; and, with respect to the consumption-income curve, it is assumed that the thriftiness

A = Consumption Function with respect to which both the marginal propensity to consume and the average propensity to consume are unity at all income levels.
B = Consumption Function with respect to which the marginal propensity to consume and the average propensity to consume are as given in the following table:

Y	$\frac{C}{Y}$	$\frac{\Delta C}{\Delta Y}$
56	1.036	0.667
62	1.000	0.667
68	0.971	0.667
80	0.925	0.667

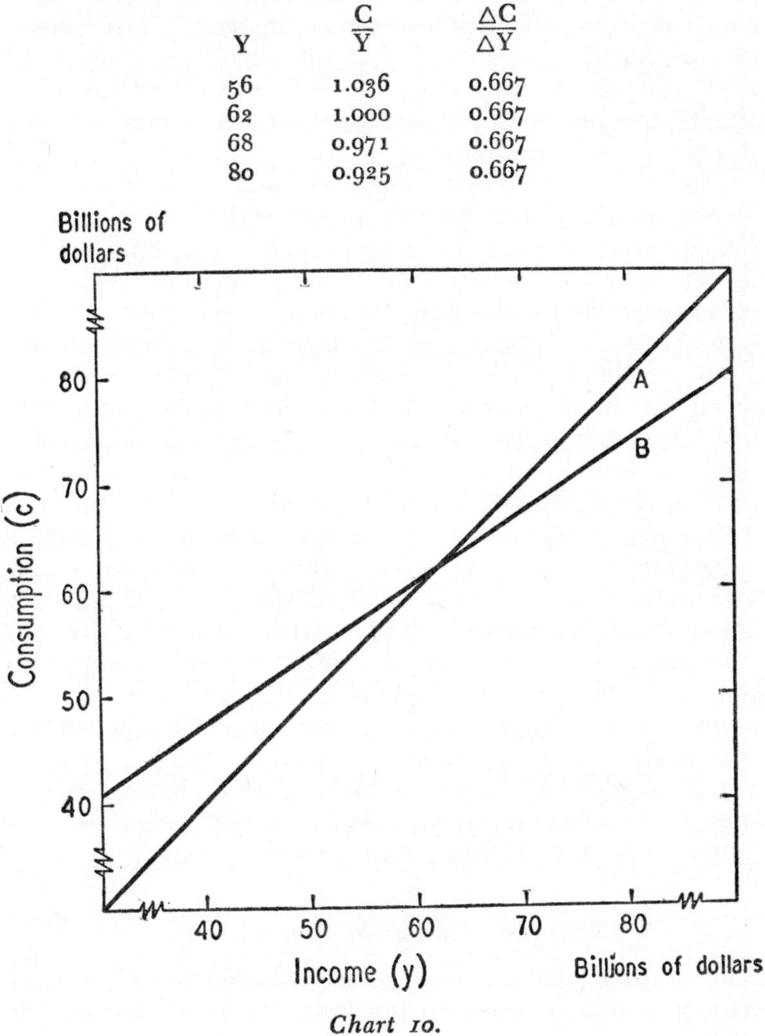

Chart 10.

of the people remains unaltered. A shift in the demand curve from left to right, for example, represents a genuine change in demand in the respect that the preferences for different types of commodities have been fundamentally changed, and similarly a shift in the consumption-income curve indicates a change in the thriftiness of the community. Thus, with a decrease in thriftiness the consumption-income curve would shift upward precisely as an increase in the demand for a specific commodity would be represented by an upward shift in the whole demand curve.

The curve, or schedule, represents the relation of one variable to the other in a "period" within which all other variables are assumed to remain constant. Thus, the consumption-income schedule, or the consumption function, represents only one single relationship—changes in consumption as income changes. Hypothetical schedules of this character are, of course, heroic abstractions. They are unrealistic in the respect that they seek to isolate from the multitude of factors which are constantly changing in a highly dynamic world a single variable which is regarded as a significant determinant in order to measure the influence of this variable upon the dependent variable. Perhaps the best illustration of such a hypothetical schedule, in so far as the consumption function is concerned, would be one purporting to show the different amounts which a given individual with certain definite, unchanging psychological attitudes would expend on consumption goods in the event that his income should change. In point of fact, of course, as his income changes, other things change also, including his psychological attitudes. A severely heroic abstraction which precludes all such changes in psychological attitudes may frequently be very useful in economic analysis, even though it is somewhat unrealistic.

Statistical Studies of Consumption

A statistical analysis more realistic, though less rigorous in its logic, might proceed on the following assumptions: that human beings, in general, are fundamentally alike when viewed in rather large statistical aggregates; that, therefore, the expenditures on consumption goods by individuals with an income of one thousand dollars represent, in some sense, a typical behavior; and, similarly, the expenditures of an appropriate sample of individuals with an income of $1,500, $2,000, $2,500, etc., may be regarded as typical. The assumption may, moreover, be made that a typical individual who expends a certain amount on consumption goods when his income is $1,000 would, if his income were increased to $1,500, $2,000, $2,500, etc., expend on consumption goods the amount which individuals in those groups typically spend. This involves, of course, the assumption that the typical individuals at the various income levels are fundamentally alike and differ in their behavior only by reason of the differences in their incomes.

An illustration of this type of statistical analysis may be found in the report of the National Resources Planning Board on Consumer Expenditures in the United States.[1] From the budgets examined it is possible to prepare a schedule showing the amounts consumed by different income classes, as is done in Table XX on page 232.

On the basis of such a table, a schedule can be constructed showing the consumption of society as a whole at various hypothetical income levels. Imagine that the income of each group suddenly rose to a higher level. The individuals of each group would now react in their consumption expenditures, it is assumed, according to the consumption-income schedules statistically ascertained in the actual budget studies. Thus, in the event that the one-thousand-dollar income class should experience a jump in income to the fifteen-thousand-dollar class, they would presumably react in their consumption expenditures just as the fifteen-thousand-dollar income class had in fact reacted, according to the inquiries made. On this assumption, a table was calculated giving the consump-

1 National Resources Planning Board, *Consumer Expenditures in the United States,* U.S. Government Printing Office, 1939.

TABLE XX

Income Head	*Consumption as Per Cent of Income*
Under $500	149.4
$500–750	112.8
$750–1,000	104.6
$1,000–1,250	100.6
$1,250–1,500	99.0
$1,500–1,750	96.5
$1,750–2,000	95.0
$2,000–2,500	91.8
$2,500–3,000	88.4
$3,000–4,000	84.4
$4,000–5,000	79.4
$5,000–10,000	70.5
$10,000–15,000	61.1
$15,000–20,000	60.1
$20,000 and over	49.3

Derived from National Resources Committee, *Consumer Expenditures in the United States*, 1939, p. 20.

tion for the economy as a whole at varying total income levels, ranging from $60 billions to $80 billions. This schedule is given in Table XXI.

TABLE XXI

National Income (billions)	*Consumption as Per Cent of Income*
$50.0	93.1
60.0	89.8
70.0	87.2
80.0	85.1

Table derived from National Resources Committee—*Consumer Expenditures in the United States*, 1939, p. 167.

What realistic interpretation might be made of such a table? Let us suppose that the national income will, in fact, rise by $10 billions per decade over the next half century. By the aid of such tables, would it be reasonable to assume that one could determine approximately the amount of consumption decade after decade from such a consumption-income schedule as the kind referred to above? Obviously, such a conclusion would be unwarranted. Were the schedule in question applied to such data, it would appear that, as the national income rose decade by decade, a smaller and smaller percentage of the total income would be consumed and a larger and larger percentage saved. Now we know in general, from past experience, that this has not happened. We know that, as incomes in all groups have risen, changes in the standard of living have forced upward the minimum consumption requirements, so that always the lower income groups, despite the fact that their incomes were much higher than fifty or one hundred years ago, still consumed all or even more than all of their incomes, their incomes being often supplemented by gifts and by borrowing. Historically, it appears probable—though the data are certainly inconclusive—that as the national income has risen secularly from decade to decade, approximately the same proportion of the income has been consumed.[2] This appears to be true for the United States down to the present time and for England, at any rate until the time of the first World War. Fundamental institutional changes may, of course, alter this relationship, but there is no conclusive evidence that, with the long-run secular rise in per capita income, any substantial increase has occurred in the relative proportion of the total income consumed and saved.

It appears evident, therefore, that the typical consumption-income schedule (which shows a tendency for the ratio of consumption to income to fall as income rises) does not hold for the long-run secular change in real income. The relation indicated holds only when large changes in income occur

[2] Preliminary estimates by S. S. Kuznets of capital formation in the United States during the past six decades, soon to be published, support this conclusion.

within a relatively short period of time. Now, in point of fact, this is precisely what happens in the violent fluctuations of income in the business cycle.

The fluctuations in consumption relative to income in the various phases of the cycle follow a more or less definite cycle pattern. The volume of consumption is determined not merely by the size of the income, but also, in part, by the particular stage in the cycle at which this income is received. Thus, the consumption is, within the cycle period, a function not merely of the size of the income, but also, to some extent, of the particular phase of the cycle in which the income occurs. Moreover, the cyclical changes in income occur for each income group. Each group experiences marked changes in income within the cycle period. The change in aggregate consumption springs from changes in the income received by all of the various income groups. This, however, is something very different from the differential consumption behavior of different income groups at any one point of time. For all these reasons, it cannot be assumed that scheddules derived from the amount consumed by various income groups at any one period—for example, 1935–36, as in the study of the National Resources Committee—could be used as a basis from which one might calculate the changes in consumption which would follow from cyclical fluctuations of income.

Cyclical Consumption-income Pattern

Fortunately, however, as we have indicated in an earlier chapter, we now have data indicating the relation of consumption to income in the various stages of two complete major cycles from 1921 to 1939, inclusive. These data give us, therefore, a fairly accurate pattern of the relation of consumption to income within the business cycle period. This pattern we may designate as the *cyclical pattern of consumption with respect to income,* or, more briefly, the *cyclical consumption-income pattern.* It should be emphasized that we are concerned with *cyclical* changes in consumption relative to income. We are not concerned with an abstract proposition about the behavior of consumption relative to income in general. The proposition is that from one phase of the business cycle to another, one can detect a pattern in the changing relationship of consumption to income. It is believed that this cyclical pattern of consumption with respect to income is of fundamental significance.

The relation of consumption to income (as measured in current dollars) for the two major cycles from 1921 to 1939 is shown in the scatter of points in Chart 11.[3] In the appendix to this chapter is presented a statistical analysis of the functional relation of consumption to income corrected for price changes and population growth.

It will be noted from the chart that, at very low income levels, consumption exceeds income. This means that disinvestment (consumption of part of the stock of capital goods) is going on. At around the $50 billion income level, consumption equals income. Judging from the raw, uncorrected data here used, one gets the impression that, at low income levels ($40 to $60 billions), consumption increases relatively more slowly as income rises than is the case at higher income levels ($65 to $85 billions). In part, this may be accounted for by the fact that in the early stages of recovery investment leads the way (see Chapter II), while consumption, being largely induced, follows with a lag. Once this lag is overcome, consumption rises more nearly in proportion to increases in income.

It is significant that the years in which the ratio of consumption to income is relatively low are the more prosperous years—1923, 1925, 1926, 1929, 1937, and 1939. From the general character of the consumption function it could be expected that consumption would be relatively low in relation to income (or, in other words, savings relatively high) in peak years. This is due in no small measure, no doubt, to

[3] The data for 1921–34 are from S. S. Kuznets, *National Income and Capital Formation, 1919–35;* and for 1935–39 from the Department of Commerce and the National Resources Planning Board.

the high corporate profits of such years, a large proportion of which is saved and retained in the business.

Apparently, the income level is very important as a determinant of the proportion of income consumed, and also

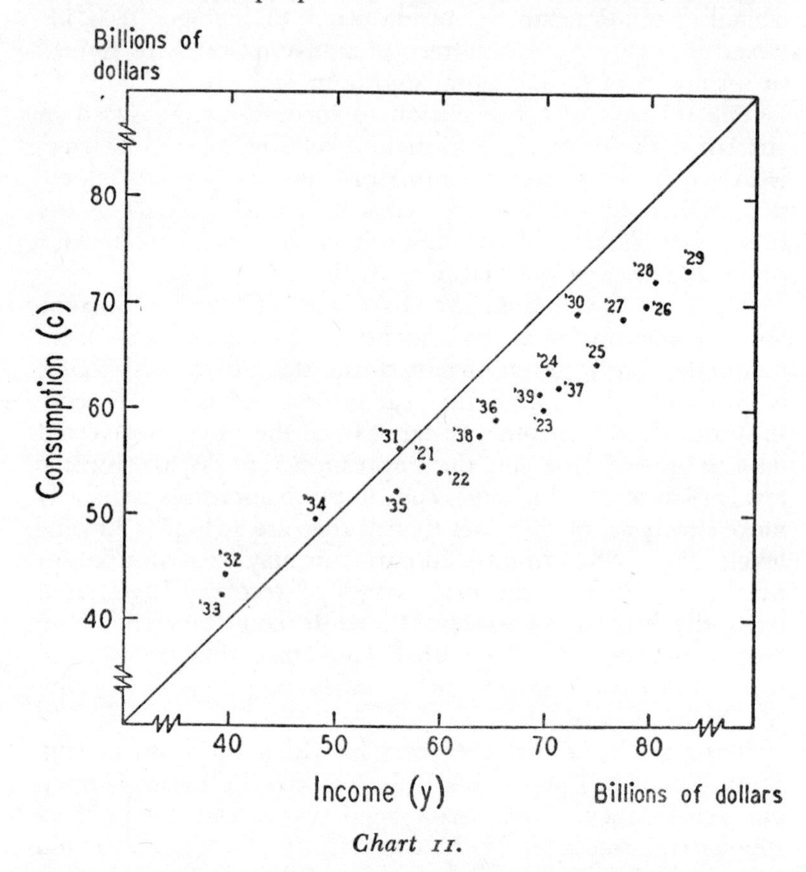

Chart 11.

The Relation of Consumption to Income

the position in the cycle. Thus, at the lower turning point (1921–22) in the first cycle 92.2 per cent of the income was consumed, while at the second lower turning point (1932–33) 109.6 per cent of the income was consumed. It requires, apparently, an extremely severe deflation, such as that in the early thirties, to bring about aggregate dissaving or disinvestment. In more normal depressions, even at the bottom, income exceeds consumption, and there takes place a considerable amount of net investment, though much less than at the peak of the boom.

During the seven relatively prosperous years 1923–29, the proportion of income consumed averaged 88.0 per cent. In 1937 and 1939, 88.1 per cent of income was consumed. The proportion of income consumed varied very little in any one year from the general average of 88.1 per cent for all these nine relatively good years. For example, the per cent of income consumed was 88.2 in 1923–24, 88.5 in 1927, and 88.0 in 1929. Such variation as there was, was probably due mainly to the rather volatile item of corporate profits and the related item of corporate savings. In the less favorable years, such as 1924, 1928, and 1938, the proportion of income saved fell off, or, in other words, the ratio of consumption to income rose. The percentage of income consumed in these years was 90.3, 89.8, and 90.6 respectively. In general, one may conclude from these data that, once a fairly high income level is reached, as for the nine years referred to, approximately the same proportion of the income is consumed.[4]

In the fairly high income years, then, about 88 per cent of the national income was consumed, and 12 per cent was saved. Gross savings for the same years amounted to 22.8 per cent of the gross national product.[5] This consumption-income pattern at relatively high income levels appears to be fairly constant. It is deeply rooted in the customs, habits, and traditions of the people, and in institutions which are not easily

[4] This conclusion holds also if one defines consumption more narrowly by excluding from this category durable consumers' goods. So defined, the proportion of income consumed averaged 76.3 in the high years, 1923–29. The figure was 76.8 in 1923–24, 77.1 per cent in 1927, 76.1 per cent in 1929, and 77.2 in 1937 and 1939.

[5] Gross national product = national income plus replacement investment expenditures. Gross savings = net savings plus depreciation, depletion, and obsolescence allowances.

changed and, indeed, very frequently not desirable to change.

In order to maintain a fairly high level of income, it is therefore necessary, as long as this cyclical consumption-income pattern persists, to expend about 22 per cent of the gross national product on real investment (new and replacement). For a $110 billion gross national product [6] (which full employment could currently make possible at a price level 10 to 15 points above the 1940 level), this means about $24 billions per annum. The difficulty of finding investment outlets for so large a volume of expenditures is a major modern problem. As long as the current consumption-income pattern persists, the economy is geared to high investment. It is the consumption-income pattern which explains why it is necessary to maintain investment at a high level in order to achieve full employment.

Stability of Consumption-income Pattern

The question is frequently asked: Why lay so much emphasis upon investment per se? Why not expand consumption? This is a perfectly sensible question. Indeed, it may well be that we ought to encourage consumption. But the fact is that the ratio of consumption to income is not easily increased. Indeed, there is reason to believe that we are right in the midst of institutional developments—structural changes in our economy—which tend, for a time at least, to lower the ratio of consumption to income and to increase the proportion of income saved.

Consider, first, the great development of life insurance—a development in itself thoroughly sound and certainly deserving of public encouragement and support. Life insurance has grown to gigantic proportions in a single generation. In 1880 the assets of life insurance companies amounted to less than $500 millions. Thirty years later in 1910, they amounted to only $3.9 billions. Then came the period of rapid growth.

[6] This would yield a national income of $98 billions. Gross national product minus replacement capital expenditures equals national income.

By 1940 the assets amounted to over $30 billions. In 1937 the income of life insurance companies from premiums and investments amounted to about $5.3. Benefit payments were $2.4 and expense outlays $1.0 billions, leaving around $1.9 billions annually for new investment.

Eventually life insurance will reach financial maturity and will pay out year by year, in benefits and costs, amounts equal to premium receipts and income from investments. When this point is reached, individuals will be able to save by the life insurance method without such individual savings resulting in any net aggregate savings. But as long as life insurance is in process of rapid growth, large reserves are being built up and an annual flow of quasi-compulsory saving is effected. We are currently just at the height of this development, and this is a factor tending to raise the savings-income ratio.

It is a striking fact that just at the point when life insurance savings were accumulating at the maximum rate a vast social insurance program was introduced, based largely on the private insurance principle of accumulation of reserves. Some modifications were made in 1939 in the original plan, reducing materially the probable future size of the old-age reserve account. Nevertheless, large accumulations have already been made and are currently in prospect for some years to come both in the Unemployment Trust Fund and in the Old Age and Survivor's Insurance Trust Fund. In the four years 1937 to 1940, inclusive, the accumulations in these funds proceeded at an average annual rate of $1.0 billions, the accumulations at the end of 1940 amounting to $4.0 billions. Thus, on top of annual life insurance savings there has suddenly been injected this important new factor adding to the flow of savings and thereby tending to reduce the ratio of consumption to income.[7]

[7] It is, of course, impossible to predict the rate at which these funds will accumulate in future. The act relating to both unemployment compensation and old-age and survivor's insurance is likely to be further amended with respect to contributions, benefit payments, and coverage. Moreover, changed economic conditions will affect the rate of accumulation. Estimates, based on

Another institutional development of relatively recent origin affecting the flow of annual savings is the introduction of amortization in real-estate loans and mortgages. Only during the last decade has anything systematic and of general application been achieved along this line in this country. From the standpoint of sound finance, it constitutes an important and, indeed, necessary reform. The real-estate mortgage situation at the end of the twenties was thoroughly bad and contributed to the deflation of the early thirties. If each real-estate mortgage had been amortized year by year to manageable proportions, the process of debt liquidation would have been very much less drastic. From this severe lesson something of value was learned. Real-estate mortgages now usually require an annual payment sufficiently large to cover interest charges and to retire the principal within a given period, ranging from, say, ten to thirty years. This development, already widely adopted, was supported and extended by the provision in the 1935 Banking Act providing that banks may not make real-estate loans having a maturity of five years or more, unless such loans are amortized according to specific requirements. Insurance companies have, in general, adopted a similar practice. And the expansion of mortgage financing (a) through federal mortgage agencies, such as the Home Owners' Loan Corporation, the Federal Farm Mortgage Corporation, and the Federal Land Banks, and (b) under the auspices of mortgage insurance agencies, such as the Federal Housing Administration, has contributed greatly to the use of the amortization device. Real-estate mortgage debt, farm and urban, amounts to around $35 billions. The amortization payments on this debt volume may quite possibly amount to around $1.5 billions per annum. This relatively new institutional arrangement is a factor of considerable magnitude and importance, adding to the flow of quasi-compulsory savings.

---

the artificial assumption that benefits and tax rates as provided in the act as amended in 1939 will continue and that economic conditions will remain the same, have been made indicating net accumulations in the Old Age and Survivor's Trust Fund of $5.7 billions by 1950.

Finally, note must be taken of the effect upon the gross savings stream of the growth of net corporate saving in the form of (a) depreciation reserves, and (b) retained earnings. The spread of the corporate form of organization and the progressive development of accounting procedures have, in the last few decades, raised charges to depreciation reserves to a level which makes this item by far the largest single source of funds available for investment.[8] The allocation of funds to depreciation reserves in 1923–29 amounted to $5.5 billions per annum and in 1936–37 to $4.6 billions.[9]

Over and above the depreciation and depletion charges are the net retained earnings of the corporate system as a whole. While the former are intended for replacement expenditures, the latter constitute an important source of funds for the financing of net additions to plant and equipment. In 1923–29 corporate net retained earnings (account being taken of corporate losses) amounted annually to $2.4 billions and in 1936–37 to $1.1 billions.[10] Thus, the internal sources of funds (depreciation, depletion and net retained earnings combined) averaged $7.9 billions per annum in 1923–29 and $5.7 billions per annum in 1936–37. How important these internal sources were for the financing of producers' fixed capital can be seen from the fact that expenditures on plant and equipment averaged $8.7 billions in 1923–29 and $6.7 billions in 1936–37.[11]

Retained earnings in 1923–29 for all corporations reporting net income in the United States amounted to 41.3 per

[8] Charges to depreciation reserves do not, of course, contribute to the flow of *net* savings. They do constitute the most important part of gross savings. They finance replacement expenditures and, not infrequently, especially in the case of corporations with new plant and equipment recently constructed, are even available to finance expansion.

[9] Solomon Fabricant, *Capital Consumption and Adjustment,* National Bureau of Economic Research, 1938, pp. 32, 33, and 38; and Charts and Tables on Savings and Investment, T.N.E.C. Hearings, 1939. See also Ruth P. Mack, *The Flow of Business Funds and Consumer Purchasing Power,* Columbia University Press, 1941.

[10] Department of Commerce, and *Statistics of Income.*

[11] *Federal Reserve Bulletin,* September, 1939, and estimates by George Terborgh.

cent of net profit.[12] In contrast, the per cent of undistributed profits in Great Britain in 1924–29 averaged only 20.1 per cent.[13] The difference between the two countries is striking. A part of the explanation of this divergence in corporate practice may probably be found in the difference in the rate of expansion in the two countries. Population increased fifteenfold in the United States during the nineteenth century and only fourfold in England. The growth of corporate enterprise and capital investment has been very much more rapid in this country. It is, therefore, not unnatural that our corporations should have formed the habit of reinvesting a large percentage of net profits—much larger than in countries experiencing a slower extensive growth. And once this has become established practice, it cannot be expected that the policy would quickly be changed, even though a slowing down of extensive expansion justified the retention of a smaller proportion of earnings.

Other sources of investment funds, in addition to those already noted, are the savings of public bodies (sinking funds and the like), individual savings which flow into commercial and savings banks, building and loan associations, individual savings directly invested in stocks, bonds, and mortgages, and the savings of farmers, unincorporated business, and home-owners used directly to purchase real investment goods.

Individual versus Aggregate Savings

Question may now be raised with respect to the main causes of the rather violent shifts in the volume of aggregate savings from depression years to years of relatively high prosperity, as revealed in the schedule of consumption in relation to income in the various phases of the cycle.[14] In answer to

[12] Treasury estimates, Hearings before the Committee on Finance, U.S. Senate, 74th Congress, 2nd Session, on HR 12395, p. 18.

[13] Colin Clark, *National Income and Outlay*, p. 187.

[14] Net savings = Income – Consumption. It should be noted that violent shifts in the aggregate of savings do not mean, as some have supposed, that the propensity to save is unstable. Under a stable consumption function, savings may fluctuate violently as income fluctuates.

this question, it is necessary to stress the fact that the most important cause of this rather violent fluctuation in the volume of aggregate savings is the fact that in depression years such a large part of the individual savings stream is used not to purchase capital goods, but to cover losses. Thus, it is necessary to distinguish between (a) the stream of individual savings which flow annually into the various savings channels (life insurance, building and loan associations, savings banks, and the like), and (b) the aggregate realized savings which remain after account has been taken of the losses incident to the decline in expenditures on investment goods and the consequent fall in income. On the other side, an important part of the explanation of the large aggregate savings in good years must be found in the high level of profits, a large part of which go into savings, either via retained corporate earnings or via individual savings from increased dividends. Thus, business profits and losses account, in large measure, for the high realized aggregate savings of prosperous years and the low aggregate savings of depression years.

A large part of the flow of individual savings, especially in the form of life insurance premiums and savings accounts, actually increased despite the fall in income in the great depression. Thus, the premiums paid to insurance companies increased from $2,235 millions per annum in 1927–29 to $2,580 millions in 1931–33, while savings in mutual savings banks rose from $8,537 millions to $9,945 millions. Account must, however, be taken of the fact that a considerable proportion of insurance policy holders, suffering heavy property losses particularly in the securities market, made large withdrawals on their cash surrender values. Nevertheless, most of them probably continued to pay their annual premiums out of current income. In general, the more steadily employed part of the population, who also hold the bulk of the insurance policies, are likely to continue to save at very nearly the accustomed rate and to cut expenditures on durable consumers' goods and, to some extent, even on other consumption goods as income declines. The fact that they save a larger proportion of their incomes in depression years as income declines does not, however, in any way invalidate the Keynesian thesis that individuals tend to save a larger absolute amount when income again rises. Moreover, if we disregard the cyclical fluctuation of income and consider only a change in income *status,* it will usually be true that some part of the net increment of income will be saved. Indeed, we can go much farther and assert with considerable confidence that normally a larger proportion of a larger income will be saved.

Business profits and losses are the volatile part of the national income (income produced). Thus the net income of incorporated businesses and of unincorporated enterprises represented 25.1 per cent of total income in 1929, and only 4.2 per cent in 1932. On the other hand, the compensation of employees, interest, net rents, and royalties, together constituted 74.9 per cent of total income in 1929 and 95.8 per cent in 1932. When, however, business savings and losses are left out of the picture, and attention is concentrated upon the income receipts of *individuals,* a fairly high stability in the percentage distribution appears.

The distribution of income receipts of individuals—property owners, employed persons, and entrepreneurs—changes only moderately in the cycle. Employed persons averaged, in the more prosperous years 1929 and 1936–37, 66.2 per cent of the income receipts of individuals. In 1930–33, they received 64.5 per cent. Property owners averaged 18.3 per cent in 1929 and 1936–37. In the depression years 1930–33 they received 19.5 per cent. Entrepreneurs received 15.4 per cent in the good years and 16.0 per cent in the depression years. Thus, there was a slight advantage in favor of the property owner and entrepreneur in the depression. Moreover, of the employed workers, the salaried persons fared better than wage earners in the depression, but by 1935 the predepression relation of salaries to wages was restored.

With respect to property owners, those drawing income largely from dividends lost ground, while those dependent on interest gained. Dividends amounted to 7.6 per cent in 1929–30, began to lose ground in 1931, and fell to an average of 5.3 per cent of total individual income receipts during the worst depression years. By 1936–37 the 7.6 level was again reached. Interest receipts gained in the depression, rising from 6.7 per cent of the total in 1929 to 10.7 per cent in 1932–33, and again falling to 6.9 per cent in 1937.

TABLE XXII

Percentage Distribution of Income Paid Out, by Type of Payment[15]

Year	*Total Income Paid Out*	*Total Compensation of Employees*	*Entrepreneurial Withdrawals*	*Earnings from Property* *Total*	*Net Rents and Royalties*	*Dividends and Int.*	*Div. and Int.* *Dividends*	*Interest*
1929	100.0	65.8	15.6	18.6	4.3	14.3	7.4	6.7
1930	100.0	64.8	15.9	19.3	3.7	15.6	7.8	7.5
1931	100.0	64.5	16.0	19.5	3.3	16.2	6.9	8.8
1932	100.0	63.7	16.3	20.0	3.2	16.8	5.6	10.7
1933	100.0	64.8	15.9	19.3	3.1	16.2	4.8	10.8
1934	100.0	65.9	15.6	18.5	3.2	15.3	5.4	9.7
1935	100.0	66.3	15.9	17.8	3.4	14.4	5.4	8.8
1936	100.0	66.2	15.3	18.5	3.6	14.9	7.5	7.5
1937	100.0	66.7	15.3	18.0	3.6	14.4	7.7	6.9
1938	100.0	67.3	16.1	16.6	3.6	13.0	5.7	7.4

Summarizing the effects of shifts in income distribution upon individual savings, it is probable that interest receivers are able to save more in depression, while dividend receivers are compelled by low incomes to save less. Wage and salary earners who are fortunate enough to retain employment probably seek to maintain their savings. Some are able to increase their savings, while others, by reason of property losses, reduction in earnings, and the necessity of giving aid to relatives, are compelled to curtail their savings. Wage and salary earners who suffer unemployment are compelled to use up their past accumulations.

On balance, the flow of institutional and individual thrift streams probably declines in deep depressions in which there

[15] From Survey of Current Business, June, 1939.

is a severe fall in income. In a moderate depression it is by no means certain that this is the case. At any rate, it appears probable that individual and institutional savings of the character referred to above fall less than the aggregate income receipts of individuals. We know, however, that the aggregate realized savings of society as a whole decline relative to national income when the aggregate income falls to low levels; and, conversely, rises proportionally more rapidly than income, at least until the income reaches a moderately high level. Since this relationship does not appear to hold for a large part of individual savings and individual income receipts, the explanation must be sought mainly in the violent fluctuations of business profits and business losses. Business profits supplement individual savings in prosperous years, and business losses offset individual savings in depression years so as to produce violent swings in aggregate or realized savings. Thus, the ratio of aggregate savings to income is low in low income years and high in high income years, as revealed in our cyclical savings-income pattern.

The attention of economists has recently been directed to the high stability of the per cent of value product of manufacturing paid out to wage earners, despite violent fluctuations in output and prices. Payrolls = Employment × Wage Rates, and Value of Product = Output × Prices. In general, wage rates fluctuate somewhat less than wholesale prices, while employment fluctuates more than output. Thus, the ratio of payrolls to value of product remains relatively stable in spite of extreme fluctuations in income. It appears, therefore, that the fluctuations in business profits are not mainly due to fluctuations in payrolls. Labor cost per dollar of sales remains remarkably stable. The fluctuations in profits are due mainly to the inability to adjust overhead costs to fluctuations in sales.

When value of sales falls off (due to a combination of decline in unit price and quantum sold—both more or less subject to control), the employer apparently is able, in general, to make sufficient adjustments so that payrolls remain, for the economy as a whole, approximately a constant ratio of value of product. This relatively constant ratio is the result of the interrelation of various factors. If in the face of a declining national income employers are confronted with rigid wage rates, they are then restricted in possible adjustments to price changes, changes in output, changes in employment, and changes in efficiency. If all employers are confronted with rigid wage rates, it may be expected that the national income will fall less than would otherwise be the case, since wage receipts constitute so large a proportion of total income. If, however, wage rates are not rigid, income will fall more rapidly. On the other side, however, the employer has available in these circumstances an additional method of adjustment, namely, the reduction of wage rates in his particular shop. This reduction is his answer to the general wage reduction and the consequent further fall in income in the country as a whole.

The fluctuation in the ratio of aggregate realized savings to aggregate income from depression to prosperity is mainly the result of large fluctuations in business profits and business losses. Aggregate income fluctuates more violently than the income receipts of individuals, and aggregate savings fluctuate far more violently than individual savings. Thus, aggregate savings fluctuate widely in relation to aggregate income from depression to prosperity.

The Consumption Function and Unsatisfied Consumer Wants

There is no evidence that the cyclical consumption-income pattern has shifted, or is likely to shift in the near future, so as to increase consumption and reduce savings. At the national income levels reached in 1923–29 the consumption-income ratio was 0.88. Again, as a relatively high income level (price changes considered) was reached in 1936–39, the ratio once more stood at 0.88. These figures, while inconclusive because of a considerable margin of error in the original data, appear to support the thesis that it is not easy to achieve, except by very slow adjustments, a high consumption economy.

It is not easy to solve the problem of full employment by raising consumption. It is true that there are untold unfilled consumer wants waiting to be satisfied. But it is not possible to leap from this fact to the conclusion that unemployed resources can, therefore, readily be absorbed in the consumption goods industries. The fact is that, at moderately high income levels, persistent institutional factors determine within rather rigid limits the ratio of consumption to income. The forces determining this ratio are, in part, the distribution of income, habitual practices (strengthened or enforced by institutional arrangements) with respect to individual savings, corporate practices with respect to depreciation reserves and retained earnings, and finally the inevitably high amplitude, as output changes, in the fluctuations of business profits owing to the high proportion of fixed costs under modern production methods.

The superficial view that the persistence of vast unsatisfied consumer wants is an answer to the problem of limited investment outlets—outlets inadequate to fill the gap fixed by the consumption-savings pattern—overlooks the stubborn fact that this pattern is, according to all the available evidence, a highly stable one. It is not likely to be radically changed from one decade to another except by important modifications in fundamental institutional arrangements. Some of these changes can eventually be expected to take place automatically, as for example the cessation of aggregate insurance savings once insurance companies cease to grow and become relatively mature. Others will come only as a result of deliberate policy, such as the redistribution of income. An increase in social benefits and a shift in the tax structure from consumption taxes to middle and upper-class incomes work in this direction. Some automatic adjustment may come through the persistence over several decades of a very low rate of interest, though it is by no means clear what the net effect on savings may prove to be. The current trend toward an increasing quasi-monopolistic control of the prices of finished manufactured products threatens to yield a lower ratio of consumption to income. But whatever the net trend, whether through automatic adjustment or conscious policy, there can be little doubt that no important shift in the consumption-income pattern can be expected within a short period. We have to recognize that we are dealing here with a function that is highly stable and is not easily changed. For this reason it is necessary, however much one may wish to emphasize consumption, to explore to the limit every available investment opportunity. Given a certain collective consumption-income pattern, it is quite impossible to achieve reasonably full employment without large investment outlays supplemented with public investment and with community consumption expenditures.

With respect to the cycle, it is just because of the high stability of the consumption function that fluctuations in the rate of investment produce the business cycle. If, for example, the consumption function shifted up and down in inverse correlation to the fluctuations in investment, no cyclical movement would follow from these fluctuations; as investment fell off consumption would fill the gap. Early investment cycle theorists did not make this point explicit.[16] But there was implicit in their reasoning the assumption that the consumption function was stable, or at least did not shift so as to offset fluctuations in investment.

[16] It is one of the important achievements of Keynes' *General Theory* to have formulated explicitly the role of the consumption function in cycle theory.

Appendix: A Statistical Analysis of the Consumption Function

by

Paul A. Samuelson

AMONG the most striking uniformities yet uncovered in economic data are the relationships between various categories of expenditure and family income. Their regularity is substantiated by studies which go back as far as the nineteenth-century investigations of Le Play and Engel.[1] In fact, so strong are these income effects that it is very difficult to find empirically the influence of price, the variable customarily related to demand by the economic theorist.

In recent years business cycle theorists have tended more and more to be of the opinion that *investment* is the strategic moving factor underlying fluctuations and determining the level of the system. This view implies as a corollary that *consumption expenditure should be related passively to income.* This is a fundamental assumption not only of the Keynesian system (e. g., the doctrine of the multiplier), but of most other schools as well.

Recent statistical material provides the opportunity to test this relationship, and numerous attempts have been made. Three general methods have been employed: [2] (a) the analysis of budgetary data, representing a cross section of the different income levels at the same time; [3] (b) the use of time series of national income, consumption, capital formation, etc.; [4] (c) more or less plausible

[1] For citations see the voluminous bibliography in *Studies of Family Living in the United States and Other Countries* by Faith M. Williams and C. C. Zimmerman, U.S. Dept. of Agriculture, Publication 223; C. C. Zimmerman, *Consumption and Standards of Living,* Van Nostrand, 1936; R. G. D. Allen and A. L. Bowley, *Family Expenditure,* P. S. King, 1935.

[2] R. and W. M. Stone, *Review of Economic Studies,* October, 1938, gives a good summary of work done up until that time.

[3] Maurice Leven's Brookings Study, *America's Capacity to Consume;* Stones, *op. cit.;* National Resources Committee and W.P.A. study, *Consumer Expenditures in U.S., 1935–36;* H. Mendershausen, *American Economic Review,* September, 1939, *Review of Economic Statistics,* August, 1940; E. W. Gilboy, *Review of Economic Statistics,* August, 1940.

[4] Colin Clark, *Economic Journal,* June, 1937, and September, 1938; Clark and Crawford, *The National Income of Australia,* Angus and Robertson, 1938; Kalecki, *Essays in the Theory of Economic Fluctuations,* Farrar and Rinehart, 1939.

rough estimating of the numerical magnitude of the marginal propensity to consume, such as have been made by Kahn, Keynes, J. M. Clark, and others. It is quite possible that the estimates under this last heading are the most useful of all for policy decisions. Nevertheless, it is impossible to appraise their validity by unambiguous statistical methods; consequently, no discussion of them will be attempted here.

However, recent data on national income provided by Kuznets[5] suggest the possibility of utilizing the second method for a new statistical appraisal of the consumption function. A rudimentary discussion of the comparability of the results of methods (a) and (b) will be attempted, but this will not be treated in the exhaustive fashion it deserves.[6]

ADJUSTMENTS OF OBSERVATIONS

Kuznets presents *national income produced* and *consumption outlay,* each in current prices, for the years 1919–35. The first two years may be presumed to contain the anomalous effects of the first World War period and are, therefore, excluded from this discussion. It would be very desirable to secure data for the five years which have elapsed since 1935, and Kuznets has presented elsewhere data for the first two of these years. However, the National Resources Planning Board has made provisional estimates of these magnitudes for the four years through 1939. While admittedly tentative, and despite their lack of strict comparability, these were considered sufficiently informative to be included in the analysis.

If dollar consumption figures are plotted against dollar national income figures for the nineteen years (see page 236), no simple relationship is apparent. Perhaps if the period were subdivided into the twenties and into the thirties, a linear relationship might be found for each half of the data. But these would differ, and the data for the whole period could be represented only by an irregular curve with a definite twist between the two levels.

A correction would seem to be in order if a reversible analytical

[5] S. Kuznets, *National Income and Capital Formation,* National Bureau of Economic Research, 1937.

[6] Cf. J. Marschak, *Canadian Journal of Economics and Political Science,* August, 1939; Hans Staehle, *Review of Economic Statistics,* August, 1937, and August, 1938.

relationship is sought rather than simply a historical description of past happenings. Because of changes in prices, changes in money income and consumption are not the same thing as changes in real income and consumption. From economic theory and from observation, we should not expect to find an invariant relationship between money consumption and money income, regardless of the real levels which these represent. A doubling of *all* prices simultaneously would presumably leave each individual in the same position as previously; we should expect, therefore, no change in real quantities, abstracting from the dynamical effects of *changing* prices. Unless a correction were made for price changes, it would appear that two different observations on the consumption function were available, and that the marginal propensity to consume were equal to the average propensity to consume. Thus, if previously money consumption equaled national income (investment being zero), and suddenly all prices doubled evenly, presumably money consumption would double as income doubled. This might be erroneously interpreted to indicate a marginal propensity to consume of unity, when in fact only one observation of the true *real* consumption function had been made, and no basis exists for inferring the magnitude of the marginal propensity to consume.

For the years before 1936, Kuznets presents a deflated series of income and consumption in terms of 1929 prices. The precise method of adjustment employed by him is a complicated one and could not be applied to the last four observations. Experimentation with the data for the 1921–35 period showed, however, that simply deflating both income and consumption by the Bureau of Labor Statistics Wage Earner's Cost of Living Index led to almost precisely the same relationship as that derived from the more complicated adjustment. Therefore, this technique was used on the whole series, homogeneity for the whole period being preferable to greater exactness in the earlier years.

A second correction readily suggests itself. The same real income divided up among more people cannot be expected to yield the same real consumption expenditure. Perfectly balanced extensive population growth, in which each individual is exactly as well off as previously (derived, for example, by combining statistics of many homogeneous countries), would, as in the case of price changes discussed above, introduce only spuriously new ranges of observation of the consumption function. A need arises, therefore, to place the data upon a standardized or per capita basis. By the use of midyear census estimates the observations were adjusted to the 1929 population level.

These two corrections yielded a series of observations of United States 1921–39 consumption outlay and national income produced, each in terms of 1929 prices and 1929 population.[7]

CONSUMPTION AND INCOME PRODUCED

In Chart 12 is plotted the scatter of real per capita consumption against real per capita income. The corrected observations present a much more unified picture, the data being no longer divisible into two heterogeneous parts. Moreover, the scatter gives at least the appearance of linearity. Determining by conventional least squares technique the regression of consumption on income, we found a constant marginal propensity to consume of .54 (i. e., a multiplier of about 2.2) and a level of income at which savings would be zero of about 59 billion dollars. The closeness of fit as indicated by the Pearsonian coefficient of correlation exceeds + .97.

This is a high correlation, even for the field of economic time series, where sizable correlations are the rule. However, detailed examination of the data suggests that the deviations from the line of best fit are not randomly distributed.

Therefore, we tested the hypothesis that a secular trend may have been operating throughout the period. We resorted to multiple correlation in which *time* was included as a linear factor. Utilizing only the pre-1936 data, a significant improvement in fit resulted, the consumption schedule being shifted upward by about .2 billion dollars per year. The point of zero saving was still around 60 billion dollars in 1929, but shifting upward at a rate of some-

[7] Without these adjustments the results would be not at all comparable with budgetary studies. These were made as of *constant prices,* and relate to individual and family decisions. Moreover, from the standpoint of a reversible relationship of relevance to the problem of (say) the effect of new investment expenditure upon income, clearly population will not increase *pari passu* with such investments. However, the case for eliminating price changes is, from this latter point of view, not so strong. If the price changes recorded in the data were rigidly related to changes in income (hence, investment), then the "pure" *ceteris paribus* relationship with prices removed may be an irrelevant one; we may seek rather the resultant of its shifts. It is precisely considerations of this latter type which we should use to justify our *not* taking into account the effects of changing distribution of income.

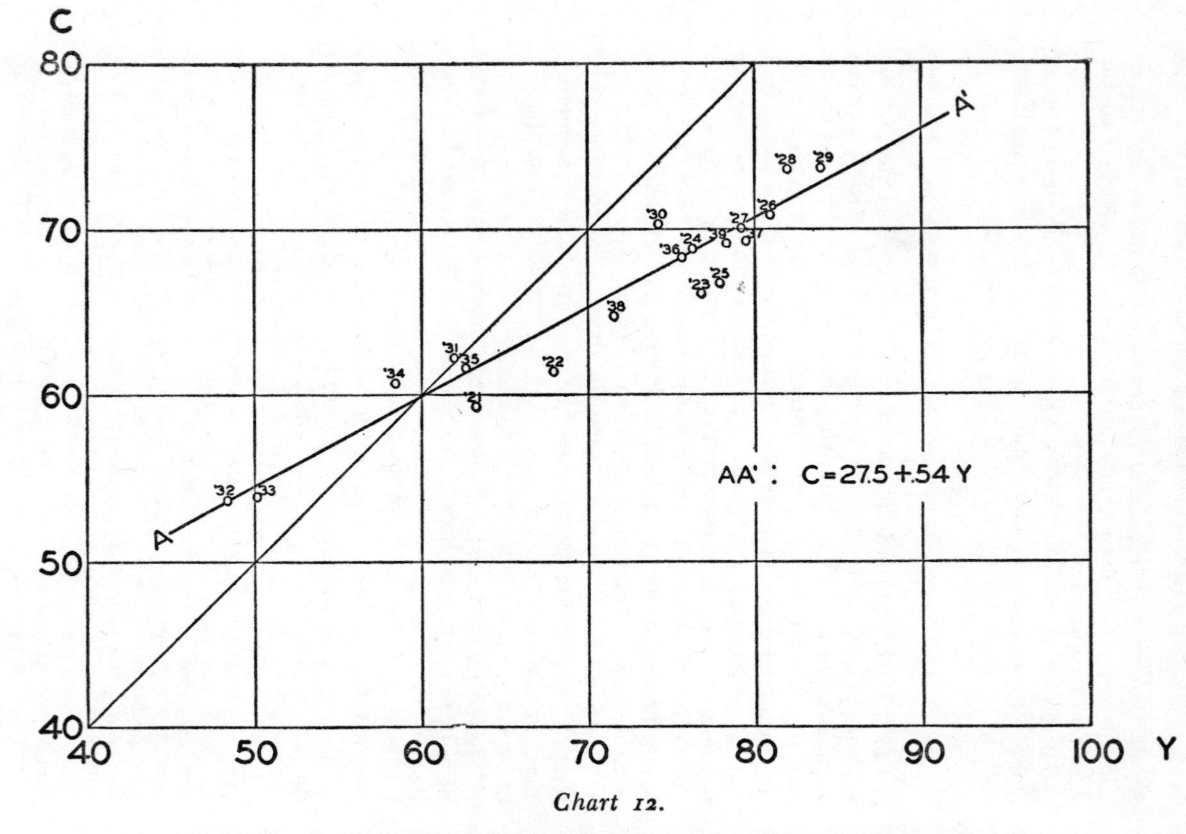

Chart 12.

The Consumption Function in Terms of 1929 Prices and Population

thing less than .1 billion dollars per year. The marginal propensity to consume was found to be only slightly higher, namely, .56; i. e., a multiplier of 2.23.

But, two considerations argued against the validity of the previous multiple correlation analysis. When the last four observations became available and were included in the analysis, there no longer appeared to be a sizable trend factor. The multiple regression coefficient of consumption on time was not found to differ significantly in a sampling sense from zero; and the slight increase in the goodness of fit of the multiple regression over the simple regression was insufficient to justify the introduction of a new parameter with a subsequent loss of one degree of freedom.

Besides, analysis of other components of Kuznets' study suggested an alternative explanation of the upward drift of consumption prior to 1936. This is explored in the next section.

CONSUMPTION, AGGREGATE INCOME PAYMENTS, AND ENTERPRISE SAVING

May not the secular trend discussed above simply be the reflection of a variable whose influence can be explicitly appraised? More specifically, in the early thirties income actually received by consumers, i. e., *aggregate income payments,* exceeded *national income produced* by billions of dollars because of calculated business dissaving and government dissaving (deficits).[8] The reverse was true in the twenties. This provides a possible explanation of the upward drift in *consumption* as compared to *income produced.* It is also in line with experience and theory which suggest that individuals' consumption outlay should depend primarily upon income received.

To check this hypothesis we plotted in Chart 13 *consumption* (1929 prices and population) against *aggregate income payments* (deflated as above for price and population changes), using the data available through 1935. The points lies almost upon a straight

[8] There has been some controversy over the problem of whether the volume of real dissavings may not be overstated because of changes in values of inventories and other business losses, and whether the volume of dissavings represents an equivalent splashing of the community with purchasing power. This is not the place to enter into this confused discussion. It will suffice to point out that *aggregate income payments* is the primary observable series, and that errors in reckoning enterprise savings will distort only the value of *income produced.*

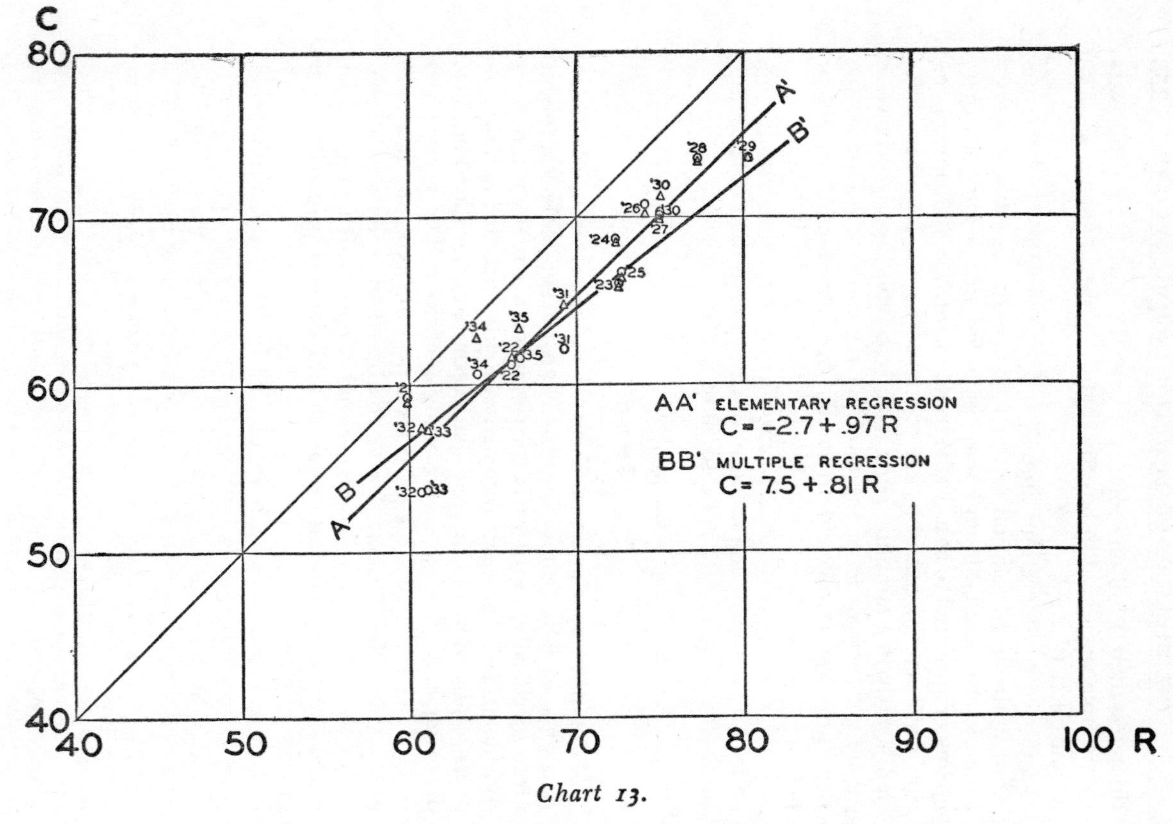

Chart 13.

The Consumption Function in Terms of Aggregate Income Payments

line, the coefficient of correlation being almost + .96. There is no noticeable drift toward increasing consumption. This was confirmed by multiple correlation analysis; the influence of time was found to be insignificant and in the opposite direction to the previous trends.

Thus, closer analysis suggests that there was no increase in consumption out of the same income received. The thirties' increase in consumption compared to income produced seems explicable on the grounds that corporations were saving less (dissaving), not that less was being saved out of income received.

Quite surprisingly, *aggregate income payments* (= national income paid out) varied *less* in this period than did consumption outlay. Savings appeared at all levels of the *aggregate income* payments. The marginal propensity to consume computed from the elementary regression of consumption on income payments has the high value of .97.

If we compute the marginal propensity to consume from the regression of income payments on consumption, we arrive at the anomalous coefficient of 1.06. This seems to indicate an unstable system in which the secondary effects of new expenditure would be unlimited and cumulative. Actually, the leakages incident upon enterprise saving induced by extra income would serve to make the system stable and all secondary effects finite.

This is illustrated in Chart 14 which shows *total enterprise savings* (1929 population and prices) against *national income produced* (1929 base). The simple correlation is + .91. A least squares calculation of the marginal propensity of total enterprise to save yields the very high figure of + .49. An increase of income produced of one dollar results in 49 cents of saving (or less dissaving). This accounts for most of the leakages incident upon net investment; as far as these data go, the leakages incident upon household savings are much smaller and possibly negative.

While income received should be expected to be the dominating determinant of consumption, income produced but not distributed might be expected to have some effect. In a perfect capital market where book and market values coincide, corporate earnings plowed back into the business would thereby increase individuals' equities and make them less anxious to save out of given income received. (Alternatively, individuals may reckon their

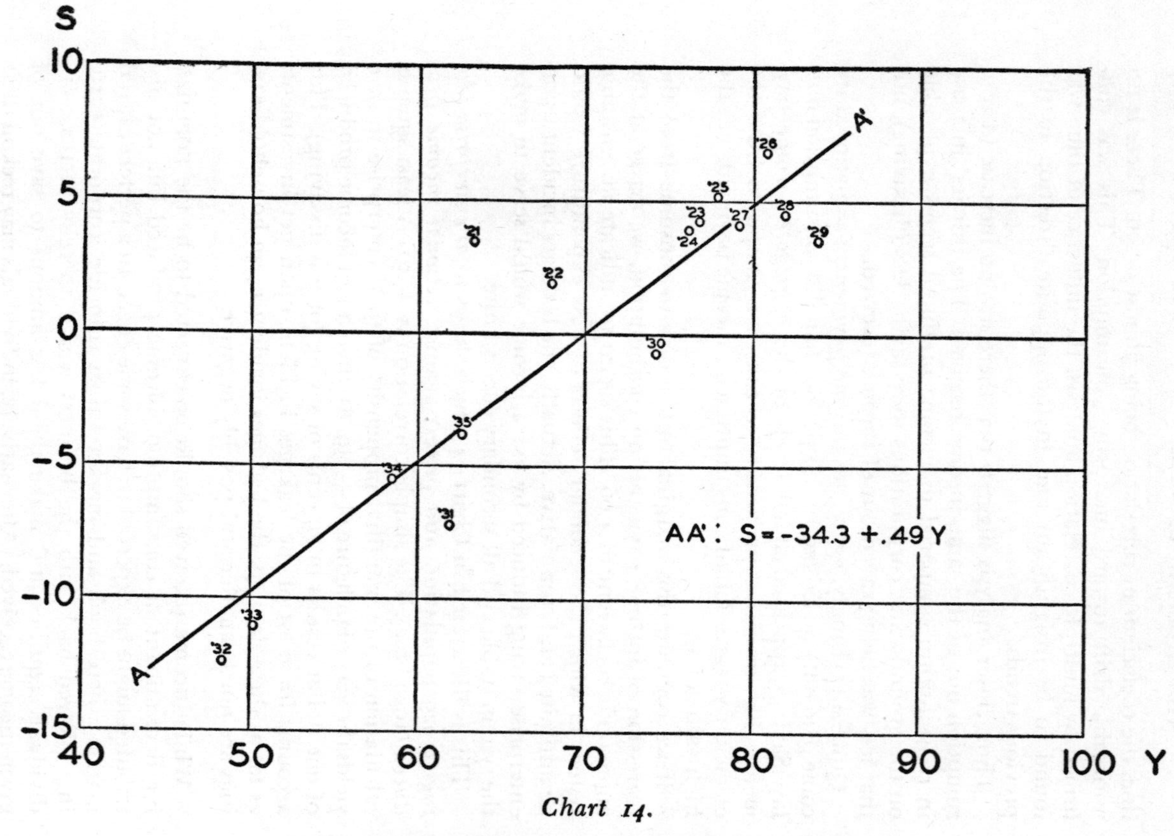

Chart 14.

Total Enterprise Savings in Relation to Income

true income as that produced, not that actually received, and would, therefore, consume more.) Similarly, when dividends exceed earnings (as in amortization of "wasting" mining properties), not all income received may be regarded as true income out of which to determine consumption.

In the real world we should expect the relationship between consumption and enterprise savings to be tenuous. By multiple correlation analysis an attempt was made to evaluate the effect of such savings upon consumption for given levels of income received.

The small triangles in Chart 13 show the net regression between consumption and income received for the level of enterprise saving in 1929. The "net" marginal propensity to consume is reduced to +.81. An increase in enterprise savings of one dollar increases consumption by approximately 23 cents; i. e., shifts the schedule up by that amount. This seems plausible; while unreceived produced income has some effect upon consumption, such "dollars" are only about one quarter as effective as dollars actually received.

The following statistical magnitudes are included for possible further exploration by others:

TABLE XXIII

A. Means and Standard Deviations

	Means of Series †	*Standard Deviations*
X_1 Consumption (corrected) (millions of $)	64,857.6 (65,490.3) *	6,286.23
X_2 Income Produced (corrected) (millions of $)	69,540.0 (70,934.5) *	11,153.69
X_3 Aggregate Income Payments (corrected) (millions of $)	69,733.3	6,207.84
X_4 Total Enterprise Savings (corrected) (millions of $)	— 189.73	6,019.13
X_5 "Time" (years; 1920 = 0)	8.0 (10.0) *	4.32 (5.48) *

† Unless otherwise indicated, all magnitudes are for the period 1921–35.
* 1921–39.

TABLE XXIV

B. Correlation Coefficients (1921–35, unless otherwise indicated)

	X_1	X_2	X_3	X_4
X_1				
X_2	+.96 (+.97)*			
X_3	+.96	+.92		
X_4	+.79	+.91	+.71	
X_5	−.29 (−.05)*	−.50 (−.15)*	+.92	+.91

* 1921–39.

The square of the multiple correlation coefficient of consumption on *aggregate income payments* and *enterprise savings* equals .95, and the square of the partial coefficient of correlation between consumption and aggregate income payments equals .85. The analysis must be taken with a grain of salt because of the high intercorrelation between the independent variables, *income payments* and *enterprise savings* (= + .7). This renders a precise determination of the respective weights of income and savings impossible. An even higher intercorrelation between savings and income produced (= .9) rendered meaningless multiple correlation analysis of these variables and consumption.

In conclusion, the opinion may be ventured that the statistical observations bear out the expectations of theory except with respect to the very sensitive relation of *consumption* to *aggregate income payments.*

Chapter XII

PUMP-PRIMING AND COMPENSATORY FISCAL POLICY

MONETARY policy is an important weapon which we cannot afford to dispense with in cyclical compensatory policy. But it has severe limitations and must be supplemented with other methods. This statement must not be interpreted to mean, however, that even a complete arsenal, involving all the known weapons of attack upon the cycle, is really adequate to stabilize a private enterprise economy. While a program of positive action is necessary, and to a degree effective, complete stability is, nevertheless, unattainable.

Cyclical fiscal policy may be discussed under two headings: first, a cyclically adjusted public spending program; second, a cyclically administered tax policy.

The policy of public spending with respect to the business cycle involves a consideration of "pump-priming," in the strict sense in which that term should be used, in contrast with a policy of public compensatory spending as an offset to fluctuations in private investment. It involves, moreover, theoretical consideration of the Multiplier Principle and the Principle of Acceleration. It involves, in addition, a consideration of the types of expenditure most effective in view of the Multiplier and Acceleration principles as instruments to lift the national income, whether through pump-priming or through compensation.

It is important to make a sharp distinction between the pump-priming concept and the concept of compensation.

Pump-priming is not to be confused with compensatory spending.

The term "pump-priming" carries with it the implication that a certain volume of public spending, varying under different conditions, will have the effect of setting the economy going on the way toward full utilization of resources on its own power without further aid from governmental spending. It is not true, as has sometimes been suggested, that the pump-priming concept implies that only a very small amount of public spending will set the economy operating at full capacity. A pump may require much or little priming, depending upon a variety of conditions; and, similarly, the pump-priming concept carries with it no implication as to the amount of spending necessary, but only the implication that, whatever the amount required, sooner or later the economy can operate on its own motive power.

The Multiplier Principle has no necessary connection with pump-priming. It carries with it no connotation with respect to whether the economy can function at full capacity sooner or later without the aid of government spending. It involves, strictly speaking, only the notion that a given amount of public spending will have an effect upon the national income in excess of the volume of expenditures made. It involves the notion of a "multiplier," but not the notion of a self-perpetuating mechanism which under normal conditions has the capacity of operating under its own "steam."

Pump-priming, using the term in the strict sense indicated above, is intended to be a remedy for a temporary maladjustment which prevents the society from functioning in a normal manner so as to recover from depression. The economy needs to be shoved off dead center, so to speak, in order to resume the normal movement from crisis and depression to revival and recovery. It may be that the missing spark is a maladjustment in the cost-price structure, which rigidities in the system make it difficult to overcome without the application of a special remedy. In this case, public expenditures may have the effect of temporarily increasing income and output in the depressed areas, thereby facilitating a readjustment of the price structure toward a more normal relationship. It may be that the missing spark is lack of confidence on the part of business entrepreneurs, owing to the depressing effects of contraction. A given volume of public expenditures may, however, start activity in an upward direction and encourage people to a less pessimistic and truer view of future prospects. It may be that the accumulation of replacement needs owing to depreciation and obsolescence has reached a point very favorable to larger capital expenditures, or that the accumulation of innovations with respect to new products and new techniques has reached a point favorable to new investment. But these investment possibilities may await a determined and vigorous leadership behind which a host of timid entrepreneurs are ready to follow. Such leadership, however, may for many reasons not be forthcoming from private entrepreneurs, but may require government action. Under these conditions, pump-priming may prove very effective.

Question may be raised how far the situations just cited are realistic descriptions of actual conditions. Such situations doubtless do more or less prevail in different depressions, varying from country to country and from one cycle to another, but their importance is difficult to appraise.

The concept of "pump-priming" is different from "compensation" in that the latter connotes no implications with respect to setting the system going on its own momentum. The latter concept, strictly conceived, implies merely that public expenditures may be used to compensate for the decline in private investment. What is the order of magnitude of the effectiveness of the compensation is not in question. A policy of compensation may be said to accomplish its purpose even though the public expenditures do not succeed in bringing the economy to full recovery. It may be said to be successful even though it succeeds in achieving a rise in the national income no greater than the volume of expenditures made. It accomplishes the purpose intended, at least in a measure, in so far as it succeeds, whether applied in the period of depression and contraction or in the period of upswing, in lifting the income higher than would have been the case had these expenditures not been made. The expenditures are intended to compensate in some measure for the inadequate volume of private investment.

The Leverage Coefficient

Expenditures made, whether with the intent of priming the pump or the intent of compensating for low private investment, *may,* however, operate with magnified effect. The force of each dollar spent may turn out to have a considerable leverage. This leverage may operate in one of two directions. An expenditure may have secondary effects (a) upon consumption expenditures and (b) upon private investment expenditures. The secondary effects of a given volume of public expenditures upon consumption are in the current literature usually discussed under the term "Multiplier Principle," while the secondary effects upon private investment are referred to under the term "Acceleration Principle." This terminology is, of course, quite arbitrary, since the initial expenditures may be regarded as having raised the national income by a "multiplier" or may be thought of as having an "accelerated effect" on the income. To avoid confusion, the coefficient which must be attached to the initial increment of expenditure in order to raise this increment to the incremental increase in the national income may be termed the "leverage." The leverage coefficient, therefore, in itself indicates nothing with respect to whether the secondary effects operate through consumption or through investment. It may measure the effect of the Multiplier Principle, or the effect of the Acceleration Principle, or a combination of both. Where it is desired to segregate the two, the terms "multiplier leverage" and "acceleration leverage" may be used.

The leverage coefficient may, of course, apply to both pump-priming expenditures and compensation expenditures. If a leverage coefficient is, in fact, applicable to pump-priming expenditures, it is clear that the volume of necessary expenditures is thereby less than would otherwise be the case. Similarly, if a leverage coefficient is applicable to compensation expenditures, it is clear that the desired increase in the national income can be achieved by a smaller volume of initial expenditures. It is, of course, clear that the distinction between pump-priming expenditures and compensation expenditures is simply a matter of the intent with respect to what it is sought to achieve; or after the event one may conclude what, in fact, was the effect of a given volume of expenditure—whether, in fact, the pump was primed or the effect was merely to compensate for the time being for current low private expenditures. Looking back over the experience after the event, it may, of course, turn out that neither effect was achieved. The expenditures might (a) fail to have any effect on the national income; (b) have an exclusively compensatory effect upon the national income; or (c) have a compensatory effect plus a pump-priming effect.

This brings us to a more detailed consideration of the Multiplier and Acceleration Principles. The Multiplier Principle, as we have just indicated, has to do with the secondary effects of the governmental expenditures upon consumption expenditures and, therefore, upon income and employment, while the Acceleration Principle has to do with the induced effects of the governmental expenditures upon private investment and, therefore, upon income and employment.

The Multiplier

The Multiplier Principle, applied to fiscal policy, relates an increment of governmental expenditures to a consequent increment of consumption expenditures. Let us assume that a billion dollars is expended on public works. The billion dollars of new funds poured out into the community is received by the contractors, who, in turn, pay out a part in wages and salaries, a part in dividends,[1] a part in the purchase of materials from manufacturers, and a part in the purchase of materials from raw material producers. These, in turn, similarly pay out a part in wages and salaries, a part in dividends, and a part in finished, semifinished, and raw materials. The Multiplier Principle is, however, concerned exclusively with the effect of the initial expenditure on *consumption,* and is, therefore, peculiarly concerned with the effect of such expenditures upon the receipt of wages, salaries, and dividends. It is clear that it is highly improbable that the full billion dollars spent by the government will materialize down through the various stages in a billion dollars of wages, salaries, or dividends. The reason for this is that many entrepreneurs in the various links in the productive chain will supply the goods sold from stock, will convert inventories into idle cash balances, or pay off bank loans and other debt obligations. Moreover, even though they supply their sales from current production, they will use a part of their profits not to pay dividends, but to accumulate cash or to pay off debts. Thus, it is clear that the billion dollars spent by the government on public works does not all materialize in income for individuals, whether wage earners, salaried employees, or stockholders. A part of the funds is diverted from becoming a part of the income stream by being drained off into idle balances or debt cancellation.

In a similar manner, the enlarged income of individuals flowing from the governmental expenditure and public works —the increased income in wages, salaries, and dividends— is not all used for consumption expenditures. The part that is not expended on consumption goods is saved. Such savings may be used either to pay off debt, held in idle balances, or used for financial investment in mortgages, securities, life insurance policies, and the like. It may, of course, be true

[1] For our purposes here the term "dividends" is understood to include dividends as such and also partnership profits or individual proprietorship profits, which in this form of business organization would be the equivalent of dividends in a corporation.

that in certain cases the individual will directly expend his savings on real investment in a house, farm equipment, or other investment goods. In this latter case it will be seen that such an individual is performing a dual function. On the one side, he is saving a part of the income and, on the other side, he is simultaneously making a purchase of real investment goods. As far as the Multiplier Principle is involved, we are concerned only with the saving function, and we shall regard his real investment purchases as quite independent, just as though they were performed by another individual.

To repeat, the initial billion dollars of private investment[2] or government outlays on public works does not all eventuate in consumption expenditures. A part is drained off directly by the entrepreneurial units engaged in the productive process in debt payments and in idle balances, and a part of that paid out to wage earners, salaried employees, and dividend recipients is saved. Thus leakages, whether in the form of debt cancellation, the hoarding of idle balances, or financial investment, occur down the entire line of business units and individuals engaged in the private investment or public works project. The magnitude of these leakages determines, in the final analysis, what the secondary effects of the initial expenditures will be upon the volume of consumption expenditures.

The ultimate effects of the initial billion-dollar investment or public works expenditures upon consumption, of course, do not stop at the stage we have reached in our analysis. The individuals participating in the private investment or public works project decide to spend a portion of the new income they have received in consumption purchases. Thus, we have reached the first stage in tracing out the secondary consequences of investment or public works expenditure upon consumption. The expenditures made on consumption goods

[2] The initial expenditure which operates through the cumulative process to raise the national income may, of course, be independent or spontaneous private investment, or it may be governmental expenditures.

now set in motion a new productive process necessary to supply these consumption goods. The funds thus expended again seep down through an entire productive process. Again, a part is not paid to wage and salary earners or dividend recipients, but is sidetracked in the form of debt cancellation and idle balances; and, again, a part of the income received by wage and salary earners and dividend recipients is shunted off into savings and utilized for repayment of debt, held in idle balances, or used for financial investment.

This process continues indefinitely into the future and may be represented by the diagram in Chart 15 which shows the successive consumption expenditures flowing from an initial private investment (or public works expenditure) of $500 millions—each consumption expenditure being smaller than the preceding volume of purchases by the amount of leakages involved.

What these leakages actually are in any given situation can, of course, be determined only by statistical investigation, though certain a priori judgments may be made with respect to their probable quantitative importance. Keynes has assumed that in England the leakages in a period of relative depression probably amount to 50 per cent, so that each successive expenditure is 50 per cent lower than the preceding one. J. M. Clark has argued that under American conditions the leakages are probably 33⅓ per cent, so that each successive expenditure is two thirds of the preceding one. This was also the rough guess of Keynes with respect to American conditions.

A point needs to be made with respect to the average period of time intervening between these successive expenditures. Distinction must here be made between the average time interval between successive consumption expenditures, here under consideration, and the average time interval involved in the income velocity of money. In the case of the latter, it is clear that, if the income velocity per year is three, the average time interval between the point at which *a dollar* becomes income for someone and the point at which it again

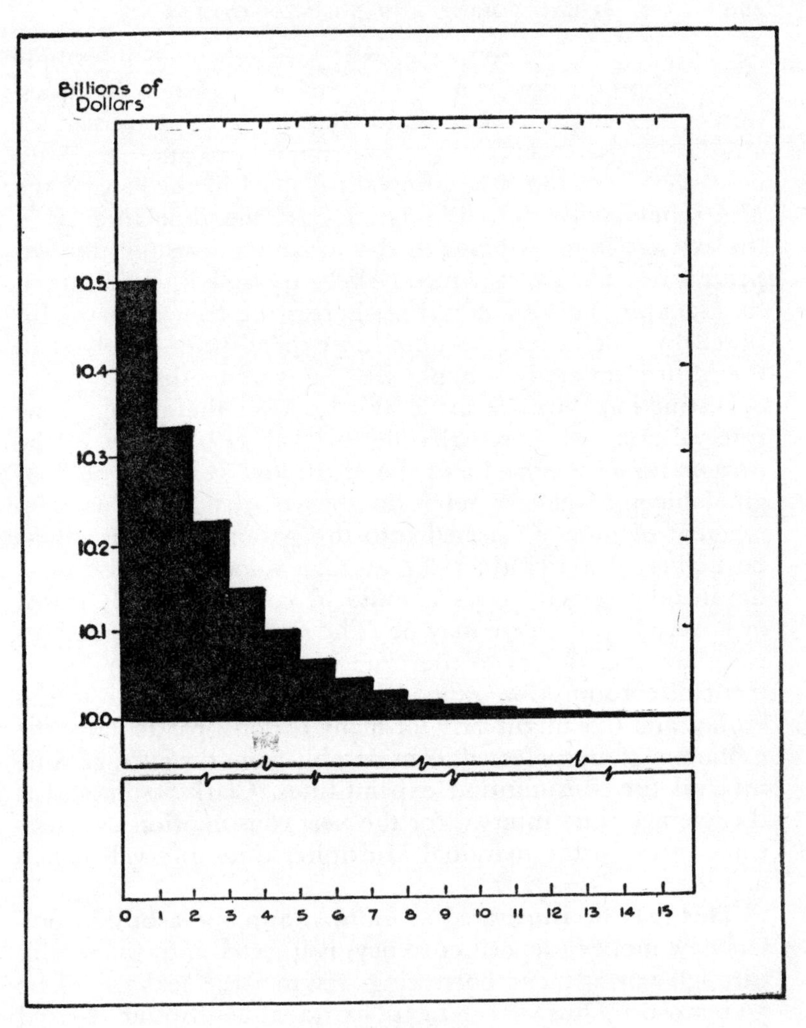

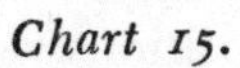

Chart 15.

Consumption Expenditures Induced by Single Investment Expenditure

becomes income for someone, as it passes through the whole circuit of production, must be four months. Here it is a question of the length of time that it requires on the average for *a dollar* to pass from one income recipient to another. This, however, is not the time interval involved in the case of the Multiplier analysis. In this latter case, the time interval is the average interval between the successive consumption expenditures. The average income velocity time interval might, for example, be four months, whereas the time interval between the successive consumption expenditures involved in the Multiplier analysis might well be two months.

Distinction must be made also between the average time interval and the marginal time interval with respect to the *income velocity period* and the *Multiplier period.* The marginal income velocity refers to the velocity of the last increment of money injected into the system, and this might be higher or lower than the average velocity. Accordingly, the income velocity period would be correspondingly raised or lowered, as the case may be. The marginal Multiplier period, however, refers to the time interval of the new increment of consumption expenditures flowing from the initial outlay, and this might vary for many reasons (particularly the economic groups affected) considerably from the average time interval for consumption expenditures. Clark assumes that the average time interval for the *new* consumption expenditures (namely, the marginal Multiplier time interval) is two months.[8]

This may be illustrated as follows: Suppose a billion dollars new money (deposit currency) is injected into the system through government borrowing. Assume the leakage to be 50 per cent. Thus, in the next "marginal Multiplier" period (say, two months) $500 millions would be spent on consumption. In another two months $250 millions, and in still another $125 millions, etc. After twelve months have passed, the initial expenditure will have added a total of $1,984,125,000

[8] At least this is my interpretation, to which, however, Clark might not agree. See his *The Economics of Public Works.*

to the national income via the functioning of the Multiplier principle. But all this tells us nothing about the marginal income velocity of the new money. New investment may have been made partly by reason of the increase in consumption (Acceleration Principle), and partly by reason of quite independent investment projects springing from the development of new industries and the like. Thus, it is quite conceivable that in a single year, after the new money was injected, the national income had increased by an increment of $4 billions. Thus, the marginal income velocity of money would be four, and the marginal income period would be three months, while the Multiplier time interval we assumed to be two months.

There remains to be considered the relation of the magnitude of the leakages to the magnitude of the Multiplier and to determine on the basis of the assumed conditions how far the level of the national income will be raised as a result of (a) a continuous flow of governmental expenditures or private investment of a given magnitude, and (b) a single injection of expenditures of a given amount.

The former is illustrated by Chart 16. Here we assume that the government (or private investment) pours out in each period (determined by the marginal Multiplier time interval, say, two months) $500 millions. From the chart it will be clear that, if the leakages are of a magnitude of 33⅓ per cent, the income will presently after a lag be raised (through the continuous expenditure of $500 millions) by $1,500 millions per period. Thus, the Multiplier is three in the sense that the national income is lifted by three times the amount of the private investment or governmental outlays. The second case is illustrated by Chart 15, which shows the effect upon subsequent national income of a single expenditure of $500 millions. If the leakages are 33⅓ per cent, it is clear that all of the succeeding expenditures flowing from the initial expenditure summated over all future time would equal twice the initial expenditure, and that the sum total of the net addition to the national income resulting from the initial ex-

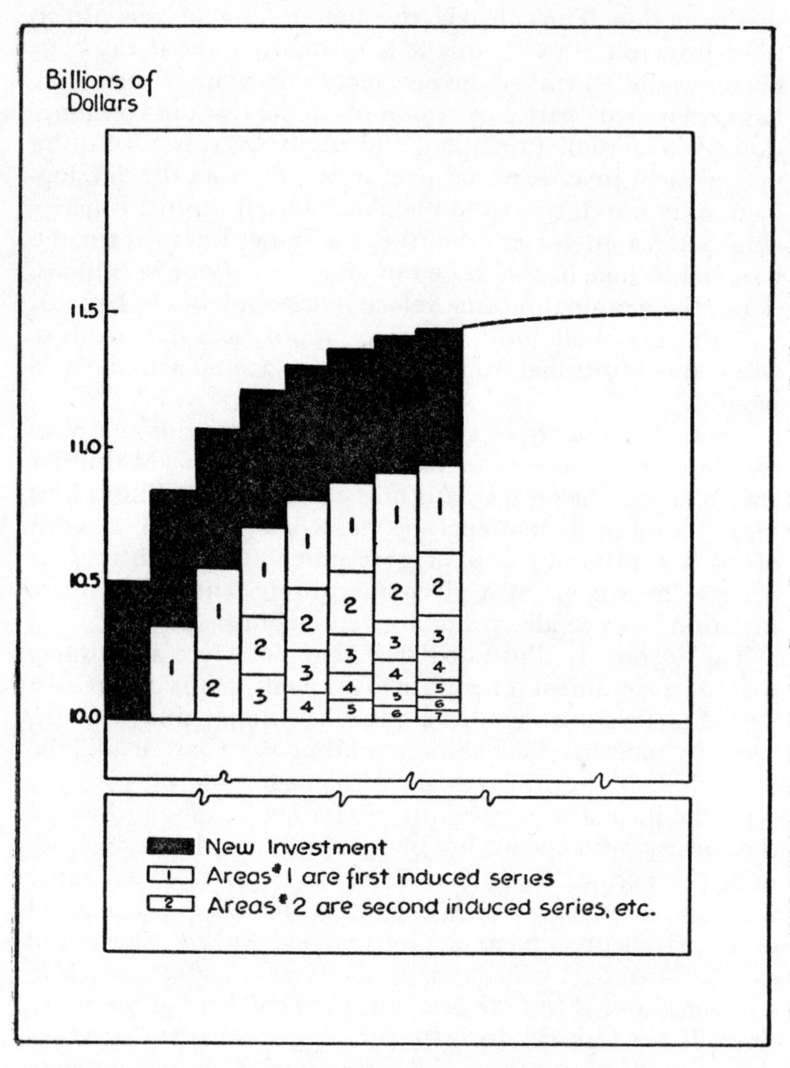

Chart 16.

Continuing Investment and Induced Consumption

penditures of $500 millions would be $1,500 millions. In this sense also, then, the Multiplier is three.

In point of fact, in both cases it is impossible to know precisely what the exact value of the Multiplier is, even though one knows the magnitude of the leakages currently experienced. This is true for the reason that one can never know what the magnitude of the leakages will be over all future time. It can readily be seen (Chart 16), however, that this point is of no great practical significance, since in a very few periods, given fairly high magnitudes of leakages, such as 50 per cent or 33⅓ per cent, the national income approaches rapidly the asymptote which, strictly speaking, could be reached only at an infinitely future date. Similarly, with the injection of a single investment outlay or governmental expenditure (Chart 15), the secondary increase of the national income quickly approaches the limit reached at an infinitely future date. Thus, while in the former case the income level would eventually rise by $1,500 millions per period, after six expenditure periods it would already have approximated this figure; and, similarly, in the second case, the secondary additional income would after six expenditure periods approximate the $1 billions additional income which an infinite progression would yield.

From the diagrams and analyses given above it is clear that the Multiplier is high if the magnitude of the leakages is low, and vice versa. Indeed, if the leakages are zero, the Multiplier is infinity, and if the leakages are 100 per cent, the Multiplier is unity. This latter case means that there are no secondary effects on the national income from the initial expenditure. Thus, the magnitude of the Multiplier can be stated in terms of the marginal propensity to save, or conversely the marginal propensity to consume, as Keynes has done in his *General Theory*. The magnitude of the leakages is determined by the portion of the marginal income which is not used for consumption expenditures, or, in other words, is saved. Thus, if the percentage saved is zero, the Multiplier is infinity. If the fraction which is saved is one tenth, the

Multiplier is ten; if one fifth, five; if one third, three; if one half, two; and, finally, if 100 per cent is saved, the Multiplier is one, and, similarly, for intervening points. The Multiplier is thus the reciprocal of the marginal propensity to save, which determines the ratio of marginal saving to marginal income received. The Multiplier can equally well be stated in terms of the marginal propensity to consume. The Multiplier (K) stated in terms of the marginal propensity-to-consume $\frac{(\Delta C)}{(\Delta Y)}$ gives the formula $K = \frac{1}{1 - \frac{\Delta C}{\Delta Y}}$.

From Charts 15 and 16 it is readily apparent that the income will not remain at the new high level reached unless the private investment or governmental outlays continue to be poured out in a continuous stream. As soon as the governmental expenditures are withdrawn, the income again falls to its previous level. This phenomenon is in no sense a peculiarity of governmental spending, but is equally true of private investment expenditures.

The Acceleration Principle

Thus, the Multiplier Principle concerns exclusively the effect of private investment expenditure or governmental expenditure, as the case may be, upon subsequent net additions to consumption expenditure. The Acceleration Principle, to which we now turn, concerns exclusively the effect of a net increase in consumption expenditures upon induced investment expenditures. If we are to measure the full effect of private investment expenditures or governmental expenditures, as the case may be, on income, we must take account of both the Multiplier and the Acceleration Principle; we must measure not only the effect of these initial expenditures upon subsequent consumption, but also the effect of the subsequent increases in consumption upon investment induced by increase in consumption expenditures.

The volume of replacement investment expenditures is determined by the volume of consumption expenditures. In the event that consumption expenditures remain constant, no *new* investment expenditures are induced, but only a given volume of replacement. In the event, however, that consumption expenditures rise, the net increment of consumption may induce a given volume of additional investment. This will occur even before existing equipment is fully utilized. If we start from the bottom of a depression, a rise in consumption expenditures is likely to induce a larger volume of replacement expenditures in the old, established industries. This follows from the fact that during depression depreciation allowances are not fully expended, and recovery tends to restore replacement to a normal level. If the increases in consumption expenditures occur in new lines, a given volume of new investment will occur, even though industry in general is still depressed. Thus, it is by no means easy to determine precisely in what degree a rise of consumption expenditures from the bottom of the depression affects, on the one side, replacement investment expenditures, and, on the other side, new investment expenditures. Statistical inquiry (see Kuznets) does, however, reveal that a rise in consumption expenditures from the bottom of the depression brings about a very smooth rise in gross investment, and there appears to be no point in the upswing at which one can clearly demarcate replacement investment expenditures from new investment expenditures; nor is there any sharp break in the gross investment expenditure curve, such as might be implied from an overemphasis on the effect of reasonably full utilization of existing equipment upon new investment, as consumption expenditures continue to rise.

The magnitude of the "Acceleration leverage"—we are here precluded by the current terminology from using the term "multiplier," since that is reserved, as we have seen, for a special case—will depend upon the concrete character of the new consumption. Certain types of consumption goods involve in their production virtually no capital equipment, while others require a very high ratio of capital to each unit of output. Thus, the "Acceleration leverage" cannot be determined on a priori grounds, but must be determined by investigation of the actual character of the new consumption. In general, we know that the average ratio of manufacturing capital to value added is about two to one.[4] It by no means follows, however, that the marginal increments of income will require this ratio of capital to output. This ratio would vary with the different phases of the cycle and with the character of the new consumption purchases.

In the diagram below we have arbitrarily assumed, by way of illustration, that the ratio is unity. In this diagram we have sought to show the effects of both the Multiplier Principle and the Acceleration Principle, in order to disclose the combined effects of both in magnifying the national income.[5]

The Cumulative Process

The diagram (Chart 17) is constructed in the following manner: It is assumed that private investment or net income-creating governmental expenditures of $500 millions are made in each "multiplier" period. The black blocks represent the magnitude of new private investment or governmental expenditures made in each successive period. The white blocks represent the total induced consumption expenditures for each period (over and above the basic income

[4] National Industrial Conference Board, *Studies in Enterprise and Social Progress*, 1939, pp. 218, 220.

[5] It may be noted that, whatever the Acceleration coefficient, the ratio of total investment to consumption will be the same. This follows from the fact that the induced investment (if any) will on its part induce, in turn, consumption expenditures, according to the value of the multiplier. If the multiplier is two, any initial investment will induce an equivalent consumption, and similarly any induced investment. Thus, whatever the ratio of initial investment to induced investment, the ratio of total investment to total consumption (both that induced by the initial investment as well as that induced by the induced investment) will be unity, if the marginal propensity to consume is one half. Hence, even though it is not possible to differentiate the total investment in any given period into its component parts—independent and induced—it is still possible to ascertain, in the statistical relation of investment to consumption, what is the marginal propensity to consume, and so the multiplier leverage.

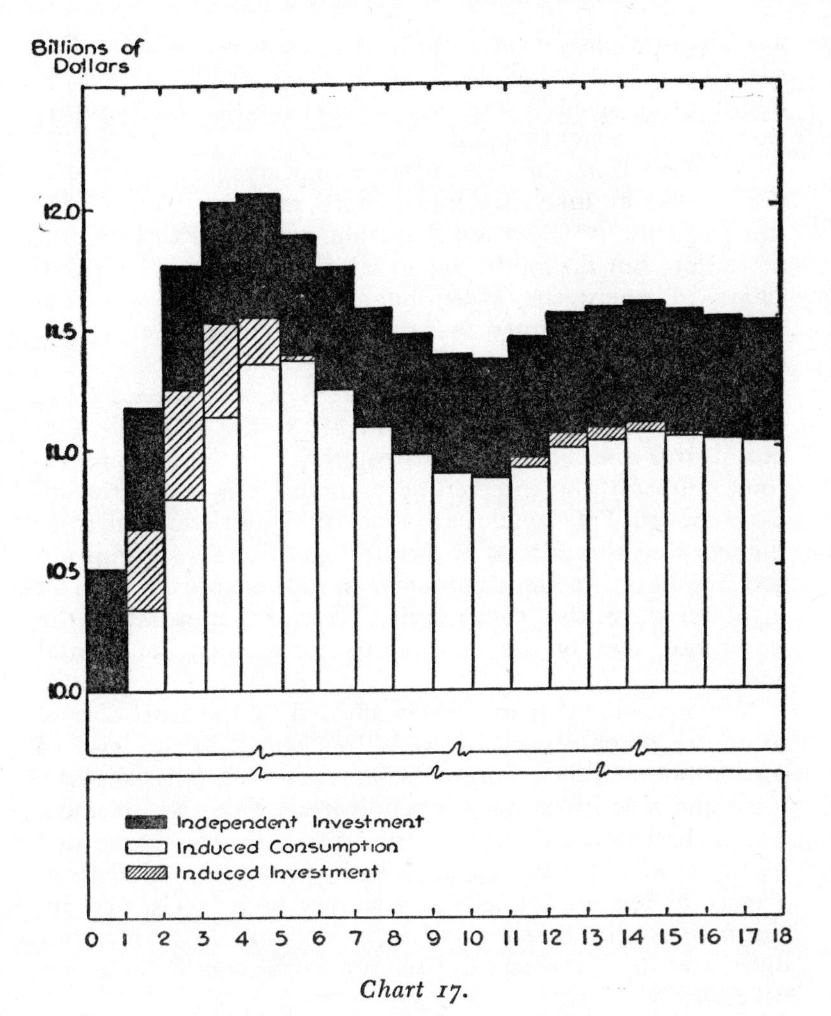

Chart 17.

Induced Consumption and Induced Investment Flowing from Continuing Independent Investment Expenditure

already prevailing when the experiment is started). The shaded areas represent the increments of private investment which are induced by reason of the net increase in consumption in the current period.

It is clear from the particular assumptions here made that the income at first rises much more rapidly than was the case when the Acceleration Principle was not taken into consideration, but it soon begins to fall,[6] unlike the situation in Chart 16 where the Multiplier Principle alone was considered. It will be noted that the income curve fluctuates up and down with diminishing amplitude around precisely the level established in Chart 16. That is to say, the addition of the Acceleration Principle to the Multiplier Principle does not, in this case, affect the ultimate level of the national income but only the intervening path through which the income moves. This somewhat paradoxical result follows from the fact that the process of creating additional consumption goods is, in our modern economy, an indirect one and in fact involves, once the consumption increase approaches the asymptote, merely the continuous replacement of capital goods.

New investment is in no way affected by the *level* of consumption expenditures, but only by *changes* in the level of consumption. When consumption rises and falls, replacement and new investment expenditures are thereby affected, but the basic level of replacement expenditures is determined by the *level* of consumption. When consumption rises from a more or less established level to new high levels, new investment is stimulated via the Acceleration Principle; but once consumption ceases to rise, new investment is no longer necessary.

It should be noted that the conclusions drawn above are derived from a specific set of data. It is, therefore, necessary to inquire into what the situation would be were the condi-

[6] It is assumed that, as soon as consumption expenditures begin to decline, disinvestment begins in accordance with the "Acceleration leverage" of unity; i.e., if consumption falls by one million dollars, one million dollars of disinvestment is induced.

tions different from those illustrated in the figure. Various model sequences, with given values of the Acceleration leverage and the marginal propensity to consume (from which the Multiplier leverage is derived) can be developed.[7] The Acceleration coefficient is here designated by the notation "β" and the marginal propensity-to-consume by "α." In the table on page 280, four selected values for these coefficients are assumed. Each pair of values results in a certain sequence of national income figures under the conditions assumed. In Column I (where $\alpha = 0.5$ and $\beta = 0$) we have the case already shown in Chart 16 above where account is taken only of the Multiplier Principle. It is, however, of interest to include it here, since it then becomes merely a special case of the more general analysis. In this case there are no oscillations and the income approaches progressively an asymptote. In Column II oscillations in the income develop, and it turns out that these are quite regular in character. In Column III the oscillations fluctuate with an increasing amplitude around an average value. In both these latter cases the average value, around which the oscillations occur, are equal to the asymptote which the income approaches when the Multiplier alone is taken account of or the Acceleration Coefficient is equal to zero. In the last column (IV) no oscillations occur, the behavior being "explosive upward approaching a compound interest rate of growth."

These columns give four selected pairs of values for α and β. But it is necessary to inquire whether other values would give still different types of results. The algebraic analysis made by Mr. Samuelson, however, reveals that these models cover all the different possible qualitative types of behavior, though the quantitative results vary, of course, with the values chosen. Thus, the whole field of possible values of the coefficients can be divided up into four regions. These regions are plotted in Chart 18. Each point in this diagram

[7] See the article by Paul Samuelson, "Interactions Between the Multiplier Analysis and the Principle of Acceleration," *Review of Economic Statistics*, May, 1939.

TABLE XXV

Model Sequences of National Income for Selected Values of Marginal Propensity to Consume and Acceleration Coefficient

("α" = Marginal Propensity to Consume;
"β" = Acceleration Coefficient)

	I	*II*	*III*	*IV*
Period	$\alpha = .5$ $\beta = 0$	$\alpha = .5$ $\beta = 2$	$\alpha = .6$ $\beta = 2$	$\alpha = .8$ $\beta = 4$
1	$1.00	$1.00	$1.00	$1.00
2	1.50	2.50	2.80	5.00
3	1.75	3.75	4.84	17.80
4	1.875	4.125	6.352	56.20
5	1.9375	3.4375	6.6256	169.84
6	1.9688	2.0313	5.3037	500.52
7	1.9844	.9141	2.5959	1,459.592
8	1.9922	—.1172	— .6918	4,227.704
9	1.9961	.2148	— 3.3603	12,211.1216

represents a certain value for α and β. For each point a modal type sequence of national income through time can be determined. These types correspond with the four sequences illustrated in the table above.

In Region A the value for the Acceleration coefficient is relatively small, though not necessarily zero. It represents the type illustrated in Column I. Here the national income approaches an asymptote, the value of which is $\frac{1}{1-\alpha}$ (in other words, the "Multiplier") times the governmental expenditure injected in each successive period plus the original income level. Whenever the expenditure ceases, the national income falls to the original level.

In Region B damped, oscillatory movements of the national income occur as in Column II. These movements gradually approach an asymptote established by the Multiplier Principle, namely, the original income plus the governmental expenditure times the Multiplier $\frac{1}{(1-\alpha)}$.

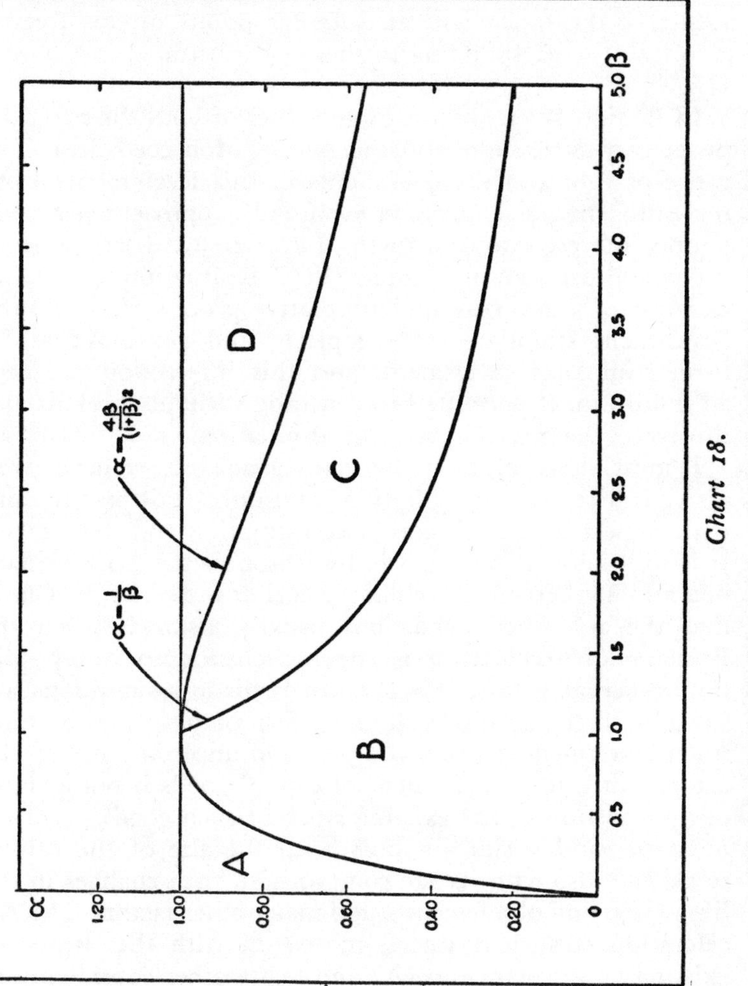

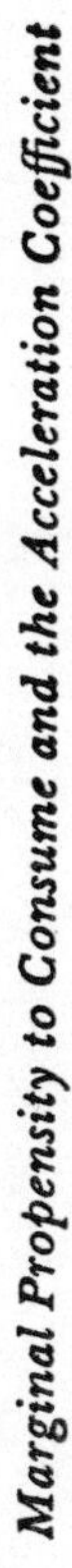

Chart 18.

Marginal Propensity to Consume and the Acceleration Coefficient

In Region C increasing oscillatory movements develop around an asymptote equal to that which would be established when the Multiplier alone is considered. The possible values of the coefficients at different points in this Region give results corresponding to the type illustrated in Column III.

In Region D we observe large values of both the marginal propensity-to-consume and the Acceleration coefficient. The range of values of the coefficients in this Region give ever-increasing national incomes, eventually approaching a compound interest rate of growth. These results correspond to the type illustrated in Column IV. This situation is a perfect example of a never-ending cumulative process of expansion. Investment stimulates consumption, and consumption, in turn, stimulates investment, and this interaction proceeds ad infinitum. If permitted to continue without check, it also illustrates the case of astronomical inflation.

It must, however, be noted that the analysis we have given above is based on very simplified and unrealistic assumptions with respect to the relation of consumption and investment. It is well known, particularly by reason of the work of Kuznets and Tinbergen, as well as the earlier work of J. M. Clark, that the simplified conditions usually assumed when the Principle of Acceleration is under discussion are rarely valid in the actual world. When more realistic assumptions are introduced, it is clear that the effect of new consumption upon investment is a very complex and uncertain one. In the actual world the replacement of capital goods is not a rigorous proportion of the existing stock of such goods. Replacement demand varies not only with the size of the capital stock, but also with its age composition, with changes in the life period and obsolescence, and many other factors. The Acceleration coefficient varies, moreover, with the degree of existing excess plant capacity and many other considerations affecting the decisions of entrepreneurs with respect to new investment. Thus, it is a mistake, at least from the short-run point of view, to place too much emphasis upon the Principle of Acceleration. Probably its most useful application to the actual world has to do with the effect of the growth of a new industry and the growth of population. Here the Principle of Acceleration appears to apply with great force. During the period of rise of a great new industry a vast amount of new investment is stimulated directly and indirectly, and when the industry reaches a plateau, all these related investments disappear, and there remain only replacement investment expenditures.

Conclusions

Certain extremely important conclusions follow from an examination of the operation of the Multiplier Principle and the Acceleration Principle. These may be summarized as follows:

1. New investment, except for short-run fluctuations in the volume of consumption expenditures, and except for very high values of the Multiplier and Acceleration coefficients, is not affected by the volume of consumption expenditures. Thus (with the exceptions noted), as far as any long-term effect is concerned, the level of consumption in no way affects the level of new investment. A firm grasp of this fundamental conclusion must minimize very much the practical significance of the Acceleration Principle. Replacement investment expenditures are obviously not to be counted at all as a constituent element in the size of the national income, since it is already incorporated in the consumption figures. The value of consumption, of course, consists of the cost of production of such goods, including the cost of replacement of the capital goods required to make the consumption goods in question. The level of consumption determines the volume of replacement investment expenditures. Net investment, however, is a function, in the short run, of *changes* in the level of consumption.

2. There is, therefore, no possibility (except for the case of high leverage values) of raising the income to higher and higher levels by the process of lifting yourself by your boot-

straps via the interrelation of increased consumption and increased investment in the familiar expansionist process. Instead, as we have shown, the Acceleration Principle, except for temporary fluctuations and the special case of high leverage values, has no effect in lifting the national income at all. The national income can, therefore, in the long run and in the normal case not rise, contrary to commonly accepted but clearly superficial views, by reason of an induced investment springing from an induced rise in consumption.

3. The volume of consumption can be increased, in so far as unemployed resources are available, by net private investment induced by factors, which we shall presently discuss, having no relation whatever to the current level of consumption, or else by governmental expenditures involving the use of new funds and, therefore, not abstracting from the current level of consumption. How high consumption can be pushed by given increments of private investment expenditures or of governmental expenditures depends upon leakages (which are determined by the propensity to save), as explained under the Multiplier Principle. But the new higher level of consumption rapidly falls to its former level unless the net private investment outlays or the governmental expenditures are continued at a constant level.

4. At a given level of income, consumption equals income, or, in other words, the average propensity to consume is equal to one. At this level of income, and at this level alone, a given volume of consumption expenditures is self-perpetuating, and income *tends* to be maintained at a constant level. If income produced temporarily falls below consumption, the gap between the two represents disinvestment. But this situation tends toward a new equilibrium at which income produced and consumption are equal. At this point also there is no *net* investment. The system is self-perpetuating in the sense that 100 per cent of the income received is consumed, and thereby current aggregate demand gives rise to production activities through which a new monetary aggregate demand is created equal to that in the previous period. This is the "cir-

cular flow" so vividly described in Schumpeter's *The Theory of Economic Development.*

The national income can, therefore, be divided for analytical purposes into two compartments: the first we shall call the "basic national income," at which the average propensity to consume is equal to one, which income level tends to be self-perpetuating; and the second, the "dynamic income," which, as we have noted, is the margin filled by net investment (private and public) and by the consumption induced by this net investment. It is this dynamic income which is extremely unstable and within the area of which the fluctuations of our economic life occur. This margin need not be wholly filled by net private investment or net income-creating governmental expenditures. But it is these two which are the dynamic factors creating the income above the minimum basic level. According to the size of the leakages (determined by the marginal propensity to save), a part of the margin between the basic income and the full income will be filled by induced consumption expenditures. If the marginal propensity to save that part of the full income which is above the basic minimum income is one half, consumption expenditures will fill one half of this margin. If the marginal propensity to save is one third, consumption expenditures will occupy two thirds of the margin. If the marginal propensity to save is one quarter, consumption expenditures will occupy three quarters of the margin, and so on.[8]

The income level at which consumption equals income may be said to be self-sustaining in the sense that no new,

[8] Erroneous conclusions sometimes follow from confusing the Multiplier coefficient with the income velocity of money. It is, of course, true that a dollar used in expenditures flows through the system and becomes income for others two or three times during the year. This, however, has nothing to do with the Multiplier as such, but has merely to do with the customs and habits with respect to the use of money, under which a given volume of income expenditures during a year is normally accomplished by a volume of money equal to, let us say, only one third of the income expenditures made. Under these conditions the income velocity of money obviously is three. But it may be that the injection of more money, instead of raising the national income, will only result in a decline in velocity.

independent, anticipatory investment is necessary to maintain this income level. It is, of course, true that the income may well fall below this basic level owing to dissaving. But this may be regarded as an abnormal, temporary maladjustment, which will sooner or later correct itself. In a progressive society, dissaving can only occur as a temporary phase of the business cycle. If consumption exceeds income (as is true in a serious depression), it follows that replacement capital expenditures are inadequate to sustain the given level of consumption and must sooner or later rise to a point at which no further disinvestment occurs.

Thus, consumption expenditures in a "circular flow" economy in which consumption equals income tend to be self-perpetuating. On the other hand, the net private investment and net income-creating governmental expenditures (together with the secondary consumption expenditures which they induce) are in no sense self-perpetuating. As long as these investment and income-creating expenditures are made, they induce a volume of consumption expenditures above the basic minimum level and thereby have a multiplying effect on the national income.

While from the long-run standpoint the Acceleration Principle (in the usual case) is incapable of raising the level of the national income, it must still be noted that it may have an effect which, under certain conditions, may be very considerable on the cyclical pattern. Without the Acceleration Principle one may argue that private investment or the net income-creating expenditures of the government may lift the national income by a certain Multiplier and hold it there until the investment or net income-creating expenditures cease, whereupon the income rapidly falls to its original level. Under conditions in which, however, the Acceleration Principle is really effective, the stimulated recovery will advance much more rapidly than would otherwise be the case. Still more important, perhaps, is the fact that it may reach a peak and decline with greater or less rapidity, even though the investment and net income-creating expenditures were continued at a constant level. Thus, it is quite possible that a volume of investment or net income-creating expenditures continuously applied may not even be able to sustain the recovery reached. Generally speaking, in the measure that the net income-creating expenditures are extremely effective in creating a burst of recovery, as would be the case when the Multiplier and Acceleration coefficients are high (though not as high as represented by Region D), it may be expected that sooner or later a serious relapse will occur. We may, therefore, conclude (within limits) that the more effectively the investment or net income-creating expenditures operate, the less sustained the recovery is likely to be. This is true, however, only to the extent that the effectiveness in question runs in terms of both the Acceleration and the Multiplier Principles and not in terms of the Multiplier alone. As far as the Multiplier Principle is concerned, the induced recovery can be expected to sustain itself as long as the expenditures continue, but not much longer. If the Acceleration Principle is operative, not even this degree of permanence can be relied upon.

Net income-creating governmental expenditures are undertaken by the government either because the community deliberately wishes to make capital expenditures in order to obtain the utilities directly flowing from the completed projects, or because the community determines to make these capital expenditures in order to raise the national income and thereby escape the wastage incident to unemployed resources. Net private investment is, on the other hand, induced purely in response to the profit motive. Spontaneous net private investment has no relation to the current level of consumption, and any increase in consumption has ordinarily only a temporary and rapidly vanishing effect upon net private investment. Thus, net private investment is fundamentally a function of factors lying quite outside of the current volume of consumption or the current volume of income—factors associated with the dynamics of economic progress. In the absence of new investment outlets adequate to maintain the boom, it is clear that any continued volume of investment, such as would be necessary to maintain income at a full level, would rapidly experience a drastic fall in the prospective rate of profit on new investment (the marginal efficiency of capital). Such a fall progressively weakens the inducement to invest, until net investment equals zero. The classicals were quite right when they argued that without technological progress the price system, including the rate of interest, would progressively drive the economy to the point at which there would be no net investment. They were wrong in assuming that the price system could also ensure a propensity to consume compatible with this investment situation so as to provide full employment.

Chapter XIII

COMPENSATORY TAX POLICY

IN the previous chapter we have discussed how private investment and governmental expenditures may affect the national income. We have examined the theoretical principles determining the leverage of such expenditures upon the national income and the necessity for the continuation of such expenditures in order to *sustain* the national income. In this chapter we consider particularly cyclical aspects of compensatory fiscal policy.

First, we concern ourselves with compensatory policy in a society which is sufficiently dynamic in terms of its private investment outlets to develop vigorous booms. What sort of tax policy is best designed to minimize cyclical fluctuations in a society which, except for periodic depressions, tends toward full employment of resources? We are thus concerned primarily with the question of a cyclical tax policy designed to minimize industrial fluctuations.

Comparison may be made between the cyclical fluctuations in a highly dynamic, high-savings economy and those in a less dynamic society which has at the same time achieved, through its fiscal policy or otherwise, a high level of consumption in relation to income—a high propensity to consume. The former will tend to have a violently fluctuating cycle; the latter a mild cycle. Both, we assume, tend toward full employment in the prosperity phase.

Chart 19 represents the consumption functions which fulfill the conditions stated. "A" represents the consumption function in a high-savings society; "B" the consumption function in a high-consumption economy. On the basis of Consumption Function A, the income will fall to 60 per cent of the full income level before consumption equals income, or, in other words, before the average propensity to consume

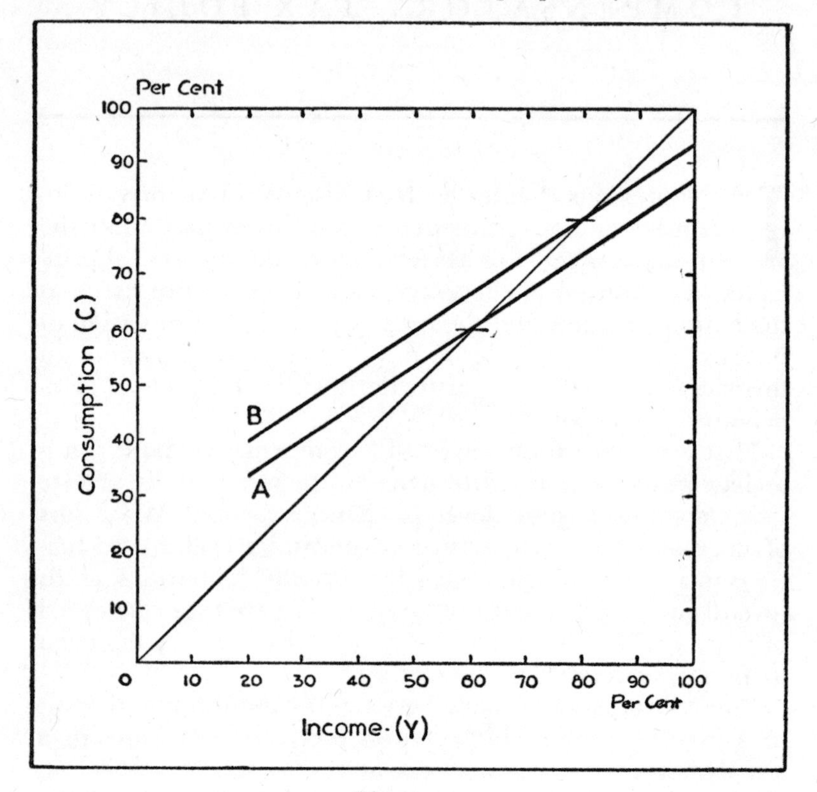

Chart 19.

The Consumption Function in a High-savings and a High-consumption Economy

equals unity. According to Consumption Function B, however, at 80 per cent of a full income level, the whole income is consumed.

Chart 20 represents the cyclical behavior of the highly

dynamic, high-savings economy, while Chart 21 represents the cycle movement in a mature, high-consumption economy. It is assumed in both cases that the amplitude of the cycle fills the whole gap between the self-sustaining income

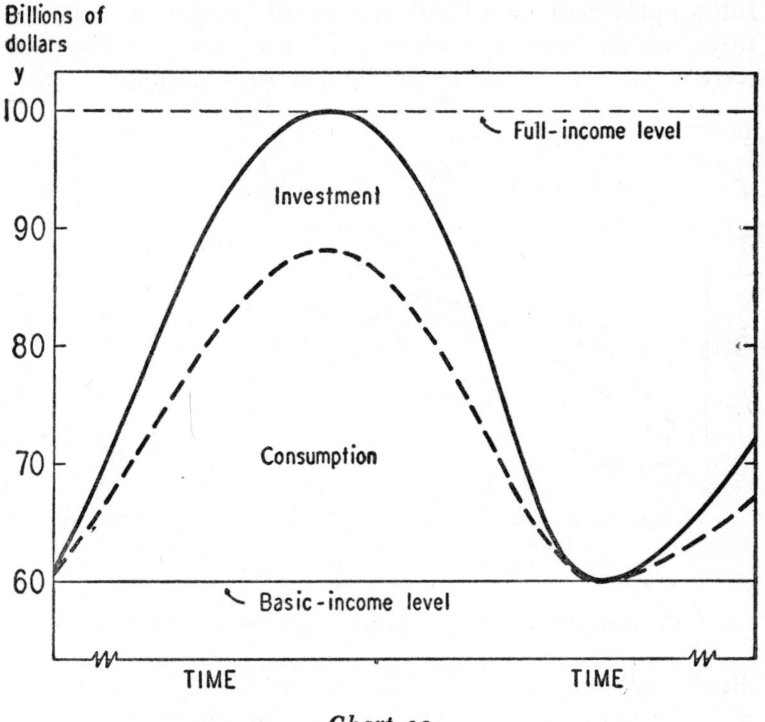

Chart 20.

Cyclical Behavior of a High-savings Economy

level (at which C = Y) and the full income level. It is also assumed that in each case the marginal propensity to consume is 0.67. Accordingly, in both cases investment is assumed to constitute one third, and consumption two thirds, of the fluctuating part of the income above the basic level. These arbitrary assumptions may be modified without invalidating the usefulness of the general scheme of analysis here employed.

Whatever may be true of the actual magnitude of the fluctuations in the two cases, it is at any rate true that a high-consumption economy (illustrated in Chart 21) can reach full employment on a lower volume of investment expenditures, unless, indeed, the marginal propensity to consume were much lower than in the high-savings economy—a con-

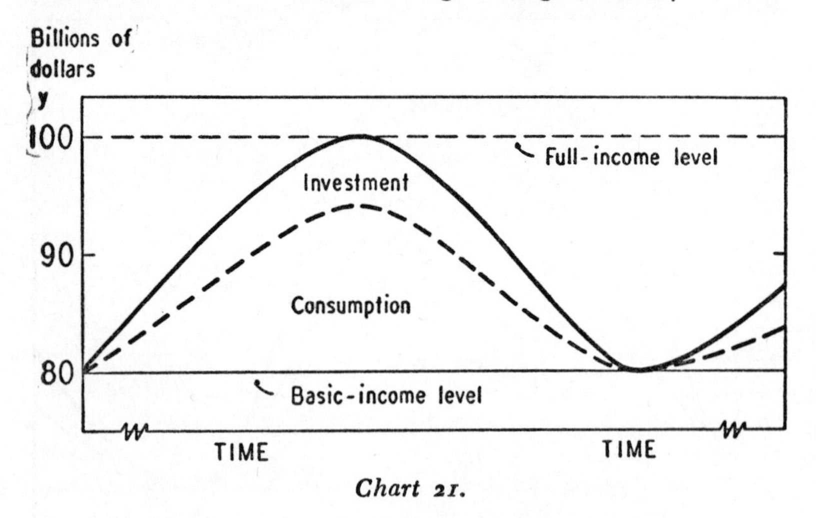

Chart 21.

Cyclical Behavior of a High-consumption Economy

dition not very probable, though theoretically not impossible. In a world in which independent investment outlets are relatively limited, a high-consumption economy is not only less likely to fall to low employment levels, but is, moreover, able to achieve full employment with relatively small investment outlays.

Stabilizing the Cycle

We may now consider the proposal to minimize the cycle movement by a system of fluctuating tax rates. There is not much use in discussing this proposal with respect to all types of taxes, since for many taxes such a scheme of timely fluctuation of rates is difficult, if not impossible. From a practical standpoint, relatively few taxes can be timed speedily. Taxes on payrolls and sales taxes can, however, very effectively be manipulated and timed according to the requirements of the cycle.[1]

Consider, first, a payroll tax collected at the source. Since we are concerned here purely with an effort to achieve stability, it is clear that the tax in question is not designed over the long run to produce any revenue for the government's operating budget, but is designed exclusively to facilitate economic stability. It follows, therefore, that when the taxes are collected, such collections should in some manner be placed in a fund which could subsequently be drawn upon and expended.[2]

Let us assume that the tax on payrolls is applied at some advancing rate during the last half of an upswing period, for example, from the point at which a half of the cyclical unemployment has been overcome. The tax would then be raised progressively as the peak of the boom is approached. As soon as it is evident that a turning point has been reached, the tax collections should cease entirely. Once it appears, however, that a recession is definitely under way and is in danger of developing into a cumulative deflation, the surplus funds previously collected should be drawn upon and poured back into the income stream.

To the extent that the payroll taxes were assessed against employers, they could be returned to aid employers to maintain current wage rates. In so far as payroll taxes had been deducted from wages, they should be returned to the wage earners to help maintain labor incomes in the depression.

In the former case, the remission of the funds would, in effect, lower the effective wage rate and thereby make it

1 Income taxes collected at the source could also be made flexible.

2 A more elaborate proposal, involving deferred wage payments, designed to help finance the war without inflationary consequences and to sustain the postwar economy, was published by J. M. Keynes in *How to Pay for the War*, Harcourt, Brace, 1940.

easier for the employer to maintain as nearly as possible a full corps of workers. In so far as this result is achieved, employment and consumption expenditures would be sustained. It is true that the employer might pocket the subsidy without maintaining or extending the volume of employment. It would not be easy to ascertain what the volume of employment would be were there no subsidy, and it is only from this bench mark that one can determine the extent to which the employer is using the subsidy for the maintenance or expansion of employment. There is thus the danger that, if the payroll tax fund is employed in this manner, the net effect would be merely to add to idle funds. But even this would at least have the favorable effect of increasing the liquidity of the firm and would thereby tend to hasten, sooner or later, expansionist activities. On balance, the imposition of a payroll tax on employers would tend to restrain the boom, and the repayment of these sums in depression would probably have some favorable cyclical compensatory effect.

In the second case, the payroll tax is a device to enforce compulsory saving upon wage earners during the boom, which savings are returned to the wage earners in the depression period. It is a deferred wage payment plan, wages being withheld in the prosperity phase and returned with interest in the depression phase. The plan would have a favorable indirect effect on employment, since the wage earners would have a larger income to spend in the depression. There is, however, the danger that employed workers receiving the deferred payments in a period of falling prices might save most of the windfall. The effect on consumption and, therefore, on employment, as far as these wage earners were concerned, might well be relatively small. The effect on consumption expenditures would, however, be definitely favorable with respect to part-time workers and unemployed workers.

Unemployment insurance financed by payroll taxes forms a special kind of tax on wages. The size of the payroll varies with the cycle and, therefore, the total tax collections rise and fall with the fluctuations in business conditions. Moreover, since the collected funds are disbursed in benefit payments to the unemployed in the depression period, the net tax collections should rapidly approach zero and even become a minus quantity. Thus, on balance, such tax funds are collected mainly during prosperity periods and are paid out to wage earners (though not to employed workers) in depression periods.

A cyclically adjusted sales tax can be implemented in a manner somewhat similar to a tax on wages. Such a tax, applied in the last phase of the upswing, would act as a drag on the rise of consumption expenditures. Under the assumptions which are here made, however, it is expected that such a sales tax would not check the advance short of full employment but would only make the advance steadier and thereby more prolonged. It is assumed that the tax is not severe enough to stop the dynamic forces which tend to drive the economy on toward full employment.

The funds collected from the sales tax might, as in the case of the wage tax, be distributed in the downswing and in the early stages of recovery. Such a plan would be a sales tax in reverse. But it does not appear probable that such a distribution could be implemented. It would require an extremely complicated and expensive accounting control to disburse the funds through the retailers to all purchasers of retail goods in some proportion to purchase vouchers. It would be much easier, from the standpoint of administration, merely to use funds so collected to finance government deficits arising from expansion of public works or relief expenditures. To make the funds most effective, it would be necessary that they constitute a *net addition* to public works (or to relief expenditures) during a depression period.

The purpose of these taxes is to check an undue expansion of consumption in the boom and, through their removal together with the return of previously collected taxes, to stimulate consumption in the depression. Moreover, they may be especially useful as a means to check a wartime inflation.

Question arises whether the best method of controlling

cyclical fluctuations is to impose in the upswing period a tax on consumption. Payroll taxes and sales taxes are peculiarly taxes which abstract from the consumption stream. This raises the very fundamental question whether the most desirable compensatory policy is to tax income which would normally flow into consumption or to tax income which would normally flow into savings. A tax which diminishes the flow of savings will impose some check upon investment in so far as investment expenditures cannot be financed adequately through monetary expansion. In so far as the taxes are imposed on income which would normally flow into consumption, not only are consumption expenditures reduced, but induced investment (via the Acceleration Principle) is also curtailed.

We are assuming here, it will be recalled, a society which is highly dynamic and in which economic progress develops surging private investment booms, and which tends, therefore, automatically toward full employment of resources. Yet, periodically, the upward march is interrupted by reason of the inherent tendency of a free enterprise economy to develop cyclical fluctuations. In such a society, be it noted, the rising income in the prosperity period is created not by government expenditures, but by net private investment. If now the mainspring of a surging investment boom has relatively little relation to the current level of consumption, but mainly to the stimulus flowing from economic progress (inventions, the discovery of new resources, the exploitation of new territory), the boom might not be seriously checked by payroll or sales taxes. Under a surging investment boom the induced consumption is likely to be very large, and the imposition of taxes on consumption might, therefore, merely steady the situation. Moreover, if consumption taxes are employed instead of income taxes, it is likely that the investment will be financed more fully from voluntary savings and less from bank credit expansion. This also would make for a healthier boom. If a sharp step up were made in income tax rates, with no restraint on consumption (via payroll or sales taxes), consumption expenditures would rise rapidly, thereby (via the Acceleration Principle) adding to the investment stimulus (already vigorously fed from the independent factors of economic progress) still more. It thus appears that, under the conditions here assumed, the boom would develop in a more stable manner under a cyclical adjustment of payroll or sales taxes than under a cyclical adjustment of highly progressive corporate and individual income taxes.

It has sometimes been argued, especially from the standpoint of the under-consumption theory of the cycle,[8] that the boom comes to an end because of a deficiency of consumption *in the boom years*. According to this view, there is something wrong with the ratio of consumption to investment during the boom. The ratio is said to be too low. But this position is, I think, not defensible. If one deducts the independent, spontaneous investment from total investment, one derives as the remainder the residue of investment which bears a relation to consumption. If consumption is increased, the investment needed to supply the flow of consumption goods will increase also. Dependent (induced) investment would rise if consumption rose. Independent investment would presumably remain unaltered. Thus, if you increase consumption, you will also increase investment. The ratio of consumption to induced investment will not be altered. Thus, the boom will be magnified if consumption is stimulated, and, if spontaneous investment is strong, such a process may even engender some considerable price inflation. Once the spontaneous investment has run out, a depression will ensue, and it will be all the more intense by reason of the extra stimulus given to consumption (and thereby induced

[8] Some readers have wrongly inferred that I subscribe to the under-consumption theory of the cycle. This is quite wrong. The depression, in my view, is caused by a decline in investment—a decline resulting not from inadequate consumption, but from the temporary saturation in spontaneously evolving investment opportunities. It is, of course, true that, if it were possible for consumption to rise as investment declines, no serious depression would ensue, although some transitional difficulties would be encountered. But the under-consumption theory alleges a difficulty in consumption in the boom period.

investment via the Acceleration Principle) in the boom years.

We have just discussed the relative effects of a tax on consumption (wage or sales tax) and a tax on the savings stream (steeply progressive income tax) upon the cycle movement, under the assumption of a vigorous expansionist tendency operating virtually exclusively in terms of private investment. The problem is to bring about a shift of the consumption function by means of a shift in the tax structure, so that the fluctuations in private investment will be overcome by offsetting fluctuations in consumption.

Raising the Propensity to Consume

We have now to consider a cycle development which is stimulated largely through net income-creating expenditures of the government. Here it is assumed that private investment outlets are, on the whole, inadequate, and that we have to deal with a long-run condition of chronic unemployment.

If the recovery is proceeding mainly under the stimulus of net income-creating governmental expenditures and to a relatively small degree under the stimulus of forward-looking private investments related to economic progress, the essential problem is that of modifying the functioning of the economy so as to render the new income, in a measure, self-perpetuating. From the analysis which we have given above, it follows that, if the larger new income is to be made self-perpetuating, it will be necessary in some manner to shift the level of the basic income (at which consumption is 100 per cent of income) to a higher plane. This means that the propensity to consume must somehow be increased, the consumption function must be shifted upward so as to reduce the margin between the basic self-perpetuating income level (at which consumption equals income) and the full-income level. The problem is not to cause a cyclical fluctuation in the consumption function (offsetting the fluctuation in the rate of investment), as in the case considered above, but to raise permanently the propensity to consume.

A redistribution of income, through social or community expenditures and a progressive tax structure, may affect the aggregate consumption function. Since the payroll and the sales taxes clearly weigh on consumption, such taxes would weaken the propensity to consume. On the other side, a steeply progressive income tax would alter the distribution of income and would tend to strengthen the propensity to consume. The income level at which aggregate consumption of the nation as a whole would equal income would be raised. Raising income tax rates would tend in the direction of making the newly created income more nearly self-perpetuating.

In the event that there is not available an adequate volume of forward-looking, anticipatory private investment, it will be necessary to substitute public investment, or else, by tax measures and otherwise, to make the newly created income as far as possible self-sustaining. In a situation in which investment activity is relatively weak, it is not necessary that as large a proportion of income shall be saved and expended on capital goods as in the case of a highly dynamic economy. It behooves such a society, therefore, to adjust itself to a higher consumption basis. Consumption is necessarily the ultimate end of economic activity. Savings perform a useful function in so far as they are necessary for growth and expansion. But, in a less dynamic society, we are confronted with the alternative of using more of our resources for the production of consumption goods, whether durable or nondurable, or else of permitting them to run to waste through nonutilization. Such a society needs peculiarly to stress consumption if it is to achieve full employment.

We have reached the conclusion that, in a highly dynamic economy in which investment booms are vigorous, the appropriate type of taxes to apply during the boom is some form of tax on consumption. On the one side, this policy would tend to hold in check an abnormal rise in consumption and thus dampen the induced stimulus (via the Acceleration Principle) to investment. On the other side, such a policy would provide funds for investment more largely from voluntary savings and thereby minimize the excesses of bank credit expansion.

In a less dynamic, less rapidly expanding (mature) economy, investment booms are less vigorous. Such a society is, therefore, less likely to reach full employment. In such a situation it is important to stimulate consumption expenditures. When booms are weak and incomplete, consumption taxes should not be applied as a cycle control measure. These circumstances suggest measures to raise the propensity to consume and develop a high-consumption economy.

Question may be raised as to whether the progressive income tax rates, designed to raise the propensity to consume, should fluctuate with the cycle, being increased in the boom and reduced in the depression; or whether the rate structure, while steeply progressive, should remain fixed in the various phases of the cycle. On balance, the latter is to be preferred. Excessively high rates in the boom cannot help the basic problem of increasing the aggregate community consumption over the entire cycle, since higher rates in the boom presuppose lower rates in the depression. The total volume of funds tapped from the savings stream and diverted into community consumption would not thereby be increased over the entire cycle period. Again, it may be argued that extra high rates should be levied during the boom phase in order to pay off cyclically incurred debt. But this is scarcely valid, since higher rates in the better years imply lower rates in depression, and hence the cyclical debt problem is not helped by such a fluctuating tax structure.

The milder cyclical fluctuations of private investment in a society such as that here under consideration could best be compensated for not by a tax program, but by offsetting fluctuations in governmental expenditures.

Thus, for a dynamic, expanding economy enjoying vigorous booms a fluctuating consumption tax may be the appropriate tax policy; for a less rapidly expanding, mature economy a fixed but steeply progressive income tax structure is indicated.

Chapter XIV

THE DYNAMIC VERSUS THE CIRCULAR FLOW ECONOMY

THE central stream of economic thought, comprising the early classical and neoclassical writers, has often been described as a system of static economics. It consisted essentially of an analysis of how the pricing process determines the allocation of productive resources. It explained how commodities and productive agents are priced in a "circular flow" economy and how, in a society so constituted, the productive process generates a demand for the products which it creates, so that the economy could continue to function at full employment. The rigorous Ricardian analysis explained how the pricing process ensures the reproduction of both the capital and the labor supply without either growth or contraction. It explained how the productive process is able to create consumer demand sufficient to absorb the whole product. In a "circular flow" economy, consumption equals net output. Saving takes the form of allocating a sufficient amount of the gross product to capital replacement. In such a society the whole of the net real income is consumed and aggregate saving is directed exclusively to capital replacement. In such a society the level of consumers' demand determines the volume of investment.

Such was the character of the equilibrium state of early classical theory. Profits tend to fall to that irreducible minimum which will just ensure a maintenance of the accumulated capital stock. Wages tend to fall to the so-called "subsistence" level, varying from country to country according to the achieved standard of living, at which the population will just reproduce itself.

This analysis correctly perceived that the price system per se could not generate economic progress. It recognized that the price system, no matter how flexible or how perfectly competitive, could not of itself provide any net investment outlet. Progress could be generated only by innovations, the development of new products, new techniques, new methods of production, the discovery of new resources, and the opening of new territory. Thus, already in early classical doctrine net investment and net saving were regarded as a function not of the operation of the price system, but rather as a function of progress in the arts.[1] Through the development of technology and the exploitation of new resources, the price system is distorted away from static equilibrium, away from the "circular flow" economy in which consumption equals production. In a progressive society, investment is no longer purely a function of consumption. The tables are turned upside down. Consumption, under the dynamic stimulus of expansion, now becomes in considerable measure a function of investment.

It is just this fact which explains the emergence of business fluctuations. The business cycle, under the automatic functioning of the economy, is the inevitable by-product of growth and economic progress.

The price system in such a society is compelled to adjust itself to an unruly, unstable economy with a violently fluctuating output. The norm of the price structure is no longer reached, as in the "circular flow" economy, at the full output level. At full employment the distribution of the product among the contributing agents is skewed toward an excess of profits. The investment boom, created by innovational developments, distorts the system away from the equilibrium position at which the cost-price system is in balance.

[1] According to the classical economists, the tendency toward the stationary state could be checked only by invention, territorial expansion, and population growth.

The norm toward which the equilibrating process in a dynamic society tends, in the event that growth and technological change prove inadequate to provide investment of boom proportions, is an equilibrium point short of full employment. How far the equilibrium norm in a dynamic society will diverge from full employment depends upon how far the expansionist forces had previously driven the price structure away from the "circular flow" *tableau economique* of a static society. This follows from the fact that the process of economic progress, with its attendant fluctuations of income and employment, has created a set of firmly rooted institutional arrangements which are not easily altered, and which do not permit an easy return to the "circular flow" norm of a static society. The economy cannot automatically pass swiftly from a condition of dynamic expansion to a full-consumption society in which consumption equals income without encountering serious unemployment. The orientation of the price system to the requirements of a rapidly growing and widely fluctuating economy has created consumption and saving patterns out of line with the "circular flow" equilibrium. The institutional framework is thus geared to produce full employment only at high investment levels.

Consumption and Net Investment

In the "circular flow" economy, replacement investment is determined by the level of consumption. But in an expanding, dynamic economy, net investment is essentially spontaneous and independent of the current volume of consumption. Indeed, a large part of consumption now rises and falls according to fluctuations in the rate of investment.

An essential difference between the type of analysis of economic crises represented by Malthus, Sismondi, and Hobson on the one side, and that represented by Spiethoff, Cassel, Robertson, and Schumpeter on the other, is to be found in the treatment of these two schools of the relation of consumption to net saving. Malthus and his followers thought that there was an inherently correct proportion between net aggregate saving and consumption. Indeed, Oscar Lange asserts that Malthus had found the precise solution of this problem. According to Lange:

> If people would spend their whole income on consumption, investment would obviously be zero, while the demand for investment would be zero, too, if they consumed nothing. Thus, mere common sense suggests that there must be somewhere in between an optimum propensity to save which maximises investment.[2]

Now the fact is that, no matter what the level of consumption, the appropriate amount of net saving and net investment necessary to sustain any given level of consumption is precisely zero. Any level of consumption, no matter how high, can be maintained indefinitely as long as the capital required to produce the given consumer real income is adequately replaced. But capital replacement involves no net saving whatever.

It is true that an *increase* in consumption from a lower level to a higher level presents a different problem. But what is often forgotten is that it is just this development which involves a dynamic and not a static type of analysis. One cannot, by taking thought thereof, add one cubit to one's stature. Neither can one raise consumption from a lower level to a higher level by making an appeal to the limitless potential wants of human beings. Consumption cannot rise without a prior increase in income and production. Some qualifications, mainly of a short-run character, are, of course, necessary. A special case is that of the more well to do, who may utilize idle funds for increased consumption. This is doubtless done more or less at the bottom of a depression, particularly with respect to durable consumers' goods, such as automobiles, and this case furnishes at times a part of the explanation of the lower turning point. But these qualifications are, at all events, limited in scope and apply only to short-

[2] Oscar Lange, "The Rate of Interest and the Optimum Propensity to Consume," *Economica*, February, 1938.

run analysis. They cannot be invoked as an explanation of the secular rise in real income during the last one hundred and fifty years. The explanation of this phenomenon can be found only in a dynamic analysis of production. The explanation is to be sought in factors external to the functioning of the price system, with its tendency to seek an equilibrium level at the "circular flow" norm. The explanation is to be sought in technological change, in the discovery of new products, new processes, and new resources. These factors, external to and upsetting the static price equilibrium, have created new productive powers and have thereby raised output and real income. Thus, *as a result,* consumption has been lifted to new high levels. It was not increased consumption that called forth net investment and net saving. On the contrary, it was net investment and net saving, springing from the dynamic factors of economic progress, which caused consumption to rise. Now, after it is discovered that consumption has in fact risen, it will not do to argue that, because consumption is now higher, new investment in plant and equipment will be required to produce it. For it was just this prior new investment which caused the rise in consumption. Thus, the new capital necessary to sustain the consumption is already present. In the "circular flow" economy the level of consumption determines the level of replacement investment. But in the dynamic economy it is net investment, generated by innovational developments, that raises and determines the new level of consumption.

The dynamic process resulting in net investment distorts the price structure away from the "circular flow" equilibrium so as to create the necessary volume of net aggregate saving. But this process cannot ensure the continuance of production at full employment. Herein one encounters an essential difference between a static, "circular flow" economy and a dynamic, progressive economy. In the "circular flow" economy any income level reached tends to be self-perpetuating. In the dynamic economy the higher levels of income reached in boom periods cannot be sustained unless technological progress and extensive growth are adequate to maintain investment at boom proportions. For, if the dynamic factors working for net investment peter out, as they have sooner or later in every boom, the distortion of the price system necessarily brought about by the dynamic process itself cannot quickly restore the "circular flow" equilibrium. In other words, customs, habits, and institutional arrangements which determine the consumption function have become firmly imbedded in the social structure, and these set up powerful resistances to the restoration of the "circular flow" equilibrium. As net investment falls off sharply, voluntary individual consumption cannot and does not rise sufficiently to fill the gap left by the receding tide of investment. Thus, total expenditures decline and the economy falls toward an equilibrial, self-perpetuating income level far short of full employment.

Technological innovations making for *intensive* expansion may be expected to continue with unabated vigor. Our society can, therefore, remain as highly dynamic as that of the nineteenth century only if we can find a substitute for the *extensive* stimulus to investment springing from territorial expansion and population growth. Geared as our economy is to a high net investment level by a deeply rooted pattern of consumption with respect to income, we shall be compelled to seek full employment of our resources by deliberately injecting a new stimulus to investment. It is just because we have developed, in our highly dynamic society, firmly fixed institutions and habits affecting the income elasticity of saving that we cannot rely upon autonomous increases in consumption to provide full employment once the extensive expansionist stimulus to investment has largely disappeared. Voluntary individual consumption can provide full employment only in the "circular flow" economy in which there is no net investment and no net saving.

Voluntary individual consumption cannot rise to higher levels except as it is lifted through the prior process of investment. It will not rise high enough through the intensive investment process alone to give us full employment. A way must be found to raise consumption independently of the autonomous investment process. This way is open through the avenue of governmental expenditures. In the past, these expenditures have been mainly for war and defense, and currently we are witnessing such expenditures on an unprecedented scale. But we may hope that in the future public welfare projects will take the place of war as a major object of governmental expenditure. War, despite all its attendant evils, has played a dynamic role in the history of modern capitalism. Outlays on public welfare projects could play an equally dynamic role. And there is reason to hope that they could be managed so as to prevent the disastrous inflation typically accompanying war expenditures. The latter cannot be curtailed when full employment is reached. Moreover, the national emergency which calls them forth is so overwhelming that all other considerations are sacrificed to the one aim of national security. But an expansionist public welfare program has as its goal not only full employment, but also the security and stability of the social structure. It is, therefore, reasonable to hope that it might serve not merely as a mainspring of expansion, but also as a balance wheel regulating the fluctuations in the rate of private investment.

The independent increase in consumption, thus deliberately created, will stimulate new investment. The relationship between investment and consumption is, therefore, reversed. Instead of autonomous investment being relied upon exclusively for the expansionist process, outlays on public welfare projects are undertaken in order to raise consumption, quite independently, to higher levels, thereby opening up new outlets for investment. Community consumption would thus lead the way, and new investment would follow.

The development of science and the requirements of modern ways of living in an urban community entail community consumption expenditures on an undreamed-of scale. Many forms of consumption cannot be engaged in on the individual basis. Consumption in large measure, under modern conditions, requires the co-operation of large groups. We cannot enjoy public roads, public health, social security, recreational and cultural facilities, low-cost housing, and the conservation and development of natural resources without community expenditures. Individual consumption expenditures need increasingly, under modern conditions, to be supplemented by community expenditures.

Through this process, as a secondary consequence, an increase in individual, voluntary consumption is induced by reason of the prior increase in the level of individual incomes. But the new higher level of income cannot be maintained, in the absence of changes in the consumption function, unless the total level of consumption is again pushed forward by deliberate action to still higher levels. For, unless stimulated by an ever-rising consumption trend, investment, autonomously supported by only the intensive expansionist factors, will not continue to increase adequately to create full employment.

A higher level of individual consumption can also be fostered by a shift in the tax structure away from consumption taxes toward greater reliance on progressive taxation. How far taxation should be used as an engine to foster a high-consumption economy depends not upon abstract notions about balancing the budget, but upon considerations relative to the volume of savings needed to supply the capital outlays required if income is pushed up to the maximum level which the productive resources make possible, and upon considerations relative to the most desirable distribution of wealth and income. Changes in the relative proportion of public receipts from borrowing and from taxation can be effectively used as a means through which control may be exercised so as to ensure an adequate supply of capital and, on the other side, prevent undue concentration of wealth.

It is, of course, conceivable that the autonomous, dynamic factors opening intensive investment outlets might develop so rapid an expansion as to equal the past effect of extensive and intensive growth combined. But I am not aware of any convincing evidence that this eventuality is at all probable.

It is certainly reasonable to expect that our economy will remain intensively dynamic, though less expansionist, owing to the relative cessation of extensive growth. Consumption, therefore, needs to play a larger role in the future. New investment will be less motivated by autonomous factors. New levels of consumption will be reached, partly through the dynamics of technical progress, as in the past, and partly through the deliberate stimulation of consumption by the community as a whole. It is this latter which must take the place of extensive expansion, if total consumption is to continue to rise as it has in the past. With a slowing down of population growth, this could well mean a more rapid rise in per capita income than ever before. Through the combined stimulation of community consumption and technological innovations, the per capita real income can be raised at a rate considerably greater than that achieved in the era of extensive growth. The potentialities for high living standards are prodigious under modern capacities for production. And if these potentialities are translated into reality by a deliberate implementation of the role of government in the consumption sphere, we may expect a reinvigoration of the role of private enterprise. The incentive to invest which, in the dynamic economy of the last century, came mainly from technical progress and extensive growth, will, in the future, be fed from the combined springs of technical progress and a greatly expanded public consumption and public investment program.

John Stuart Mill on the High-consumption Economy

Some of the economists of the nineteenth century were quite aware that the era of great extensive expansion would some day come to a close. There is much in the early literature of economics which looks toward the so-called "stationary state." The term "stationary state," which the earlier economists used, while satisfactory as a concept for static analysis, is somewhat unfortunate when applied to a historical period, for it implies, among other things, the cessation of the progress of economic technique. The term "mature economy" is perhaps to be preferred, and, in fact, this term appears to describe better what John Stuart Mill had in mind when he used the term "stationary state." The essential characteristics of this state are, first, a decline in population growth, and, second, a decline in the ratio of new capital formation to national income. But it does not imply, as some have inferred, a cessation of progress. Indeed, Mill said quite plainly:

It is scarcely necessary to remark that a stationary condition of capital and population implies no stationary state of human improvement. . . . Even the industrial arts might be as earnestly and as successfully cultivated, with this sole difference, that, instead of serving no purpose but the increase of wealth, industrial improvements would produce their legitimate effect, that of abridging labour.

The nonexpansionist economy may be aptly characterized as a high-consumption economy, an economy in which all, or nearly all, of the total income is spent on consumers' goods. The nonexpansionist economy can, however, still remain a progressive economy with an ever-rising standard of living.

A mature economy may, as Mill stated, under certain conditions modernize and improve its capital equipment, introducing continually new techniques, without tapping any new savings or making any net additions to capital formation. If the progress of technique in the capital goods industries outruns the rise in wage rates, then the accumulated depreciation reserves will be adequate to finance the replacement of an old machine by a new one more productive than the old. On the other hand, if there has been no technical progress in machine production, if the efficiency of a machine requiring for its production a given amount of labor is not increased, it follows that the depreciation reserve, based on original cost, will be adequate only in the event that wages [8]

[8] Labor is here used, for short, to represent all the factors employed in the production of machines.

have not risen. Thus, depreciation reserves will be adequate to finance capital renewals more productive than the old only in the event that the productivity of labor in the capital goods industries has increased more rapidly than wage rates.[4] But if innovations are made which are capital saving, plant and equipment may be modernized and made more productive merely by the expenditure of depreciation allowances, without tapping any new savings or making any net additions to capital formation. A mature economy is prepared to make large replacement capital expenditures, and these will raise the productive capacity if capital-saving innovations are taking place. Replacement capital outlays are, however, financed from depreciation allowances and not out of new savings. Such a society can make a considerable degree of progress, even though it consumes all of its income.

John Stuart Mill by no means regarded an economy which consumes all, or nearly all, of its income as an undesirable one. The ultimate end of production is, of course, consumption, and a high-consumption economy achieves this end to a maximum degree. Yet such an economy may make progress with respect to new processes; it may also make progress with respect to new products.

While some progress, given technological developments of the character described above, is not incompatible with even a full-consumption economy such as Mill envisaged, such a society nevertheless clearly fails to realize to the full the potentialities of technical progress. To achieve this requires a volume of savings adequate to ensure all the new investment which changes in technique make possible. Unless sufficient investment is made to exploit these to the limit, the full potential of productive power and rising standards of efficiency will not be reached. Thus, a 100 per cent consumption economy can never attain the economic progress which improving technique can offer.

[4] One may state the proposition also as follows: When capital-saving innovations are made, less capital per unit of output is required than before. This means that the expenditure of replacement allowances will yield a net increase in productivity.

There *is,* thus, an optimum ratio of consumption to income at the full income level. In a world in which extensive expansion is largely gone, and in which investment outlets are mainly limited to those opened by technical progress, this optimum will be higher. Such a society, in order to operate at full productive capacity, needs to become a high-consumption economy. The free functioning of the price system will not necessarily bring this about. If the price system (including wage rates) is distorted by monopolistic practices, matters are still worse. It may thus become necessary in a nonexpansionist economy to supplement private consumption with public expenditures financed by borrowing the savings of the public, or by tapping these savings through a progressive tax structure.

Chapter XV

PRICE FLEXIBILITY AND FULL EMPLOYMENT OF RESOURCES

A DISCUSSION of the role of price flexibility in the functioning of the economy must begin with a definition of terms. The phrase "price flexibility" is subject to two possible interpretations which need to be sharply distinguished. These are (*a*) structural price flexibility [1] and (*b*) cyclical price flexibility.[2]

By structural price flexibility I mean the long-term secular adjustment in the price structure. It is concerned not with the *level* of prices, but with the *interrelation* of individual prices. Thus, for example, changes in technology and the methods of production continually alter the unit cost of production of one commodity relative to other commodities. The cost of producing an automobile has, by reason of changes in technique and mass production methods, fallen greatly in the last two decades relative to the unit cost of production of the great bulk of manufactured commodities. Structural price flexibility implies an adjustment of prices to changes in unit costs [3] springing from unequal rates of

1 This involves in part, of course, the problem of monopoly price: the divergence of price from marginal cost.

2 In general, these terms correspond to those used in *The Structure of the American Economy,* Part I, pp. 126, 129, under the headings: (1) "Sensitivity to Basic Factors Conditioning Economic Activity"; and (2) "Sensitivity to Depression and Recovery."

3 Unit costs may, of course, under conditions of monopolistic competition, be enhanced through large advertising expenditures. This element of cost constitutes one of the important factors causing maladjustment in the price structure.

technological progress in different industries, or from shifts in the pattern of wants. Without structural price flexibility the full gains of economic progress could clearly not be realized. Structural price flexibility implies that the price system is functioning in a manner to yield the largest possible product of goods and services which a given stage of technique makes possible. A structurally flexible price system operates to direct the productive resources into channels which will yield the largest social product. Without structural price flexibility an uneconomic allocation of resources would prevail.[4]

Cyclical price flexibility or inflexibility is a quite different matter. Unfortunately, in much of the literature, the distinction between cyclical and structural flexibility is not made.[5] Cyclical price flexibility has to do with the sensitivity of prices to fluctuations of the business cycle. Commodities whose prices move quickly in response to changes in the national income and whose amplitude of fluctuation is relatively large are said to be cycle-sensitive commodities with respect to price. Raw materials, both agricultural and industrial, are, by and large, cyclically price sensitive, while finished manufactured products in large measure are insensitive to cyclical changes in employment, output, and income. In the case of farm products the sensitivity is limited to price responses, while in the case of certain industrial raw materials the sensitivity relates both to price and to fluctuations in output.

There is, as far as I am aware, no disagreement among economists with respect to the desirability of structural price flexibility. Without structural price flexibility it is quite impossible for the community to obtain the full fruits of economic progress. Arbitrary interferences which obstruct structural price flexibility necessarily result in an uneconomic utilization of resources. Moreover, any marked derangement in

[4] See discussion under the heading, "Sensitivity to Basic Factors Conditioning Economic Activity," pp. 126–29 in *The Structure of the American Economy,* Part I, National Resources Committee, 1939.

[5] This aspect of price behavior is discussed at length in *The Structure of the American Economy,* Part I, Chapter VIII.

the structural adjustment of the prices of important commodities in relation to unit costs may have a disrupting effect upon consumption and investment expenditures, intensifying or contributing to the initiation of a decline in industrial activity. Thus, at times, structural price maladjustment may contribute to cyclical movements. For example, the enormous increase in agricultural tariffs in the great raw-material importing countries in the last years of the twenties doubtless affected unfavorably the terms of trade of the primary producing countries and contributed to the Great Depression. For the most part, however, structural price maladjustments probably accumulate relatively slowly and have little influence on cyclical movements. They do, however, retard the secular advance in real income and in the standard of living. Under modern conditions, with the great development of institutional controls, corporate, trade-union, agricultural, and governmental, there is danger that structural price maladjustments may present serious obstacles to economic progress. This area, though largely neglected, offers an important field for the exercise of price policy.

Price Flexibility and the Cycle

It is, however, with reference to cyclical price flexibility that most discussions of price policy are concerned. Unemployment and underutilization of resources, it is said, are caused, or at least intensified, by the depression insensitivity of a large and important group of commodities. It is suggested that depression might, in large measure, be prevented or remedied by making all commodities as price sensitive as are most raw materials.[6] It is argued that the deficiency in effective demand which results in depression is, in greater or less degree, caused or intensified by the cyclical insensitivity

[6] This position, for example, has often been attributed to Gardiner C. Means. While Means does lay great stress on the lack of balance in the price structure growing out of the cyclical dispersion of administered and free market prices, nevertheless he apparently does not believe that *in practice* an adequate remedy can be found in a policy aiming to make all prices flexible.

of administered prices. Any incipient deficiency in effective demand could, it is believed, largely be corrected, were it possible to achieve short-run price sensitivity. To the extent that prices do fall in depression, some considerable increase in real buying power, over and above what would otherwise be the case, would be achieved, according to this thesis. A high degree of cyclical price sensitivity, it is said, would help to sustain effective real demand and would prevent fluctuations in output and employment.

In support of this thesis, it has been urged that price dispersion—the divergence of agricultural prices from administered prices, the divergence of raw material prices from the prices of finished products, the divergence of price-sensitive commodities from price-insensitive commodities—is highly correlated with fluctuations in output and employment. The inference is that it is the dispersion of prices which causes the fluctuation of the cycle.

These considerations raise two crucial questions. First, what is the causal connection between price dispersion and the business cycle; is price dispersion cause or is it effect? Second, if it were possible to extend the area of price sensitivity to include all commodities, would cyclical fluctuations be minimized?

Broadly speaking, the main explanations of business cycle fluctuations can be classified under two heads: First, those which explain business fluctuations in terms of price movements, and second, those which explain business fluctuations in terms of fluctuations in the rate of investment.

The former explanation of the cycle, in terms of price movements, may be subdivided into two groups: First, the monetary explanation which seeks the causes of industrial fluctuations in terms of general price movements, and second, the price dispersion explanation which finds the cause in terms of maladjustments in the cost-price structure. According to the former, public policy directed toward the maintenance of the total money flow is the all-important desideratum. According to the latter, appropriate adjustment of the cost-price structure is the remedy for depression.

It is not possible here to go into an exhaustive examination of the causes of business fluctuations. An examination of the trend of thought over the last four decades, however, will disclose the fact, I think, that a growing body of opinion stresses fluctuations in the rate of investment as the dominant factor in cyclical movements. It is not necessary for the purpose of this chapter to go into the various factors which bring about fluctuations in the rate of investment. They relate to factors which cause violent changes in the marginal efficiency of capital in relation to relatively small changes in the rate of interest.

What is all-important for our purposes is the fact that a decline in the rate of investment results in an accelerated decline in income and in effective demand, and that any such decline of necessity produces a wide dispersion of prices. This follows from the fact that certain prices are highly sensitive to changes in effective demand, while others are insensitive. It is clear that, granted a decline in income, price dispersion is bound to follow. It is, therefore, reasonable to suppose that the correlation of price dispersion with fluctuations in income represents a relationship in which the latter is cause and the former effect.

A decline in income, by reason of the high price sensitivity of certain commodities, results simultaneously in price dispersion. This conclusion is reasonable in so far as one can find independent outside factors—familiar in the investment theories of the business cycle—which cause the decline in income. In similar manner, as soon as income rises under the spur of increased investment, it is to be expected that the price-sensitive commodities will quickly respond, and so the price dispersion will narrow. It may, therefore, be argued that it is not only the fluctuation in the rate of investment, and, therefore, in income, which causes the price dispersion—the maladjustment in the price structure between price-sensitive and non-price-sensitive commodities—but also that this price dispersion can, in fact, be remedied not by a direct attack on the price dispersion itself, but only by policies which aim to correct the root difficulty, namely, the low level of income.

There can be no doubt that a balanced cost-price structure is favorable to the proper functioning of the economy. A balance in the cost-price structure, as we have already noted, is of peculiar importance from the standpoint of structural changes and differential cost reductions (or, conversely, changes in productivity) in different industries. But while a balance in the cost-price structure is a favorable condition, it does not necessarily follow that, once forces are at work deranging a balanced cost-price structure, an effort at correction of such price maladjustment per se can be relied upon to improve the rate of business activity. Instead, what is needed is an attack upon the general factors causing the price dispersion. A mere artificial rectification of the price dispersion may get at the root causes of the decline in income and employment no more than a tampering with the thermometer can change the temperature. The price dispersion is, indeed, a fairly accurate thermometer registering disturbances in the economic temperature.

Consider, for example, the situation at the beginning of a period of depression. A vigorous boom has come to an end, has died "a natural death." By this I mean that the currently available outlets for investment in plant and equipment have been temporarily exhausted. This situation is not uncommonly the basic cause of the termination of a boom. All of the available new developments which the progress of science and technology, together with the growth of population, have made possible have been exploited to the utmost extent economically feasible, and not infrequently even beyond this point. Once industry has been equipped with the capital facilities which technology has made available, there remains little that can be done profitably for a time, except to maintain the capital plant already constructed. Typically, economic progress is made by spurts, by leaps and bounds. The essence of a boom is a gigantic spurt in capital formation. This involves not only plant and equipment of industries and utilities, but also office buildings, hotels, houses, and apartments. Frequently, a backlog of housing requirements, or the rise of a new industry, results in an accelerated pace of construction. When the new developments have been exploited to the full, the boom dies. The spurt in capital formation cannot last at the pace set. The boom subsides because a saturation point has temporarily been reached. For the moment, there is no room left for further investment expansion or for new capital outlays. It takes time before the cumulative effects of new developments can again manifest themselves, before the discovery of new techniques, new resources, and new industries, and the growth of population, will set the stage for another boom.

In such a situation, and this is the typical one at the end of a period of moderate or high prosperity, it is clear that the driving force which causes a decline in income is the sharp reduction in investment expenditures; and as soon as this occurs, a price dispersion develops between the cyclically flexible prices of agricultural and raw material commodities on the one side, and the cyclically rigid prices of many finished products on the other. The price dispersion is not the cause of the depression. It is a result of the decline in the national income and in employment caused by the initial decline in investment expenditures.

Consider now the question whether in such a situation a program designed to make the administered prices as cyclically flexible as those of agricultural and some other raw materials would improve matters and cure the depression.

It is not possible to make a general statement about every individual commodity or every individual industry. In certain specific cases, particularly if these cases do not become generalized for the economy as a whole, a downward readjustment of a rigid administered price may frequently prove beneficial. That such may be true proves nothing about the desirability of a program designed to make rigid prices cyclically flexible.

The problem is peculiarly pertinent to the capital goods industries that are most affected by the temporary saturation referred to above. Once the period of temporary saturation has been worked through and the conditions are ripe for a recovery in investment expenditures, owing to the accumulation of depreciation, obsolescence, and the emergence of new products, a price reduction in the capital goods industries would be beneficial. But it is quite a different matter to argue that at the beginning of the depression, while the temporary saturation of the capital goods market prevails, cyclical flexibility of prices would avail as a depression remedy. For example, it is certainly not clear that, at the end of 1929, a reduction in the prices of building materials and building labor commensurate with the decline in agricultural prices could again have induced anyone to continue to erect gigantic office buildings such as the Empire State Building in New York City. And much the same held true for metropolitan areas throughout the United States. It is the fact of the *temporary saturation* which is all-important. During this state of affairs no price reduction, commensurate with that of price-sensitive commodities, will again bring about a recovery in investment expenditures. In so far as there are areas—as is certainly the case—in which there is no pronounced saturation, a more favorable price might, in fact, in some measure sustain investment expenditures. But it is to be doubted that such cases are sufficiently numerous and important in the economy as a whole to sustain, in a significant degree, the volume of investment expenditures in the downswing of the cycle.

If in industry as a whole, and particularly in the capital goods and durable consumers' goods industries, prices and wages were reduced drastically to an extent commensurate with the decline in the prices of cyclically flexible commodities—agricultural and other raw materials—it is to be expected that, by and large, such price and wage declines would merely reduce the gross volume of monetary expenditures made in the capital goods and durable consumers' goods area, without appreciably affecting the physical volume of output. Since these cost payments are also income receipts of individuals, incomes fall along with a decline in costs. In these circumstances, the effect of the price reduction is merely to accelerate the decline in the national income [7] and thus intensify the downward movement in business activity. Moreover, the uncertainty created by the disruption of reasonable stability and normality with respect to the industrial price and wage structure would only serve to intensify the already unfavorable business expectations engendered by the decline in investment.

If income and effective demand could be maintained or expanded at the moment that costs are reduced, the effect would, of course, be different. Once the deflationary aspect of the cycle has ceased, once the passage of time makes increasingly necessary the replacement of plant and equipment required to maintain the minimum volume of consumption purchases, once obsolescence and new developments begin to improve the outlets for investment, it is certainly clear that a reduction in prices in the capital goods industries, made possible by cost-reducing improvements effected during the depression, would be favorable to expansion. Such price reduction, it should be noted, would conform with the requirements of structural price flexibility. It has to do with cyclical price policy, mainly with respect to timing. Similarly, in conjunction with a governmental expansion of public investment, a program of cost reduction in the industries directly involved would facilitate expansion of output and employment.

[7] Reduction in price need not *necessarily* lead to a reduction in money income. For example, if at the same time that corporations reduced their prices they maintained wage payments by drawing on idle bank balances or other cash resources, the total income and the money volume of consumption expenditures might not decline, and so the physical volume of sales would increase. Obviously, there are severe limits to this possibility.

Cyclical price flexibility all around, including administered prices and wage rates in addition to agricultural prices, under the conditions prevailing at the end of a boom, might well accelerate the downswing. The expectation by business and consumers that prices will fall tends to generate a cumulative decline in expenditures and to intensify the downswing. There results not only inventory disinvestment, but also the curtailment of investment and durable consumers' expenditures in the expectation of a further fall in the national income and in costs and prices.[8]

The deflationary movements cannot be remedied by chasing administered prices and wage rates down to the level of agricultural and other flexible prices. It is not possible to remedy the disparity in the cost structure by adjusting the inflexible prices to the flexible price basis, for this process merely accelerates the decline in income, and this, in turn, creates a fresh price disparity. Combined, however, with monetary and fiscal policies designed to maintain the total volume of consumption and investment expenditures, an orderly program of cost-price readjustment does facilitate recovery. In other words, a direct attack must be made upon the cycle itself and not merely upon the price dispersion, which, for the most part, only reflects the cycle movement. Cost-price adjustments, thus implemented, are very different in their effect on business expectations from a general crumbling of prices. How far such cost reductions are desirable will depend, in part, upon the progress made in cost reduction; in other words, upon the extent to which certain costs and prices have gotten structurally out of line.

Just as forced cyclical downward adjustments of administrative prices are to be avoided, so also an advance of administrative prices in the upswing is to be avoided. Such an advance similarly creates business expectations which tend to

[8] "In most countries there are a large number of prices which, for one reason or another, are fairly insensitive to economic forces, at least over short periods. . . . But, for whatever cause rigidity occurs, it means that some prices do not move upward or downward in sympathy with the rest—they may consequently exercise a stabilizing influence." J. R. Hicks, *Value and Capital,* p. 265.

cause the accumulation of excessive inventories, leading to subsequent relapses.

In the upswing, price advances are not justified, strictly speaking, from the standpoint of the cycle movement. At any rate, no price advance can be economically justified until the industry approximates full capacity, and even then a small increase in price may be adequate to stimulate a sufficient amount of new investment to satisfy the enlarged demand. If a greatly expanded output in a given industry is required, this itself is an indication of a structural change in the economy.

It follows from the above analysis that price policy ought, above all, to be concerned with the problem of structural price flexibility. In the event that there is a structural shift in demand, involving an increased output of a certain industry, it may well be that a price advance is necessary in order to divert productive resources, including capital, into this expanding area. Such a situation would reveal itself in a genuine scarcity of the product in terms of the insufficient capacity of the industry to supply the demand.

Structural price flexibility involves the continuous adjustment of price to unit costs. Under the impact of changes in technology, the unit cost of some commodities fall, while the unit costs of other commodities are necessarily increased. This is peculiarly true in view of a fairly persistent wage structure which holds wage rates in different occupations approximately in line, regardless of the technological developments in different areas of the economy. Note needs here to be made of the fact that structural price flexibility avoids the difficulty of the variation in unit costs according to fluctuations in output. Structural price flexibility implies the adjustment of prices to unit costs at a normal percentage of capacity production.

With respect to wage rates, it should first of all be noted that throughout the last hundred years wage rates have exhibited an upward trend relative to the commodity price level. This, of course, is a reflection of technological change by which labor costs have been kept down despite the advance in wage rates. The general fact is, then, that as far as the long-run trend is concerned, technological improvements, under a condition of stable commodity prices, justify a rising wage rate trend.

Just as cyclical price flexibility may intensify the cyclical problem because of the effect of such price changes upon business expectations, so sharp wage reductions are likely to be deflationary. It was not altogether an accident that the most violent deflationary movement in the Great Depression came in 1931 in the midst of wholesale wage cuts. Economic thought in recent years, led by the Swedish and more recently the English economists, is coming more and more to the conclusion that a relatively high degree of wage stability from the cyclical standpoint is the preferable wage policy. It follows from this that, if the long-run trend of wage rates may be expected to rise relative to commodity prices, in view of increasing productivity, such an advance ought to occur in the upswing phase of the cycle, in other words, in periods of rising output when unit costs normally tend to decline. Assuming continued changes in technique, the community needs to be educated to understand that an increase in wage rates in the upswing phase is perfectly compatible with price stability, in so far as the advance in wage rates does not exceed the offsetting increase in productivity springing from technological developments. Wage advances, therefore, do not in themselves justify a price increase. In general, the public and employers are inclined to take the rigid position that wage advances and price advances inevitably go hand in hand. This is certainly erroneous and leads to wrong price policies. The advance in wage rates, it is true, does frequently necessitate structural price adjustments as between different industries by reason of the relatively fixed wage structure in terms of occupational differentials on the one hand, and the differential rates of technological progress in various sectors of the economy on the other.

It is quite impossible for administrative agencies to determine accurately the appropriate price or the appropriate wage. The flexible functioning of the economy requires that this be left largely to the private determination of the parties concerned. It is, however, probable that better price and wage policies could be implemented by a governmental review of proposed price or wage increases. The burden of proof would then be put upon the industry or the trade-union to show that the facts in the economic situation really justified the price or wage increase. In the case of wage rates, this problem has been attacked in various countries through the instrumentality of labor courts and through boards of compulsory or voluntary arbitration. The problem is, indeed, a difficult one and requires a high degree of voluntary participation through collective bargaining units. Experience indicates the greatest measure of successful achievement where the responsibility for the determination of the rate has been placed upon the parties involved—the employers and the employees or their representatives. The problem confronting a price review board would seem to be relatively simpler than that confronting a wage review board. In most cases, it should not be too difficult to determine whether a general price advance in an industry is justified by the economic situation. Particularly is this the case if it be admitted that cyclical price adjustment is, on the whole, an unsound policy, and that price adjustment should be reserved mainly for changes required by reason of structural movements incident to differential rates of technological progress in different sectors of the economy.

From the standpoint of prolonged underutilization of resources, or more or less chronic depression, it is equally to be doubted that a realistic solution can be found in price reduction designed to bring about expansion of output in the various separate industries. The individual industry could, indeed, afford to reduce the prices of its commodities if it could reasonably assume that it is confronted by an elastic demand situation. This, in point of fact, however, is usually not the case. New product industries are, of course, typically confronted during the period of their development with an elastic demand situation. This was the case with respect to the automobile industry, up to, say, the middle twenties, the radio industry until a few years ago, and currently the electric shaver. But most industries are confronted, at best, with a unit elasticity of demand. This means that a price reduction will bring no increase in the dollar volume of sales, while at the same time the expanded output clearly results in some increase in the total money cost. Thus, each individual industry in a condition of chronic depression is unable to contribute to expansion by price reduction. The expansion of each industry calls for a general increase in effective demand. The increase in effective demand cannot be achieved via a program of price reduction in each individual industry. It can be achieved only by an expansion in the area which is fundamentally responsible for the low level of income and employment, namely, an expansion of investment.

A full recovery requires an expansion of investment quite independent of the current level of output, employment, consumption, and income. These outside independent investments must spring from new technological developments—cost-reducing improvements that call for capital outlays, the development of new products, the growth of new industries—or else new areas of investment must be made possible through monetary policy or fiscal policy. As income rises, replacement investment expenditures will add impetus to the upswing. With a general expansion of effective demand, it is important, however, that the increased demand shall not at once be offset by an increase in prices, thus forestalling any volume expansion which otherwise might be expected. The increased effective demand can eventuate in increased volume and increased employment only on the assumption that prices remain stable or are reduced if and when increased productivity justifies a price reduction from the standpoint of structural price flexibility.

The Income Elasticity of Demand for Consumption Goods

The argument is frequently made that the persistence, even under modern high standards of living, of a large volume of unfilled consumer wants in and of itself guarantees full employment of resources, provided only that the price system is functioning properly.

This analysis overlooks the fundamental fact that people desire to save a part of their income and that they would wish to continue to do so, regardless of how low the prices of consumption goods might fall relative to money income. Indeed, the higher the real income, the greater the amount saved tends to be. It is true, as the data analyzed in *The Structure of the American Economy,* Part I, reveal, that American experience, and, indeed, that of other countries, indicates rising consumption in almost all lines as income increases. But it is equally true, as is shown on page 91 of the same volume, that with higher incomes a larger and larger amount is saved. Cyclically, the percentage of income saved rises and falls as income rises and falls. If, however, one concentrates attention exclusively upon the rising secular trend in real income, there is no conclusive evidence that a higher *percentage* of income is saved now than formerly. But if we save the same percentage of income (at corresponding phases of the cycle) as in earlier periods, it follows that the *amount* saved is higher, since real incomes have risen.

It does not follow, therefore, that the mere persistence or consumer wants will automatically ensure a sufficient market to absorb all the output which the economy is able to produce. In an economy which even at full employment consumed all of its income,[9] this might, indeed, be the case. But

[9] Such an economy would still be able, through the expenditure of its depreciation allowances, to maintain its capital equipment. If capital-saving inventions are made, or if wage rates do not rise as fast as productivity in the capital goods industries, the expenditure of depreciation allowances may even raise the productive capacity of the stock of capital goods without any net saving.

in a society in which people desire to save, it is only at very low income levels that they will consume their entire income. At higher income levels a considerable portion of the income is set aside as savings.

Thus, when all the resources are employed, it would be necessary that the stream of savings at the full income level should be offset by a volume of net investment in new capital goods commensurate with the stream of savings.

It is extremely important to see clearly that the mere fact that the public desires to save in no way ensures automatically that there will be a corresponding and offsetting demand for savings in the form of investment expenditures on capital goods. This follows from the fact that, whatever the level of income, it is clear that the maintenance of any income level requires no net additional investment at all, but merely replacement investment expenditures. Savings, however, if they are to be utilized, must be expended on net investment, since replacement capital expenditures are merely a part of consumption, constituting as they do simply an indirect way of utilizing the labor resources in the production of final consumption goods. Thus, while savings are a function of the income level, investment is in no sense a function of this level.[10] Net investment, on the contrary, is a function of (*a*) economic progress, including new developments in the field of technology, discovery of new resources, the opening up of new territory, and the growth of population, and (*b*) changes in the rate of interest (brought about, for example, by monetary policy) independent of changes in thrift. Changes in these factors account for and make economically feasible net investment expenditures.

It is important to distinguish between price elasticity of

[10] It is true that a *change* of income from one level to another, higher or lower, will, during the interval of change, affect investment. A *change* in income induces fluctuations in investment. This is the relationship involved in the well-known Principle of Acceleration. A shift from a chronically depressed income level to a full income level would certainly entail a considerable increase in investment in plant and equipment. But once this additional capital formation, commensurate with a full income level, was completed, net investment would again tend toward zero.

demand for consumption goods and income elasticity of demand for consumption goods. Those who stress the functioning of the price system are likely to overlook the elasticity of demand for consumption goods with respect to income. They fail to recognize that, while consumption of a specific commodity is a function of price, consumption as a whole is fundamentally a function of income. The mere existence of consumer wants, and the mere fact that with larger incomes more is consumed, do not of themselves ensure the full utilization of the productive resources. What is required is that the gap between the volume of consumption at a full income level, which gap is fixed by the savings pattern of the community, must be filled by investment expenditures. And these investment expenditures have no relation per se to the level of income or of consumption expenditures, but are determined by outside factors having to do with changes in the real factors inherent in economic progress and, under certain conditions, with changes in the rate of interest.

According to the static economic analysis, it is assumed that an increase in saving would bring about a decline in the rate of interest, and that this decline in the rate of interest would itself open up new investment outlets. The defect in this type of analysis is that it fails to take account of the dynamics of the problem. It fails to take account of the impact of an increase in thrift upon consumption expenditures and, therefore, upon the income level. An increase in thrift at any income level of necessity must cause a decline in consumption expenditures, and this decline would result in a fall in the demand for replacement investment and thus accelerate the decline in income.[11] It is true that a low level of income would bring about a decline in the rate of interest.

[11] An increase in thriftiness on the part of individuals does not necessarily result in an increased flow of aggregate savings. For, if the decisions of individuals to save result in the contraction of consumption expenditures, such decline in consumption may so affect the national income that the realized savings of others in the economy are reduced. Thus, an increase in thriftiness may cause a decline in the realized aggregate savings of the community as a whole; and, conversely, an increase in the propensity to consume (a decline in the propensity to save) may enhance the aggregate flow of savings.

The low rate of interest is, however, the result of the fact that the economy is depressed. The depressed condition causes the low rate of interest, and the rate of interest continues low only as long as the economy is depressed. Under these circumstances, the decline in the rate of interest will not stimulate investment sufficiently and, therefore, cannot bring the economy back to full employment.

This is not to say that a low rate of interest achieved through monetary policy has no effect upon the volume of investment. If one assumes no change in thriftiness and, therefore, no decline in the volume of consumption expenditures, a fall in the rate of interest brought about through the action of the monetary authority would inject a positive new factor into the situation. Consumption expenditures being maintained, the low rate of interest might in certain areas bring about an expansion of investment.

There is increasingly, however, considerable doubt among economists as to how effective, even under these circumstances, the low rate of interest would be, at least within realizable limits, as a means of increasing investment and, therefore, income. The fact seems to be that with respect to short-lived capital goods, such as machinery, the rate of interest within realizable limits, of, say, 2 to 7 per cent, is not an important consideration. Decisions to make new capital outlays are made on quite a rough basis, such as that a machine must be able to pay for itself within four or five years. These considerations are so rough and uncertain and the time element is so short that obviously the rate of interest has little bearing upon such decisions. The rate of interest clearly has a more important bearing upon very durable, long-term, fixed capital projects, such as public utilities, railroads, and building structures. But in this area one encounters the important offsetting fact that the longer the project in question, the more uncertain is the future. Risk, therefore, looms as an overwhelmingly important consideration and becomes in many cases a more important determinant of investment than moderate variations in the rate of interest.[12]

Next we turn to the problem of how effective a lower rate of interest may be in deflecting the flow of savings into larger consumption expenditures. It has long been recognized by economists that a lower rate of interest may or may not, according to different circumstances, tend to induce individuals to save a smaller proportion of income. One of the important motives for saving has found expression in modern times in the dramatic rise of life insurance. In so far as one saves for this purpose, it is clear that the lower the rate of interest, the greater is the incentive to save, since the purpose of saving is to make adequate provision for old age or for dependents. The lower the rate of interest, the greater the amount of saving required. The increasing significance of life

[12] On this point Professor J. R. Hicks, in his recent volume on *Value and Capital,* Oxford University Press, 1939, says:

"So long as we are concerned with movements of rates of interest which fall within the ordinary range of such movements, say between two per cent and seven per cent per annum, the effects of such changes . . . in the near future will be very slight. Very often they will be slight enough for the business man to neglect them altogether; and it is only in special cases that they are likely to have much appreciable effect on business policy. . . . The length of time for which an entrepreneur will be prepared to plan ahead depends upon technical conditions (in some kinds of business it is more necessary to plan ahead than in others) . . . but it also depends in a very important way on risk. . . . Now the farther ahead the future output is, the larger this risk allowance is likely to become . . . ; after a certain point, therefore, the risk allowance will become so large as to wipe out any possible gains and the effective 'expected price' will become nil. . . . But it is these very outputs upon whose *pull* interest must mainly rely if it is to cause large adjustments in the plan; we now see that their *pull* is likely to be much less strong than we might have expected. Interest is too weak for it to have much influence on the near future; risk is too strong to enable interest to have much influence on the far future; what place is left for interest between these opposing perils? How far it can find a place depends upon the strength of the risk factor; and that, as we have seen, is largely a psychological question. In a state of grave mistrust people will live from hand to mouth; if they do, changes in the rate of interest (the moderate changes we are talking about) can have little influence on their conduct. In a state of confidence, on the other hand, risk allowances are much smaller; and a space will probably be left between the extremes where interest is ineffective, within which it can have a significant influence. . . ."

insurance premiums in the flow of savings indicates that a low rate of interest may be a stimulus to savings rather than a factor deflecting savings into larger consumption expenditures.

On the other side, it has been asserted that a low rate of interest of itself tends to redistribute income. The return to property is less; the return to labor is more. But the distribution of income is relatively little determined by the yield accruing to creditors. It is much more the result of factors operative in the active productive process. The far-reaching and ramifying rewards of entrepreneurship, broadly conceived, are more important in the distribution of income than the yields on loan capital.

Thus, we are confronted with the fact that in a world of high risk, a low rate of interest is relatively ineffective as a stimulant to long-term fixed investment. On the other side, the effect of a low rate of interest on savings is a mixed one. To some extent, a low rate of interest stimulates saving, particularly in such areas as life insurance savings. In some respects, a low rate of interest tends to reduce the volume of savings. On balance, it is not at all clear how effective a low rate of interest is in deflecting the flow of savings into consumption. Moreover, the adjustment process is a slow and difficult one.

Thus, the existing state of abstract theorizing about the rate of interest leaves us very uncertain about its possible effect on the volume of investment and consumption, while statistical and case studies enhance this skepticism.[13]

Prices and Wage Rates

It is sometimes asserted that chronic unemployment of resources must indicate that prices are too high in relation to

[13] J. E. Meade and P. W. S. Andrews, "Summary of Replies to Questions on Effects of Interest Rates," Oxford Economic Papers, No. 1; J. F. Ebersole, "The Influence of Interest Rates upon Entrepreneurial Decisions in Business—A Case Study," *Harvard Bus. Rev.* Volume XVII, pp. 35–39; J. Tinbergen, *An Econometric Approach to Business Cycle Problems,* Paris, 1937.

the level of purchasing power. On the one side, it is said that this situation could be remedied by a progressive reduction of prices, while others assert that the appropriate remedy is an increase in wages. With respect to this type of reasoning, some comments are necessary at the outset to ensure the avoidance of certain misunderstandings.

To begin with, it is certainly clear that high monopoly prices, for example, may have the effect of reducing the volume of employment. Monopoly prices tend to reduce the real purchasing power of wage earners and to enhance profits. This abnormal distribution of income tends, accordingly, to reduce the flow of consumption expenditures and to increase savings. Accordingly, if monopoly prices are reduced to the level of competitive prices, consumption will be increased and employment will tend to rise.

Equally, it is clear that employment will tend to rise when consumers' goods prices fall incident to a technological innovation which reduces unit cost. This manner of stating the case, however, confuses somewhat the causal relationship between the variables involved. The fact is that both lower consumers' goods prices and increased employment follow from the technological innovations. The cost-reducing innovation induces new investment, and this results in an increase in employment while the new investment is made, and, subsequently, in a reduction in consumers' goods prices after the new investment pours out an increased production of goods. Thus, the reduction in consumers' goods prices is not the *cause* of the increased employment, but is the end result of the expansion of investment and output incident to the change in technology.

In the absence of monopoly prices or of technological change, price reductions cannot be used as a means to increase employment. If competitive prices are arbitrarily reduced, wage rates remaining unchanged, marginal firms will be driven out of business, and disinvestment will occur, causing a reduction in employment. It is quite impossible to cure the problem of unemployment by reliance upon the potentially larger purchasing power which, it is assumed, will appear if prices are arbitrarily reduced below the point determined by competition.

A perfectly flexible price system, undisturbed by technological change, will always tend toward an equilibrium position in which there is no net investment. But there is nothing in the functioning of a perfectly flexible competitive price system that yields a distribution of income which will ensure a consumption function which makes this condition compatible with full employment.

The argument which finds a solution in wage rate increases, prices remaining the same, encounters precisely the same difficulties as those raised above. Indeed, the two proposals are essentially alike. A decrease in prices, wage rates and technology remaining the same, is essentially the same thing as an increase in wage rates, prices and technology remaining unchanged.

Sometimes it is argued that we are suffering from both too high prices *and* too high wage rates. But this is not possible. If prices are too high, that in essence means that wages are too low. If wages are too high, that in essence means that prices are too low. They cannot both be too high in the economy as a whole.

Finally, we encounter the argument that a reduction in wage rates can bring about an increase in investment adequate to produce full employment, whatever the consumption function. It is, of course, true that wage reductions in a specific industry, such as residential building, may stimulate employment. But that is not the argument. The thesis under consideration is that, starting from a balanced wage structure, a general all-around reduction in wages can increase investment and raise the level of employment.

What is overlooked in this type of reasoning is the fact that wage reduction is a two-edged sword. On the one side it cuts down on costs, but on the other side it equally reduces demand. If, indeed, it could be assumed that employment would increase when wages are cut, then, of course, unit costs would fall while demand was sustained. But this *assumes* the result which is sought. The wage reduction cuts both cost and demand, and this change cannot assure any increase in employment.

The case may also be stated in terms of the effect of wage changes upon the degree of capital intensity in the process of production. From this standpoint, the argument shifts, however, and it is urged that wage reductions will tend to reduce investment and employment, since lower wage rates will tend to make the less capitalistic processes—those using much labor and little capital—more profitable than the more capitalistic ones. Thus, investment would decline. But this argument overlooks the fact that, unless there is a change in technique or in the rate of interest, there is nothing in the change in wage rates which can alter the relation of costs (and, hence, of prices) in the less capitalistic industries compared with those that are more capitalistic.

If wages and interest are the only ultimate costs, then a doubling of the wage rate in a highly capitalistic industry doubles the unit cost, interest rates remaining unchanged, precisely as the unit cost will also be doubled in an industry employing only labor. If, however, wage increases occur in the final goods industries, but not in the industries making the machines producing the final goods, then, of course, such a wage increase will tend to stimulate investment in machines in order to economize on labor. But this is a special case and cannot be applied to general all-around wage increases. In fact, the case just cited could equally well be stated in terms of a wage *reduction* in the machine-making industry with no change in wages in the final goods industry. Thus, the two seemingly contradictory arguments, as often popularly stated —(1) that wage *increases* will stimulate investment and (2) that wage *reductions* will stimulate investment—are really identical. Both arguments assume a change in the level of wages in the final goods industries *relative* to the machine-producing industries so as to favor the introduction of machinery, thereby making the process of production more capitalistic. Thus, depending on which wage rates one is talking about, the argument that wage changes stimulate investment can be stated either in terms of wage increases or wage decreases. Obviously, the argument cannot apply to all-around wage increases or decreases in the economy as a whole.

Conclusions with Respect to Price Policy

At any rate, it is definitely clear that the mere fact that there are seemingly unlimited consumer wants cannot of itself ensure full employment of resources even with the most perfectly functioning price system. This is true for any society which does not consume its entire output.[14] In a society where people desire to save, the mere fact of unlimited consumer wants will not of itself bring about full employment of resources. The savings process per se does not automatically develop a corresponding offsetting flow of investment. An increase in thriftiness not only reduces consumption expenditures, but tends to diminish investment opportunities. The volume of net investment, with the qualifications noted, is independent of the level of consumption and saving. Investment outlets are created by technological progress and, to some extent, by monetary policy designed to lower the rate of interest. Since the efficacy of the latter is very much to be questioned, for the reasons indicated above, it follows that the gap between a full income level and the consumption expenditures which individuals are willing to make at that income level may or may not be filled by investment expenditures induced, as they largely are, by the more or less accidental development of technological factors. Positive governmental action, partly in the form of monetary and fiscal policy, will be necessary at times to stimulate and supplement private investment, so that the gap between the potentially

[14] The classicals were convinced that wage rates controlled the labor supply (population) and that the rate of interest controlled consumption and saving. The trend of economic thinking during the last half century casts serious doubt on both conclusions.

realizable full income and voluntary consumption shall be tolerably well filled.[15]

Price policy is not likely to be adequate either to control the business cycle or to ensure reasonably full employment of resources. As far as the cycle is concerned, a downward adjustment of rigid prices for the economy as a whole is not an adequate remedy, and, indeed, under many circumstances might well be positively harmful. In the recovery phase it is equally important that cyclical price advances shall not be made. Appropriate price policy from the cyclical standpoint ought to aim at relative price stability both in the downswing and in the upswing, while general cycle policy should seek to minimize price dispersion as far as possible by the maintenance of general effective demand on a high level. From the long-run standpoint, or the standpoint of the changing structure of the economy, price policy ought to aim to achieve a continuous adjustment of prices between different commodities corresponding to structural changes in the unit cost of production. Without such adjustment, uneconomic utilization of the productive resources would result. Thus, while price policy does play an important role, it does not constitute an adequate remedy for the business cycle and for chronic underutilization of resources. Price policy must be integrated with monetary and fiscal policies. It is mainly upon these latter that reliance must be placed to prevent any large decline in business activity and in the national income. If this is done, cyclical price dispersion between cycle-sensitive commodities and cycle-insensitive commodities will be greatly minimized. From the long-run standpoint, reasonably full

[15] See my paper "Economic Progress and Declining Population Growth," *American Economic Review*, March, 1939, pp. 13–15, for a discussion of the possible dangers of pushing recovery, by governmental measures, so close to full employment that the control of costs becomes difficult. Impressed with the "stubborn economic realities of a rapidly changing world, on the one side, and the frailties of human nature in its power to make the appropriate adaptation to change, on the other," we may "prefer to take a course that risks neither a negative policy nor a breakdown of collective management."

utilization of the productive resources will facilitate the adaptation of individual prices to structural changes incident to the differential rates of technical progress in different industries.

Part Four

INVESTMENT INCENTIVES PAST AND PRESENT

Chapter XVI

THE ROLE OF INVESTMENT IN THE MODERN ECONOMY

IN earlier chapters we have considered the special role of private investment as a dynamic factor controlling the rise and fall of income. We have explained that, by and large, consumption plays a passive role, rising and falling according as income rises and falls. Thus, in a noninterventionist society full reliance, in effect, has to be placed upon private investment as the means to secure full employment.

Private consumption, except for minor qualifications, is determined by the level of private income, and can, therefore, not play a dynamic, active role in securing full employment. If consumption is to play such a role, supplementing the active role of private investment, it is necessary to invoke the aid of government. Community consumption expenditures, or publicly financed private consumption expenditures (such as relief for the unemployed), need not be conditioned by the level of currently received private income. Thus, through government action, consumption can be made to play an active, dynamic role in income creation.

The Role of Investment

In this chapter, however, we are particularly concerned with the role of private investment. In the past it was almost exclusively *private* investment which called the tune and rang the changes in the movement of the cycle. Even public expenditures, whether for public investment or for consumption, regularly followed the lead given by private investment. If prosperity prevailed, the society felt itself rich enough to embark on public projects. If the economy were depressed, public economy was rigorously enforced. Thus, in the heyday of capitalism, private investment was king.

Nor can an inquiry into the current functioning of our system of production overlook the continuing predominant role of private investment. Admittedly, an investigation into the reasons why our society is not functioning as effectively as it might, why it is not succeeding in producing the maximum output of which it is capable, or in giving full employment to our labor and capital resources, must take account of many factors. Yet, any consideration of these problems must include not only the theory of imperfect competition and the decline of price competition; it must take cognizance also of the role of saving and capital outlays in our economy.

Too frequently, when the functioning of the productive process is under consideration, attention is focused almost exclusively upon the commodity markets and the price system. To leave an inquiry into the functioning of the economy with a consideration of commodity prices alone would, in my judgment, overlook a sector which is more important than any other for an understanding of the operation, the maladjustments, and the instability of modern economic life.

The income stream flows day by day to everyone participating in the productive process, including the production not only of commodities but also of services of every kind and description—trade, professional, and governmental. This income stream is large or small according to the volume of purchases currently made. These purchases are of two kinds: one type consists of the purchase of consumption goods and services; another type consists of the purchase of capital equipment, industrial plant and machinery, public utility and railroad equipment, commercial and residential building, and the like. There are, therefore, two streams of expenditures continually going on: one stream consists of expenditures for consumption and the other consists of expenditures on capital outlays on plant and equipment.

How large the income stream will be, whether $60 billions or $100 billions, depends upon the volume of these two expenditure streams. But the outlay made on capital goods of all sorts is the expenditure stream which is mainly responsible for the rise and fall of the total income.

Reasonably full employment and a fairly satisfactory income level, such as we had in 1923 to 1929, require a quite extraordinarily large volume of private investment if no reliance is placed on government action. In such a society it is the margin of income which is created by private investment which fills the gap between prosperity and depression. No high level of employment and income has ever, in a non-interventionist society, been achieved without a large outlay on inventories, equipment, plant and new residential and commercial construction.

Let us consider what is necessary in order to keep the income stream flowing on a high level, once it has reached that level. The income received or realized out of the productive process of the prior week or month will either be expended for consumption or it will be saved. The part that is spent on consumption goods and services automatically becomes the source of a new income stream. The part that is saved may or may not feed into the income stream, depending upon whether or not these savings are used either by the saver himself or by a borrower for the purchase of capital goods.

But when the national income is already at a low level, it avails nothing that under the depressed conditions there is no excess of savings over investment. What is needed under these circumstances is to raise the level of investment, thereby increasing the income level out of which a larger flow of savings will spring.

Assume that the national income is at a high level and that savers do not themselves use the funds, or fail to find borrowers who will use them to purchase plant, equipment, and other capital goods. Then the income stream dries up and unemployment prevails in the capital goods industries. It is highly essential that all that part of the current flow of income which is not expended on consumption goods, namely, that part which is saved, shall be expended either directly by the saver himself or indirectly through a borrower on new plant, equipment, or investment goods of some sort. If the amount which is saved is large, as it is likely to be at a high income level, it is necessary that equally large outlets be available for these savings in equipment and plant expansion, and in residential construction.

In every boom period, the flow of savings is expended on capital outlays of this sort, and frequently these funds are augmented by additional sums created out of an expansion of bank credit. In a depression, expenditures on capital projects fall off, savers are unwilling themselves to purchase capital goods with their savings, or are unable to find borrowers to do so. The income stream thus dries up. In addition, owing to the fall of employment, the stream of expenditures on consumption declines, and so the income stream shrinks still more.

At low income levels, the aggregate savings stream also dwindles away, and the economy runs along on a low level of output and employment. At this low equilibrium level there is no excess of aggregate savings over investment.

Why is it that no boom, in a purely private enterprise economy, has ever been able to perpetuate itself year by year and so maintain income on a high level? Special causes have, from time to time, brought particular booms to an end, but apart from these we can say that every boom eventually dies a natural death. Available outlets for capital expansion have been temporarily exhausted.

The boom is a period in which we exploit to the full all the available new developments which the progress of science and technology, together with the growth of population, have up to that point made economically possible. Once all factories have installed the new machines, once a city has been equipped with the municipal utilities which technology has so far made available, once the construction of houses, apartments, office buildings, hotels, school buildings, and the like has caught up with the growth of the population, there remains little that can profitably be done except to maintain the capital plant already constructed. When this point is reached, the boom dies a natural death.

This is essentially what happened in 1929. Nearly all over the world, England excepted, there had been going on for some years a gigantic constructional boom. This was true not only of the United States but of Germany, France, Canada, Latin America, and even the Orient. The vigor of this boom was due, in part, to the backlog of housing requirements which had accumulated by reason of the cessation of building during the war; in part, it was due to the impetus to the industrialization of backward countries which the war itself had caused; and, in part, it was due to the growth of new industries.

The boom of the twenties was a gigantic spurt in capital formation, in capital outlays. Progress typically is made by spurts—by leaps and bounds. Progress typically is discontinuous, jerky, and lumpy. New developments are exploited to the full, and then the boom dies. It peters out because a saturation point has temporarily been reached. The spurt cannot last at the pace set.

It is not difficult to see that if we had kept on constructing office buildings, apartments, hotels, houses, commercial and industrial structures, and the like, at the rate they were being constructed in the late twenties, we should very soon have bankrupted all the owners of old property.

For a time there was no room left for further plant expansion or for other new capital outlays. It takes time before new developments can again accumulate, before the discovery of new techniques, new resources, new industries, and the growth of population can again set the stage for another boom.

In the depression, even a severe one, gross capital outlays, including plant replacement and renewals, will not sink to zero, but there is danger that the capital expenditures will not be large enough to absorb depreciation allowances. Thus, in such a period there is no room whatever for new savings.

Now the total stream of gross savings consists, in part, of net savings from current income and, in part, of depreciation and depletion allowances designed to maintain intact the plant and equipment. If the total expenditures on capital structures and equipment is not even enough to absorb the depreciation allowances earned by business year after year, a twofold deflationary effect to the income stream is present: first, the failure of new savings to be expended on expansion of plant and equipment; and, second, the failure of business concerns to expend earned depreciation allowances on the replacement and renewal of plant and equipment.

Under the impact of the unemployment thus created, consumption expenditures will fall to low levels. Thus, the total income stream will be reduced by an amount not only equal to the decline in investment, but also by the induced decline in consumption. Every dollar of capital outlays has a multiplier or leverage effect on income and, similarly, every dollar of savings or depreciation allowances not expended on capital outlays drives the income down with a magnified effect.

Thus, a society geared to a high peak load of capital goods production is likely to experience violent fluctuations in income and employment. A high savings economy will remain a highly dynamic economy as long as it is able to experience periodically great bursts of capital outlays on plant and equipment. It is then a dynamic, rapidly expanding, and progressive economy, despite its instability. But if such an economy fails to find adequate investment outlets for its new savings and for its depreciation allowances, it will lose its dynamic quality and become a depressed economy, with a large volume of chronic unemployment, unless, indeed, the government assumes a more positive role. The high savings economy, barring government intervention, can escape a fall in income and employment only through the continuous development of new outlets for capital expenditures. As far as private investment outlets are concerned, this requires continuous technological progress, the rise of new industries, the discovery of new resources, the growth of population, or a combination of several or all of these developments.

A Century of Expansion

One overwhelmingly important fact characterized the century which preceded the first World War. It was a unique epoch. It was a century of rapid expansion into new territory, and it was a century of prodigious growth of population. Population poured into America, into the great West, into Brazil, the Argentine, Canada, Australia, and flowed back from the agricultural communities into giant urban centers which grew and fed on this expansion. This one central fact of growth and expansion dominated the whole of economic life. It minimized the risk of new ventures. If optimism had carried railroad building too far at the moment, if a city had temporarily overbuilt, the damage was short lived. Expansion and growth soon made good the error. Businessmen could look far into the future with gigantic plants, with anticipatory capital outlays, with investment plans which had no relation to the present, and which were based upon the expectation of growth and expansion.

It is important to reduce to the utmost possible extent the risk and uncertainty that confront the business community. The modern world, even apart from war, is loaded with a high risk factor. We are living in a period of rapid institutional change in our internal economy.

In our complicated modern world we are confronted with intricate and seemingly insoluble problems of human organization. We are in process of developing new institutions controlling the relations of employers and employees. The Social Security Act, the regulations of the capital market, of public utilities, and the like, confront business executives with new and difficult problems. For the most part, these changes in our institutional arrangements are, in some form or other, here to stay, and business cannot go forward without recognizing this fact.

Many of the reforms recently introduced in this country were long overdue. Where mistakes have been made, they must be corrected, as rapidly as possible. We must consolidate and improve these institutions in a statesmanlike manner. This, I think, we can all take for granted. Business has learned to live with changing situations in the past; flexibility and versatility to meet new conditions in a rapidly changing world are essential for survival of a free enterprise economy and for political democracy.

The highly dynamic nineteenth-century world was also a world of high risks. Technical progress itself implies the risk of obsolescence and depreciation of capital values. Nevertheless, confronted with alluring investment projects springing from rapidly expanding population, the occupation of new territory, the exploitation of new resources, and the growth of new industries, capital outlays were eagerly made, despite the high risk factors. A rapidly expanding economy can afford to undertake, and willingly does undertake, risk.

Yet it cannot be denied that, even under the favorable conditions of rapid expansion, heavy losses alongside rich gains were sustained. Yet, despite these losses, hope always ran high with respect to new ventures. Our current, less rapidly expanding economy is perhaps in a stronger position to safeguard itself from the risks of technological innovations, but it is compelled to face larger risks from institutional change and from social and international upheaval. It does not enjoy the buoyancy and optimism under which the rapidly expanding economy of the prewar century was capable of riding roughshod over risk. I think we must face the fact that we live today in a peculiarly risky world, and this fact has a repressive effect. It makes the problem of adequate private investment outlets more difficult.

Chapter XVII

EXTENSIVE AND INTENSIVE EXPANSION

THROUGHOUT the modern era, ceaseless change has been the law of economic life. Every period is, in some sense, a period of transition. The swift stream of events in the last quarter century offers, however, overwhelming testimony in support of the thesis that the economic order of the Western world is undergoing in this generation a structural change no less basic and profound in character than that transformation of economic life and institutions which we are wont to designate loosely by the phrase "the Industrial Revolution." We are passing, so to speak, over a divide which separates the great era of growth and expansion of the nineteenth century from an era which no man, unwilling to embark on pure conjecture, can as yet characterize with clarity or precision. We are moving swiftly out of the order in which those of our generation were brought up, into no one knows what.

Overwhelmingly significant, but as yet all too little considered by economists, is the profound change which we are currently undergoing in the rate of extensive expansion. It is important to integrate population growth intimately with the other factors making for expansion, including territorial expansion and technological progress. Indeed, it can scarcely be questioned that a continued growth of population at the rate experienced in the nineteenth century would rapidly present insoluble problems. This, of course, is due to the fact that we no longer have the rapid extensive expansion territorially throughout the world that we formerly had. The important thing to note is the decline in extensive expansion which involves both population growth and territorial expansion.

In the decade of the nineteen-twenties the population of the United States increased by 16,000,000—an absolute growth equal to that of the prewar decade and in excess of any other decade in our history. In the current decade we are adding only half this number to our population, and the best forecasts indicate a further decline in the decade which we are now entering.

Inadequate as the data are, it appears that the prodigious growth of population in the nineteenth century was something unique in history. Gathering momentum with the progress of modern science and transportation, the absolute growth in western Europe mounted decade by decade until the first World War; and in the United States it reached the highest level, as I have just noted, in the postwar decade. The upward surge began with relatively small accretions which rapidly swelled into a flood. But the advancing tide has come to a sudden halt and the accretions are dwindling toward zero.

Thus, with the prospect of actual contraction confronting us, already we are in the midst of a drastic decline in the rate of population growth. Whatever the future decades may bring, this present fact is already upon us; and it behooves us, as economists, to take cognizance of the significance of this revolutionary change in our economic life.[1]

Schooled in the traditions of the Malthusian theory, economists, thinking in terms of static economics, have typically placed an optimistic interpretation upon the cessation of

1 With respect to the cycle, some economists, while agreeing that a high rate of population growth may play a large role in a recovery movement, have argued that it cannot alleviate a depression when much unemployment already prevails. It is, however, precisely with respect to the recovery of 1935–40 that the thesis applies. The recovery in investment (notably housing) was less rapid than would have been the case had population grown as rapidly as in the twenties.

population growth. This, indeed, is also the interpretation suggested by the National Resources Committee, which recently issued an exhaustive statistical inquiry into current and prospective changes in population growth. In a fundamental sense, this conclusion is, I think, thoroughly sound; for we cannot look with equanimity upon a continued growth of population in a world in which territorial expansion is largely past. But it would be an unwarranted optimism, nevertheless, to deny that there are implicit, in the current drastic shift from rapid expansion to cessation of population growth, serious structural maladjustments which can be avoided or mitigated only if economic policies, appropriate to the changed situation, are applied. Indeed, in this shift must be sought a basic cause of not a few of the developments in our changing economy.

Adam Smith regarded growth of population as at once a consequence and a cause of economic progress. Increasing division of labor would, he argued, bring about greater productivity, and this would furnish an enlarged revenue and stock, from which would flow an enlarged wages fund, an increased demand for labor, higher wages, and, therefore, economic conditions favorable for population growth. Now, a growing population, by widening the market and by fostering inventiveness, in turn facilitated, he thought, division of labor and so the production of wealth. Thus, he arrived at an optimistic conclusion. Population growth, he held, stimulated progress and this, in turn, stimulated further growth and expansion. In contrast, the pessimistic analyses of Malthus and Ricardo stressed the limitation of natural resources and the danger of an increasing population pressing down the margin of cultivation to a point at which real income would be reduced to a bare subsistence level. In this static analysis the more dynamic approach of Adam Smith was quite forgotten. If we wish to get a clear insight into the economic consequences of the current decline in population growth, it is necessary to return to the suggestion of Adam Smith and to explore more fully the causal interconnection between economic progress, capital formation, and population growth.

Expansion and Economic Progress

Economic analysis from the earliest development of our science has been concerned with the role played by economic progress. Various writers have included under this caption different things; but, for our purpose, we may say that the constituent elements of economic progress are: (a) inventions, (b) the discovery and development of new territory and new resources, and (c) the growth of population. Each of these in turn, severally and in combination, has opened investment outlets and caused a rapid growth of capital formation.

The earlier economists were concerned chiefly with the effect of economic progress upon the volume of output, or, in other words, upon the level of real income. For them, economic progress affected the economic life mainly, if not exclusively, in terms of rising productivity and higher real income per capita.

Not until the very end of the nineteenth century did an extensive literature arise which stressed the role of economic progress as a leading, if not the main, factor causing fluctuations in employment, output, and income. Ricardo had, indeed, seen that there was some relation between economic progress and economic instability; but it was left for Wicksell, Spiethoff, Schumpeter, Cassel, and Robertson to elaborate the thesis that economic fluctuations are essentially a function of economic progress.

More recently, the role of economic progress in the maintenance of full employment of the productive resources has come under consideration. The earlier economists assumed that the economic system tended automatically to produce full employment of resources. Some unemployment there was periodically, owing to the fluctuations incident to the business cycle; but in the upswing phase of the cyclical movement the economy was believed to function in a manner tending to bring about full recovery—maximum output and employment. This view was inspired by a century in which the forces of economic progress were powerful and strong, in which investment outlets were numerous and alluring. Spiethoff saw clearly that technological progress, the development of new industries, the discovery of new resources, and the opening of new territory were the basic causes of the boom, which, in turn, was the progenitor of depression. Indeed, he believed that once the main resources of the globe had been discovered and exploited, once the whole world had been brought under the sway of the machine technique, the leading disturbing factors which underlie the fluctuations of the cycle would have spent their force and an era of relative economic stability would ensue. But he did not raise the question whether such stability would be achieved at a full employment and full income level.

The business cycle was, par excellence, the problem of the nineteenth century. But the main problem of our times, and particularly in the United States, is the problem of full employment. Yet, paradoxical as it may seem, the nineteenth century was little concerned with, and understood but dimly, the character of the business cycle. Indeed, as long as the problem of full employment was not pressing, it was not necessary to worry unduly about the temporary unemployment incident to the swings of the cycle. Not until the problem of full employment of our productive resources from the long-run, secular standpoint was upon us were we compelled to give serious consideration to those factors and forces in our economy which tend to make business recoveries weak and anemic and which tend to prolong and deepen the course of depressions. This is the essence of secular stagnation—sick recoveries which die in their infancy and depressions which feed on themselves and leave a hard and seemingly immovable core of unemployment.

In every great crisis the struggle of contending groups maneuvering for an advantageous position amidst rapid change whips up the froth and fury of political and social controversy. Always there is present the temptation to explain the course of events in terms of the more superficial phenomena which are frequently manifestations rather than causes of change. It is the peculiar function of the economist, however, to look deeper into the underlying economic realities and to discover in these, if possible, the causes of the most obstinate problem of our time—the problem of underemployment. Fundamental to an understanding of this problem are the changes in the "external" forces, if I may so describe them, which underlie economic progress—changes in the character of technological innovations, in the availability of new territory, and in the growth of population.

The expanding economy of the last century called forth a prodigious growth of capital formation. So much was this the case that this era in history has, by common consent, been called the capitalistic period. No one disputes the thesis that without this vast accumulation of capital we should never have witnessed the great rise in the standard of living achieved since the beginning of the Industrial Revolution. But it is not the effect of capital formation upon real income to which I wish especially to direct attention. What I wish to stress is rather the role played by the process of capital formation in securing at each point in this ascending income scale fairly full employment of the productive resources and, therefore, the maximum income possible under the then prevailing level of technological development. For it is an indisputable fact that the prevailing economic system has never been able to reach reasonably full employment or the attainment of its currently realizable real income without making large investment expenditures. The basis for this imperious economic necessity has been thoroughly explored in the last half century in the great literature beginning with Tougan-Baranowsky and Wicksell on saving and investment.

Deepening and Widening of Capital

A growth in real investment may take the form either of a deepening of capital or of a widening of capital, as Hawtrey has aptly put it. The deepening process means that more capital is used per unit of output, while the widening process means that capital formation grows *pari passu* with the increase in the output of final goods. If the ratio of real capital to real income remains constant, there is no deepening of capital; but if this ratio is constant and real income rises, then there is a widening of capital.

According to Douglas,[2] the growth of real capital formation in England from 1875 to 1909 proceeded at an average rate of 2 per cent per annum; and the rate of growth of capital formation in the United States from 1890 to 1922 was 4 per cent per annum. The former is less than the probable rate of increase of output in England, while the latter is somewhat in excess of the annual rise of production in the United States. Thus, during the last fifty years or more, capital formation for each economy as a whole has apparently consisted mainly of a widening of capital. Surprising as it may seem, as far as we may judge from such data as are available, there has been little, if any, deepening of capital. The capital stock has increased approximately in proportion to real income. This is also the conclusion of Gustav Cassel; [3] while Keynes [4] thinks that real capital formation in England may have very slightly exceeded the rise in real income in the period from 1860 to the first World War. If this be true, it follows that, in terms of the time element in production, which is the very essence of the capital concept, our system of production is little more capitalistic now than fifty or seventy-five years ago. It requires, in other words, a period of employment of our productive resources no longer than formerly to reproduce the total capital stock. The "waiting," so to speak, embodied in our capital accumulations is no greater today than half a century or more ago. Capital has, indeed, grown relative to labor. Thus, the technical co-

[2] Paul H. Douglas, *The Theory of Wages*, Macmillan, 1934, pp. 464–65.

[3] Gustav Cassel, *On Quantitative Thinking in Economics*, Oxford, 1935, Chapter 6.

[4] J. M. Keynes, "Some Economic Consequences of a Declining Population," *Eugenics Review*, April, 1937.

efficient of production, with respect to capital, has increased. While this indicates a more intensive application of capital relative to other factors, it does not necessarily imply any deepening of capital.

In important areas the capital stock has not increased significantly even in relation to population. This is notably true in the service industries. Moreover, in the field of housing, real capital has little more than kept pace with population growth. In manufacturing, as a whole, it is certainly true that real capital formation has not only far outstripped population, but has also risen more rapidly than physical product. The studies of Douglas for the United States and Australia show that real fixed capital invested in manufacturing increased more rapidly than physical output of manufactured goods. On the other hand, Carl Snyder's [5] data, which run in terms of value of invested capital and value of product, indicate that for important separate industries, such as textiles, iron and steel, and petroleum, capital has grown little or no faster than output since 1890. With respect to the automobile industry, according to his findings, capital investment has risen no more rapidly than value of product, while in the electrical industries invested capital increased at a slower rate than output after 1907. Considering the economy as a whole, including fields of economic activity other than manufacturing, there is no good evidence that the advance of technique has resulted in recent decades, certainly not in any significant measure, in any deepening of capital. Apparently, once the machine technique has been developed in any field, further mechanization is likely to result in an increase in output at least proportional to, and often in excess of, the net additions to real capital. Though the deepening process is all the while going on in certain areas, elsewhere capital-saving inventions are reducing the ratio of capital to output.

In order to get some insight into the effect of population

[5] Carl Snyder, "Capital Supply and National Well-Being," *American Economic Review*, June, 1936.

growth upon capital formation, it is necessary to consider the role it plays in conjunction with other factors in the widening and deepening process. The widening of capital is a function of an increase in final output, which, in turn, is due partly to an increase in population and partly to an increase in per capita productivity, arising from causes other than a larger use of capital per unit of output. On the other hand, the deepening of capital results partly from cost-reducing changes in technique, partly (though this is probably a much less significant factor) from a reduction in the rate of interest, and partly from changes in the character of the output as a whole, with special reference to the amount of capital required to produce it.

Now the rate of population growth must necessarily play an important role in determining the character of the output; in other words, the composition of the flow of final goods. Thus, a rapidly growing population will demand a much larger per capita volume of new residential building construction than will a stationary population. A stationary population, with its larger proportion of old people, may perhaps demand more personal services; and the composition of consumer demand will have an important influence on the quantity of capital required. The demand for housing calls for large capital outlays, while the demand for personal services can be met without making large investment expenditures. It is, therefore, not unlikely that a shift from a rapidly growing population to a stationary or declining one may so alter the composition of the final flow of consumption goods that the ratio of capital to output, as a whole, will tend to decline.

Often the question is raised: How can an increase in population per se raise the effective demand? It is not human wants which determine the rate of output and employment, but effective demand. The answer is that investment (and, therefore, income and employment) may be increased merely as a result of a *shift* in demand. The pressure of population growth tends to shift demand toward housing, and raises rents. But the demand for housing requires more investment of capital than most other kinds of consumer demand. It is not true, as some critics have inferred, that the population argument implies a prior increase in aggregate demand, which increase it leaves unexplained. What these critics overlook is the fact that a mere *shift* in demand, through the ensuing stimulus to investment, may raise income and so the aggregate effective demand.

In the beginning stages of modern capitalism both the deepening and the widening processes of capital formation were developing side by side. But in its later stages the deepening process, taking the economy as a whole, rapidly diminished. And now, with the rapid cessation of population growth, even the widening process may slow down. Moreover, it is possible that capital-saving inventions may cause capital formation in many industries to lag behind the increase in output.

An interesting problem for statistical research would be to determine the proportion of investment in the nineteenth century which could be attributed (a) to population growth, (b) to the opening up of new territory and the discovery of new resources, and (c) to technical innovations. Such an analysis it has not been possible for me to make, and I shall venture only a few rough estimates together with some qualitative judgments. With respect to population growth, some insight into the problem may, perhaps, be gained by considering first the role of population growth in the rise of aggregate real income. The various estimates agree that the annual rate of growth of physical output up to the first World War was roughly 3 per cent in western Europe and nearly 4 per cent in the United States. Of this average annual increase something less than half of the 3 per cent increase in western Europe can be attributed to population growth, while something more than half of the annual increase in the United States can be assigned to the increase in the labor supply. Thus, it appears that per capita output has increased both in western Europe and in the United States at approximately

1½ per cent per annum. This increase can be attributed mainly to changes in technique and to the exploitation of new natural resources.

We have already noted that capital formation has progressed at about the same rate as the rise in aggregate output. Thus, as a first approximation, we may say that the growth of population in the last half of the nineteenth century was responsible for about 40 per cent of the total volume of capital formation in western Europe and about 60 per cent of the capital formation in the United States. If this is even approximately correct, it will be seen what an important outlet for investment is being closed by reason of the current rapid decline in population growth.

Obviously, the growth of population affects capital formation most directly in the field of construction, especially residential building. But the effect of population growth on capital formation is, of course, felt in other spheres as well. This is notably true of all the various municipal and public utilities, and also of the manufacture of essential consumers' goods.

An interesting excursus would lead us into a consideration of the problem how far an increase in population itself contributed to a more efficient technique and thus was, in part, responsible for the rise in per capita real income. According to the old Malthusian view, the growth of population would act counter to the effect of technological progress upon per capita productivity, and would thus slow down the rise in per capita real income. If this were correct, population growth considered by itself alone would tend to check the rise in per capita consumption, and this, in turn, via the so-called Acceleration Principle, would affect the volume of capital formation. According to the optimum population theory, however, it may not infrequently be the case, and indeed probably was during the greater part of the nineteenth century, that population growth itself facilitated mass production methods and accelerated the progress of technique. If this be correct, population growth was itself responsible for a part of the rise in per capita real income, and this, via the influence of a rising consumption upon investment, stimulated capital formation. Thus, it is quite possible that population growth may have acted both directly and indirectly to stimulate the volume of capital formation.

It is not possible, I think, to make even an approximate estimate of the proportion of the new capital created in the nineteenth century which was a direct consequence of the opening up of new territory. The development of new countries was, indeed, so closely intertwined with the growth of population that it would be difficult to avoid double counting. What proportion of new capital formation in the United States went each year into the Western frontier we do not know, but it must have been very considerable. Apparently, about one fourth of the total capital accumulations of England were invested abroad by 1914, and one seventh of those of France.

These figures, while only suggestive, point unmistakably to the conclusion that the opening of new territory and the growth of population were together responsible for a very large fraction—possibly somewhere near one half—of the total volume of new capital formation in the nineteenth century. These outlets for new investment are rapidly being closed. The report on *Limits of Land Settlement* by President Isaiah Bowman and others may be regarded as conclusive in its findings that there are no important areas left for exploitation and settlement. As far as population is concerned, that of western Europe has already virtually reached a standstill; but that in eastern Europe, notably in Russia, is still growing, and so also is that in the Orient. And much of this area will probably experience a considerable industrialization. But it is not yet clear how far the mature industrial countries will participate in this development through capital export. Russia still has a long way to go before she becomes completely industrialized; but foreign capital is not likely to play any significant role in this process. India will offer some opportunity for British investment, but the total is likely to be small relative to the volume of British foreign investments in the nineteenth century. China and the Orient generally offer, in view of the present and prospective turmoil in that area, relatively meager investment opportunities. At all events, no one is likely to challenge the statement that foreign investment will, in the next fifty years, play an incomparably smaller role than was the case in the nineteenth century.

Thus, the outlets for new investment are rapidly narrowing down to those created by the progress of technology. To be sure, the progress of technology itself played in the nineteenth century a decisive role in the opening of new territory and as a stimulus to population growth. But while technology can facilitate the opening of new territory, it cannot create a new world or make the old one bigger than it is. And while the advance of science, by reducing the death rate, was a major cause of the vast nineteenth-century increase in population, no important further gains in this direction can possibly offset the prevailing low birth rate. Thus, the further progress of science can operate to open investment outlets only through its direct influence on the technique of production.

Intensive Expansion and New Industries

We are, thus, rapidly entering a world in which we must fall back upon a more rapid advance of technology than in the past if we are to find private investment opportunities adequate to maintain full employment. Should we accept the advice of those who would declare a moratorium on invention and technical progress, this one remaining avenue for private investment would also be closed. There can be no greater error in the analysis of the economic trends of our times than that which finds in the advance of technology, broadly conceived, a major cause of unemployment. It is true that we cannot discount the problem of technological unemployment, a problem which may be intensified by the apparently growing importance of capital-saving inventions. But, on the other side, we cannot afford to neglect that type of innovation which creates new industries and which thereby opens new outlets for real investment. The problem of our generation is, above all, the problem of inadequate private investment outlets. What we need is not a slowing down in the progress of science and technology, but rather an acceleration of that rate.

Of first-rate importance is the development of new industries. There is certainly no basis for the assumption that these are a thing of the past. But there is equally no basis for the assumption that we can take for granted the rapid emergence of new industries as rich in investment opportunities as the railroad, or more recently the automobile, together with all the related developments, including the construction of public roads, to which it gave rise. Nor is there any basis, either in history or in theory, for the assumption that the rise of new industries proceeds inevitably at a uniform pace. The growth of modern industry has not come in terms of millions of small increments of change giving rise to a smooth and even development. Characteristically, it has come by gigantic leaps and bounds. Very often the change can best be described as discontinuous, lumpy, and jerky, as, indeed, D. H. Robertson has so vividly done. And when a revolutionary new industry like the railroad or the automobile, after having initiated in its youth a powerful upward surge of investment activity, reaches maturity and ceases to grow, as all industries finally must, the whole economy must experience a profound stagnation, unless, indeed, new developments take its place. It is not enough that a mature industry continues its activity at a high level on a horizontal plane. The fact that new railroad mileage continued to be built at about the same rate through the seventies, eighties, and nineties was not sufficient. It is the *cessation of growth* which is disastrous. It is in connection with the growth, maturity, and decline of great industries that the Principle of Acceleration operates with peculiar force. And when giant new industries have spent their force, it *may* take a long time before something else of equal magnitude emerges. In fact, nothing has emerged in the decade in which we are now living. This basic fact, together with the virtual cessation of public investment by state and local governmental bodies, as indicated by a decline of $2 billions in their net public debt since 1932,[6] explains in large measure the necessary rise in federal expenditures.

Spiethoff was quite right when he argued that a vigorous recovery is not just spontaneously born from the womb of the preceding depression. Some small recovery must, indeed, arise sooner or later merely because of the growing need for capital replacement. But a full-fledged recovery calls for something more than the mere expenditure of depreciation allowances. It requires a large outlay on new investment, and this awaits the development of great new industries and new techniques.

We have noted that the approaching cessation of population growth and the disappearance of new territory for settlement and exploitation may cut off a half or more of the investment outlets which we were wont to make in the past. We are, thus, compelled to fall back upon that measure of capital formation which is associated with the advance of technique and the rise in per capita output. But current institutional developments are restricting even this outlet. The growing power of trade-unions and trade associations, the development of monopolistic competition, of rivalry for the market through expensive persuasion and advertising, instead of through price competition, are factors which have rightly of late commanded much attention among economists. There is, moreover, the tendency to block the advance of technical progress by the shelving of patents.

Under vigorous price competition, new cost-reducing techniques were compulsorily introduced even though the scrapping of obsolete but depreciated machinery entailed a capital loss. But under the monopoly principle of obsolescence new

[6] *Debts and Recovery 1929 to 1937,* The Twentieth Century Fund, 1938, p. 230.

machines will not be introduced until the undepreciated value of the old machine will at least be covered by the economies of the new technique. Thus, progress is slowed down and outlets for new capital formation, available under a more ruthless competitive society, are cut off. Capital losses which could not be avoided under rigorous price competition can be and are avoided under an economic system more closely integrated by intercorporate association and imperfect competition. If we are to save the one remaining outlet for private capital formation, deliberate action of a far bolder character than hitherto envisaged must be undertaken in order to make the price system and free enterprise sufficiently responsive to permit at least that measure of capital formation to which the rate of technological progress had accustomed us in the past.

With respect to the nineteen-thirties, it seems probable that the combination of the decline in population growth,[7] particularly the slow rate of growth in our urban communities, plus the failure of the development of large new industries, was of great importance, but one cannot consider the population factor alone. With respect to the future, important new industries are, of course, likely to develop as in the past, but the combination of the decline in territorial expansion and the decline of population growth will together present a new situation—one never before experienced during the last two hundred years.

In general, it is the decline of extensive expansion that must be stressed. I am not able to see how anyone can doubt that extensive expansion will play a smaller role in the future. The question then resolves itself as follows: Can intensive expansion develop sufficiently to take up the investment slack? It seems to me—and this is also the opinion of Myrdal in his recent book on population [8]—that the decline

[7] It is important to note—a point which I have continually stressed—that it is the *absolute increment* of growth that is significant, *not the percentage rate of growth.* This also holds with respect to the Acceleration Principle in business cycle analysis.

[8] Gunnar Myrdal, *Population,* Harvard University Press, 1940, p. 150.

of extensive expansion itself makes intensive expansion more difficult. This, however, does not imply an inevitable impasse. Adjustment to the diminished rate of expansion is possible, and it becomes the problem of economic policy to ascertain how far this adjustment may be expected to take place automatically and how far deliberate action is required, and of what character (monetary policy, fiscal policy, cost-price policy, etc.), in order to achieve full employment and that higher standard of living which a cessation of population growth per se presents as a realizable possibility.

Chapter XVIII

EARLY FINANCING METHODS

IN considering the question of the impact of the tax structure upon the inducement to invest, it is of interest to inquire into the origin of new industries, the early beginnings of great fortunes, and the changes which have occurred over the last hundred years in methods of financing new enterprises.

An examination of the biographical literature on great fortunes and on the beginnings of great corporations [1] ought to throw some light upon the problem of the effect of a tax structure on investment in new enterprises. It is useful to inquire how an individual and corporate income tax, an undistributed profits tax, and a capital gains tax, had they been in existence a hundred years ago, might have modified

[1] The following biographies were examined: L. H. Seltzer: *A Financial History of the American Automobile Industry,* Boston, 1928; A. D. H. Smith: *Commodore Vanderbilt,* New York, 1927; J. H. Appel: *The Business Biography of John Wanamaker: Founder and Builder,* New York, 1930; J. T. Flynn: *God's Gold: The Story of Rockefeller and His Times,* New York, 1932; B. J. Hendrick: *The Life of Andrew Carnegie,* 2 vols., New York, 1932; J. G. Pyle: *The Life of James J. Hill,* 2 vols., New York, 1917; G. T. Clark: *Leland Stanford,* Stanford University, California, 1931; Oscar Lewis: *The Big Four, The Story of Huntington, Stanford, Hopkins and Crocker, and of the Building of the Central Pacific,* New York, 1938; George Kennan: *E. H. Harriman: A Biography,* 2 vols., Boston, 1922; Harvey O'Connor: *The Guggenheims: The Making of an American Dynasty,* New York, 1937; Harvey O'Connor: *Mellon's Millions,* New York, 1933; George Harvey: *Henry Clay Frick: The Man,* New York, 1928; C. W. Ackerman: *George Eastman,* Boston, 1930; J. K. Winkler, *The Dupont Dynasty,* New York, 1935; Gilson Gardner: *Lusty Scripps: The Life of E. W. Scripps,* New York, 1932; and also the histories of many American business corporations which appeared in *Fortune* magazine from April, 1930, to May, 1938.

the remarkably rapid emergence, frequently within a few years or at any rate within a few decades, of enormous private fortunes, and the rise of great new industries with which these fortunes were often associated.

Financing in Nineteenth-century Capitalism

The biographies of rich men in America all conform, in large measure, to a certain more or less uniform type. Typically, an energetic and ambitious young man, living in an environment of rapid expansion, vast unexploited natural resources, rapid growth of population, rapid extension into new territory, and rapid changes in techniques, found an opportunity to take advantage of the highly dynamic factors in such an economy. Typically, the future captain of industry or financier had the capacity for hard work, the capacity to accumulate small savings out of a very small salary or income, and the imagination to see possibilities for profit in the rapidly changing scene about him. Typically, he made a small beginning with his own resources and, not infrequently, the profits springing from the new enterprise or from the exploitation of virgin resources furnished the entire capital for a giant new industry. Again and again great new industries and the private fortunes to which they gave rise have grown almost exclusively out of profits plowed back into the enterprise.

In addition to the typical development from small beginnings, there was the case of the ambitious young man who succeeded in borrowing from others the funds necessary for the initial and developmental capital. Subsequently, such industries also grew mainly from the reinvestment of profits —from internal growth. Falling in one category under this general class are those industries for which the outside borrowed capital was obtained from a number of friends, each of whom had little capital but had accumulated small savings from small incomes. There is, however, another typical category in which the enterprising young promoter succeeded in obtaining financial support from capitalists of large means.

A fourth category is one in which men of large means themselves started new enterprises. This case differs from the second case in the respect that, while a high income surtax structure might well deter wealthy men from lending in a risky enterprise, it is less likely to deter them from investing in an enterprise which they themselves organize. This is due partly to the fact that men engage in enterprise not merely for profit, but also because of the allurement of the activity related to organizational development itself. Moreover, if men organize businesses themselves, they are more likely to feel confident that they will really succeed, and that the investment will yield a larger rate than could be obtained elsewhere. The assumption of risk is more likely to be undertaken in enterprises which carry with them pleasure and prestige in the responsibility of management than would be the case in an enterprise in which the capitalist occupied a purely passive position as a lender. A fifth type is that in which new enterprises are started not by individuals, but by old-established and successful corporations. Here the problem of individual income taxes, including surtaxes and capital gains taxes, does not feature, but only such taxes as weigh upon corporations themselves.

Broadly speaking, it is probably true that the historical evolution of the emergence, the establishment and the financing of new enterprises has moved more and more toward the latter types. In the earlier part of the nineteenth century, the first type was clearly the preponderant one, supplemented by the second and third types. More and more, as the nineteenth century wore on and the twentieth century emerged, the fourth and fifth types became important means of establishing and financing new businesses.

The early conditions in the automobile industry peculiarly favored the entrance of small units into the field. Scores of small enterprises, in fact, tried their fortunes, most of which were weeded out by sharp competition. In the early history of the industry, a typical automobile plant consisted simply of a small assembly unit. Established factories were already in existence, prepared to adjust their equipment to the making of bodies and parts. Carriage makers, buggy manufacturers, machine shops, metalworking factories, woodworking mills, electrical equipment factories, and rubber goods factories all could readily shift from their established trades to the requirements of the new automobile industry. Thus, the automobile producer was originally essentially a designer who placed orders for parts and who assembled the parts into the finished automobile. The process of assembling was a short one. It required no elaborate plant and equipment and, therefore, no large fixed capital. It did not even require any large amount of working capital, since the parts manufacturers were ready to extend from thirty to ninety days' credit, and this adequately carried the automobile manufacturers over the assembling period. Moreover, working capital was not required to finance sales, since the demand for the product was such that the retail dealers were willing to advance a certain amount of cash and to pay cash on delivery. It was not even necessary to have working capital invested in any large inventories of finished products, since the cars could be loaded onto dealers as soon as produced, thus placing the inventory burden upon the retailers. All of these conditions were peculiarly favorable for the entrance of small-scale units into the field.

The development of the automobile industry illustrates, more or less, all of the types referred to. Conspicuously, the Ford Motor Company is an illustration of the second type—a small beginning financed by a small group of individuals, all of meager means. When Ford organized the Detroit Automobile Company, he succeeded in raising the paltry sum of ten thousand dollars in cash to finance the venture. Dissatisfied with this organization, a few years later he organized the Henry Ford Automobile Company, and this time he raised from individuals with small means the almost equally insignificant sum of thirty-eight thousand dollars. When he finally organized the Ford Motor Company, small subscriptions were obtained from several individuals, including the Dodge brothers, machine shop proprietors; Malcolmson, a coal dealer; Cousens, a clerk in the Malcolmson firm; and a few other friends and associates. Each contributed small sums ranging from one thousand dollars to five thousand dollars in cash or in promissory notes. All told, only twenty-eight thousand dollars was collected in cash, and an additional twenty-one thousand was subscribed in the form of promissory notes. From these relatively small savings of men of small means grew, by the reinvestment of profits, the vast Ford properties.

Of other successful firms, Hudson was started with a small capital of ten thousand dollars collected from individuals of small means.

Many of the companies sprang from established related industries. Thus, Buick began with the entrance of a parts manufacturer into the automobile field, was later taken over by the Flint Wagon Works, and was subsequently reorganized by Durant, a carriage manufacturer. Cadillac started from a machine company with relatively large new capital funds obtained from a group of backers. Studebaker represents the clearest case of the switching of an established carriage and wagon manufacturing business into the new line. Overland sprang from a buggy manufacturing business, and Dodge was developed by the Dodge brothers, who originally ran a machine shop and later became automobile parts producers, particularly for Ford.

A number of the companies were started full blown, so to speak, on a rather extensive scale backed by wealthy financiers. Thus Maxwell, later developing into the Chrysler Company, was early financed by J. P. Morgan. Packard was organized by second-generation, rich young men, and Nash, as a result of reorganization, began with a large capital investment. Reo represents, perhaps, an intermediate position, with an original investment of one hundred and seventy thousand dollars obtained from a group of Lansing citizens.

A long list of great fortunes represents the first type of

development of new industries referred to above. Brief reference will be made below to some of the outstanding examples. They extend over the nineteenth century and also into the twentieth. They are certainly more typical of the earlier period, though examples continue down to the present time.

One of the earlier examples of this type is Cornelius Vanderbilt, who at the age of sixteen began to operate a ferryboat. This cost him one hundred dollars, with which his parents started his business career. He soon succeeded in saving from the business a thousand dollars. Harbor traffic increased enormously during the War of 1812, and from the war earnings he built a schooner. Soon another vessel was added for coastwise traffic, and by 1817 he owned three vessels and nine thousand dollars in cash. In the meantime his wife had operated the Halfway House, from which business she had accumulated thirty thousand dollars. This Vanderbilt put into steamboat ferries. Once it became evident that the new railroad method of transportation was really here to stay, Vanderbilt entered this field, acquiring interests in the Hudson and Sound lines and in the Boston and Stonington Railroad. In addition, he ventured into iron works and shipyards, and developed a steamship route via Panama, thus capitalizing on the California gold rush. Thus, he ran eight steamers from New York on the Atlantic coast side and five steamers on the Pacific coast side, making connection with California. By the time of the Civil War, he was worth fifteen million dollars. In this period he turned to railroads in earnest and developed out of smaller lines the consolidated New York Central and Hudson River line in 1869.

John Wanamaker started as an errand boy for a publisher in Philadelphia, became a stock boy in a clothing store, and for a short time was the first paid secretary of the Y.M.C.A. in Philadelphia, at a salary of one thousand dollars a year. From this he saved nineteen hundred dollars, formed a partnership with his brother-in-law, who had saved a similar amount, and entered the clothing business. The store fixtures cost the partners three hundred and seventy-five dollars, and the first stock of fabrics seven hundred and forty dollars. From this small beginning business grew rapidly, and branch stores were opened in other cities. By 1876 they had built the largest store in America. Wanamaker never borrowed any funds. He financed his business exclusively out of profits and only in recent years issued bonds to the public.

John D. Rockefeller at the age of ten had accumulated fifty dollars from raising and selling turkeys. Later, from a small salary, he was able to save enough to start his partnership with Clark in the produce commission business. Clark put two thousand dollars in the business and Rockefeller one thousand of his own money plus one thousand borrowed from his father. The expansion of his properties during the produce commission period and later in the oil business grew from two sources—partly from internal profits, but heavily from borrowed funds. Rockefeller represents the daring type. He was continuously venturing out far beyond his own means and was an inveterate borrower almost from the beginning. His career, therefore, falls partly in the first category and partly in the third category outlined above.

Andrew Carnegie started work as a cotton mill operator and later was a telegrapher. He was then offered an opportunity, more or less by accident, to invest in the newly organized Woodruff Sleeping Car Company. When his first subscription of $217.50 fell due, he did not have the funds to pay it but succeeded in borrowing at a bank. Each installment, as it fell due, was met from borrowing. This investment rapidly yielded large dividends which became the nucleus from which the Carnegie investments sprang. These extended into railroads, oil, the manufacture of iron bridges, iron rails, locomotives, rolling mills, an express company, banks, insurance companies, street railways, and steel mills.

James J. Hill began as a clerk in a village store at the age of fourteen. Four years later found him as a shipping clerk in St. Paul for the Packet Company. Later he became agent for other companies, organizing a warehousing business with two partners, into which each put twenty-five hundred dollars. Later a new partnership was organized in the warehousing and commission business, dealing particularly in wood and coal. Separate partnerships were organized on the side to carry on a merchandising and transportation business in the Red River country. And still another partnership was organized to build and operate steamboats. From the profits of these various companies came the capital which enabled him to play a role in the organization of the bankrupt St. Paul and Pacific Railroad. This venture, of course, entailed the enlistment of a large amount of outside capital support. In the main, his wealth came from the appreciation of the value of reorganized railroad properties which, under his management, became highly profitable institutions.

Leland Stanford entered a law office and was admitted to the bar at twenty-nine. He opened a law office in Wisconsin, where he remained four years. He sailed from New York for San Francisco in 1852, where his brother had already gone with the gold rush and had opened a store in 1850. Two other brothers were also engaged in the store business, and a fourth was acting as purchasing agent in New York. The brothers had organized a wholesale business in Sacramento with stores in various places. Leland opened a store at Cold Springs, where, however, the gold prospects gave out. He then moved to Michigan Bluff and later joined in the Sacramento store venture. He invested in a gold mine in which he made a profit of four hundred thousand dollars. Thereupon, he entered politics and was elected governor in 1862. The project of a transcontinental railroad was in the air, and Stanford, in conjunction with Huntington, Crocker, and Hopkins, raised money for explorations. The Central Pacific Railroad was incorporated in 1861 with the so-called "Big Four" on the board of directors. In 1862 the Pacific Railroad Act was signed and the building was started on the Union Pacific westward and the Central Pacific eastward, with the aid of heavy government loans in the form of second mortgages, the assumption by the state of California of the interest burden on a large bond issue for a twenty-year period, and with other state and county aid. The Crocker Construction Company, a subsidiary, was organized, and in this Stanford invested heavily.

The careers of the three associates were very similar to that of Stanford. Huntington, at the age of fourteen, had saved $184 and invested it in a country store. On the side he peddled jewelry and bought up defaulted notes. He joined the California gold rush and sold goods, whisky, and blasting powder to the miners, at one time cornering the "shovel market." Hopkins started as a clerk in a New York village store and later was a partner in a commission house in New York City, after which he joined Huntington in California. Crocker had saved a small sum of money from boyhood and, at twelve, bought a news agency, for which he went into debt two hundred dollars. He later worked on his father's farm in Indiana and, at seventeen, worked in a sawmill. He discovered a deposit of iron ore on an Indiana hillside and set up a crude furnace, from which, however, he made no profits. Thereafter, he joined the gold rush and opened a store at Sacramento. There Crocker became acquainted with the other members of the Big Four.

E. H. Harriman began as an office boy in a brokerage firm and later was a messenger clerk and a managing clerk in a brokerage firm. He borrowed three thousand dollars from a wealthy uncle and bought a seat on the New York Stock Exchange, opening an office of his own. He engaged in extensive speculation, making large sums of money and sometimes losing large sums. He purchased a steamer, a small Hudson River boat, and in 1881 acquired an interest in a small railroad which he reorganized and sold to the Pennsylvania Railroad. Other railroad properties were acquired in New York, Pennsylvania, Illinois, and Ohio. He became president of the Illinois Central, reorganized the Erie, and in 1898 reorganized the Union Pacific. His main fortune, like that of Hill, was made from the appreciation of the value of railway properties which came under his control.

Meyer Guggenheim first peddled shoestrings, shoe polish, glue, stove polish, and the like, set up a tailor shop, later a grocery store, and then a wholesaling business in Philadelphia. In this last venture he made a considerable amount of money and during the Civil War made large profits in selling foodstuffs to the army. An uncle in Switzerland sent him a consignment of machine-embroidered lace, the sale of which proved to be extremely profitable. He later invested as a partner in two mines in Colorado, which also proved extremely profitable and, in the late eighties, brought him a large income. By 1870 one of these mines was valued at fifteen million dollars. From mining he went into smelting and rapidly rose to a top position in the copper industry.

Andrew Mellon's father, Thomas Mellon, set up a law office in Pittsburgh. From small savings he entered upon speculation, particularly the purchase of small judgments. After five years in the law practice he had saved twelve thousand dollars. With these savings he speculated in real estate, buying up properties and lending on mortgages and notes. During the Civil War he owned a fleet of coal barges and profited from government business. Andrew Mellon, born in 1855, was set up, together with his three brothers, by his father very early in life in the realty and lumber business. From the outset the brothers made large profits. Mellon money flowed into railroads, a tractor company in Philadelphia, coke ovens, banks, insurance companies, steel works, glass factories, coal mines, blast furnaces, bridge building, structural steel, steamers, barges, glass works, electric power, gas, aluminum, pipe lines, coke, etc. Few fortunes have played so significant a role in the starting of new enterprises.

Henry C. Frick began life as a farm boy and later became a bookkeeper. He began business by borrowing a little over ten thousand dollars, two thousand from his sister and the rest from his mother's estate. Frick was always full of big ideas and ready to persuade others to lend him money for his ventures. In 1870 he borrowed ten thousand dollars from Andrew Mellon, to which additional sums of ten thousand were added from time to time, and one hundred thousand in 1876.

George Eastman had a business school training. He had saved some five hundred dollars as a bookkeeper in an insurance office and later in a savings bank. By 1876 he had saved thirty-six hundred dollars. He then became interested in photography, first as an amateur, later investing in a machine for coating plates. He went to England to learn more about the business, obtained patents, and in 1880 leased a floor of a large building and began operations. He induced a friend to invest one thousand dollars and later five thousand dollars. All the profits went back into the business, and soon a company was organized with a capital of two hundred thousand dollars, one half of the stock being issued to Eastman and his associates for patents and the rest sold to friends in small lots of twenty-five hundred to three thousand dollars. In addition to profits plowed back into the business, capital was later raised by the sale of stocks to old stockholders, and, subsequently, the capital was further increased through stock dividends. Large profits were plowed back into the business.

Other examples of less spectacular individual fortunes, of business corporations springing from meager individual savings, and of small beginnings with growth financed mainly from reinvested profits, fill the pages of American business annals throughout the nineteenth century and even down to the present day. McCormick patented a reaper in 1834 and started a small factory from which developed one division of the great modern farm implements industry. John Deere, a Vermont blacksmith, succeeded in making a steel plow and in a few years had made over one hundred such plows. He then built a foundry in Moline, Illinois. In 1886 the John Deere Company was incorporated with a capital of five hundred thousand dollars and this later developed into Deere and Company, partly through the plowing back of internal profits and partly through the issuance of stock to the public. Studebaker, to whom reference has already been made in connection with the automobile industry, started as a wagon manufacturer in 1853 with a capital of sixty-eight dollars and two forges. In 1858 he was joined by his brother, who came back from the gold rush with eight thousand dollars in gold nuggets. From this modest capital investment the company rapidly grew, until in 1868 it was making three hundred and sixty thousand wagons a year.

Simmons started as a clerk in a general store in Kenosha, Wisconsin, in 1849. He later bought out his employer and accidentally, through a customer, had an opportunity to buy up a bankrupt telegraph company, which he developed into the Northwestern Telegraph and leased to the Western Union. He later built a small railroad, invested in the Burlington and Northern Pacific Railroads, and built a cogwheel railroad. He then established a cheesebox factory and, upon meeting the inventor of a woven wire mattress, bought the patent and began to make mattresses. From these small beginnings sprang the Simmons Company.

Weyerhauser started as a hand in a sawmill, worked hard, and saved his money, and in the panic of 1857 was able to buy up a bankrupt lumberyard. He built barns and houses for farmers and in two years succeeded in making eight thousand dollars. Thereupon, he bought a larger lumbermill and went into the logging business from which the Weyerhauser fortune sprang.

George A. Hormel began running a small retail butcher shop in Austin, Minnesota, and soon established a local reputation for making sausages. In this manner, through internal growth and development, sprang the George A. Hormel Packing Company.

The Crane Company began with a small brass foundry started by Crane in a shed which he himself built in Chicago. He received financial assistance from an uncle and was joined by his brother, an iron foundry mechanic. The Civil War brought a profitable business, and after the war the Northwest Manufacturing Company was organized with a capital of two hundred thousand dollars. Crane embarked upon the construction of elevators, but this business was later sold to the Otis Elevator Company.

Other illustrations which follow the typical pattern of an energetic young man with meager savings establishing a small business which expanded through internal growth are found in the history of R. H. Macy and Company, the Caterpillar Tractor Company, the Coca-Cola Company, Cluett, Peabody and Company, Budd Manufacturing Company, Minneapolis-Honeywell Company, Wayne Pump Company, Sherwin Williams Company, Campbell's Soup Company, Axton-Fisher Company, Montgomery Ward, and the United Fruit Company, among many others.

Some interesting recent illustrations, indicating that this type of growth is not yet over, are to be found in the growth of the Walgreen Drugstores, W. T. Grant Company, Real Silk, Life Savers, Planter's Nut and Chocolate Company, Philco Radio, J. E. Prentiss Company, and Greyhound Lines.

With respect to the last-named company, Wickman, a diamond drill operator at Hibbing, Minnesota, began by carrying miners across the range in his car. Bus bodies were later built and put on truck chassis. In 1915 Wickman and his partner had earned eighteen thousand dollars, in 1916 sixteen thousand, in 1917 forty thousand. In 1916 the Misaba Transportation Company was organized, and, in 1918, it had a fleet of eighteen buses. In 1922 Wickman sold his share for sixty thousand dollars and began operations around Duluth. He continued to buy out small bus lines and, in this manner, gradually built up the Greyhound Lines.

The Schick Shaver, the Covered Wagon Trailers, Schultz Trailers, and Palace Travel Coaches are recent illustrations from the late twenties and early thirties of rapid development from meager beginnings. The Covered Wagon Trailers started with Sherman, a bacteriologist, building a trailer for himself and then one for a friend. He then decided to risk a few thousand dollars and began to build trailers in a garage. In 1930 he exhibited his product in the Detroit Auto Show and in the next year sold one hundred and seventeen trailers.

Until 1933 all the capital had come from initial outlays together with plowed back earnings. Then, however, a company was formed which issued a block of common stock and preferred stock, which brought in seven hundred and fifty thousand dollars for the expansion of the business.

Illustrations of industries that have grown from small beginnings with small outside capital support, together with the reinvestment of profits, may be found in the A. G. Spaulding and Brothers Company and the Hookless Fastener. Companies that have been organized with fairly large outside capital support are Dry Ice Company, Anaconda Copper, St. Joseph Lead Company, Gulf Oil, Aluminum Company of America, Climax Molybdenum, Markrum Company, Pacific Coast Borax Company, Cannon Mills, Campo Shoe Manufacturing Company, and the Columbia Broadcasting Company. Examples of companies that have been organized either by established companies or by wealthy men starting new companies are Phelps-Dodge, Grigsby-Grunow, United Shoe Machinery, Continental Can, Anheuser-Busch Company, American Radiator, Newport News Shipbuilding and Drydock Company, and Beechnut Packing Company.

It will be seen from this brief survey that most of the great fortunes started with small savings, together with small support from friends of meager means. Profits were plowed back into the business and expansion came from internal growth. In some cases the beginnings of the fortune were based essentially on borrowing and on more or less risky investment. This was particularly true of Frick, Carnegie, and Harriman.

Corporate Research and Current Financing of New Ventures

An examination of nearly six hundred prospectuses recently issued under the Securities and Exchange Commission regulations indicates that, under modern conditions, established companies with well-developed engineering and research staffs, and frequently with a largely diversified line of products, are constantly developing new products and expanding into new lines. In general, it may be said that the day of the energetic lad starting a new business in a small shop with meager savings of a few hundred dollars is past. It is true that the development of new businesses and large private fortunes via this historic route is not yet over, as we have seen in some of the illustrations given above. But, for the most part, it is evident that new developments no longer are started in this manner. Small individual beginnings were typically the product of a rapidly expanding economy in which extensive growth and development incident to the opening of new territory, the exploitation of new natural resources, and the growth of population were characteristic features. Today, in a more mature economy and with the phase of extensive growth largely over, with growth and development limited more completely to intensive expansion, and with great aggregates of capital covering a wide range of industry, it is less easy to start small new enterprises and develop new products. Great established corporations with research laboratories are peculiarly in a position to take advantage of opportunities for intensive expansion. Starting frequently from a diversified line of products, research departments continually improve and increase the variety and range of products and, in addition, develop new sidelines which may themselves become important new industries. Thus, just as business organization has, for the most part, shifted from the small-scale individual proprietorship type to the huge corporate type, so the development of new products and new industries rarely comes through the route of small individual beginnings, but rather through the branching out into new lines of established corporations.

This development obviously is important for a consideration of the impact of the current tax structure upon the exploitation of new investment outlets. Many individual instances have been cited in recent years, particularly of wealthy capitalists being restrained from venturing upon new risky businesses by reason of the high individual surtax rates or the capital gains tax. It is argued that, whereas in former times risky business was amply able to get such capital, nowadays this is lacking. The history of the development of great fortunes and new industries in the nineteenth century, however, indicates that wealthy individuals have played a relatively inconspicuous role in the founding of new industries, while today these developments come mainly through established corporations. To be sure, as we have seen, it is evident that, in the past, men of means have frequently aided the development of new enterprises by large investment of funds—if not at their earliest beginnings, at least later on in their development. But, typically, new industries have sprung from internal growth and sometimes, after they have been well established, by the issuance of securities to the general public, while nowadays new developments spring largely from established corporations.

Undoubtedly, the vast expansion of the nineteenth century would have proceeded less rapidly had as heavy a tax burden applied to income and property then as now. Whereas now the wealthy are compelled to pay a very large portion of their income to the government, then all their savings were available for new investment. This undoubtedly played a role in the rapid expansion of the nineteenth century. Frequently in this period the limiting factor was a scarcity of capital. Today, despite the heavy load of taxes, with more limited investment opportunities it is probable that the limiting factor is rather a sufficient advance in technique to develop promising new products and, in particular, the cessation of extensive expansion.

We have seen that also in recent years some new industries have developed outside of the great corporate laboratories. These have available a source of capital in the great middle class with fairly high incomes, yet subject to relatively low income taxes. In relation to currently available investment opportunities of this rather small-scale character, the capital supply available for small individual ventures must be enormously greater than was the case in the early half of the nineteenth century.

Chapter XIX

THE EFFECT OF THE TAX STRUCTURE ON INVESTMENT

WHILE a recovery may be induced, in part, by net income-creating governmental expenditures, public policy must in a system of private enterprise be directed mainly toward providing the necessary conditions under which private enterprise can go forward. To this end, it is necessary to create the most favorable possible basis for the emergence of new private investment.

In this connection, it is important to consider the tax structure with a view to the elimination or modification of taxes tending to prevent the normal flow of private investment. Among the taxes which, it has been charged, operate in this direction—and this was particularly the case in the upswing of 1936–37—are the undistributed profits tax and the capital gains tax.

The undistributed profits tax operated, it is said, in this direction because corporations are more likely to assume the risks of forward-looking, anticipatory investments by expending corporate surpluses than is the case if they must go to the market and raise capital through new issues. Similarly, the capital gains tax is said to prevent large private investors from undertaking new ventures, if the profits which it may be expected will be made in the first years of new undertakings were, for such individuals (in the event that the enterprise, once it reached stability, were sold to others), taxed at the top bracket. Historically, it is said, venturesome capitalists have embarked on attractive and promising speculative projects and, as soon as the promotional stage was completed, have sold the business at the capitalized value of the then-expected income and turned their capital to other new ventures. With the development of the stock market as an important source of funds, new issues were first placed directly with wealthy individuals, and these, in turn, after a lapse of time resold to the general public through the stock market.

Current Sources of Funds

Broadly speaking, the rise of the great modern corporation has profoundly affected both the channels through which savings flow and the character of investment activity. In the days of small-scale, individual proprietorship investment activity was undertaken by individuals. Today it is largely a function performed by corporations. Typically, the innovator in the nineteenth century was a daring individual. Typically, the innovator today is a great corporation engaging in elaborate organized research, deliberately and systematically developing new things instead of hitting upon them by luck or accident, as was formerly frequently the case.

Since innovation, entrepreneurship, and real investment are nowadays carried on so largely by corporations, it would appear that a normal adjunct to this activity would be a fund of quasi-automatic savings in the form of depreciation and depletion allowances and of corporate surpluses available for the exploitation and development of new investment projects. In the days of small-scale, individual proprietorship, savings naturally flowed directly in the normal case into investment, just as is still the case today when the farmer (the one remaining field where, in general, individual, small-scale proprietorship still prevails) puts his savings directly into farm equipment. With the rise of the great corporation, industrialization, urbanization, and the decline of individual businesses into which small savings could be poured, it was inevitable that institutions should grow up through which would be canalized the flow of savings from millions of individuals. Thus, we have witnessed the great growth of the savings bank, of postal savings, of building and loan associations, of life insurance companies, and mortgage companies offering an outlet for millions of small savings streams.

The extent to which gross capital expenditures are financed by internal corporate sources, including (1) depreciation and depletion allowances and (2) retained corporate earnings, is well recognized by business executives with respect to their own concerns; but it is not generally appreciated with respect to corporate enterprise as a whole. For the period 1925–29, depreciation and depletion allowances of all nonfinancial enterprises averaged $5,524 millions per annum, while retained earnings amounted to $2,365 millions.[1] Together, these two internal sources accounted for $7,889 millions available for capital outlays on plant and equipment. In comparison with this sum derived from internal sources, only $1,738 millions was obtained, through productive issues, from the outside capital market.[2] Thus, of the total of $9,627 millions available from both internal and external sources, 82 per cent came from internal sources and only 18 per cent from the outside capital market.

It is, moreover, of interest to note that industrial corporations are responsible for only a relatively small part of the total productive issues of nonfinancial corporations. According to the study by George Eddy,[3] railroads, public utilities, and real-estate corporations raised $1,160 millions from productive issues in the capital market in 1929, while industrial concerns raised only $730 millions. The great industrial concerns are very largely self-sufficient with respect to their capital requirements. Thus, the United States Steel Corporation, for example, expended $1,222 millions for plant and equip-

1 *Statistics of Income;* Fabricant, *Capital Consumption and Adjustment;* Hearings, Temporary National Economic Committee, Part 9, p. 4041.

2 Moody's Investors' Service; Hearings, Temporary National Economic Committee, Part 9, p. 4041.

3 *Review of Economic Statistics,* May, 1937.

ment in the period 1921–38 inclusive. In the same period depreciation and depletion allowances provided the vast sum of $938 millions, while retained earnings amounted to $192 millions. These two internal sources combined, therefore, furnished $1,130 millions, or 93 per cent of total capital outlays.

In 1936–37 the depreciation and depletion allowances of all nonfinancial enterprises averaged $4,575 millions per annum, while retained earnings amounted to $1,084 per annum. Thus, internal sources furnished on the average, in this period, $5,659 millions compared with $7,889 millions per annum in 1925–29. Productive issues in the capital market, according to Moody's, yielded only $505 millions per annum in 1936–37, compared with $1,738 millions in 1925–29. According to George Eddy, however, the productive issues were $1.0 billion per annum in 1936–37.[4] The explanation which he gives for the difference between his figures and those of Moody's is that the latter have eliminated in recent years, from "productive issues," issues for working capital. This he regards as a questionable step, inasmuch as the purposes of many issues are now vaguely described in prospectuses as additions to working capital. Internal sources of funds furnished 92 per cent (86 per cent, according to Eddy's data) of the total in 1936–37, compared with 82 per cent in 1925–29.

It is evident that business enterprises rely relatively little upon the capital market for their investment funds. The role of the capital market as a source of funds has evidently been enormously exaggerated. Moreover, there is reason to believe that the role of the capital market is declining in terms of a long-run trend. It is true that we do not as yet have an adequate statistical basis for the calculation of a long-run trend, in view of the incomplete recoveries of 1936–37 and 1939–40.

With respect to the external sources of funds, it is important to note that the stock market is of less importance

[4] *Review of Economic Statistics,* August, 1939.

than formerly. An increasing proportion of new corporate bonds and notes are placed privately with large financial institutions outside of the stock market, and even without the intermediary, except in a perfunctory way, of investment bankers. Thus, of total corporate bonds and notes issued in 1938, 37 per cent were privately placed, in comparison with 11 per cent in 1936 and 27 per cent in 1937.[5]

Attention was called above to the fact that increasingly the flow of savings is being canalized into institutional channels. The total premium income of life insurance companies in relation to the total national income has risen steadily since 1880. From one hundred thousand dollars in the middle eighties, premium payments have grown at a constant percentage rate until they reached over $3,500 millions in 1937. The assets of life insurance companies have risen from $4.0 billions in 1910 to $28.8 billions in 1938, savings and time deposits from $7.4 billions to $26.0 billions, building and loan association assets from $1.0 billion to $5.7 billions, government pension and trust funds from nothing to $6.2 billions, postal savings and baby bonds from nothing to $2.5 billions. Combined, then, savings accumulations have risen from $12.4 billions in 1910 to $69.0 billions in 1938. These accumulated savings amounted to 44 per cent of the national income in 1910, and by 1938 totaled a sum in excess of the national income.[6]

Now, while these institutional savings are, indeed, available to finance the real investments undertaken by corporations, there is, nevertheless, the difficulty that these institutional savings inevitably seek almost exclusively, as hitherto constituted, fixed debt obligations, such as bonds and mortgages. Thus, the financial institutions which are the reservoirs of savings held $14.4 billions ($11.9 billions when commercial banks are excluded) of the $21.7 of mortgages on urban real estate in 1929 and $8.9 billions of the total of

[5] *The Commercial and Financial Chronicle;* Securities and Exchange Commission; Hearings, Temporary National Economic Committee, Part 9, p. 4065.

[6] Hearing on Savings and Investment, Part 9, T.N.E.C., p. 4052.

$17.3 billions in 1937. They held $1.4 billions of farm mortgages in 1938 and $22.0 billions ($8.4 billions when commercial banks are excluded) of the federal direct and guaranteed obligations.

Characteristically, the modern institutional savings mechanism tends to develop the holding of wealth in the form of debt claims. If borrowers wish to tap this source of savings, they must do so by issuing debt obligations. And this they are encouraged to do by reason of the fact that the volume of the savings stream seeking this particular form of financial investment is large and is offered at an attractive rate of interest.

Equity Capital

These developments, with respect to both the demand and the supply of capital funds, indicate a tendency away from the absorption of savings into equities and toward the use of fixed debt obligations. The increasing ratio of debt to wealth makes for a sort of rigidity which is highly dangerous and in itself tends to intensify economic instability. Investment of a larger part of the savings stream in equity capital ought to be encouraged.

Question may be raised whether institutional savings ought not to be forced, in a certain measure, into the equity field. The Canadian Sun Life alone of North American insurance companies has ventured far into the field of investment of its funds in common stocks. At the beginning of the Great Depression over 50 per cent of its assets were so invested. This was doubtless excessive, particularly in view of the terrific deflation in the early thirties. In consequence, the Canadian Parliament passed a statute compelling insurance companies to reduce their holdings of common stock to 15 per cent of their assets. This, however, probably goes too far in the opposite direction. In any case, it would be quite unsound, from the standpoint of the economy as a whole, to compel corporations to adopt and practice financial policies designed to withstand periodically deflations of the magnitude experienced in the Great Depression. It is incumbent upon government actively to pursue policies which will not make it necessary for business to face such risks.

As a tentative figure, it may be suggested that insurance companies might well be permitted to invest up to 25 per cent of their assets in equity holdings and might be required to invest not less than 15 per cent in this manner. The same requirements might also well be made of banks. Partly through a modification of the outlets for funds flowing through institutional savings channels, and partly through the freedom of corporations to accumulate surpluses, adequate equity money may, even under modern savings-investment conditions, be found to permit large anticipatory private investments.

Reinvestment of corporate earnings is an important and desirable source of equity capital. Under conditions of less rapid extensive growth, American corporations may, however, tend to retain too large a proportion of earnings. Moreover, some modification in our tax structure in order to achieve equality of taxation between partnerships and corporations, and to prevent tax evasion by wealthy individuals, is necessary. These aims could be reached by amending the individual income tax so as to require each stockholder to include in his taxable income his pro rata share of the undistributed profits of corporations. In addition, it may also be necessary to prevent corporations from piling up undue idle balances in their excessive desire for corporate security by taxing those undistributed profits (after making reasonable allowances for liquidity) which are not invested in plant and equipment. There is, however, the danger that such a tax might result in earnings being invested in plant and equipment in excess of the amount which could economically be justified, leading to misdirected and excessive investment.

With respect to the capital gains tax, the fact that anticipatory real investments are now typically made by large corporations minimizes very much the objection to the capital gains tax as a deterrent to real investment, since corporations are under less inducement than individuals to realize on their capital gains through sale. With respect to individuals, numerous cases may be found, even in our highly industrialized corporate society, in which individuals may have been deterred from making anticipatory real investments by reason of the capital gains tax. But the net effect of all these upon the whole economy is probably not great. New developments are not likely to be stifled long if they are really promising. Moreover, in so far as venturesome capitalists retain their holdings in the new enterprises, as was true of the Mellon investments, the capital gains tax does not act as a deterrent.

It is said, however, that the capital gains tax affects real investment in a quite different manner. Admitting that investments are made by large corporations, and that they are financed in some considerable measure through the security markets, it is said that the capital gains tax so affects the functioning of the security markets that important anticipatory real investments are prevented by reason of this tax. This raises the question what sort of capital market condition is most favorable for investment.

In the first place, a high price of securities represents a favorable situation, since this means that issues can be placed very favorably in terms of yields or interest rates. In the next place, it is sometimes said that a very stable security market is favorable for investment. This, however, is more problematical, since statistical investigation clearly reveals that the volume of new issues has a high correlation with the *movement* of security prices. If the prices are rising rapidly, issues also are increasing rapidly. From this it would appear that a rapidly rising market is the most favorable condition for the stimulation of new investment. If one takes the entire cycle into consideration, however, it is conceivable that a stable security market might, over the entire cycle period, be more favorable for investment than a market which fluctuated violently. Granted that new issues are stimulated when the market is rising, they are clearly choked off almost completely when the market is falling rapidly.

These considerations raise the question of how the capital gains tax affects (a) the level of security prices and (b) their stability. Would the reduction or the abandonment of the capital gains tax induce a larger volume of funds to flow into the market and thereby affect the level of security prices? Would not such revision afford greater stability by encouraging the taking of profits when the market is rising, and by removing the inducement to establish losses in the downswing?

The complete removal of the capital gains tax (except for professional speculators) could scarcely fail to stimulate speculation by wealthy individuals and would, therefore, have, in a measure, the effect of transferring investment-seeking funds from bonds and mortgages to stocks and real estate. But the magnitude of the shift, considering the fact that the vast bulk of the common stock is already held by wealthy persons, would probably not be great.

From the standpoint of the Treasury, it is not altogether clear that a fair capital gains tax, which allows adequate loss offsets, is likely to be of any great value in the long run. In a rapidly expanding economy, particularly one experiencing a rising trend of commodity prices, the Treasury would stand to gain handsomely. But in a less rapidly expanding economy losses are more likely to offset the gains, and, on balance, the Treasury will secure relatively meager tax revenues over the entire cycle, unless, indeed, it plays a "heads I win, tails you lose" game by not permitting adequate loss offsets.

George A. Eddy, in an article in the *Review of Economic Statistics,* August, 1939, questions the thesis that the tax structure was an important factor in the relatively low new productive issues in 1936–38. In the first place, his estimates indicate larger productive issues for these years than that hitherto assumed—$900 millions for 1936, $1,100 millions for 1937, and $825 millions for 1938. The average for the three years amounted to 48 per cent of the 1929 level and 53 per cent of the 1921–30 level. For the twelve months July, 1936, to June, 1937, the new productive issues were $1.4 billions, or 70 per cent of the 1929 level and 77 per cent of the

1921–30 average. The decline relative to the twenties was mainly in the real-estate field and in public utilities. Moreover, the theory that the tax structure was responsible for the inadequate flow of funds into new issues in 1936–37 is not compatible with the low yields then prevailing on both bonds and stocks.

How important tax-exempt securities are in causing a flight from equities is not altogether clear. Mr. Wesley Lindow of the United States Treasury Department, at the meeting of the American Statistical Association, December 29, 1938, presented some estimates of the holdings of tax exempts. According to his findings, individuals owned $8.3 billions of the $19.3 billions of wholly tax-exempt state and local bonds, and $3.9 billions of the $17.3 billions of wholly tax-exempt federal bonds or bonds of federal instrumentalities. Thus, all told, individuals held $12.2 billions of the total of $36.6 billions of wholly tax-exempt bonds, or exactly one third. The wholly exempt bonds are the only ones which, in any significant way, come into question from the standpoint of the problem here under discussion.

According to H. L. Lutz,[7] large estates held, during the period 1926–36, state and local bonds amounting to only 9.8 per cent of the total value of the estate, and wholly exempt federal bonds amounting to only 1.9 per cent. E. E. Oakes[8] denies that there has been a precipitate flight of wealthy investors into tax exempts. He gives as reasons for this: (1) that very wealthy men are rather adventurous and are more interested in large gains than in a stable income; (2) that the estates for which we now have statistics took form largely at a time when the rates were not severely burdensome, and when earnings from stocks were very high; (3) that the assumed threat of inflation of recent years has left large estates heavily in stocks; and (4) that the low depression values of stocks prevented a transfer to tax exempts, since a strong market was expected.

[7] H. L. Lutz, *The Fiscal and Economic Aspects of the Taxation of Public Securities,* Bar Press, 1939.

[8] *Bulletin of the National Tax Association,* June, 1938.

According to the second point, however, it could be expected that estates in future would go more heavily into tax exempts, and, according to the fourth point, it might be expected that the relatively high stock market of 1936–37 would have resulted in large transfers to tax exempts.

TABLE XXVI

Percentage of Estates Held in Tax-Exempts

Value of Estate, $ 000's	*1922*	*1930*	*1937*
Total	7.66	7.34	10.64
Under 50	5.39	3.27	6.86
50–100 (1922, 50–150)	6.11	4.22	7.52
100–200 (1922, 150–250)	6.48	4.92	9.48
200–400 (1922, 250–450)	7.78	5.75	10.33
400–600 (1922, 450–750)	7.24	5.01	11.15
600–800 (1922, 750–1,000)	7.57	4.74	13.88
800–1,000		9.40	13.06
1,000–1,500	8.04	6.44	11.53
1,500–2,000	10.66	7.50	14.69
2,000–3,000	13.64	10.01	19.88
3,000–4,000	12.03	16.26	14.97
4,000–5,000	14.94	16.73	14.98
5,000–6,000	8.21	19.42	19.49
6,000–7,000	6.07	3.98	24.24
7,000–8,000	16.32	11.24	15.02
8,000–9,000	14.69	13.90	42.73
9,000–10,000		23.12	
10,000 and over	8.39	16.52	23.33

Colm and Lehmann's study,[9] based on inadequate samples, indicates an increasing trend toward tax exempts in recent years. This trend is also suggested by the Bureau of Internal Revenue's figures [10] on "Statistics of Income," from which the above table is constructed.

[9] "Economic Consequences of Recent American Tax Policy," Supplement I, *Social Research,* 1938.

[10] Includes federal government bonds wholly tax exempt and partially exempt and state and municipal bonds.

While these distributions are not regular and uniform, but are, on the contrary, multimodal, they nevertheless exhibit a tendency for the percentage of estates held in tax-exempt securities to increase as the size of the estate increases. Again, while it is not true of every size group, the figures show a decline in the percentage of estates held in tax-exempts in 1930, and a rise in 1937 to a level above the 1922 figure. Fluctuations in the yields of other types of assets, such as equities, would provide a partial explanation of this shift in type of assets held. It is likely that the reductions in the income and estate tax rates, the raising of exemptions in the Revenue Act of 1926, and the higher rates and lower exemptions of the Revenue Acts of 1932, 1934, and 1935 also had their effect in causing variations in the percentage of estates held in tax-exempts.

Taxation and Corporate Profits and Losses

With respect to the cyclical aspect of the structure of taxation, problems relating to extreme fluctuations in business income are important. One consideration has to do with the evaluation of inventories for tax purposes. Such valuation may profoundly affect the cyclical fluctuation of corporate incomes and, therefore, affect the cyclical fluctuations in taxes. If inventories are valued on a "first in, first out" basis, it follows that there will be large inventory profits in the upswing and large inventory losses in the downswing. The result is to exaggerate enormously the cycle of profits and losses in a manner that is quite artificial. From the standpoint of taxation, this result may not be undesirable if one wishes to impose heavy taxes in the prosperity period and low taxes in depression. The valuation of inventories for tax purposes, on the "last in, first out" basis, as permitted in recent legislation, however, tends to make the corporation accounts reflect more accurately the actual course of profits and losses.

One feature of federal taxation of recent years which, it was said, acted as an impediment to investment was the discrimination between corporations with highly fluctuating incomes and those with stable incomes. When one takes into account the losses and profits over a period of years, the effective tax rate as then applied varied very greatly with different corporations according to the fluctuation of income. Certain types of industries are of a fluctuating character, and others are of a stable character. Thus, it was found that, for a period of general prosperity, the taxes for all manufacturing industries was 16.0 per cent of the net income of the entire period, while that for paper and pulp products was 15.3 per cent; for printing, publishing, and allied industries 15.4 per cent; and for chemical and allied products 14.8 per cent. On the other hand, in the period of the Great Depression, 1930 to 1935, it was found that for this entire period the proportion of net income taxed for all manufacturing industries was 94.6 per cent; for paper and pulp products 53.7 per cent; for printing, publishing, and allied industries 31.2 per cent; and for chemical and allied products 34.8 per cent.[11]

In order to obviate this difficulty, either the tax should be applied to an average income over a period or there should be provision for loss carry-over. The latter remedy was adopted in the Revenue Act of 1939. It was provided that net operating losses could be carried over for two years, effective for income received after December 31, 1939.

Both of these methods have been used in England. From 1882 to 1926 the British method of dealing with this problem was to permit a three-year averaging of income for tax purposes. This procedure, however, was terminated by the House of Lords in the Whelan vs. Henning case of 1926. The method involved auditing and administrative difficulties and, at times, resulted definitely in tax avoidance. Industrialists appearing before the Colwyn Committee entered vigorous protests against this method. Following the case referred to above, the Finance Act of 1927 introduced the loss carry-forward method, under which losses may be carried forward against subsequent profit for a period of six years.

11 See J. Keith Butters, "Discriminatory Effects of the Annual Computation of the Corporation Income Tax," *Quarterly Journal of Economics*, November, 1939.

Another matter bearing on the problem of the impact of taxation upon investment relates to the general effect of the tax structure upon business profits in recent years. Has the tax structure prevented business from making sufficient profits to justify new investment?

Professor Crum's study of profits in the May, 1939, issue of the *Review of Economic Statistics,* measured in terms of "rate of return on equity," gives the following results, for various types of corporations, for the year 1936 compared with the average for 1926–29.

TABLE XXVII

Business Profits: Rates of Return

	1926–29 (average)	*1936*
Manufacturing	7.68	7.94
Trade	5.85	7.16
Public Utilities	5.95	2.69
Finance	6.47	3.98
All Corporations (including other divisions not listed above)	6.27	4.83

Absolute figures for corporate profits are available in the *Statistics of Income.* If we compare 1926–29 with 1936–37, we get the results shown in Tables XXVIII and XXIX.

These extremely interesting data indicate a low rate of return for financial corporations and for public utilities in 1936, but a high rate for manufacturing and a quite extraordinary rate for trading corporations. The results for manufacturing and trade are the more remarkable in that the national income in 1936 was only $64 billions compared with $80 billions in 1926–29. Industrial production stood at 104 in 1936 compared with 111 in 1926–29, while wholesale prices were 81 in 1936 compared with 100 for 1926, and 95 for 1929. Department store sales stood at 88 in 1936 compared with 108 in 1926–29. Apparently, manufacturing corporations had been able to make adjustments (involving, in part,

TABLE XXVIII

Statutory Net Income of All Corporations Showing Net Income [12]

	1926–29 (in millions)	*1936–37* (in millions)
Manufacturing and Mining	$4,972	$3,858
Trade	1,190	1,014
Transportation and other Public Utilities	1,804	1,133
Finance	1,757	495
Total (including groups not listed above)	10,263	6,824
Taxes	1,192	752
After taxes	$ 9,071	$6,072

TABLE XXIX

Statutory Net Income of All Corporations
(net income less deficit) [12]

	1926–29	*1936–37*
Manufacturing and Mining	$3,943	$3,307
Trade	813	788
Transportation and other Public Utilities	1,634	720
Finance	1,090	(− 434)
Total (including groups not listed above)	7,745	4,388

revaluation of assets) which enabled them to make as high a rate of profit, despite lower output and lower prices, while trading corporations were able to make a higher rate of return on a lower value of sales. What these facts may mean with respect to the growing power of monopolistic competition in the modern world is not easy to say, but apparently there is a field here for economic research. A part of the explanation of the high profits rate of 1936 is, perhaps, to be found in the rise in inventory values, a phenomenon particularly conspicuous in that year.

[12] *Statistics of Income.* Dividends for domestic corporations and tax-exempt interest excluded for all years.

Finance and public utilities earned, in 1936, rates of return far below that 1926–29 level. There are special reasons for this, particularly in the case of financial institutions and of the railroads. In view of the profits made in the manufacturing and trade fields, however, it is scarcely probable that a general explanation can be found in the tax structure.

Consumption Taxes and Investment

It is highly probable that taxes on consumption played a far greater role as a deterrent to full recovery in 1936–37 than did corporate and personal income taxes. The heavy weight of new consumption taxes, including the federal and state social security taxes, was of primary significance here. Attention has been directed to this in earlier chapters. Especially to be noted is the sudden imposition of heavy social security taxes (unemployment and old-age) on payrolls in 1937, which resulted in a withdrawal of nearly one and a quarter billion dollars in excess of benefits paid. This, undoubtedly, had an important bearing upon the decline in total consumption expenditures beginning early in 1937.

In general, taxes weighing heavily on consumption bulked very large. Thus, for example, in the fiscal year 1938 federal, state, and local taxes on liquor, tobacco, gasoline and motor vehicles, sales taxes and other excises, and payroll taxes amounted to $5,700 millions.[13]

In so far as these revenues had the effect of curtailing private consumption expenditures, it is clear that equivalent offsetting governmental expenditures were in no sense income generating. The receipt of these taxes and the expending of these sums by the government merely *diverted* the income stream from private to governmental purposes.

To the extent that our tax system could be shifted away from regressive taxes bearing on consumption to progressive taxes on that part of the income stream which flows into the savings channel, private consumption expenditures would

[13] *Bulletin* of the Treasury Department, August, 1939.

rise. Such increase in expenditures would stimulate private investment. A major reform of our whole federal, state, and local tax structure, designed to reduce consumption taxes, would be of crucial importance in any program aiming to enlarge the outlets for private investment.

Chapter XX

THE DUAL ECONOMY

THE economy which developed and flourished in the nineteenth century throughout the Western world was pre-eminently a private capitalistic economy. This economy enjoyed relatively little interference from the state, and even from private institutional controls such as trade-unions or cartels. To be sure, as the century wore on, both private institutional interferences with the free working of the private system and state interferences became more and more general. Within the framework of these interferences, however, the private capitalistic economy continued to occupy nearly the entire field of industry.

Economic activities on the side of consumption as well as on the side of production were carried on by private individuals or private organizations. With respect to production, the individual entrepreneurial type of production organization receded more and more with the increasing development of the corporate form of organization. Moreover, consumers' co-operation in retail buying, in distribution, and even in manufacturing, came to play a considerable role. Here and there in certain restricted areas the state played a relatively minor but increasing role as producer, particularly on the Continent of Europe, in the field of railroads and public utilities. Expenditures for consumption purchases were made almost exclusively by private individuals or by private organizations.

Toward the close of the nineteenth century and gaining momentum rapidly in the twentieth century, particularly from the second decade on, there developed a pronounced tendency in the direction of the socialization of income and of the growth of community consumption expenditures. On the side of production, there also developed some considerable increase in socialization. Quasi-governmental corporations were organized, such as the British Broadcasting Corporation, the Port of London Authority, the Central Electricity Board, the London Passenger Transport Board; the various governmental corporations developed in Germany in the decade of the twenties, such as the Vereinigte Industrie-Unternehmungen Aktiengesellschaft, and the German Railway Company; and, in the United States, the Port of New York Authority, the Reconstruction Finance Corporation, the Home Owners' Loan Corporation, the Tennessee Valley Authority, the United States Housing Authority, and the like.

These two tendencies, one looking toward a socialization of the means of production and the other looking toward a socialization of income and consumption, suggest two possible alternatives to the simon-pure system of private enterprise. Each alternative represents a dual system. One type of dual system would be a private-public consumption economy; the other, a private-public production economy. To each of these types we shall now direct our attention, with particular reference to fiscal policy and the problems of economic stability and full employment of resources.

A Dual Production Economy

A dual production system, which is clearly a hybrid between a private capitalistic economy and a socialized economy, might perhaps be said to offer the disadvantages of mixing two contradictory schemes of organization of production, while on the other side failing to achieve the advantages of a fully developed system, whether of the purely private capitalist type or the thoroughgoing socialist type. This point of view has been much elaborated in recent literature. It has been suggested that either type of economy in the hands of an intelligent and resourceful people with character and self-discipline could be expected to function well, but that the mixture of the two systems presents inherent contradictions which would make such a hybrid system unworkable. A mixture of the two systems interferes, it is said, with the proper functioning of the private capitalist segment of the economy.

One advantage which the dual system clearly has, however, over the thoroughly socialist state is that it offers a greater scope for individual freedom from the coercive restraint of a highly centralized authority. This is true for the reason that in the dual system there would, of necessity, be a much wider distribution of power than is possible in a highly centralized collectivism. Under modern conditions of high concentration of economic power in the hands of giant corporations and in the hands of centralized trade-unions, with hundreds of thousands and even millions of members, it is by no means certain that the private capitalistic economy offers a wider distribution of power than a dual economy. It may, indeed, be argued that the dual economy offers a way of escape from a highly regimented private industrial system, on the one side, and an equally highly regimented collectivist system on the other. Much is to be said, under present conditions of high development of corporate and labor organization and the concentration of power which these imply, for the balance created by the weight of governmental activities as an offset against the growth of private organizational control.

Aside from the problem of the distribution of power is the purely economic problem of high efficiency and workability, including the increasingly important aspects of stability and full utilization of resources. From this standpoint, much may be said for the dual system in contrast with either the purely private system, on the one side, or the highly collectivized system on the other. The highly collectivized system is likely to result in a deterioration of efficiency. On the other side, the purely private capitalistic economy, while capable of achieving high operating efficiency, nevertheless is tending, through the development of monopolistic restraints, toward restriction of production and is not well adapted to cope with the problems of stability and full employment of resources.

The dual production system, if it is to avoid the difficulties which have been feared for a hybrid economy, probably would have to be developed in terms of a fairly high compartmentalization of different phases of economic life, certain areas being reserved for private enterprise and others for state enterprise. The economic trends in the last fifty years indicate that the most natural field for state enterprise lies in the area of railroads and public utilities. These fields were not able to continue to operate under a competitive or free enterprise system. Close regulation and control of the rate structure was early seen to be necessary in this sphere of economic life. Regulation, however, we know now, has proven to be thoroughly unsatisfactory and has prevented that rapid adaptation to change and adjustment necessary for the growth and expansion which are potentially latent in these areas. Private operation of the railroads under the type of governmental control which has been forced upon them has made the railroads ineffective in meeting rapidly changing conditions. They have not been capable, working within the framework of regulation, of circumventing the tendencies at work making the railroad industry a declining one. In like manner, private management of the electric power and light utilities under the type of regulation which has been imposed has resulted in a rigidity of the rate structure in contrast with the developmental prices designed to tap an ever-widening circle of demand such as has been exhibited in a striking manner by the automobile industry. The railroads and the public utilities, by reason of the fact that regulation under private management is unescapable, thus offer an area in which all of the unfavorable effects of a hybrid system are displayed.

A thorough analysis of the reasons, both in terms of experience of countries which have engaged in state ownership and operation of public utilities, as well as in terms of the inherent characteristics of the industries which tend to make them most suitable for state enterprise, cannot be developed here. Such an examination may or may not result in the conclusion that state enterprise in this area could reasonably be expected to be successful in the United States. Without such extensive study it is not possible to offer any conclusions on this point. What we do wish to do is to examine the particular advantages which a dual system would have (granted, for the sake of argument, that state enterprise is feasible in certain areas) from the standpoint of the special problems of stability and full employment of resources, and particularly from the standpoint of fiscal policy.

A dual economy in which railroads and public utilities operate under state enterprise, leaving trade, manufacturing, and finance under private management, would offer certain advantages from the standpoint of stability and full employment of resources. The first clear gain which would follow from such a dual system is that the total area of economic life which is under the control of the state would be very much greater. This means that a very large sector, perhaps one third, of the total national income would spring from governmental expenditures. The state is freer to regularize these expenditures than is private competitive management. If, for example, the railroads had been under the control of the federal government in the last decade, investment expenditures modernizing railway equipment would have been possible during the depression. A long-range investment plan with respect to passenger and freight equipment, terminal facilities, bridges, and safety devices could have been carried forward in a period of depression by state enterprise in a manner very difficult for private management. The regularization of expenditures in state enterprise, whether operating expenditures, replacement expenditures, or expenditures on new investment, would provide a continuous flow of income. State enterprise would thus serve as a central pivot around which the rest of the economy would revolve. This in itself would serve to limit the cumulative deflationary influences flowing from one sector of the private economy to other sectors. The stability of the state enterprise sector of the economy would act as a resisting wall against deflationary tendencies coming into play in the private sector.

A dual system would thus offer a compromise between stability and flexibility. Private initiative would continue to have free play over a large area of the economy and would continuously reinvigorate unprogressive bureaucratic tendencies that might develop in the state enterprise sector. Such an economy would be far from a completely stable one, but the instability could likely be kept within a narrower range of fluctuation than could be achieved in a purely private economy.

Difficulties inherent in a dual system would certainly be present, particularly with respect to the control of wage rates. These difficulties are already more or less upon us and are probably, in any event, unescapable. It is the kind of problem which we are compelled to face in greater or less degree and which demands the development of self-discipline and intelligent understanding by leaders as well as by the rank and file of labor organizations. That this necessary goal is not altogether hopeless is indicated in the experience of the most advanced industrial countries, which have had the longest experience with the systematic development of collective bargaining. The history of labor relations indicates that the demands of labor by no means run exclusively in terms of wage rates, but also in terms of the satisfaction of understandable and legitimate wants regarding conditions of work and labor relations in the narrower sense of the term, as well as satisfactory housing, public health, social security, and general social and community conditions. A resistance to unreasonable wage demands may well lead to revolutionary and disruptive activities, if other legitimate demands of human beings in the modern social community are not reasonably provided for. But the more labor becomes a participant in, and beneficiary of, a wide range of community and social services, the more likely it is that labor will assume a reasonable relation with respect to the problem of wage rates, which counts so heavily in the price structure. It is possible that the problem of keeping the cost structure, particularly wage rates, within economic limits may be intensified by the expansion of state enterprise. But the sphere of the state in modern communities is, in any event, a large one, and we are, therefore, compelled to face the problem in large measure, whether or not state enterprise is expanded, to the limits here discussed, into a dual economy.

A Dual Consumption Economy

A second type of dual economy represents a considerable socialization of income and consumption. The important distinction between these two types of systems is that the dual production system has, perhaps, certain advantages from the standpoint of stability. This is true because such a system would have, of necessity, a large control over investment expenditures. Since it is clear that fluctuations in investment are the heart and core of business cycle fluctuations, a dual production system makes possible a higher degree of regularization of the rate of investment than is possible in a purely private enterprise economy.

A dual consumption economy, on the other hand, offers, perhaps, greater opportunities to provide full employment of resources than is the case with a dual production economy. This is true for the reason that a mature economy requires, for full employment of its resources, a high ratio of consumption to income. Indeed, a fully matured economy, such as the classicals envisaged, requires that the entire income must be consumed. Such an economy will have a high rate of replacement of its capital equipment, which replacement (if the inventions are capital saving) may continuously assume the form of improved machines and equipment with capacity for larger and larger output. But, under these circumstances, the replacement allowances are adequate for the purpose, and there is no need for the utilization of part of the income for additional or new capital equipment. The whole income is consumed and, indeed, if the whole income were not consumed, unemployment of resources would result, since no new investment outlets in such a fully matured economy would be available.

The earlier economists looked forward, indeed, to the ultimate development of an economic order where consumption would equal, or substantially equal, income. It was a stationary state, in the sense that there was no growth factor taking the form of an increase in population, addition of new territory, or the accumulation of capital. It is, however, improbable that we shall ever reach the stationary state. For even though extensive expansion may be expected to play a much smaller role than in the past, intensive expansion incident to technological progress can be expected to play as important, or even a more important, role than formerly. And in so far as changes in technique are not capital saving, they will call for net capital investment.

The earlier economists looked forward to the stationary state as a highly desirable one—a state in which one was not compelled to sacrifice the present for the future, but could enjoy in the present the full productive power of the society. Such a state would not have to carry the burden incident to continuous expansion and growth. And the earlier economists conceived that the transition could be made from an expanding economy to a mature economy smoothly and without difficulty through the automatic adjustment of the price system. As investment outlets declined, consumption would rise, and no problem would present itself. There would always be full employment of resources.

The first really revolutionary change in economic thought came in consequence of the injection of business cycle theory into the general framework of economic analysis. All the other modifications in economic theory, such as the Austrian approach to the problem of value, were in the nature of clarifications. The acceptance of business cycle theory constituted an admission, however, that the economic system cannot, in fact, make the smooth adjustments which the older economic theory presupposed. Business cycle theory, in essence, amounts to a statement of the frictional impact of institutional arrangements, of customs, habits, and behavior patterns, upon the functioning of the price system. In like manner, the broader development of dynamic economics, of which business cycle theory is a part, makes it clear that the smooth, incremental, continuous adjustment, presupposed by the earlier economists, fails to take account of the frictional impact of human institutions.

The fact is that it requires an extraordinary readjustment of customs, habits, and behavior patterns to change from a rapidly growing society to a mature society, from a society which has practiced a high ratio of saving to income to one in which a low ratio of consumption to income is called for. It is, indeed, true that the maladjustments incident to this transition period will affect the interest rate—the element in the price structure upon which the earlier economists pinned the greatest faith for smooth adjustment.

Put briefly, there are two reasons [1] why this price adjustment, taken by itself alone, is likely to prove wholly inadequate to achieve the high ratio of consumption to income required by an economy with a less rapid extensive development. The first is that established customs, habits, and behavior patterns impose obstacles to the smooth adjustment of the rate of interest, so that the lower rate of interest which the new situation calls for is achieved only with a long institutional lag which may well extend over several generations. In the second place, it is clear that the propensity to save is not purely a function of the rate of interest, but is also a function of the size of the income. Even though the rate of interest were zero, saving by individuals would take place at a high income level. Thus, it is highly improbable that we could ever reach the satisfactory adjustment to the requirements of a fully matured economy, as envisaged by the classicals, through the functioning of the price structure—in par-

[1] See discussion in Chapter XI.

ticular, the rate of interest. To reach the condition required by a fully matured economy, state intervention in the form of an increased socialization of income and consumption would probably be necessary. Without this, a rich community could probably not achieve at a full-employment income level a ratio of consumption to income equal to unity (as required in a stationary state), or in a less mature economy a sufficiently high propensity to consume to permit full employment. A dual consumption economy could, however, from the standpoint of full employment of resources, satisfactorily fulfill the requirements of a purely private economy in the production sphere. While the dual production economy offers certain advantages from the standpoint of stabilizing the income, the dual consumption economy supplies the conditions requisite for the relatively matured society.

The socialization of income in the twentieth century is rapidly developing, notably in the field of low-cost housing, recreational facilities, public health, social security and social welfare, including old-age and unemployment insurance, mothers', widows', and dependents' allowances, and the like. In the event that an actual decline of population is impending, a further powerful push in this direction is probably inevitable. For, once a society is actually confronted with a population decline, it is almost certain to seek desperately to provide incentives for an adequate maintenance of the birth rate. Such incentives may take the form of family allowances, granted proportionally or progressively in terms of the number of children per family. How effective such financial incentives may be it is impossible to gauge, but modest experiments in Germany and Italy would indicate that they would have to be on an extremely generous scale in order to be really effective. Indeed, the possible financial inducements necessary to maintain population could easily reach such an order of magnitude that it would simply spell the doom of private capitalism altogether. Certainly, a rapidly declining population, such as is already indicated in the current net reproduction rates, is by far the most revolutionary event in modern times, and its impact on the industrial order cannot possibly be forecast by a priori reasoning. On the other hand, we do not yet know how effective an educational campaign popularizing moderately large families might be made. It is conceivable that totalitarian states might prove their superiority for survival at just this point. In the event of a truce or inconclusive peace, the capacity to grow, or at least prevent a decline, even more than the impending armament race, might well prove, in the end, to be the decisive issue.

Part Five

DEFENSE AND ITS AFTERMATH

Chapter XXI

MONETARY AND FISCAL CONTROLS IN WARTIME

THE present European War necessarily alters, in greater or less degree, the economic situation in the United States. We have been trying, in one way or another, for ten years to stimulate economic activity and restore our income and employment to a reasonably full level. Monetary policy has been utilized extensively to bring about an advance in commodity prices. And, while the general commodity price index was lifted from a low of 60 to a high of 88 between 1933 and 1937, we are confronted with the fact that the price level in the fourth quarter of 1940 stood at 80 compared with 100 in 1926. A 40 per cent reduction in the gold content of the dollar and billions of excess bank reserves were not able to prevent the apparent long-run downward price trend from 1920 to 1940.

This experience, to be sure, has added powerful empirical support to the theoretical analysis which has more and more come to the fore during the last forty years and which has tended to push into the background purely monetary explanations of price movements. Nevertheless, the general public has become increasingly educated to a crude quantity theory, and even among many professional economists there is the belief that an increase in the monetary gold stock inevitably spells a price inflation. That the inflation has, in fact, not come is explained away on various grounds, but the thesis is still firmly maintained that the inflation bonfire has been laid, that the inflammatory material has been gathered in enormous quantity, and all that is needed is a spark to set it off. Question now arises whether the present European War does not supply that spark; therefore whether we may not be compelled to turn our attention away from expansionist and inflationary measures to repressive controls designed to hold in check an undue expansion of commodity and security prices.

Let it be noted at once that September 3, 1939, found the British economy in a very different situation from that of the American economy. At the beginning of the second World War, the United States had ten million people unemployed with potential capacity for output in nearly all sectors of the economy far in excess of the level then prevailing. In Great Britain, on the other hand, the available productive resources (so we were told by competent British observers) were already utilized to a point approaching full capacity. It is of interest to recall, however, that in August, 1939, there were still one million workers wholly unemployed (not including the two hundred thousand unemployed owing to temporary stoppages), or 7 per cent of Britain's fifteen million workers.

Britain, having already reached nearly full employment of resources, faced immediately, in view of the additional war expenditures, the problem of control of inflation. Swiftly, she set in motion a battery of direct controls. This is merely another way of saying that she was prepared to force her productive resources, even more than had previously been the case, into war purposes without resorting to monetary inflation. Monetary inflation permits a reorientation of an economy to a wartime basis via the functioning of the price system. Direct controls—taxation, rationing, government purchasing, and supply boards—are designed to commandeer the nation's resources for war production without resort to price inflation. It remains to be seen whether we shall at last witness, for the first time in modern history, a major war without a violent commodity price inflation.

There has been much alarmist talk about inflation in the United States during the last seven or eight years. Much of the discussion has been quite irresponsible and without a sound theoretical basis. It has spread fear and uncertainty without justification. But under the impact of the war exports and our huge defense program a new situation confronts us. It would be foolish if, having listened to the cry of "Wolf! Wolf!" so long, we now failed to be on the alert. If the war and the defense stimulus now bring us rapidly to practical full employment of resources, the real problem of price inflation will, at last, be upon us.

While we must always be on the alert to detect new combinations of circumstances and to resist the easy generalization that history repeats itself, it is worth while to remind ourselves of the experiences in the first World War. At the beginning of that war, the United States was in the depression phase of the cycle, though the volume of unemployment was less than now. It required nearly eighteen months of war, with ever-increasing purchases by the belligerents, to start a rise of our price level. Of the nine commodity groups for which index numbers are calculated by the Bureau of Labor Statistics, only the "chemicals and drugs" index rose significantly above the 1913 level prior to December, 1915. It is true that here and there the prices of special commodities, such as wheat, rose much earlier; but in this particular case it is to be noted that, while wheat prices rose sharply in the first ten months of the war, a serious relapse was sustained, and the final price increase began as late as June, 1916.

Contrast of Current with First World War Conditions

The conditions confronting us today are, however, very different, both from the short-run and from the long-run standpoint. From the short-run standpoint, business expectations in the first World War were dampened by the outbreak of hostilities. In the present war, the first impulse was strongly favorable. Twenty-five years ago businessmen were impressed with the disruptive effect of war upon the economy, and the first impact was, therefore, deflationary. Today, by reason of the memory of the prosperity finally engendered by the four years of prodigious expenditures in 1914–18, business expectations reacted favorably upon the outbreak of the war. Hence the rush of orders and the building up of inventories, and here and there the expansion of productive facilities which we witnessed in the autumn of 1939. And, after a lull in early 1940, the vast defense program, undertaken following the spring invasion of the Low Countries and France, powerfully reinforced the upswing of employment and output.

With respect to our export markets, the long-run aspects are very different today. The British Empire is incomparably more self-sufficient today, with respect to agricultural foodstuffs and raw materials, than was true twenty-five years ago. America is neither the actual nor the potential supplier of British food supplies today that she was in the first World War. Prior to 1914, the proportion of total imports entering Britain from empire countries was 20 per cent. In recent years, it has been not far from 45 per cent. The Dominions have, in large measure, supplanted the United States as a supplier of foodstuffs for England. Her own agriculture has been greatly expanded by artificial measures. With respect to industrial products, the Dominions, notably Canada and Australia, have reached a high degree of industrialization. The British economy itself is more productive. Not only had the first World War built up from almost nothing a gigantic chemical and munitions industry (recently greatly expanded by the rearmament program) but a highly protective tariff has, for some years past, built up and strengthened a whole range of industries formerly weak or nonexistent.

We must, moreover, recognize that the almost instantaneous introduction of direct, or, if you prefer, authoritarian, controls affected American exports. If reliance is placed upon a free price system as the mechanism through which war supplies are to be obtained, all suppliers, whether in Britain, in the Dominions, or elsewhere, are placed on the same footing. When, however, the British government takes over, at one stroke, the whole Australian wool supply and concentrates the purchases of foodstuffs and important raw materials in government boards, the situation is very different. Moreover, when civilian purchases are rigorously controlled through rationing and taxation, the British market for general American exports is obviously restricted. These direct controls imply not only a determination to commandeer productive resources for war purposes without resort to inflation, but also a determination to tighten the belt and thereby restrict imports for domestic consumption. Imports no less than domestic output are commandeered for war purposes.

Nevertheless, some sectors of the American economy (including munitions, airplanes, trucks, machine tools, and steel products) have experienced a vast expansion of exports. These, moreover, are just the areas upon which our own armament program is concentrated. The areas enjoying an increase in demand are far more specialized than in the first World War. The direct war demands are not spread throughout the whole economy, including agriculture, in the degree then experienced. But even more significant is the undoubted fact that the *induced* investment springing from the general expansion is likely to be less now than in 1914–18. This is true for the reason that the first World War found us a relatively undeveloped industrial country. The investment in plant and equipment in American manufacturing industries in the decade of the first World War reached an all-time high, creating whole new major industries, such as the chemical industry, and raising all industries within a few years to a far higher plane of productive capacity. Considering the current productive capacity of leading American industries, no such prodigious spurt of induced investment springing from an accelerated war demand or our own defense program can be expected except in the industries closely related to the war effort.

If the war continues, aid to Britain and our own defense program will certainly result in a great expansion of output and employment. It will, nevertheless, be difficult and probably impossible to diffuse this expansion in a balanced manner. This is, of course, more or less true in every war period. But it is especially true today, particularly with respect to agriculture. By reason of the changed demand situation, and also our own surplus producing capacity, American agriculture is not today in a favorable position to profit from the war. The prospect for cotton, tobacco, wheat, corn, and lard is not very favorable. The inflation problem, as far as agricultural and raw material prices are concerned, is quite different today from that confronting us in the first World War. The fact that the continent of Europe has been cut off as a market, together with the fact of great productive capacity in the primary producing countries—the United States, Canada, New Zealand, Australia, and South and Central America—means overhanging surpluses in a long list of important commodities. Witness the depressed international markets and large current stocks of cotton, tobacco, wheat, lard, and corn. The current situation points toward relatively low prices of basic agricultural commodities. The current supplies and prospective output capacity of raw materials and foodstuffs and of a broad range of consumers' goods tend to impose a powerful check on general price inflation.

Speculative Booms and Bottlenecks

But the war has intensified two control problems which do immediately concern us. One is the increasing tendency of American business to respond to short-run speculative stimuli leading to intense but brief inventory booms with subsequent relapses. Within five years, we have twice witnessed such disrupting movements. The second is the problem of bottlenecks. Our economy has been so long depressed in the constructional and capital goods industries that, at certain vital points, equipment and labor shortages threaten the moment halfway levels of higher activity are reached. The present European War and our own expanded armament program strike precisely at points which intensify this problem. With respect to bottlenecks, it is necessary to expand plant capacity and to increase the supply of specialized skills where needed. But, even though this program is carried out with utmost speed, the requirements of the defense are likely to be so great that it will be necessary in some areas to resort to priorities control and to rationing. In certain cases, it may be permissible to allow some distortion of the price and wage structure in order to encourage a redirection of resources toward the bottleneck areas.

Both these situations create specialized price inflation problems. It is not a question of general price inflation, but of violent speculative flurries and an abnormal distortion in the price system caused by the development of bottlenecks.

For neither of these problems is the monetary mechanism of control adequate or even applicable. Thus far, the only valid attack on the speculative inventory problem, short of direct controls, is to counter these herdlike movements by the check which an up-to-date index of inventories may be expected to furnish. It may be suggested that the problem could be attacked by a sort of "commodity exchange-equalization account," of which the "ever-normal granary" is a concrete illustration. Something of this sort may be necessary in a major defense program.

Lopsided and distorted as it must almost inevitably be for the reasons indicated above, it appears probable that a great expansion of output and employment lies immediately before us, based partly on aid to Britain and partly on our own defense effort, reinforced by some induced investment incident to lifting the national income to levels much higher than have prevailed in the past. Consumption, accordingly, will rise to new high ground. Payrolls will be higher and farm incomes in certain areas—notably meats, vegetables, and dairy products—will increase. Once the productive capacity of the consumption goods industries can no longer be increased, owing to the imperious competing demands of the armament industries and the limitation of the labor supply, the stage is set, unless appropriate measures are taken, for a general price inflation. The current *monetary* basis for such an inflation is, as is well known, of almost astronomical proportions.

Direct and Indirect Methods of Control

Broadly speaking, there are two possible methods of control—one the indirect control through familiar monetary restraints which operate in the direction of a sharp increase in interest rates, and the other the direct controls through taxation and rationing.

With respect to the monetary controls, it is, perhaps, not extreme to say that we are badly at sea. The monetary restraints imposed in 1936–37—the raising of the reserve requirements and the gold sterilization program—whatever their actual effects, have left us with even less confidence than we formerly had in our capacity to manipulate the monetary levers in a manner that contributes to stability. Moreover, the reserves have reached such gigantic proportions that the authority of the Federal Reserve Board, unless wider powers are granted by Congress, is quite inadequate to impose the necessary restraint. Treasury powers are perhaps ample, but they involve the holding idle of large balances at a cost which, negligible though it be in terms of our economy, nevertheless makes such action politically difficult.

Unfortunately, the monetary method is quite incapable of differentiating those sectors of the economy that need to be held in check in contrast with those upon which no restraint ought to be imposed and those which need stimulation. Indeed, it operates in a perversely selective manner. It cuts at the roots of prosperity in the general run of staple, consumption goods industries, and leaves largely unaffected the alluring speculative industries unduly inflated by the boom. Moreover, there is the equally serious fact about the monetary method of restraint that it appears incapable of bringing the expansion *gradually* under control. The brakes need to be put on vigorously in order to have any effect at all and, once the mechanism really begins to grip, the economic machine starts headlong into a downward spiral. Accordingly, there is a growing conviction that other methods of restraint have greater prospect for moderating the advance without starting a nose dive in the opposite direction. It may be that experience will prove this to be a false hope; it may be that the trouble is not with the machinery of control but with the violent swings in business expectations incident to a change in the direction of activity or even in the rate of expansion.

It was possible for England in a war emergency to introduce the whole paraphernalia of authoritarian controls—government boards, price fixing, rationing, and other quantitative restrictions. These devices may equally have to be resorted to by this country under the conditions imposed by a huge defense program.

In the event that the control of governmental expenditures and taxation are relied upon to check a threatening commodity price inflation, different situations call for different procedures. If the stimulus to the undue expansion springs from governmental expenditures, then the remedy lies, obviously, in the curtailment of such expenditures. But if the inflation-threatening expenditures in question are for armaments which are deemed essential, it is clear that this remedy can be applied only in so far as nonarmament governmental expenditures can be curtailed. The current high level of extraordinary expenditures, such as for the WPA, affords rather wide scope for checking an undue expansion through the process of progressive curtailment. Yet, here it is necessary to introduce a caution. The public is likely to face an unwelcome surprise in the number of persons that will remain on the rolls eligible for WPA even after employment has risen by five, six, or even seven millions. There were about eight millions unemployed at the beginning of 1941. As industrial employment increases, two to three million farm boys and unneeded farmers will be drawn into urban industry. This movement is already going on. Moreover, there are still about one million persons eligible for WPA but not on the payroll owing to lack of funds. Finally, some unascertained part of the unemployed force is quasi unemployable. Yet, these could usefully be employed on work-relief projects rather than put on the dole. Thus, even at peak employment levels, there is likely to remain an important function for the WPA.

After all expenditures directly relating to unemployment have been eliminated, a point is sooner or later reached when further curtailment involves an encroachment upon normal governmental functions. Resort must then be had to taxation. Such taxes, in the first instance, ought not to impinge on consumption expenditures. Corporate and personal income taxes and estate duties are indicated—direct, not indirect, taxes. By these means, unnecessary private expenditures would be drained off into armament expenditures. Governmental expenditures would take the place of, instead of being added on top of, private expenditures.

Once full employment is reached, a further increase of expenditures, if inflation is to be avoided, becomes absolutely necessary. If the armament expenditures must go on, private expenditures will, of necessity, have to be curtailed. But the mere fact that the armament expenditures are tax-financed will not, of itself, ensure price stability. A surge of investment in the armament industries, stimulated by domestic armament purchases and war exports, together with investment in other industries induced by a full-employment income level, might be financed by bank credit, or by the more active utilization of existing balances. In these circumstances, it would be necessary to hold in check, or even to reduce, the volume of demand deposits. Without resorting to the familiar monetary controls, this could be accomplished by a federal tax surplus used to retire the bonds held by the commercial banking system. Note should be made, however, of the important fact that, in so far as the tax surplus was used to retire debt held by individuals and institutions other than commercial banks, the funds would flow back into the capital market and thence again into investment and consumption expenditures. And even though the tax surplus were applied to the retirement of obligations held by the commercial banks, a powerful war-orders boom might, nevertheless, in the absence of monetary checks, continue to expand on the basis of new bank loans and investments more than offsetting the restrictive action of the Treasury. Unless the monetary control mechanism were brought into play, we should have to resort, in these circumstances, to consumption taxes. These would have the effect of diverting at the full-employment level the resources of the community from consumption to the war export and armament trades, which it is deemed necessary to support even at the expense of reduced consumption. A forced curtailment of consumption would, moreover, check investment in the general run of nonarmament industries and prevent an undue general expansion.

To minimize the subsequent relapse to a peacetime basis, it might be desirable not merely to hold the total level of consumption expenditures in check, but to apply the restraint in a selective manner. Thus, it might well be sound public policy to starve the durable consumers' goods industries in order to build up a large accumulation of backlog demand with which to cushion the depression once armament expenditures were curtailed. Postponement of expenditure in the durable consumers' goods area can, for a limited period, be carried out without serious infringement upon the standard of living. But the nondurable consumers' goods sector in the economy ought to be sustained during the boom at as high a level as the limitation of productive resources and the magnitude of the armaments program permit.

Chapter XXII

DEFENSE FINANCING

WHEN the vastly expanded defense program was undertaken in 1940, we were still a long way from full employment. It was, accordingly, possible to expand output and employment to take care of the needs of defense and even to increase civilian production. The national income for 1940 was about $74 billions, some $4 billions above the 1937 level. The Federal Reserve index of production averaged around 122, compared with 113 in 1937 and 110 in 1929. Employment averaged about 47 millions, slightly above the 1937 level, and about one million below that of 1929. The labor force for 1940 was estimated at about 56 millions. Thus, there were about nine million unemployed —about eight millions by the end of the year. While some part of this number is more or less unemployable, on the other side it should be remembered that there are probably two to three million surplus workers, counted as employed in agriculture, who are ready to seek jobs in urban industries whenever opportunity affords. Moreover, the first World War experience indicated that there is always a vast potential labor supply which can readily be drawn into the labor market—when labor scarcity becomes intense. Thus, in 1918, 44 millions were employed, including those drawn into the armed forces, while the normal labor force was only 41 millions. Three million potential workers, not normally in the labor market, had been drawn into employment. This indicates that the potential increase in labor resources is greater than indicated by the formal and somewhat artificial figures with respect to the so-called normal labor supply.

With respect to plant and equipment, the possibilities for expansion, as Terborgh showed in the July issue of the *Federal Reserve Bulletin,* is enormous in the noncontinuous process industries. Two or even three shifts could, if necessary, be introduced. This would provide greatly expanded output without any large capital outlays. To some extent, a lengthening of the work week in the more essential industries, on the basis of overtime, would be helpful. (The system of overtime may, indeed, be a quite scientific method of automatically adjusting wage rates in boom industries). The situation is most critical in steel, a continuous process industry. Here, at the end of 1940, we were already operating at close to 100 per cent capacity. Exports to Britain, the defense requirements, railroad equipment purchases, together with the increased demand for consumers' durables, notably automobiles—all these converge upon the steel industry. Steel thus threatens to become our most serious bottleneck. Steel ingot capacity is about 12 per cent above 1929. A projected trend based on iron and steel production from 1899 to 1929 indicates a peacetime consumption of these products, at full employment, of about 30 per cent in excess of the 1929 output. Wartime consumption of steel is, however, a quite different matter.

The Defense Program

How rapidly we shall encounter bottlenecks in certain types of equipment and labor will depend, in part, upon the magnitude and speed of the defense program and the stimulus it gives to income and employment. The President's Budget Message estimated total military expenditures, during the fiscal year 1941, at $6.5 billions. In view of the greatly enlarged army program (which offers easier opportunity for quick expenditures), it is possible that this figure may be reached. In July, 1940, the defense expenditures were only about $150 millions. From this point on, they were stepped up by over $50 millions per month, reaching $475 millions by December, 1940. It is estimated that expenditures will average nearly $800 millions per month during the last half of the current fiscal year, or at the rate of well over a billion dollars per month by July, 1941. Should this rate be reached, it would appear possible to achieve a total defense expenditure far in excess of the $10.8 billions estimated for fiscal 1942. But it must be remembered that the new budget does not include aid to Britain, which, as fixed in the Lend-Lease Bill, reaches $7 billions.

The international situation might, of course, easily become so menacing that we should be compelled to push on as rapidly as possible to a full defense effort. This, however, would involve a drastic increase in the defense program as now anticipated. The present program contemplates:

(1) A navy of 3,000,000 tons (approximately three times the size of our present effective navy).

(2) Full equipment for an army of 1,400,000 men, and, in addition, equipment of critical items (not readily obtainable on short notice through commercial channels) for an additional 800,000 men. Housing facilities for 800,000 draftees and for 200,000 National Guardsmen.

(3) An air fleet of 35,000 planes, including fighting, bombing and training planes, with production facilities for an output of 50,000 planes per year.

To raise the navy, army and air force to this level would entail an "expansion" cost of nearly $20 billions. Pay and subsistence of draftees during training, and the cost of training 40,000 air force personnel annually, are not included in this figure. In a certain sense, these items, at least in the earlier years, really constitute a part of expansion and, if they were so included, the total cost of lifting the armed force to the contemplated strength would approach $25 billions.

The army expansion program is expected to reach a peak in fiscal 1942 and to be practically completed in 1943. The navy expansion program, it is thought, will reach a peak in 1943 and be completed by 1945. In the meantime, however, the operating expenses, including maintenance and training of personnel, and the upkeep and replacement of the military plant and equipment would rapidly rise. Thus, total expenditures would amount to nearly $40 billions in the next five years. The program now laid out, as nearly as it can be pieced together with respect to timing and magnitude (including expansion and maintenance), is given in the table below:

TABLE XXX

Defense Program

Fiscal Year[1]	*Grand Total (billions) Expansion and Operating Expenses*
1941	$ 6.5
1942	10.5
1943	9.0
1944	8.0
1945	6.0
Total	$40.0

If the present program were carried out without revision upward, a tapering off in defense expenditures would thus begin in fiscal 1943. It is rather difficult to believe that an upward revision will not occur. In the event, however, of a negotiated peace—say, this year—in which England emerged as the undisputed sea power, we should probably feel relatively safe, even though Germany were left in command of the European continent. The present defense program might, therefore, appear adequate while, on the other side, the situation would not be sufficiently safe to warrant its abandonment or curtailment. Under these circumstances, the model given in the table above might be substantially realized.

Two other eventualities are, however, perhaps more prob-

[1] The fiscal year 1941 runs from July 1, 1940, to June 30, 1941, etc.

able. On the one side, Germany may conquer England. In this event, it would appear certain that we shall step up our defense expenditures with utmost speed, perhaps reaching $15 to $20 billions in 1942, and $25 to $30 billions in 1943. This would put us definitely on a war basis as far as expenditures are concerned. On the other side, England may withstand the attack and continue the war indefinitely. This outcome presents two alternatives for us. Either we shall speedily enter the war, or we shall continue to give maximum support to England short of war, meanwhile rapidly increasing our own military strength. In the former case, our expenditures might rapidly rise to $30 or $40 billions. In the latter case, we might spend $10 to $15 billions in fiscal 1942 and $18 to $20 billions in fiscal 1943.

Rising Income and Higher Tax Yields

It is scarcely worth while to attempt an estimate of the effect of the defense program on national income for 1943. But some tentative figures may be suggested for the calendar years 1941 and 1942. The defense expenditures will enlarge the total income stream directly by a certain amount. Moreover, there will be certain repercussions upon private investment in plant and equipment induced by the general expansion. A considerable part of the increase in plant and equipment required for the production of military equipment will, however, be financed directly by the government. Nevertheless, the general expansion of income will doubtless induce a considerable amount of private investment in plant and equipment which will be financed quite independently of the defense outlays. In 1940, with a national income of $74 billions, capital outlay on plant and equipment amounted to about $7.5 billions. At a national income of $90 billions, it is expected that expenditures on plant and equipment might rise to $11.0 billions; and at $100 billion income level to $13.5. As indicated above, however, a considerable amount of these outlays relating to the defense effort will be financed directly or indirectly by the government. In so far as this is the case, one would be guilty of double counting if one added to the stimulating effect of the defense outlays the plant and equipment expenditures directly or indirectly financed out of defense outlays.

Everything considered, it is not unreasonable to suppose the national income might rise from $74 billions in 1940 to $80 or $85 billions in 1941 and $90 or $95 billions in 1942, assuming no major changes in the defense program and only a moderate increase in the price level.

In 1940 output and employment were running at, roughly, 80 per cent of potential capacity. It should, therefore, be possible to raise the national income at attainable full employment to about $90 billions at current prices or $100 billions at, say, 10 per cent higher prices. At the end of 1940 the general wholesale index number stood around 80 (1926 price being 100).

Total federal expenditures in fiscal 1941 are estimated at around $13.2 billions with probable tax receipts at $7 billions. Expenditures for the fiscal year 1942 are estimated at $17.5 billions, with probable tax receipts at $8.3 billions. Thus, the probable deficits are $6.2 billions for 1941 and $9.2 billions for 1942. It is expected that approximately $2.0 billions of the 1941 deficit would be financed by the sale of new issues to government trust funds and baby bonds purchasers. Thus, it would be necessary to sell in the open market (to banks, insurance companies, corporations, and individuals) about $4.2 billions in fiscal 1941 and, perhaps, $7.0 billions in fiscal 1942. In the event that tax rates are increased, less would need to be raised from borrowing.

It is important to emphasize the fact that even the existing tax structure will yield very large revenues—much larger than the public is generally aware of—once the national income has risen to the attainable full employment level of $90 to $100 billions. During the interval in which the national income is rising, there is a lag in the increase in tax receipts. This follows from the fact that corporate and individual income taxes are normally paid in four quarterly installments, overlapping the two fiscal years following the calendar year upon whose income the taxes are assessed. Thus, for example, the taxes assessed on the income of 1940 are paid in March and June of fiscal 1941, and September and December of fiscal 1942. Because of this lag in tax collections, tax receipts are relatively low, compared with what may finally be expected, while the national income is still rising. The deficit will, therefore, of necessity be large during this interval. The Treasury estimates that a national income of $100 billions would yield on the existing tax structure, after a lag of about one year, a revenue of $13.4 billions. Some estimates run as high as $15 billions.

Methods of Financing

For some years prior to 1941 all available evidence indicates that the savings stream of the nation—flowing from corporations (depreciation reserves and retained earnings); from financial institutions, such as life insurance companies and savings banks; and directly from individuals—has been adequate to finance the demand for funds, including government requirements for deficit financing. In terms of broad, global figures this is evident from the fact that the increase in bank credit from 1937 to 1940 was offset by the continued accumulation of idle funds. Monetary expansion was being offset by hoarding. Thus, the increase in demand deposits from $25.8 billions in 1937 to $31.7 billions in 1940, instead of reflecting an increase in the national income, only produced a decline in the income velocity of circulation from 2.8 to 2.2.

If the national income should rise to, say, $100 billions, no major expansion of bank credit would be necessary to finance the combined demands of private industry and the federal deficit. As the national income rises, the savings of corporations and individuals will substantially increase. And there is, moreover, the large backlog of accumulated idle funds, totaling approximately $10 billions, to fall back upon.

From the standpoint of the MV type of analysis, no substantial increase in demand deposits is necessary to circulate a national income even of $100 billions. At the current volume of demand deposits, the income velocity would be 3.1 compared with 3.5 in 1923–29. Using both demand deposits and currency combined (to represent M), the income velocity would be 2.6 compared with 3.0 in 1923–29.

These considerations raise the question of the appropriate method of financing the deficit incurred by the defense expenditures.[2] What part, if any, should be financed from borrowing from the commercial banks? What part should be financed from borrowing from the public and what part from taxes? Should the proportion financed from each of these three sources vary at different levels of business activity?

In general, it may be argued that, in the earlier stages of recovery from depression, considerable reliance should be placed on borrowing from banks. In the deflationary phase the volume of demand deposits, as well as their turnover rate, typically declines sharply. An increase in the level of income can, in these circumstances, be facilitated by monetary expansion (both M and V) to a level corresponding to the requirements of a larger volume of transactions. Thus, some expansion (varying with the magnitude of the prior contraction) can be justified. If considerable reliance is placed upon governmental expenditures as a means of securing recovery, it is appropriate to borrow from the banks, since this procedure increases or maintains a high degree of liquidity for private enterprise and facilitates recovery by keeping interest rates low.

As the national income rises, it is appropriate to turn increasingly (a) to borrowing from the nation's savings stream

[2] See also John H. Williams, "Economic and Monetary Aspects of the Defense Program," *Federal Reserve Bulletin,* February, 1941; and "Federal Budget: Deficit Spending," *American Economic Review,* Papers and Proceedings, February, 1941.

and (b) to taxation. As the national income rises, savings will tend to increase, thereby making available funds from which the government can borrow and tax. As the recovery approaches full employment, increasing reliance on taxes rather than on borrowing is indicated, since taxation is, on balance, more restrictive than borrowing. To be sure, it is important that the banks should be restrained not only from taking new issues, but also from indirectly mopping up the new issues through the purchase of bonds from the public. Admittedly, this is not easy to accomplish, but a more or less effective approach doubtless could be implemented, and particularly with reference to the larger institutions. Borrowing from the commercial banks is most expansionist in effect, borrowing from other sources and taxation of the savings stream (progressive taxes) occupies an intermediate position, while consumption taxes are definitely restrictive. Thus, the normal sequence in financing governmental outlays in different phases of recovery is: first, borrowing from banks; second, borrowing from the savings stream; third, progressive taxes; and fourth, consumption taxes.

This sequence more or less automatically takes place without conscious planning or design. At higher levels of business activity, commercial banks are able to find, in some measure, other outlets for their funds. Moreover, at higher income levels the volume of savings increases and it is possible to sell more bonds to savings institutions, government trust funds, and the public. Finally, the progressive sector of the tax structure yields much larger revenues when the national income has risen.

These tendencies partly explain the changing proportion of the federal expenditures financed from (1) borrowing from commercial banks, (2) borrowing from other sources, and (3) taxes, in the period 1933–36 compared with the period 1937–40.[3] The first period was one of rapid increase in the national income from $40 billions to $65 billions. The second was a period of relative stability at around a $70 billion in-

[3] Fiscal years, inclusive.

come level. In the first period, 50 per cent of the federal expenditures was raised from borrowing, of which over one half was from commercial banks and the Federal Reserve Banks, while less than half came from savings institutions, trust funds, and the public. In the second period, only 30 per cent was raised from borrowing, all of which came from savings and none of it from the commercial banks. The decline of commercial bank holdings of governments in the recession of 1937 largely accounts for this fact, while the growth of government trust funds partly accounts for the increasing role of savings in government financing operations. Moreover, larger receipts from the progressive taxes at higher national incomes enabled the government to raise nearly 70 per cent of its requirements from taxation in 1937–40. It is not suggested that the relative proportions raised (a) from taxes, (b) from banks, and (c) from borrowing from the savings stream were the correct ones. It is only suggested that the change taking place from the first period of rapid recovery to the later period of relative stability at moderately high income levels was in the right direction.

Starting from the income level of $74 billions in 1940, how far should the defense expenditures be financed by borrowings from the commercial banks? We have already noted above that there may be sufficient savings (including funds now held idle) to finance both the federal deficit and the private demand for capital through fiscal 1942. It does not appear necessary, as far as the global figures are concerned, to resort to any considerable expansion of bank credit. But this may not necessarily mean very much. The mere fact that corporations and financial institutions have funds available does not ensure that they will purchase government bonds in so far as private investment outlets are not adequate to absorb their idle balances. Thus, the mere availability of funds does not ensure that banks will not have to be relied on to finance a part of the deficit. Yet, bank credit expansion on a large scale, plus the utilization of currently accumulated idle balances, when the national income has already reached

$74 billions, and huge federal outlays have been appropriated or authorized to be expended as rapidly as feasible, might invite dangerous price inflation as the economy approached full employment. And, if the banks finance the deficit, while the corporations use idle balances for working capital and for the expansion of plant and equipment in nonmilitary and nonessential lines, the combined effect might yield an undue monetary expansion.

Borrowing from the national savings stream tends to restrain inflationary developments. But there is, nevertheless, no assurance that price inflation may not, in fact, come—even though the federal deficit is not financed by borrowing from the commercial banks. In the first place, individuals may be induced to subscribe to defense bonds in excess of their savings, covering the difference by borrowing from the banks. During the first World War banks loaned about $3 billions on government securities. If large reliance must be placed on bank credit expansion to finance a war deficit, this method does have certain advantages over direct borrowing from banks, but the effect on prices is the same. In the second place, a substantial rise in business activity might result in a considerable demand for bank loans and might induce banks to enlarge their holdings of private bonds and mortgages. Indeed, it was this development which accounts mainly for the enormous credit and price inflation of the first World War.

Conditions are now in many respects different. There are currently no good reasons for urging the public to buy bonds beyond their capacity to save out of income. Private business concerns have large internal sources of funds available for expansion, and are relatively little in need of bank funds. Moreover, since much of the plant and equipment required for the defense program will be financed by the government directly or indirectly, it is evident that this minimizes the requirements of private enterprise.

Paradoxical as it may seem, until an approach to full employment is reached expansion will help to prevent inflation. This is true because, until full employment is reached, the main danger of inflation lies in the development of bottlenecks. Unless these bottlenecks are broken, we shall be compelled to choke off further expansion in order to prevent the scarcities caused by the bottleneck from resulting in inflationary price and wage increases in the areas affected. From these areas there is danger that the inflationary development may spread to the whole economy. The only sound way to prevent bottleneck inflation is to break the bottlenecks. There is considerable warrant for the statement that the fear of inflation is exaggerated, and there is danger that the important weapon of specific price increases where these may help to eliminate bottlenecks may not be sufficiently used. In so far as the bottlenecks *cannot* be forestalled by the provision of adequate plant and equipment capacity and by an adequate supply of skilled mechanics, priorities and rationing may be necessary. Inflation is even more serious and insidious than unemployment. It will not do to let it get started in any area.

If we succeed in avoiding, or at any rate holding to a minimum, bottleneck inflation and speculative price developments in the security and commodity markets, we shall finally encounter, as we approach full employment, the problem of general inflation. For the control of general inflation, taxation bearing on consumption is technically a potent weapon, but practically and politically the matter is very difficult. Theoretically, the most desirable method is probably a tax on payrolls deducted from wages. According to the well-known Keynes plan, such deductions should, however, be credited to the wage earners in the form of blocked postal savings accounts. These accounts would be unblocked by proclamation of a designated monetary authority after the war emergency is over, and, specifically, when a slump was beginning to develop. Various statistical series might be invoked to guide the monetary authority, for example, the index of industrial production, income paid out, wholesale prices, employment, etc.[4]

[4] If corporations accumulated during the prosperous war years a fund to be made available for dismissal wages, such a scheme would accomplish much the same purpose as the Keynes plan, and would act as a cushion against a post-defense slump.

The difficulty with the Keynes plan is that there is probably little hope that it would be acceptable to wage earners. Wage earners can be appealed to on a voluntary basis to purchase government bonds and even to pay onerous taxes, but they are not likely to accept a compulsory deferment of wage payments. It will not be easy to convince them that such compulsory deferment is really in lieu of taxes. They will want their wages as earned. There is, moreover, the difficulty with payroll taxes (whether actual or in the form of deferred payment) that such taxes in a period of buoyant expansion and labor scarcity may lead to demands for wage increases sufficient to cover the tax. Should this occur, no curtailment of consumption would result from the imposition of the tax.

It is possible, however, to apply the fundamental principles of the Keynes plan on a voluntary basis. A modified baby bond, with 3 per cent interest payable annually, and with subscription privilege limited to five hundred dollars per year so as to limit the sale to the lower income groups, might be made very attractive and, if properly advertised and pushed with a patriotic appeal, could reach wide masses of the population.

The defect in a voluntary plan, of course, is that its magnitude will necessarily be small compared with what might be achieved by a compulsory plan. It may, therefore, become necessary, once an approach to full employment is reached, to resort to other forms of consumption taxation. A tax levied on "value added" has been suggested. Such a tax is said to be preferable to a sales tax by reason of greater simplicity of administration. It has, however, the disadvantage that, in practice, it will probably tend to encourage price increases at every stage in the productive process. To some extent, sales taxes also give the retailer an opportunity to raise the price by more than the amount of the tax. But it is probable that the impact of a sales tax on price increases is relatively less than in the case of a "value added" tax. A flexible normal income tax, with somewhat lower exemptions than at present and collected at the source, has been suggested. At the lower income ranges such a "tax" deduction might be blocked as a compulsory savings account and "unfrozen" by administrative order to help cushion a postdefense slump.

With respect to the indirect monetary controls, it would be a mistake to leave them out of account, or to regard them as obsolete. While direct methods of control, supplemented by fiscal devices, should be used in the first instance, the time may nevertheless come when it will be necessary to apply monetary checks to expansion. It is, therefore, desirable that the Federal Reserve Board be granted the powers necessary to reduce the excess reserves to manageable proportions so as to make open-market operations effective as a check upon bank credit expansion.

In January of this year the Federal Reserve Board asked Congress for legislation enabling the Board to cope more adequately with the problem of credit control. Congress was asked to provide means for absorbing a large part of the existing excess reserves and for the removal or control of various sources of potential increases in reserves, including the power to issue greenbacks and the monetization of foreign silver and of gold imports. It was urged that the financing of the federal budget, including the defense program, be accomplished by drawing upon the existing large volume of deposits rather than by creating additional deposits through bank purchases of government securities. It was urged that the special limitations of defense financing, restricted to short-term issues as passed in the Revenue Act of 1940, be removed and that the Treasury be authorized to issue securities which would be especially suitable for investors other than commercial banks.

In taking account of inflation potentialities, the situation differs from that of the first World War in two significant respects. In the first place, there are currently available vast overhanging surpluses of agricultural products; there is, moreover, very large productive capacity not only of agricultural products and foodstuffs, but also of consumers' products generally. In the second place, at the very outset of the defense program we start off with a strong tax structure capable of yielding enormous revenues as we approach income levels attainable at reasonably full employment. Thus, we approach the problem of preventing wartime inflation from a stronger vantage ground than in the first World War. But this fact should not cause us to relax our efforts to the utmost. Our economic structure cannot endure either deflation or inflation.

Chapter XXIII

THE POSTDEFENSE SLUMP

TWO considerations must be taken account of in appraising the problem of a postdefense slump. The first is the withdrawal of heavy consumption taxes imposed during the major defense effort as a means to check inflation. The relief from several billion dollars of consumption taxes would act as a powerful counterweight to the reduction of military expenditures. Just as resources were diverted from supplying private demand to satisfying the requirements of a defense program through heavy consumption taxes, so also they may be diverted back again to private use by the release of consumer purchasing power incident to the cancellation of emergency consumption taxes.

The second major factor to take account of is the probable revolutionary change which the changed international situation will likely make in our federal budget, even after the major defense program is completed. It is estimated that even the currently contemplated military strength, once completed, will require an annual outlay of about $6 billions in upkeep, maintenance, and replacement. And it is more than probable that we shall sharply revise our defense program upward, perhaps doubling currently planned expansion. It does not appear probable now, at any rate, that anything can happen in the near future which will turn Europe and Asia into stable, peaceful continents during the next two or three decades. Even though we suppose that, somehow, Hitlerism completely collapses in Germany, the problems of Europe would not thereby suddenly be solved. A new Europe will have to be created. It will have to be policed by somebody until stable political conditions can be restored. Moreover, the increasingly menacing position of Japan in the Pacific, in addition to the European turmoil, points toward a large permanent defense program.

Postdefense Budget

Nonmilitary federal expenditures have, in recent years, amounted to about $7 billions. A considerable part of these, such as WPA, were, in effect, emergency relief expenditures. It is to be hoped that in the postdefense period we shall be able to manage our affairs so that it will not be necessary to provide work relief, except for a limited number of quasi unemployables. Instead, we need to spend more on genuine public improvement projects. We must rebuild America for peace no less than for defense. Express highways, modernized urban transportation systems, reforestation, soil erosion control, flood control, hospitals, slum clearance, together with the accumulated backlog of ordinary public works held in abeyance during the defense effort, will call for large expenditures. An adequate program of public improvements, federal, state, and local, should be carefully planned and held in reserve to meet the eventuality of a postdefense slump. Low-cost housing by private enterprise and private capital if possible, but, if not, then supplemented by government subsidy, is urgent. Moreover, a number of changes are inevitably impending in our social service and public welfare programs. Old-age assistance should be greatly expanded. This could be done in various ways. Under the 50–50 federal matching system, the benefits now range from $6.00 per month in the poorer states to $38 per month. In order to remedy this situation, it will be necessary for the federal government to make larger grants to the fiscally incompetent states. The federal government might make an outright minimum grant of $15 per old person assisted in all states, with the requirement that each state contribute at least $3.00 in addition. This would establish a minimum benefit of $18 per month in the poorer states. In addition, the federal government should match each additional dollar contributed by the states until a maximum benefit of $40 per month was reached. In addition, the means test should be liberalized so as to admit any aged person to benefits whose income was judged inadequate.

A good case could be made to support the thesis that old-age assistance ought to be taken over entirely, both with respect to administration and cost, by the federal government. This could help to relieve the states' fiscal situation and tend to check further increases in state consumption taxes.

Other methods designed to liberalize benefit payments to aged persons are as follows: (1) All persons over the age of seventy might be given outright a federal pension of $30 (man and wife together, $45) without having to meet a means test. This proposal would reserve the old-age insurance plan and old-age assistance now in operation to those aged sixty-five to seventy inclusive. About 3,250,000 persons are included in each group. This proposal follows, in general, the British system. (2) Every person over the age of sixty-five might be paid a pension of $15 without a means test, this pension to be supplemented by the current provision for old-age insurance benefits, and (for those not covered by insurance) by old-age assistance on the simplified income means test. The latter proposal is complicated by the fact that, under it, most persons would receive benefits from two sources.

There is much to be said for the dual system—insurance benefits for those aged sixty-five to seventy inclusive, and noncontributory pensions beyond seventy. In the first place, this plan would preserve intact the old-age insurance system already firmly established and well received by the general public, but would limit its application to those aged sixty-five to seventy. The noncontributory plan would cover all aged persons over the age of seventy, thereby restricting the means test (at best difficult to administer and undesirable socially) to those aged sixty-five to seventy not covered by the old-age insurance. Together with a federally administered old-age assistance plan for uncovered persons under seventy, a federal pension plan for those over seventy would greatly relieve the burden of the states, and facilitate reduction in state consumption taxes, or, at any rate, enable the states to participate on a federal grant-in-aid basis in other expanded social welfare programs without raising consumption taxes beyond the present high level.

Public health and federal aid to education are equally pressing. The recent interdepartment committee on medical care recommended a program consisting of three parts: (1) expansion of general public health services, including the strengthening of public health facilities, increased efforts to eradicate tuberculosis, venereal diseases, and malaria, to decrease the mortality rate from pneumonia and cancer, to provide mental hygiene and industrial hygiene services, to provide more adequate maternal and infant care, medical care for children, and treatment for crippled children; (2) to provide greatly enlarged public hospital facilities, including general and special hospitals, and sanitariums for tubercular and mental cases; (3) to provide medical care in the home for the medically needy—those on relief or with incomes below $1,000 (about one third of the population). Such a program would involve expenditures ranging from about $250 millions in the first year to about $900 millions in the tenth year.

Related to an enlarged public health program is the Food Stamp plan. More than twenty millions in the lower income groups are limited in their food consumption to 5 cents per meal per person. The Food Stamp plan has revealed that the consumption of foodstuff can be very greatly increased in the lower income levels, thereby relieving in some measure the agricultural surpluses. In addition to food, cotton has been experimented with on a small scale. It is estimated that a subsidy of $600 millions through a Cotton Stamp plan would increase the domestic consumption of cotton by two million bales.

A large number of bills are currently before Congress, calling for federal aid to education in order to relieve the pressure on the state budgets and to provide more adequate services (for example, adult education).

Assuming an expansion of social security and welfare programs along the lines indicated, with the federal government carrying a larger part of the cost, we may envisage a postdefense federal budget roughly of the proportions indicated in the table below. According as less is spent on defense, more funds would be available for public works, internal improvements, and social welfare. It is assumed that the federal works program, together with federal grants to local bodies for public works, would increase along lines discussed above. It is assumed that the agricultural program, while continued at about the former level, would be heavily shifted toward the Food Stamp and Cotton Stamp plan type of outlays. In this manner the agricultural program would aid relatively more than in the past to expand the domestic market for agricultural products.

TABLE XXXI

Postdefense Federal Budget

(in billions)

1. Ordinary operative functions of government:	
Legislative, judicial, and civil establishments, and interest on the public debt	$2.5 to 3.0
2. Defense:	
Maintenance of operation of enlarged military force	5.0 to 6.0
3. Welfare functions of government: [1]	
Public improvements, social security, public welfare, agricultural program	6.0 to 7.0
Total, range centering around $14 to $15 billions	

[1] The amount that would need to be spent on public improvements in order to achieve substantially full employment would vary with the rate of private investment. While the fluctuation in private investment would be very much damped down if the government undertakes a strong compensatory program, it would nevertheless not entirely disappear. Progress in capital formation would still proceed by spurts, followed by temporary saturation.

To those schooled in the traditions of an era that is forever behind us a federal budget of $14 to $15 billions will appear to be nothing short of disastrous. Yet, if the analysis of this book is correct, it will require a budget of some such magnitude to keep our economy functioning at attainable full employment. At a $100 billion income level, the tax structure enacted in 1940 could be expected to yield $13 to $14 billions of revenue. The 1940 tax rate level (with modification of the tax structure to make it more workable) would not constitute an intolerable tax burden at a reasonably full national income. Moreover, some measure of controlled borrowing can be justified.

We need to change our ideas about the true meaning of economy. It is pure waste to economize by policies which condemn labor and capital to idleness. The first job of public policy is to make the system function so as to provide opportunities for employment. But when this is done, the efficient way to "economize" our productive resources is to see that they are employed efficiently and on the projects socially most useful. Fortunately, with the vast bulk of the productive processes operating under private enterprise and under the guidance of the price system, the part left for the more or less arbitrary decisions of public authorities is relatively small.

How such a budget should be financed—what proportion from borrowing and what from taxes—depends in the final analysis, as we have seen, upon one's judgment with respect to the socially desirable distribution of wealth and income. The tax revenues, whatever the magnitude, should in any case be drawn as far as possible from sources which impinge lightly on consumption. For only if the expenditures are so financed will they have an income-generating effect. It is certainly quite possible to finance such a budget wholly from taxation, if that is deemed desirable. We have noted above, however, that loan expenditures of, say, $2 or $3 billions per annum offer a suitable outlet for the secure investment of the annual accrual of savings in trust funds and thrift institutions. It should be noted also that the tax method of financing, even though the rates are progressive, is at best more restrictive in effect than loan financing—in other words, has a smaller income-generating effect—and this is all the more true of the last increments of taxes collected. These two facts favor the more conservative policy of financing a part from borrowing.

Fiscal Reorganization

From the standpoint of long-range planning relating to full utilization of resources and antidepression policy, two defects in our institutional arrangements present serious obstacles to a full realization of the desired objective. One has to do with the current federal-state fiscal setup, and the other with the lack of a fiscal authority with power to administer a flexible fiscal program with respect to expenditures and taxation.

Any proposal to introduce an effective national fiscal program adequate to cope with modern problems encounters at once the anomalies and conflicts inherent in the overlapping functions and taxing powers of the federal, state, and local governments. Moreover, the expanding functions of government, particularly in the field of social welfare, place upon the states financial burdens beyond their capacity without resort to heavy consumption taxes. This form of taxation runs precisely counter to the main objective of fiscal policy—that of securing reasonably full employment. Thus, in recent years, many states have been compelled to levy sales taxes in order to provide old-age assistance and other expanding social services. Indeed, the leadership of the federal government, through the traditional 50–50 matching system, has compelled the states, by reason of their fiscal incapacity to levy adequate progressive taxes, to resort increasingly to consumption taxation. Thus, by 1938 the state and local bodies were collecting $3,250 millions in sales, liquor and tobacco, gasoline, and payroll taxes.

This situation will sooner or later necessitate a thorough

reorganization and reallocation of functions and taxing powers. Such a reorganization has been recommended in Canada in a recent report by the Royal Commission on Dominion-Provincial Fiscal Relations. It may be that the time is not ripe for a complete overhauling of the federal-state fiscal relations in the United States. We are not confronted with anything like so acute a crisis as that confronting Canada. The federal government has been able to step into the breach through the assumption of a major part of the burden of urban and agricultural relief and grants-in-aid to local public works projects. The public debt of states and municipalities has accordingly, for the country as a whole, ceased to rise. The credit position of the local governments has thereby been strengthened materially. But while we are not confronted with an immediate crisis, the cumulative effect of growing social services, financed largely by consumption taxes, is to place an increasing drag upon economic expansion and full employment of our resources.

Short of a drastic reorganization, the problem can be eased by a modification of the federal grant-in-aid program and by the assumption by the federal government of certain responsibilities now carried wholly or in part by the states. Thus, the old-age assistance program (perhaps converted into an outright pension for those over seventy) ought probably to be taken over entirely by the federal government. Other social welfare programs, which by reason of administrative problems or otherwise (education, for example) should be left under state control with federal supervision, could be financed by a variable federal grant adjusted according to the fiscal capacity of the various states. Without far-reaching modifications in this general area, we shall not be able to undertake an effective fiscal program with respect to full employment of our productive resources.

Nor can fiscal policy ever become a really potent device for economic stability and expansion without placing its operation on an administrative basis. We have long been accustomed to the administrative control of monetary and banking policy. *Ad hoc* legislation by Congress with respect to open-market operations and rediscount rates would patently be impossible. Precisely the same is true of fiscal policy, if it is to be used effectively as an instrument to control employment. The only reason legislative enactment, from time to time, is regarded as adequate in this field is that governmental expenditures and tax rates are still expected to fulfill only their traditional functions. Fiscal policy has not yet won a place as an instrument of economic control continuously to be applied as a means to secure employment stabilization and expansion. When such a place shall have been won, comparable with that achieved by monetary policy, it will be recognized that the intermittent use, by specific and *ad hoc* legislative enactment, of public expenditures and taxation after each special emergency has arisen is quite inadequate for the purpose in hand. It will become necessary to subject these powerful instruments to continuous administrative management in order to render the control sufficiently flexible to cope with the ever-changing economic situation and to prevent disastrous cumulative movements from getting under way.

These considerations are peculiarly pertinent to the problems raised by the defense program. Gearing fiscal policy to the rapid changes in economic conditions which the defense program will call forth requires the development of new procedures. For the time being, one type of tax policy is appropriate. But we may very soon encounter a situation in which a quite different tax policy is called for. Such conditions cannot be managed by piecemeal legislative enactment.

Congress should set up a long-run fiscal program adequate to cope with the defense and postdefense problems. Such a program calls for a comprehensive, long-range plan. For one thing, Congress should establish a Monetary and Fiscal Authority. Such an Authority should be assigned the responsibility of advising and recommending to the Executive with respect to the implementation of a comprehensive tax program. The Executive, acting under the advice of the Monetary and Fiscal Authority, should be empowered to increase or curtail at the appropriate time a specially designated category of public improvement expenditures designed to promote employment stability and expansion. He should, moreover, be empowered, with the advice of the Monetary and Fiscal Authority, to determine the imposition and withdrawal of taxes designed to check inflation or deflation and to change existing rates within limits imposed by the comprehensive tax program. Congress might specify certain criteria which the Monetary and Fiscal Authority would be required to take cognizance of in the determination of the appropriate timing of such adjustments. The determination ought certainly to be discretionary, but it is possible that the objective criteria could be sufficiently definitive so that limits could be imposed upon the range within which discretion could be exercised. Upon such determination and proclamation by the Executive the respective provisions of the comprehensive tax measure previously passed by Congress would become effective.

Admittedly, Congress may be reluctant to delegate power to the Executive on so vital a matter as the timing of the application of tax rates and expenditures. But, if we are to make the economy workable under modern conditions, it will be necessary to engage in bold social engineering. And especially is this true with respect to the defense program and its aftermath. If the magnitude of the defense effort is sharply revised upward, the time is coming when high consumption taxes should be imposed in order to prevent inflation. If we leave it to Congress to determine when this time has arrived, there is the gravest danger that action will be taken too late. And similarly with respect to the timing of appropriate fiscal measures when the postdefense slump begins to set in.

Chapter XXIV

FISCAL POLICY AND INTERNATIONAL STABILITY

MANY persons vitally interested in sound international relations are too frequently disposed to assume that a high level of economic prosperity in all countries would be ensured if trade barriers were largely removed. It is undoubtedly true that the erection of postwar agricultural tariffs, together with the increasingly protectionist policies of primary producing countries, the reparations payments, and the unsound policies pursued with respect to foreign lending, were important factors intensifying the terrific world depression beginning in 1929. While this may certainly be granted, it would be a great mistake to assume that sounder international economic policies of the character referred to above would themselves ensure an avoidance of serious depressions. Indeed, one can go much farther and assert that even in a world which was completely under one political sovereignty the fundamental factor producing depressions would still be present, namely, the fluctuation in the rate of real investment.

A second point to be noted is that in laying plans for a durable peace it would be very dangerous to overlook the threat to the stability of any arrangements that may be made which would arise in case we had a recurrence of deep depressions.

American Prosperity and World Peace

It is increasingly the view of many economists that the depression starting in 1929 is, in very large measure, responsible for the present plight of the world. There was a very good chance—though no absolute certainty—that, in the absence of the Great Depression, a solution might have been found for the central problem of Europe, namely, the place of Germany in international relations. Despite the mistakes of the Versailles Treaty, progress was being made toward a solution in the relatively prosperous years of the late twenties, and could this prosperity have been maintained on a fairly high level it is not unreasonable to assume that, progressively, a solution would have been found and war thereby averted.

The thesis can, therefore, be advanced with a good deal of reason that the really acid test of international economic co-operation runs in terms of deliberate international policy with respect to the control or moderation of depressions.

With respect to the United States, it may be asserted with confidence that this country could make no greater contribution toward the solution of the international political as well as economic problems than that of achieving a high degree of internal economic stability at a level of fairly full employment of labor and other resources. It is a fact that the extraordinary instability of the American economy presents one of the most serious problems confronting Europe. The Great Depression itself was, of course, a result of the interplay of a great many factors, partly internal and partly international, but there can be little question that the tremendous investment boom of the twenties in the United States (and in other countries aided by American foreign loans), the succeeding high degree of temporary investment saturation and the ensuing collapse in the output of fixed capital goods, particularly in this country, were the central core of the great world depression and determined mainly its intensity and duration. A bad international setup, of course, magnified the impact upon the outside world, and this impact, in turn, reflected itself back upon our own country in a cumulative fashion. Thus, as always in a depression period, it is quite impossible to unravel the interplay of cause and effect relationships. But through it all it is important to see the internal situation in the United States which would have created a profound depression regardless of the international setup.

Europe, and also the primary producing countries from whom we import so heavily, and whose prosperity or depression is, therefore, in large measure a reflection of our own, have every reason to fear the impact of America upon world affairs if we are to continue (a) a high degree of economic instability, or (b) chronically depressed conditions, or (c) a combination of both (as in recent years).

It is a striking fact that the movements of the Federal Reserve index of industrial production in the last decade bear a close resemblance to the movements in the quantum of world trade. To illustrate from one episode in this decade, the sharp depression in the United States in 1937–38 spread to the rest of the world through the sudden decline in American imports induced by our depression. The continued low rate of activity in America inevitably throws the American trade and service balance of payments into disequilibrium. At low activity and low income levels our imports (notably, raw materials and tourist expenditures) tend to prove inadequate to balance our current international account. A violently fluctuating American economy is a menace to economic stability in the rest of the world. A chronically depressed America, unless Europe can in some manner isolate itself from this depressional influence, tends to infect the rest of the world.

Under these circumstances it is highly probable that, unless the United States can do a better job of managing its own economy and can effectively co-operate with other countries on monetary policy, fiscal policy, and on such measures as, say, a co-ordinated international program of public works in a period of depression, it will become necessary for the European countries to insulate themselves as far as possible from the American influence. It is by no means improbable that, without an adequate internal American policy, combined with international collaboration along the lines indicated, after this war the European countries will find it essential to their political stability and to the security of any international program to collaborate on policies designed to isolate themselves from the United States.

In the nineteenth century and, indeed, until the breakdown of the international price system in the Great Depression of the early nineteen-thirties, international trade, while more or less hampered by tariffs, nevertheless extended far beyond political boundaries and was relatively little affected by political power. During the last decade the world has, however, become increasingly broken up into more or less watertight trade area compartments. In particular, the trading policies of the totalitarian states have fostered a high degree of self-sufficiency in the areas brought within their sphere of influence. And, of course, the war has now cut off the entire continent of Europe from trade with the Western world.

America's Place in Postwar World Trade

The prospect for a satisfactory political organization of Europe is not bright, regardless of the outcome of the war. Europe in our generation will not easily be able to achieve a satisfactory political settlement. If the outcome of the war is such that Germany will dominate the continent of Europe, this would entail the continuance of autarchic trade policies, resulting in largely cutting off this area from trade with the rest of the world. Barter deals no doubt would be made where they could be effected advantageously, but general international trade intercourse on a free price basis between a German-dominated Europe and the rest of the world would be a thing of the past.

On the other hand, it can reasonably be expected that in the event of a British victory the independent states of Europe will be reconstituted, and that international trade across political boundaries will be resumed. Thus, the outcome of the war has important implications with respect to world trade and, in particular, the trading area available for the United States.

In the event of a complete German victory, including the

conquest of the British Isles and perhaps the loss of British India and much or all of the African British Empire, the American trade area would shrivel to include virtually no more than the North American continent and the Caribbean countries. In the event of a British defeat, the United States could not, singlehanded, control the Atlantic and Pacific Oceans. Our defense would have to be drawn on close lines. It would involve a restricted area, including the North American continent and the Caribbean countries. It would, of course, include the protection of the Panama Canal and an area, say, fifteen hundred miles beyond. With the defeat of Britain, we could not afford to risk far-flung, distant outposts.

The economic and trade implications of this limited defense area are rather obvious. The United States does not constitute a powerful economic magnet drawing the countries of South America into our trade orbit. Their great export products are, with the exception of coffee in Brazil, precisely the products of which we have huge agricultural surpluses.[1] Nor should we be able to hold the Far East, Australasia, the Dutch and British East Indies, China, the Philippine Islands, and Japan within our trade orbit. This area in the event of a smashing German victory would increasingly fall, both on military and on trade lines, under the control of Japan and the Axis Powers.

The limited trade area thus left for the United States does, indeed, contain rich raw materials, and we could in time develop a high degree of self-sufficiency, but it would mean a

[1] The difficulty of integrating the South American countries in the orbit of American trade I explored in some detail in an article on "Hemisphere Solidarity" in the October, 1940 issue of *Foreign Affairs*. See also the article by P. W. Bidwell and A. R. Upgren on "A Trade Policy for National Defense," *ibid.*, January, 1941. Quantitatively, our own agricultural export surpluses aggregate about $700 millions per annum. But, if the Western Hemisphere as a whole is considered, these surpluses cumulate to a total of no less than $2 billions. Our own surpluses include cotton and wheat, tobacco and meat, and mineral surpluses of copper and petroleum, to name but two of the latter class. Canada and the Argentine together have even greater surpluses of meat and wheat, Brazil has a large surplus of coffee and cotton, and other countries of the hemisphere have very large surpluses of copper and petroleum.

drastic reallocation of our productive resources. Within this narrow trade area we have an enormously overdeveloped agricultural capacity. This would have to be liquidated. Our economy has developed within a world market, and our trading area cannot shrivel to small dimensions without entailing drastic reorganization and readjustment.

The key to the solution of this dilemma is Britain. In recent years the proportion of the total European purchases of Western Hemisphere agricultural surpluses taken by the United Kingdom is striking indeed. Of total hemispheric exports of wheat, Britain absorbed over 60 per cent. In the case of meat—a critical export for the Argentine—the proportion of total Western Hemisphere exports to all of Europe absorbed by Britain was 90 per cent; for lard, 58 per cent; for cotton, tobacco, and corn, the proportion ranged from 32 to 40 per cent; and, finally, in the cases of copper and petroleum, the figures are 49 and 38 per cent respectively. Coffee is the only important Western Hemisphere export not purchased in large volume by Britain.

If Britain holds and the British Empire survives, our trade outlook would accordingly be very different. With British and American control of the seas, a large trading area would be available for this country, even though Germany should retain control of the continent of Europe. Such a trade area would include the British Isles and the whole of the British Empire, the whole of the Western Hemisphere, and the Far East. This represents a reasonably satisfactory triangular trade area, including by far the most important part of our former world trade. Important trade routes would thus be preserved across the Atlantic and the Pacific. In this area, by reason of the market offered in the British Isles, the South American countries could also find their place. And we, on our part, would import important raw materials from the Far East.

The outlook for the United States in such a world would be fairly optimistic from the trade standpoint. But, in terms of world organization and permanent peace, a world divided between a great land power (Germany) and sea powers (Britain and the United States) presents a gloomy picture.

International Economic Collaboration

But the political solution of the problem of world organization is not enough. The League of Nations, imperfect as it was, could in all probability have survived and improved had it been possible to maintain a sound economic foundation in terms of world prosperity. In the next attempt at world organization there is no likelihood that any scheme, however wisely conceived, can survive widespread unemployment. The war is demonstrating how great are the fiscal powers of the state to commandeer the resources of a society for purposes of destruction. Is it Utopian to hope that countries may learn to use this powerful instrument of public policy for building and preserving the economic foundations of enduring world peace?

In the London *Times,* February 9, 1940, a statement of the Executive Committee of the British Labour Party on "The War and the Peace" is made. This statement further calls attention to the economic difficulties which will confront all nations at the end of the war, particularly the danger of mass unemployment. In addition to political reconstruction, bold economic and financial planning on a world-wide scale is required, involving perhaps international public works and the development of great colonial territories under the direction of an international authority with a budget of its own. Such a plan, of course, goes farther than my own suggestion, which involves international collaboration with respect to internal expansion within each country, undertaken simultaneously with a view to disrupting as little as possible the structure of exchange rates.

Similarly, in an article in the *New Statesman and the Nation,* February 17, 1940, reference is made to the perilous situation which will confront all the belligerent countries when the armies are demobilized and returned to civilian life. The worst error, it is urged, committed by the statesmen following the first World War was not the Treaty of Versailles with its doubtful political frontiers, but rather their failure to grapple effectively with the economics of the postwar world. The first chapter in a peace settlement ought to include, it is stated, an ambitious plan of public works, development, and restoration.

Undoubtedly, intelligent opinion in Europe would prefer a policy of international collaboration with America. But this is true only on the assumption that there is reason to suppose that America can and will stabilize her economy at a high employment level and can and will participate in effective international collaboration on monetary, trade, and fiscal lines.

What I have tried to state briefly is my conviction that it is necessary to think of international economic collaboration in more thoroughgoing terms than has commonly been the case. It is important not merely to think in terms of the optimum international division of labor which at full employment would give us the largest realizable real income. In the kind of world in which we live today it is even more important to think in terms of reasonably full utilization of our resources and to consider both domestic and international policy which will tend to promote this end.

INDEX